THE KOKODA CAMPAIGN 1942
Myth and reality

The fighting on the Kokoda Track in World War II is second only to Gallipoli in the Australian national consciousness. The Kokoda campaign of 1942 has taken on mythical status in Australian military history. According to the legend, Australian soldiers were vastly outnumbered by the Japanese, who suffered great losses in battle and as a result of the harsh conditions of the Kokoda Track.

In this important book, Peter Williams seeks to dispel the Kokoda myth. Using extensive research and Japanese sources, he explains what really happened on the Kokoda Track in 1942. Unlike most other books written from an Australian perspective, *The Kokoda Campaign 1942: Myth and reality* focuses on the strategies, tactics and battle plans of the Japanese and shows that the Australians were in fact rarely outnumbered.

For the first time, this book combines narrative with careful analysis to present an undistorted picture of the events of the campaign. It is a must-read for anyone who is interested in the truth of the Kokoda campaign of 1942.

Peter Williams is a researcher for the Defence Honours and Awards Tribunal and is a military historian for the Darwin Military Museum.

OTHER TITLES IN THE AUSTRALIAN ARMY HISTORY SERIES

(Series editor: David Horner)

Phillip Bradley *The Battle for Wau: New Guinea's Frontline 1942–1943*

Mark Johnston *The Proud 6th: An Illustrated History of the 6th Australian Division 1939–1946*

Garth Pratten *Australian Battalion Commanders in the Second World War*

Jean Bou *Light Horse: A History of Australia's Mounted Arm*

Phillip Bradley *To Salamaua*

Peter Dean *The Architect of Victory: The Military Career of Lieutenant-General Sir Frank Horton Berryman*

Allan Converse *Armies of Empire: The 9th Australian and 50th British Divisions in Battle 1939–45*

John Connor *Anzac and Empire: George Foster Pearce and the Foundations of Australian Defence*

THE KOKODA
CAMPAIGN 1942

MYTH AND REALITY

PETER WILLIAMS

CAMBRIDGE
UNIVERSITY PRESS

477 Williamstown Road, Port Melbourne, VIC 3207, Australia

Published in the United States of America by Cambridge University Press, New York

Cambridge University Press is part of the University of Cambridge.

It furthers the University's mission by disseminating knowledge in the pursuit of education, learning and research at the highest international levels of excellence.

www.cambridge.org
Information on this title: www.cambridge.org/9781107015944

First published 2012

Cover design by Rob Cowpe

A catalogue record for this publication is available from the British Library

A Cataloguing-in-Publication entry is available from the catalogue of the National Library of Australia at www.nla.gov.au

ISBN 978-1-107-01594-4 Hardback

I dedicate this book to my children,
Catherine and Michael Williams

CONTENTS

PHOTOGRAPHS

Maps

TABLES

Key to military symbols

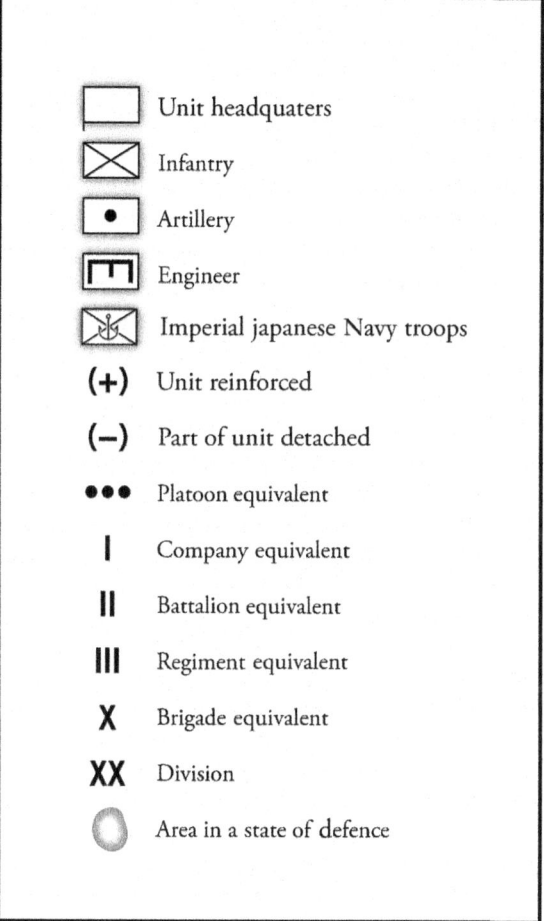

Unit headquaters

Infantry

Artillery

Engineer

Imperial japanese Navy troops

(+) Unit reinforced

(−) Part of unit detached

●●● Platoon equivalent

I Company equivalent

II Battalion equivalent

III Regiment equivalent

X Brigade equivalent

XX Division

Area in a state of defence

ACKNOWLEDGEMENTS

Thanks must go first to Dr Steven Bullard and Professor David Horner. Steven, with his extensive knowledge of Japanese sources for World War II, steered my PhD in the right direction. When it became a book, David guided me through publication. The book could not have been completed without them.

I am grateful to Yoshida Haruki for meticulous translations of Japanese documents over many years.

Thanks to my brother John Williams for his constructive criticism. Others who read chapters were Peter Collidge, Greg Blake, Jim Gandy, Renfrey Pearson, Tom Lewis, Michael Shevak and Hugh Dolan. At the always helpful Army History Unit thanks to Roger Lee and Dr Andrew Richardson.

At the Australian National University Professors Frank Fenner (dec.), Hank Nelson and Drs Bryant Allen, Michael Burke and Michael Clarke allowed me to interview them about their various fields of expertise. Thanks also to Dr Tamura Keiko and Dr Christopher Forbes-Ewan, Clive Baker, Frank Taylor (for taking me along the Kokoda Track) and Kasis Inape of the Papua New Guinea Meterological Service.

In Japan thanks are due to the staff at the National Institute for Defense Studies, in particular Major-General Yoshinaga Hayashi and Dr Shindo Hiroyuki. Marutani Hajime provided, as ever, fine translations. Thanks also to Nakagawa Naoko and Akaboshi Yayoi. My oldest friends in Japan are Sato Go and Sato Yukiko, who helped in every way that they could. Major Horie Masao, a New Guinea veteran, arranged for me to meet many others.

Finally, thanks to my wife Sammy for her constant encouragement.

NOTE ON THE TEXT

Names are written in their correct order. Australian and American names have the family name last, Japanese names have the family name first.

The country now called Papua New Guinea was in 1942 divided into two. The northern half was New Guinea and the southern half was Papua. When referring to the whole of what is now Papua New Guinea the term 'New Guinea' has been used.

Villages in Papua are often not where they were in 1942. For this reason it is useful to refer in the text to a village's wartime or postwar location.

Buna is the word Australians use to describe the 18-kilometre strip of Papuan coast between Gona and Cape Endiadere, where the Japanese landed, developed their base for the advance along the Kokoda Track, and made their last stand in January 1943. But as Giruwa, near Sanananda, was the command, administrative and supply centre of the Japanese base, it has been used instead when referring to the base in general.

'Nankai Shitai' (South Seas Detachment) has been used to include all IJA and IJN forces in the Giruwa–Owen Stanley Range area. Strictly speaking, the air flotilla and a number of small IJN units were not under army command, so were not part of the Nankai Shitai.

After the war for official purposes the fighting in Papua 1942–43 was divided into three parts: the battles of Kokoda, Buna–Gona and Milne Bay. This book concerns the Battle of Kokoda, but the term 'Kokoda campaign' has been used instead.

The six Japanese infantry battalions in the Nankai Shitai were in two regiments, the 144th and 41st. The battalions were numbered 1/144th, 2/144th, 3/144th, 1/41st, 2/41st and 3/41st. Other infantry battalions in the text with a prefix 2/ are Second Australian Imperial Force battalions. Other Australian infantry battalions without the prefix 2/ are militia battalions.

GLOSSARY

AAF	Allied Air Force
adj	adjutant
AIF	Australian Imperial Force
AJRP	Australia–Japan Research Project
AMF	Australian Military Force
ANGAU	Australian New Guinea Administrative Unit
ATIS	Allied Translator and Interpreter Service
AWM	Australian War Memorial
BCC	bridge construction company
Bde	brigade
Bn	battalion
BnHQ	battalion headquarters
butai	Japanese military unit
C in C	commander in chief
CIB	Commonwealth Investigation Branch
Coy	company
daitai	Japanese battalion-size unit
DCC	division cavalry company
DNI	Director of Naval Intelligence
ER	engineer regiment
FAAAB	field anti-aircraft artillery battalion
go	unit of measurement for rice; 1840 grams
HMG	heavy machine-gun
IER	independent engineer regiment
IGS	Imperial General Staff
IHQ	Imperial Headquarters
IJA	Imperial Japanese Army
IJAHQ	Imperial Japanese Army Headquarters
IJN	Imperial Japanese Navy
IJNHQ	Imperial Japanese Navy Headquarters
IMTB	independent motor transport battalion

IO	Intelligence officer
LOCH	line of communication hospital
MAR	mountain artillery regiment
MFHQ	Maroubra Force Headquarters
MMG	medium machine-gun
MPC	military police company
MO	Japanese plan to attack Port Moresby
NAA	National Archives of Australia
Nankai Shitai	South Seas Detachment
NCO	non-commissioned officer
NGF	New Guinea Force
NGVR	New Guinea Volunteer Rifles
NIDS	National Institute of Defense Studies
NLA	National Library of Australia
NP	Naval Pioneers
NSHQ	Nankai Shitai Headquarters
PCB	Patient Collecting Butai; a field ambulance
PIB	Papuan Infantry Battalion
QF	Quick Firing (gun)
RAAF	Royal Australian Air Force
RAE	Royal Australian Engineers
RAN	Royal Australian Navy
RAP	Regimental Aid Post
rentai	regiment
RGC	regimental gun company
RHQ	regimental headquarters
RN	Royal Navy
RPC	Royal Papuan Constabulary
RSC	Regimental Signals Company
RSM	Regimental Sergeant Major
SDC	sea duty company
SER	shipping engineer regiment
sho	unit of measurement for rice; 1.4 kg
SNLP	Special Naval Landing Party
Stanley Shitai	(Owen) Stanley (Range) Detachment
SWPA	South West Pacific Area
USAAF	United States Army Air Force
USN	United States Navy

CHAPTER 1

INTRODUCTION

This book is an examination of the Kokoda campaign – from the Japanese landing in Papua in July 1942 and their advance along the Kokoda Track, to their defeat at Oivi–Gorari in November. The Kokoda campaign is catching up with Gallipoli in popularity, as is apparent from the number of books on it that have appeared in the past twenty-odd years and the thousands of Australians who now walk the Kokoda Track each year.[1] As the events of 1915 pass into distant memory, it is possible that Kokoda might come to rival Gallipoli as the representative Australian military experience. While there are positive aspects to this, as its popularity increases errors in the Kokoda story have a tendency to be repeated until they take on the outward appearance of fact. Other aspects of the campaign, some arising from Australian wartime propaganda, have not been subject to postwar investigation. These two strands combine to create the Kokoda myth. Recent popular accounts, concerned more with colour than precision, perpetuate the myth.[2]

The core of the Kokoda myth is that during the Japanese advance towards Port Moresby the Australians were greatly outnumbered. Those in the front line were convinced of this, and their word has been accepted. Japanese veterans often say the same thing – that the Australians significantly outnumbered them. It may be that in jungle fighting, where the enemy is rarely seen, there is a tendency to imagine that he is in great strength. In truth, during the Japanese advance, the Australians were rarely outnumbered by their enemy. While Australia's 39th Battalion and the Papuan Infantry Battalion faced superior numbers in the small

1

July clashes, it was not as many as two to one. The forces engaged at Isurava, the first large action, have always been thought to have been at the very least three to one against the Australians and perhaps six to one. In fact the numbers were equal with about 2300 being engaged on either side. With the exception of the first Eora–Templeton's Crossing fighting, where the Japanese did have almost twice as many troops as the Australians, the Australians fought the Japanese at one to one until Ioribaiwa in September, where it was the Australians who outnumbered the Japanese by two to one, yet the Australians were still defeated. During the Australian advance after Ioribaiwa they always maintained a great superiority of numbers over the Japanese.

Numbers are important in war. To have a good prospect of success the attacker should usually have more men than the defender. The fire-power of modern weapons so advantage a defender that a three-to-one local superiority is said to be needed to be reasonably certain of success if all other factors are equal. A two-to-one advantage provides a lesser chance of success but will sometimes be enough, and one to one is usually not enough for the attacker to prevail. When numbers alone do not explain victory or defeat – and it is rarely as simple as that – we look to the quality of the troops, their weapons, morale and supply, and how well they were commanded. Each of these elements can power-fully increase fighting power or, to use terms not in use in 1942, they are force multipliers that enhance combat effectiveness. For example, if the attacker's men were of higher quality than those of the defender, or if the attacker had much more artillery or was better supplied, then he might not need any superiority in numbers to win. According to the Kokoda myth, it was the large Japanese numerical superiority that ena-bled them to advance as far as they did towards Port Moresby. If that is not true then other reasons for the series of Australian defeats on the Kokoda Track between July and September 1942 would be required. One possibility is that the Japanese were qualitatively superior to the Australians.

A central fact of land warfare in the first year of the Japanese offen-sive in the Pacific from December 1941 is that, man for man, the Japanese proved to be better soldiers than those who opposed them. The proof is that up to the second half of 1942 the Japanese rarely had superior num-bers engaged in land battles, yet they rarely lost one. They achieved their victories in Burma, the Dutch East Indies, during the Malayan campaign, in the final battle at Singapore and in the Philippines without a numerical advantage. Only when the Allies had a very considerable superiority, as at Milne Bay and Guadalcanal, were they able to defeat the Japanese. The Kokoda campaign fits this pattern.

Another force enhancer that might help to explain the early Japanese success and later prolonged defence during the Kokoda campaign is their artillery. Australian postwar accounts show little awareness of the importance of Japanese artillery in explaining the outcome of the battles and have tended to suppose that the Japanese had many mortars but few guns. This error has arisen in part from the mistranslation of the Japanese term for their 70mm battalion gun, the 'gun-mortar', as 'mortar'. There were no Japanese medium or heavy mortars (as distinct from the ubiquitous short-range 'knee mortar') in the Owen Stanley Range. Instead the Nankai Shitai (South Seas Force) carried 16 light artillery pieces to Papua. Most of them were 70mm and 75mm guns; well supplied with ammunition, they had a major influence on the fighting.

It might not be too much to say that most issues of the campaign ought to be reappraised if it can be shown that the Japanese engaged in the battles along the Kokoda Track were many fewer than has been believed. This word *engaged* holds a clue because, while the Nankai Shitai was more than 16 000 strong, the number the Japanese actually committed to battle on the Kokoda Track, which runs from Kokoda south over the Owen Stanley Range towards Port Moresby, was much smaller. In Kokoda in 1967, 39th Battalion held a reunion. There Bert Kienzle, a famous identity of the campaign, spoke of the fighting portion of the Nankai Shitai. He said, 'Ten thousand experienced and highly trained soldiers plus 3000 naval personnel [were] against the Australians.'[3] The Australian official history agreed, calculating that the Nankai Shitai included 'a well-balanced fighting force of 10 000 men'.[4] These numbers have generally been accepted, and accounts continue to claim that the Australians were outnumbered by, for example, ten to one at First Kokoda.[5] The myth of Japanese numerical superiority has continued unaltered since Keinzle spoke more than 45 years ago. The problem for the myth is that of a 16 000-strong force, of which 7000 were fighting troops, no more than 3500 of these actually advanced along the Kokoda Track.

What has occurred in postwar Australian historiography might have something to do with the saying that the victors write the history. This is true as far as it goes, but much of what the victor later writes might not be accurate as it can arise out of his own wartime propaganda. The defeated too has wartime propaganda, but this is swept away postwar as it is immediately seen for what it usually is – falsehood. The victor's propaganda is not subject to the same rigorous reassessment and has a chance to seep into later accounts and, over time, become entrenched there. Two examples of Australian wartime propaganda still read today, and which stress the Japanese numerical superiority, are George Johnston's *New Guinea Diary* and Osmar White's *Green Armour*, published in 1943 and 1945 respectively.

The Kokoda myth is not only concerned with the relative size of the Japanese and Australian forces. The other elements of the myth are that:

- the Australian fighting retreat along the Kokoda Track saved Port Moresby
- the Japanese were ignorant of conditions in the theatre of war
- the Australians inflicted huge losses on their enemy
- the Japanese conducted the campaign on a shoestring budget; their retreat and defeat was largely because they ran out of supplies
- Allied air power made a major contribution to the Japanese defeat
- the Australians were better prepared medically and lost fewer men to disease, and
- senior Allied commanders were out of touch and junior commanders were sacked unfairly.

Taking each in their turn, the first aspect of the Kokoda myth is that the Australian fighting retreat from July to September saved Port Moresby. While Australian strategy in 1942 has been dealt with in a number of books, little work has been done from the Japanese perspective.[6] The strategic factor that most influenced the strength of Japanese forces in the Owen Stanley Range was Guadalcanal. Within days of the US invasion of that island on 7 August 1942 the Japanese recast their plans. Lieutenant-General Hyakutake Harukichi, commander of Seventeenth Army, ordered Major-General Horii Tomitaro, commander of the Nankai Shitai, to halt his attack on Port Moresby and keep the major part of his force on the northern side of the Owen Stanley Range. Hence from mid-August, before the battle of Isurava, Japan's advance on Port Moresby was put on hold. That Horii was never released from this restriction constitutes the single most important strategic influence upon the course of events along the Kokoda Track. The small force that was permitted to advance south along the track and fought at Efogi (also known as Mission Ridge–Brigade Hill) and Ioribaiwa was tasked with finding a useful position just past the crest of the range and holding it until the situation at Guadalcanal was resolved. Then the main body of Horii's force, with reinforcements, would be released to enter the mountains and march on Port Moresby in combination with an amphibious assault mounted from Milne Bay. The Japanese failed to take Milne Bay and were defeated at Guadalcanal, so Horii was never given permission to advance on Port Moresby. In short, the Australians on the Kokoda Track cannot have saved Port Moresby when, before the main body of the Nankai Shitai even arrived in Papua, the attack on Port Moresby, the MO operation, was postponed, never to be reactivated.

It is generally held that Japanese intelligence on the theatre of war was poor. This is the second part of the myth. It is said the Japanese knew 'little or nothing of the inland area' of Papua.[7] A commonly used example is that the Japanese believed there was a road from Buna to Port Moresby via Kokoda. It is true one can find the odd ignorant statement of this kind in Japanese soldiers' diaries, but these are rare, often written while the writer was still en route to New Guinea or by low-ranking soldiers with no access to the intelligence used by their commanders to plan the operation. Japanese studies on the tracks over the mountains to Port Moresby, based on prewar visits to Papua and information provided by residents, were reasonably accurate, and they were in no doubt about the difficulty of crossing the Owen Stanley Range along the Kokoda Track and that there was no vehicular road there.

Eastern New Guinea had been under investigation by the Japanese since 1931. By 1938 there was some interest in the route from Sanananda to Kokoda to Port Moresby. In March 1941 Major Toyofuku Tetsuo, later senior intelligence officer of the Nankai Shitai, visited Port Moresby incognito. Armed with Toyufuku's report, serious intelligence studies of the Kokoda Track commenced in January 1942. Two months later Toyufuku was in contact with his main source of information about the track, Josef Anton Hoffstetter, a Swiss resident of New Guinea with Nazi sympathies. By the time the campaign was launched, the Japanese probably knew more about the Kokoda Track than did the Australians.

One author has accused the Japanese of 'creative accounting' in their estimates of the number of enemy they fought and the number of casualties they inflicted.[8] This is a fair criticism. The Japanese in Papua often overestimated the number of Australians they fought and the number of casualties they inflicted. However, the third myth is that the Australians inflicted many more casualties than they lost. In fact the Australians were equally guilty of fabricating impressive but inflated numbers of enemy killed. After the battle of Isurava the Australians reported that they had killed or wounded 700 Japanese. This was an estimate as they could not have known the true figure. The essence of the Kokoda myth is to exaggerate, and decades after World War II the number grew to 1500.[9] Japanese casualty records are not always as accurate as Australian ones, but they are quite adequate to show that the actual number of Japanese killed and wounded at Isurava was very close to 360.[10] From the Japanese landing in Papua in July 1942 to the end of the battle of Ioribaiwa in September, both sides had lost about 900 battle casualties. Lindsay Mason, a veteran of the campaign, was right to say, 'The fact is we were killing them at about one for one.'[11]

A fourth aspect of the Kokoda myth is the view that the Japanese conducted the Kokoda campaign with a narrow supply margin. Operating on a tight timetable, the Nankai Shitai expected to get from Giruwa, near Buna, to Port Moresby in two weeks carrying virtually all their requirements on the backs of their men. On the contrary, the Nankai Shitai was, from July to September, as well supplied as the Australians. After two months in Papua the most advanced elements of the Nankai Shitai did experience severe shortages for several weeks. Some of this force, the Stanley Detachment of fewer than a thousand men, did suffer all the trials, starvation, even cannibalism, attributed to the whole of the Nankai Shitai in the Kokoda myth, but Japanese supply difficulties have been overstated. The Kokoda myth is narrowly focused on the track itself and, as with some other aspects of the myth, it is necessary to look beyond the track to understand what happened during the Japanese supply crisis. Their food shortage was caused not by unpreparedness but rather by the weather. Four days of heavy rain in mid-September washed away their supply line from Giruwa to Kokoda, north of the Kokoda Track itself, and for two weeks nothing could move along it. Repairs to roads and bridges were made, and supply recovered to an acceptable level.

Linked to Japanese supply is the issue of Allied air interdiction of the Japanese line of communication. The Allied air bombardment of Japanese supply lines is reputed to have caused heavy casualties and contributed to the breakdown of the supply line. Most aspects of the myth have arisen well after World War II, but this one appears to have its origins, like Japanese starvation, in the propaganda of the time. Nankai Shitai casualty returns show that losses to air attack were small and that the Allied destruction from the air of the Japanese bridges over the Kumusi River, a supposed choke point, had little effect on Japanese supply.

The sixth myth is that the Australians took better care of their soldiers and suffered fewer casualties to sickness. The reverse is true. Australian losses to dysentery were extremely high, and it was not until the end of the Kokoda campaign that Japanese losses to medical causes caught up. This error also arose in part from wartime publicity. Much was made in Australian newspapers of the terrible circumstances in which the

Japanese found themselves at the disastrous end of the fighting in Papua at Buna, Sanananda and Gona in January 1943, when they did run out of medical supplies and food. However, this was not the case during the prior Kokoda campaign as the Japanese came to Papua better prepared medically than the Australians and, in the fighting in the mountains up to November 1942, the period covered by this book, the Australians lost far more men to sickness than the Japanese.

The seventh myth concerns senior Allied commanders. It is said that they were out of touch and sacked the operational commanders unfairly: 'Allied victory in Papua had little to do with Blamey and MacArthur and everything to do with the prodigious abilities and courage of a few outstanding officers, and the dogged loyalty and bravery of their men.'[12] General Arthur Allen and Brigadier Arnold Potts, both relieved during the campaign, are two of the 'outstanding officers' commonly associated with this claim. Here it is argued that replacing Potts and Allen was a reasonable course of action. Potts was beaten repeatedly and driven back by a force not at all superior in number to his, and Allen, who outnumbered the Japanese by three to one during the later Australian counter-offensive towards Kokoda, advanced slowly and cautiously, the opposite of what his seniors required and the strategic situation demanded.

There is a part exception to the Kokoda myth. It is the last battle of the campaign at Oivi–Gorari, in early November 1942, where the Australians won a decisive victory. Oivi-Gorari was quite unlike any of the previous battles in that Australian generalship was good, morale was high and the Australians were successful in attacking a prepared position without a very great superiority in numbers. They drove the Japanese from it, and they inflicted far more casualties than they lost.

A curious feature of the widespread yet mistaken view of the Kokoda campaign, here called the Kokoda myth, is that it took hold well after the war ended. The core facet, Japanese strength, was not greatly exaggerated at the time. In September 1942 President Roosevelt complained that the Australians were being pushed back by an inferior enemy force, no more than 4000 strong.[13] The Australian headquarters in Papua, New Guinea Force, had roughly accurate estimates of the size of the Japanese force not too far from Roosevelt's number, and in October Australian newspapers carried stories that the Japanese on the Kokoda Track were not as strong as previously believed. As Sydney's *Daily Telegraph* reported on 8 October 1942, 'Correspondents cautiously suggest … the Japanese were weaker in the Owen Stanleys than we thought …'

There was no change in the 1950s. Raymond Paull's 1958 book *Retreat from Kokoda*, and the official histories, contain only a little of what would become the Kokoda myth. The Australian official history said there were 6000 Japanese on the Kokoda Track, and the United States history, *Victory in Papua*, calculated there were 5000.[14] Scott's 1963 book *The Knights of Kokoda* seems to be the first in which all elements of the myth are in place: the Japanese were in immense strength, 10 000 or so; they knew nothing about the theatre of war; MacArthur treated his Australian subordinates poorly; the Australians inflicted huge losses on the Japanese, and so forth.[15]

With the increasing interest in Australia about the Kokoda campaign, myth-making gathered steam. In 1981 Timothy Hall wrote *New Guinea 1942–44*, followed by Lex McAulay's 1991 *Blood and Iron* and Peter Brune's book *A Bastard of a Place* in 2003. In 2004 Paul Ham and Peter Fitzsimons both published books called *Kokoda*, and in 2005 there was Patrick Lyndsay's *Spirit of Kokoda*. Some, like Sublet's *Kokoda to the Sea* (2000) and McAulay's *Blood and Iron*, do not intentionally mythologise, but others do. Garth Pratten's comment on Peter Brune's series of books, which was combined into *A Bastard of a Place*, could be applied to other authors. Brune, wrote Pratten, desired 'to turn the Papua campaign into a great national myth, replete with heroes and villains'.[16] Two biographies, Bill Edgar's *Warrior of Kokoda* about Brigadier Arnold Potts, and Stuart Braga's *Kokoda Commander* about Major-General Arthur Allen, do of necessity embrace elements of the myth to defend the subjects of their books. If, for instance, Potts was not outnumbered at Isurava and Efogi – and he was not – then it is more difficult to argue that he did extremely well. Edgar assessed that there were 6000 Japanese facing Potts at Efogi, four times the actual number.[17]

The myth-making has not gone unnoticed. Professor Hank Nelson has pointed to aspects of it, which he summed up in a 2009 article. The Kokoda campaign, he said, 'has been burdened with exaggeration':

> Kokoda did not save Australia from invasion, or even Port Moresby
> from capture. The limited numbers, firepower and fitness of a
> Japanese force that had struggled across the Owen Stanley Ranges
> was not going to take Port Moresby unaided, as both the Australian
> and the Japanese commanders knew before the Japanese began
> their retreat in September 1942. Kokoda was not as important as
> Guadalcanal in determining the direction of the war in the south and
> south-west Pacific; Guadalcanal involved more ships, aircraft and

ground troops and consumed Japanese units from the three services that would otherwise have been used in Papua.[18]

Dr David Stevens has also written of problems in the way the Kokoda campaign has been presented in a chapter of *Zombie Myths* entitled 'Australia's Thermopylae? The Kokoda Trail'.[19]

The attempt to debunk Kokoda myths is not intended to denigrate the Australians who fought on the Kokoda Track. Their bravery and fortitude is not in question. It is rather that the current interpretation of the campaign is invalid. This book is an attempt to set aside the myth of Kokoda and replace it with the reality and, as the evidence that undoes the myth comes mainly from Japanese sources (see Note on Sources), it follows that more than half the book concerns the Nankai Shitai. The unfortunate contribution of Australian popular military history to the strength of the Kokoda myth was discussed earlier, but the problem is broader than that. The Kokoda myth has arisen because there exists a gap in Australian historiography: a wide range of Japanese sources have not hitherto been examined, although Raymond Paull, Lex McAulay and Paul Ham have all made some effort to do so. The result is a lack of balance in our understanding of the Kokoda campaign, a natural outcome, for if we try to explain an historical event involving two belligerents using sources from only one of them, then we should hardly expect to get it right.

CHAPTER 2

STRATEGY

The Japanese plan for the invasion of Papua had a solid strategic foundation and was much more than the opportunistic and rapid dash for Port Moresby it is characterised as being in the Kokoda myth.[1] The opportunism was supposed to have occurred when, after the failure of the sea attack on Port Moresby at the Battle of the Coral Sea, the Japanese suddenly switched to a landward approach whereby the main attack came along the Kokoda Track and was to arrive at Port Moresby at the same time as a secondary amphibious attack launched from Milne Bay. In fact a land approach from the north coast of Papua was always the preferred option. The myth, with its sights firmly on the Kokoda Track, also misses the point that the Japanese were not in Papua just to take Port Moresby. They were there to forestall an Allied offensive by occupying sites of importance regardless of whether or not their assault on Port Moresby went ahead. Japanese strategy in Papua in 1942 was essentially defensive – an Allied counter-offensive was expected from Australia, and Papua was to be seized and the Allied advance halted there. Major bases were to be built in the Buna–Giruwa–Gona area and at Milne Bay, with a lesser base at Kokoda. Port Moresby was a highly desirable, but not essential, part of the plan.

AIRFIELDS AND AIRCRAFT CARRIERS

The strategic consideration that persuaded the Japanese to launch a land campaign in Papua, which would probably involve an attempt to take

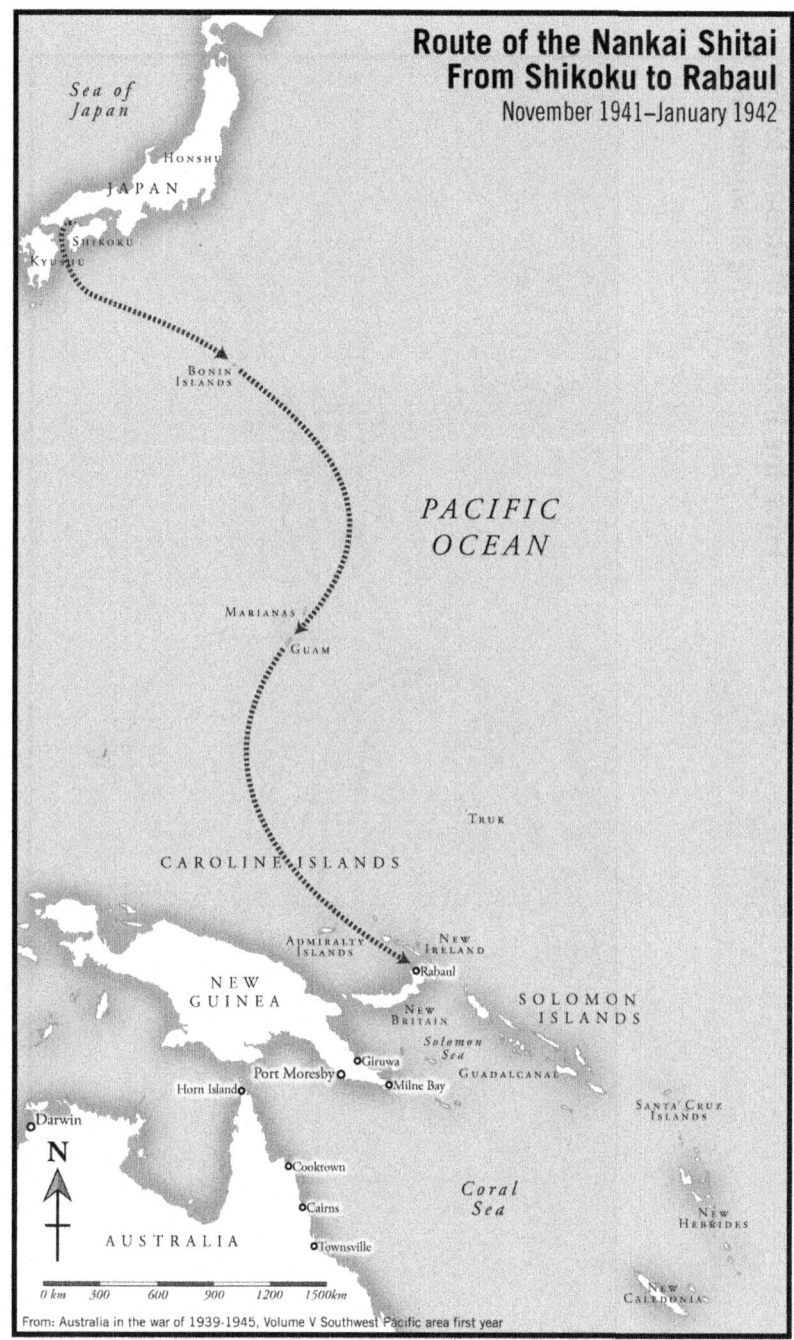

Map 1 The route of the Nankai Shitai from Shikoku to Rabaul,
December 1941 – January 1942

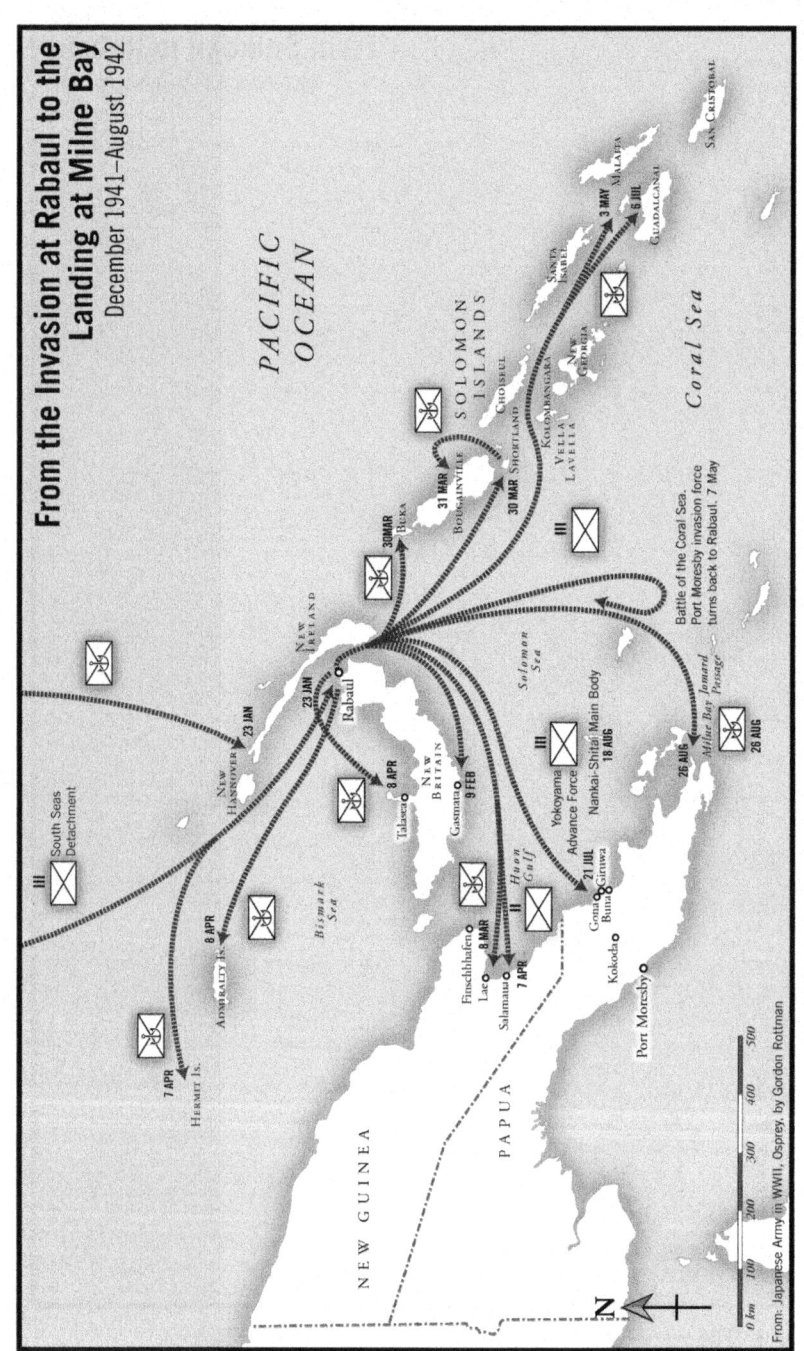

Map 2 From the invasion of Rabaul to the landing at Milne Bay,
January–August 1942

Port Moresby via the Owen Stanley Range, is concerned with airfields. The Pacific War was first an air war, second a sea war and last, a land war. Regardless of victories on land, armies on Pacific islands eventually starved if denied food coming by sea. The ships carrying supplies would be sunk by aircraft unless the air above them was denied to the enemy. In 1942 carrier-borne air power was weak against land-based air power. Carriers did briefly move within range of land-based aircraft for a surprise strike then withdraw, but they would lose any protracted contest with land-based aircraft. Carriers did not fear high-level long-range bombers such as the B17 as they quickly demonstrated an inability to hit a ship at sea. It was medium bombers, the Japanese Mitsubishi G4M Betty and the United States' B25 Mitchell or B26 Marauder, that proved able to do so. We rarely find examples of carriers being sunk within medium-bomber range of land in this period because the relative superiority of land-based versus sea-based air power was well understood by both sides: at the Battle of the Coral Sea, fleet carriers of the Imperial Japanese Navy (IJN) took care never to come within medium-bomber range of Port Moresby, weak as was Allied air strength there in May 1942. At Midway, where IJN carriers were risked within range of land-based air power, the first priority was to destroy the American aircraft quickly. It was this otherwise sensible prioritising that undid the Japanese, as they had not finished knocking out American land-based assets before aircraft launched by United States Navy (USN) carriers attacked their fleet. The carrier battles of Eastern Solomons and Santa Cruz were similarly, and purposely, fought outside or at the edge of the range of American land-based aircraft at Guadalcanal. A consequence of this relationship between land-based air power and carrier-based air power was that the side able to maintain and defend well-placed airfields could project air power out to sea and hence would win any campaign in the long run.

Both the Guadalcanal and Papuan campaigns are suitable illustrations of the rule that strong land-based air power was the major determinant in shaping the outcome of the Pacific campaigns. In both places the Allies held the air bases even though their strength in the air was not so powerful in mid-1942, but by early 1943 the Japanese could neither reinforce nor resupply their soldiers in Papua so they gave up the contest and attempted evacuation. In Guadalcanal, this was successful, in Papua not so.

For the Japanese the relationship between the carrier and the air base did not alter in the course of the war as the IJN never had enough carrier aircraft to risk staying long within the range of enemy land-based bombers. For the Americans it did alter, as their carrier-based air strength increased to become vastly more powerful than the ever-decreasing Japanese land-based strength. Off Leyte in the Philippines in October 1944, the USN had 18 carriers with 1500 aircraft, ten times their average fleet air strength in 1942. The USN was able to swat Japanese land-based air attacks while with the other hand it destroyed Japanese airfields. Until the end of the war USN carriers could, although not without cost, conduct extended air operations within range of airfields, something unthinkable for both sides in 1942.

If strategy was determined by taking airfields or airfield sites, then there were very few to take in the south-west Pacific. In March 1942 the Japanese, having identified Guadalcanal and Buin on Bougainville as potential airfield sites, began looking for others in the intervening 800-kilometre-long Solomon Island chain. By August they still had not found one. Across the Solomon Sea in Papua there were just four good locations with a functioning airfield, or the potential to develop one or more airstrips. They were Port Moresby, Milne Bay, Buna and Kokoda. There were other second-rate abandoned airstrips, at Yodda and Wanigela, which neither side considered using in the early stage of the campaign. Before the Pacific War began the Japanese had noted airfields and identified potential airfield sites in Papua. Samarai Island near Milne Bay was considered a possibility until it was discovered there were Allied airfields in Milne Bay that could be taken. The suitability of the plains about Buna was also known to the IJA by November 1941.[2] Although the coast was swamp, close inland there was bare, flat and mostly dry land with small anchorages nearby. These were the prerequisites for a large airfield complex, not easily found on south-west Pacific islands, which tended to be mountainous, with lowlands prone to flooding. Coral reefs severely limited coastal navigation, and land communications were poor.

Moreover, a square kilometre of suitable land was needed for each runway of an airfield complex, together with its dispersal area, repair facilities, fuel farm, accommodation and storage space. Basic inland strips, like Kokoda in Papua and Wau in New Guinea, could be used by small air units but could not become large concerns because an air base consumed huge amounts of fuel, bombs and spare parts, not to mention the supply requirements of the 20 to 40 men who worked on the ground to keep each aircraft aloft. In theory the necessities might be flown in, but in practice that would require more than all the air transport available to either side in 1942. Large air bases had to be supplied by sea and had to be near to the coast to exist at all. The Dobodura–Buna complex of airfields built by the Allies in 1943 illustrates the point. Such a large establishment, with six runways and a capacity to handle several hundred aircraft a day, was possible only because sea supply was available from nearby Oro Bay.

A DEFENSIVE STRATEGY

The Japanese aim at the start of the Pacific War was to seize locations of strategic importance, then to establish a defensive perimeter around them. By the first half of 1942 they had succeeded in the first and were in transition to the second part of the plan. In this transition phase thought was given to further conquests, and an invasion of Australia was briefly considered and rejected. The naval defeat at Midway in June 1942 confirmed that there would be no more extensive Japanese conquests in the foreseeable future, and intelligence warned of an Allied counter-offensive from Australia. Their strategic problem in the south-west Pacific became to seize a line that could be defended. The advance to Papua and Guadalcanal was an attempt to seize links in the new defensive line. Hence the move of the Nankai Shitai into the Owen Stanley Range, while tactically and operationally offensive in nature, was a defensive measure strategically. The Japanese correctly believed the Allied counter-offensive would come via the Coral Sea, although they thought it would advance from Papua on the sea's western shore. They did not anticipate that there were two counter-offensives planned, one via Papua and one via Guadalcanal.[3] The IJN's distribution of submarines to inhibit the counter-offensive is one measure of their confidence that the Allied attack would originate in Australia. Eleven submarines were available in the region, and six of 21st Submarine Division, based in Rabaul, were sent down the east coast of Australia where, in mid-1942, they sank seven ships and damaged another six.[4] This left five boats to patrol the remainder of the south-west Pacific, and only two of these were anywhere near Guadalcanal when the Americans landed there on 7 August 1942.

By the end of January 1942, the new thinking at Imperial Headquarters (IHQ) resulted in an order for the Japanese Fourth Fleet and the Nankai Shitai to invade Port Moresby. Initially the IJA did not respond as enthusiastically as the IJN. Colonel Hattori Takushiro, chief of operations of the Imperial General Staff (IGS), related after the war that the army was not initially concerned about Rabaul or Port Moresby. Their interest was Asia, and their policy was to send troops south only as the navy requested and, in early 1942, the Nankai Shitai was the only army regiment in the

Photo 1 Lieutenant-General Hyakutake Harukichi, commander of Seventeenth Army. The Nankai Shitai became a part of Seventeenth Army from 20 May 1942. (Source: author's collection)

South Pacific.[5] From February 1942 Allied air attacks on Rabaul from Port Moresby increased in intensity, which persuaded the army to agree to act with the navy against Port Moresby, where Japanese air reconnaissance noted that the two airfields were being increased to four. Army Chief of Staff Sugiyama Hajime wrote on 11 July 1942, before the anticipated counter-attack had occurred, 'We must hold the fronts in eastern New Guinea and Rabaul to the end. If they fall, not only will the Pacific Ocean be in peril, but it will allow the western advance of MacArthur's counterattack through New Guinea and herald the fall of our dominion in the southern area.'[6]

The threat from growing Allied air strength, which had brought the army's opinion into line with the navy, was a serious one. It was thought the Allies had 400 combat aircraft in New Guinea and north-eastern

Australia,[7] which was roughly correct. There were about 250 operational aircraft in the Allied Air Force (AAF) alone operating from North Queensland and Port Moresby. This number increased in the course of the campaign and to it must be added US aircraft based on Guadalcanal from August 1942. No IJA aircraft were present in the region until November 1942 and, from February to November, IJN land-based air strength fluctuated between 50 and 120 operational aircraft, less than half that of the Allies.[8] Rear-Admiral Kanazawa, commander of 8th Base Force of Fourth Fleet in Rabaul, noted in his diary in March 1942 that there were already 'conspicuous signs of defeat in the air war'.[9]

The reason for taking air bases in Papua, or sites where they could be built, was also connected to Rabaul and Truk. In a postwar interview Rear-Admiral Tomioka Sadatoshi explained his and Admiral Yamamoto Isoroku's view of the Rabaul–Truk–Port Moresby nexus,[10] which was that fleet bases were vulnerable to air attack. At the start of the war the Allies held Rabaul and could bomb Truk from there. Truk was the major Japanese naval base outside the homeland, so Rabaul had to be seized to secure Truk.[11] After Rabaul was taken in January 1942 and the Japanese realised there would be an Allied counter-offensive from Australia, it seemed that Rabaul was the logical place to base the fleet to oppose it. In the new strategic circumstances, the relationship between Rabaul and Port Moresby became similar to that which had existed between Truk and Rabaul. One of the most air-minded of the Japanese admirals, Vice-Admiral Inoue Shigeyoshi, commander of Fourth Fleet, expressed the view that Rabaul was simply not a viable base if the fleet at anchor could be regularly bombed from Port Moresby and that, if the Allies built an air base at Guadalcanal, the same problem could arise. For this reason Port Moresby and the potential airfield site at Guadalcanal were to be secured.[12] Rabaul was also suitable for development as a large air base. Eventually it had four runways, and reconnaissance aircraft could fly from there as far as Queensland. Other IJN considerations were that ownership of Port Moresby created an option to ferry aircraft, if required, from the Dutch East Indies by a short route directly along the front line to Guadalcanal. Later, Milne Bay was included in the plan as a link in the chain of proposed air bases on the outer defensive line and, if Port Moresby was attacked from Kokoda, a secondary Japanese amphibious attack on Port Moresby could be launched from Milne Bay.[13]

Great Navy Instruction 47 and Great Army Instruction 596, which governed Japanese operations in eastern New Guinea in early 1942, ordered the taking of 'all key locations in British New Guinea'.[14] It was envisaged that Port Moresby, Lae, Salamaua, Wau, Giruwa, Kokoda and Samarai would be occupied. By June, after the failure of the Coral Sea operation it was apparent to Fourth Fleet staff that it might not be possible to extend as far as Port Moresby at all in which case Rabaul would be of only limited use as a major fleet base. They still recommended that advanced air bases in Papua were a necessity even if the attack on Port Moresby did not go ahead.[15] Expectations were reduced, and a line that had appeared in the Great Army and Navy Instructions in January was now taken seriously: that Port Moresby was to be taken only 'if at all possible'.[16] Of the approximately 25 000 Japanese to be landed in eastern New Guinea in 1942 to construct and occupy bases, it was thought about 5000 might be used for an attack on Port Moresby over the Owen Stanley Range, should one occur. A permanent base for 10 000 men at Giruwa and a permanent airfield at Buna and another at Kokoda were part of the plan, whether or not the mountain campaign occurred and whether or not it was to be a quick thrust or a measured advance.

The order of battle of the Nankai Shitai is a further reminder that the Papuan operation was a serious long-term plan to occupy eastern New Guinea regardless of whether or not the MO operation to take Port Moresby went ahead. Seventeenth Army's order of 18 July to Horii to commence operations against Port Moresby ordered three-quarters of all engineers in the southern area, and the only bridging company available, to go with him to Papua to build bases and to maintain and improve communications.[17] When later the decision was taken that Guadalcanal would be the main focus of Japanese efforts and Port Moresby would have to wait, none of these engineer units was withdrawn. In October 1942, when it was plain to the Japanese that the postponed Port Moresby attack might never be made, thousands of Japanese engineers still laboured to build a motorable road between Kokoda and Giruwa because without Port Moresby a significant base at Kokoda was all the more important to the Japanese.

THE BATTLE OF THE CORAL SEA

The over-the-mountain attempt to take Port Moresby is usually seen as an alternative approach adopted by the Japanese after the failure of their seaward attempt at the Battle of the Coral Sea in May 1942. In fact the landward option was always the preferred one, especially by those who would carry it out, the Nankai Shitai. In mid-April 1942 a carrier division, two fleet carriers and their escorts and supply vessels, unexpectedly became available so a seaward option suddenly came to the fore. It was attempted but abandoned after the Coral Sea defeat in May, and then planning returned to the preferred option.

The first IJA document that discussed what to do about Papua appeared in November 1941. It was written by Lieutenant-General Adachi Hatazo, who later commanded Eighteenth Army in New Guinea. Its recommendation was that Salamaua should be taken, then there should be an advance down the coast 'to the plains about Buna'.[18] From January 1942, when serious staff work on a Port Moresby plan began, three options were considered in army and navy discussions. One of these was not long entertained. It was to land in the Basabua–Giruwa area, then transfer to barges and move along the coast to Port Moresby at night, via Samarai Island (near Milne Bay), in five short hops. Work was still being done on this plan up to April, but it was decided that the coral reef running along the coast from Port Moresby to Milne Bay would make inshore navigation too risky. The second plan was to land on the north coast of Papua, either at Giruwa or at the mouth of the Mambare River, then advance via Kokoda to Port Moresby. The third plan was a direct amphibious assault from transports on to the beaches of Port Moresby, the plan that resulted in the Battle of the Coral Sea. The reason this plan was less favoured was that it could not be done without fleet carrier support and it was well known in the IJN that, with other projects in mind at Ceylon and Midway, Yamamoto was reluctant to part with carriers for southern operations.[19]

Both Fourth Fleet and Nankai Shitai senior officers favoured the Owen Stanley plan. Their opposition to the seaward approach was this: the Jomard Passage, 650 kilometres from Port Moresby, one of several options to round the eastern tip of New Guinea, was assessed to be the best sea route from Rabaul to Port Moresby. The difficulty was that 'the convoy [would be] forced to conduct this operation across the sea, all the while susceptible to attack from allied air bases at Townsville and Cooktown. If the Jomard Passage was navigated during the evening and the convoy maintained a constant 20 kilometres an hour, then it would be exposed in the Coral Sea during the following day for about 12 hours. An expectation of success was only possible once air and sea superiority was secured in the Coral Sea.'[20]

It was not a fear of aircraft from Port Moresby so much as from north Queensland that influenced Japanese strategy regarding an invasion of Port Moresby. That this was the vital factor is reinforced by the alternative plan to land in Papua at Giruwa. Giruwa is 200 kilometres by air from Port Moresby, well within the range of all types of allied aircraft from Port Moresby but, very importantly, it is north-east of Port Moresby and not within medium-bomber range of Queensland. The Japanese were aware that Port Moresby held few Allied aircraft permanently. Japanese air attacks on it ensured that most of the AAF was kept safely out of range in north Queensland. Squadrons were flown forward and refuelled at Port Moresby, then they attacked Japanese targets and returned to Queensland, sometimes refuelling again at Port Moresby. This method lessened the chance of the aircraft being attacked on the ground. It also lessened, by a factor of about four, the number of sorties that could be flown. It was also precisely what the Japanese planned to do once they captured Port Moresby: maintain fighters there but stage bombers from Rabaul through there for raids on Queensland.[21] Japanese thinking was that an amphibious landing at Giruwa could come under only limited Allied air attack because of the Allied requirement to refuel at Port Moresby, and a Giruwa landing could receive more IJN air cover from Lae, Gasmata and Rabaul. In contrast, at any point south-east of Port Moresby in the Coral Sea troop transports would face the full weight of the AAF operating from its permanent bases in north Queensland without the necessity to refuel at Port Moresby.

In March two events further inclined Fourth Fleet and the Nankai Shitai towards the Owen Stanley plan. On 9 March IJN aerial reconnaissance discovered that there was a new Allied air base on Horn Island at the northern tip of Queensland. The Horn Island strip, 1200 metres long, enabled both medium and heavy bombers to strike along the whole of the southern coast of Papua east of Port Moresby to the Jomard Passage, thus increasing the Allies' ability to attack a convoy bound for Port Moresby.

The second event occurred on 10 March, when one battalion of the Nankai Shitai participated in the invasion of Lae and Salamaua, during which several transports were sunk and more than a hundred personnel from the army and the navy were killed by air attack from two USN carriers. On 20 March Horii wrote, 'When considering the experience of the Salamaua–Lae operation, particularly the appearance of the enemy navy's carrier task force, I believe it will be very difficult to assign protection for the transport convoy by land-based air units, and to protect the air base establishments and the landing point after embarkation.'[22] Moving on to discuss land-based air opposition, Horii recommended both a parachute drop on Port Moresby airfields in advance of a landing to disrupt Allied air operations, and more anti-aircraft artillery for the transport fleet. He also thought the escort carrier *Shoho* could not provide sufficient air cover

over the transports and wanted double the land-based air support before the seaward option could be considered. Two of Horii's three battalion commanders supported the land option even if only some of the troops could be got over the mountains 'rather than risking them all should the convoy be sunk in the Coral Sea'.[23] It is a part of the Kokoda myth that Horii was dubious about the plan to advance along the Kokoda Track, but it has not been made clear that his misgivings about a seaward route were even stronger. Going over the Owen Stanley Range was, in his view, the lesser of two evils.

In the reorganisation following the IJN's April carrier strike on Ceylon, Fourth Fleet was offered, for a Port Moresby operation, the large fleet carrier *Kaga* in addition to the small *Shoho*. Vice-Admiral Inoue, Fourth Fleet's commander, was not satisfied and asked for the Fifth Carrier Division, the *Zuikaku* and the *Shokaku*. This was agreed to so, from mid-April, planning suddenly switched to a direct seaward approach to Port Moresby. The carrier division was not tasked with direct cover of the transports as we have seen that fleet carriers were not usually risked in this way. Rather the *Zuikaku* and *Shokaku* were to do battle with USN carriers should any appear. If none did, they would approach north Queensland at night and launch raids on air bases on the day the transports were exposed to air attack from there. They would then withdraw beyond range, hopefully before they were found and attacked by land-based aircraft. The *Shoho*, a small escort carrier, was to stay with the invasion fleet and run the risk of attack by land-based aircraft.

At the Battle of the Coral Sea the USN carriers did appear and one, the *Lexington*, was sunk. The IJN lost the *Shoho* and succeeded in landing a force at Guadalcanal to build an airfield, but their Port Moresby invasion force turned back to Rabaul. The peculiar outcome of the Battle of the Coral Sea, a drawn game, is relevant to the campaign in the Owen Stanley Range. Had the Japanese been victorious, Port Moresby would probably have been in Japanese hands following a seaborne invasion in May 1942 and there would have been no campaign over the range, although large bases would still have been developed at Giruwa and Milne Bay. Had the Coral Sea been a clear Japanese defeat resulting in the loss of their fleet carriers, then the US naval ascendancy in the region would have been assured and the Japanese plan to take Port Moresby would probably have been dropped. What actually occurred was that the Japanese cancelled the sea option but still saw a landing on the north coast of Papua as viable. Officially, the rejection of a seaward approach to Port Moresby did not occur until 7 June when an army and navy agreement postponed both it and the FS operation to take Fiji and Samoa.

From this point, Imperial Headquarters implied that there was no longer a need to conduct research on any large operation involving a seaward approach to Port Moresby. Seventeenth Army, when it took over planning in June, studied only one option, although it was still in doubt whether the landing would be at the mouth of the Mambare River or at Giruwa.[24] A final illustration that a landward approach over the mountains to Port Moresby, together with an operation to take Milne Bay, was seen in Rabaul, if not Tokyo, as the long-term realistic option is that, while orders were issued that the Nankai Shitai should prepare itself for an opposed landing on a coral coast, no exercise was conducted. What was done repeatedly was that the members of the Nankai Shitai were loaded with heavy packs full of volcanic dust to march up and down Rabaul's volcanoes to increase mountain-climbing fitness and in order to assess what weight of pack could be carried over a mountain range.[25]

The Kokoda myth entirely misses the strategic context of the Kokoda campaign. The Japanese attack on Papua was a large and complex operation, and the advance on Port Moresby was to be a part of it, but not an essential part. If it did not go ahead the Japanese still planned to permanently occupy as much of eastern New Guinea as they could and from there defend against the anticipated Allied counter-attack. The route taken to Port Moresby, along the Kokoda Track, was always the favoured option, and it was rather the Coral Sea attempt that was opportunistic.

CHAPTER 3

MILITARY
INTELLIGENCE

On 13 March 1941, nine months before the Japanese made their move in the Pacific, Major Toyufuku Tetsuo stepped ashore at Port Moresby. He walked around asking questions, visited the Government Land Office to buy maps, and drove a short distance inland. Toyufuku was an IJA intelligence officer disguised as a seaman on the Japanese merchant ship *Takachiho Maru*. He was not the first Japanese officer to go to New Guinea for intelligence purposes, but he was the most important. Later the senior intelligence officer of the Nankai Shitai and wounded at Isurava, Toyufuku wrote a report that undermines the Kokoda myth that when the Japanese began the campaign they knew very little about Papua.[1]

The best-known example of the myth is that the Japanese believed a vehicular road existed over the Owen Stanley Range, and a few comments to that effect can be seen in documents and diaries:[2] 'It is thought there is a poor motor road between Kokoda and Port Moresby.'[3] No doubt some Japanese, those without access to intelligence reports, believed this, but the Nankai Shitai senior officers and planning staff knew it was not so. In fact the term 'road' meant little; both sides freely use the words 'road', 'track' or 'trail' almost interchangeably.[4]

Toyofuku's report on British New Guinea, written within weeks of his visit, lists the length and location of all vehicular roads in Papua. Of the roads about Port Moresby, Milne Bay and Giruwa, Toyofuku wrote: 'It is recognised that these roads only connect the villages in the vicinity of the coast.'[5] In January 1942 Captain Kanemoto Rinzo, a staff officer of Seventeenth Army, recorded in his diary that he had been talking to Toyufuku, who assured him that there was no road over the Owen Stanley Range.[6] Later, when Kanemoto returned from a reconnaissance flight along the Kokoda Track, he was questioned by Horii: 'The commander did not think that motorable roads were running over the Stanley range at an altitude of 3000 metres. He only wanted to know how far inland automobiles could go.'[7]

The supposed Japanese ignorance of Papua and the Kokoda Track highlighted by the Kokoda myth does, however, raise an interesting question, one asked by Captain Geoffrey Vernon, New Guinea identity and doctor to Maroubra Force. In his diary Vernon wrote: 'From Kagi towards Kokoda there are many tracks. I know of three which cross the range at different places. Enemy captured maps show at least four. Where their information comes from is a mystery.'[8] The following is an attempt to answer Vernon's question: what did the Japanese know, and how did they know it?

Ten years before Toyufuku went to Port Moresby, when the Japanese Ministry of Foreign Affairs in conjunction with the IJA and the IJN began a study of the 'southern area' (bounded by the equator in the north, India in the west, Australia in the south and Hawaii in the east), New Guinea and Papua were not of much interest. The first IJA report on Guam was completed in 1932, but none was produced on eastern New Guinea until an IJN research paper of September 1940, which listed it as an outlying but necessary acquisition, and Toyufuku's IJA report of March 1941.[9] In the southern area in the 1930s, the IJN and IJA sent officers on information-gathering missions, often in the guise of employees of research and business enterprises, some established or subsidised by the ministry. Botanical research was a favourite cover for espionage.[10] By the mid-1930s in the Netherlands East Indies there were 40 Japanese companies employing more than a thousand Japanese citizens.[11] In Rabaul and at Guadalcanal, resident Japanese passed on intelligence to their homeland.[12]

The level of Japanese interest in eastern New Guinea stepped up in 1937. When the *Caroline Maru* visited five times that year, for no obvious commercial reason, the Australian Directorate of Naval Intelligence (DNI) and the Commonwealth Investigation Branch (CIB) took notice. In 1938 the Defence Department notified the Prime Minister's Department that the Japanese were taking a keen interest in the Australian mandate of New Guinea: 'A Japanese naval officer travelled to Rabaul in a Japanese vessel as a passenger but landed dressed as a member of the crew and whilst on shore carried out reconnaissance.'[13] In Papua there was an

Photo 2 The *Takachiho Maru* in which Major Toyufuku Tetsuo arrived at Port Moresby on 13 March 1941. (AWM 304004)

Australian effort to keep Japanese influence to a minimum. By 1940 there were, officially at least, no permanent Japanese residents in Port Moresby and the only Japanese company there was the Nanyo Kohatsu Kaisha.[14] The company had Japanese government contracts for the construction of piers, oil tanks and defensive works at Palau and also operated in Dutch New Guinea. It maintained an air link to Japan, employing pilots on secondment from the IJN. An Australian report of 27 February 1941 on Japanese activities in New Guinea confirmed that the company was working with the Ministry of Foreign Affairs, and it was strongly suspected of intelligence activities on behalf of the IJN. The report concluded that 'there is also evidence that the Japanese are [now] giving attention to the whole island of New Guinea'.[15] Japanese trade with Port Moresby was also stepped up in 1940–41, thus providing increased opportunities for intelligence-gathering.[16]

The trading vessels *Caroline Maru* and *Takachiho Maru* began a further series of visits to New Guinea from 1938 to 1941. The *Caroline Maru* carried three English-speaking Japanese known only as Kobayashi O, Iida H and Yashi N. They visited Rabaul, Salamaua and Wau. They hired an aircraft, took photographs of the Wau airstrip from the air and asked to buy maps.[17] They were observed taking grass samples, a procedure used in China before a campaign to see whether suitable local forage was available for the horse-reliant Japanese army.[18] They then sailed to Basabua, between Gona and Giruwa, and where the Nankai

Shitai landed in July 1942. They measured the depth of water at Basabua anchorage and at Milne Bay checked the location of coral reefs against their charts. Australian authorities were convinced that Kobayashi and the others were spies. If they were not spies, then there were certainly IJN officers examining the coast of Papua doing similar things, for in January 1941 an IJN officer travelling incognito on a ship from Lae to Milne Bay wrote that he 'was in a position to see many small islands which I could not have visited in a warship [and] it was by this means I was able to survey the work of my compatriots'.[19] The Japanese prewar investigations along the Papuan coast contributed to the information that appeared on the maps the Nankai Shitai used.[20]

In September 1940 the IJN's report on eastern New Guinea was produced. It used Kriegsmarine charts that had their origins in older Imperial German Navy charts. An Australian naval officer judged that they were better than the Royal Navy (RN) charts used by the Royal Australian Navy (RAN).[21] The IJA also had RN charts but seem to have preferred the Kriegsmarine ones. In German with Japanese translation, the charts were used in 1942 to land forces at Lae, Salamaua, Basabua and Milne Bay. Another German source of intelligence for the Japanese about New Guinea opened up with the success of the Nazi Party in the German elections of 1933. Although Germany had not had a colony in New Guinea since 1914, there were still Germans living there. Many were involved in the Lutheran Church and were thought to wield a great deal of influence locally, a matter of concern to the Australian CIB. The CIB also noted Germans taking aerial photographs of New Guinea and were aware that German maps of the area were supplied to the Japanese.[22] The contact between Japanese sailors and Germans was known, and it was later discovered that the Nankai Shitai brought German-speaking officers to Rabaul to work with Peter Matthies, a half-German half-New Guinean who had avoided the round-up of German citizens in New Guinea at the start of the European war. The CIB thought Matthies to be a part of an extensive network of German and Chinese spies in Rabaul. That might be true, but it is certain that he helped the Japanese recruit labourers in Rabaul for the Port Moresby operation.[23]

In December 1941 General Adachi, while writing a paper about a possible advance from Salamaua to Buna, requested more information about the state of routes over the Owen Stanley Range, and in January 1942, the Japanese began to look at the Kokoda Track closely as a result of orders from IHQ to Nankai Shitai and Fourth Fleet that they should examine possible land invasion routes to Port Moresby.[24] The preferred route was through Kokoda, and a series of studies was inititated. Sources of food, the rainfall, roads and bridges were among the topics examined, and the results were impressive. In March 1942 a summary of intelligence gathered about eastern New Guinea advised that 'on an average two pigs are raised by each family in a village ... they are small and thin, average weight 30kg ... wild pigs are found all over the mountains but it is difficult to catch them.'[25] The summary also provided information on local fruit and vegetables, an estimate of the numbers of eggs that might be found in a village and the types of fish in the streams.[26] For an army whose doctrine emphasised local foraging this was vital information.

Some of the Japanese maps Vernon saw were purchased in Australia, a fact the CIB was aware of:

> Prior to the war the Japanese had organised, along the lines of the general pattern elsewhere, a number of agents and spies throughout Australia. The consulate must have passed back a vast amount of information ... and numerous special agents were sent to Australia to obtain information. One of these, a major in the army, made a complete tour of the country, noting down all the information of value to Japan. Others arrived in the guise of 'trade missions' etc and contacted local Japanese in the various states.[27]

In addition to Japanese agents visiting the country, the DNI and the CIB were also concerned to discover in 1941 that Japanese residents of Australia, of whom there were about 3000, were purchasing maps of New Guinea in Sydney.[28] Apart from commercial and very general 1:300 000 maps of the Territory of Papua, the only detailed maps available in the late 1930s and early 1940s were those made by explorers and patrol officers. In June 1942 Prince Takeda Tsuneyoshi of IHQ gave 'an English explorer's map' to Seventeenth Army staff before their departure for Rabaul.[29] Prince Takeda's map was probably made by one of the explorers who mapped eastern New Guinea from 1913 to 1930: Ernest Chinnery, Cyril Jackson or Wilfred Beaver. The Chinnery, Jackson and Beaver maps were available in Australia in a number of archives, including the Parliamentary Library and the New South Wales State Archives, and in private collections. They frequently appeared in the *Papuan Annual Report*, which could be obtained in Australian state public libraries. Two of Jackson's maps appearing in the 1916–17 *Papuan Annual Report* show the route from Buna via Kokoda to Port Moresby, and the similarity between the Chinnery maps and maps used by the Nankai Shitai's 41st Regiment in Papua in 1942 is too marked to be coincidental.[30] The annual reports also made frequent reference to road construction and provided photographs of the region.

Japanese intelligence gatherers in Australia were also interested in obtaining books. Just before the Pacific War began a bookshop owner in Canberra supplied to the CIB a list of books purchased or requested by a Japanese.[31] There is no way of knowing whether this was a perfectly innocent purchase; however, one book that was definitely used by Seventeenth Army cartographers, as it appears as a source on Japanese maps, was an account of several months spent in the Eora Creek–Kokoda–Buna area by Evelyn Cheesman entitled *Two Roads of Papua*. Cheesman was an entomologist who had spent many years in the South Pacific. When the war began she wanted to use her detailed knowledge of New Guinea to aid the Allied war effort. Among other endeavours she gave lectures on New Guinea in London in early 1943.[32] Evelyn Cheesman probably never realised that she was of even greater help to her enemy. Half of Cheesman's book concerns her several months based at Kokoda in 1933. Twice she walked along the Kokoda Track to just north of Templeton's Crossing, and she made two trips to Buna. Cheesman wrote that 'the road crosses Papua from coast to coast, starting at Port Moresby, passing through Kokoda and finishing at Buna'. She stated that there are airfields at Yodda and Kokoda, and her sentence 'Roads are unusually good about Kokoda compared with some parts of the territory' is repeated word for word on Japanese maps.[33] The trip from Kokoda to Buna, 68 miles according to Cheesman, was described in daily stages. Wairopi was identified as a particularly fertile area with renowned taro gardens, and sweet potato was said to be plentiful around Kokoda. Cheesman also described the locations of government administration, patrol officers and armed police.[34] She complained that decent maps of Papua were unobtainable in London, and her own were purchased in the same place Toyufuku visited, the Government Land Office in Port Moresby.

Cheesman's contribution to Japanese knowledge of the landward approaches to Port Moresby pales before that of Josef Anton Hofstetter, who gave the Japanese a great deal of information derived from personal experience. His name, as the sole source of information, appears on half a dozen Nankai Shitai maps of the Wau–Buna–Kokoda–Port Moresby area, and the information he provided reveals his extensive knowledge of the region gained as a result of 22 years living there. Hofstetter was a Swiss, a national of a neutral country, so he had escaped the Australian round-up of Germans in New Guinea. Hofstetter's family was originally from Bavaria, and Hofstetter was born in St Gallen, Switzerland, on 10 April 1895. He came to Australia in 1914 and told customs officials he had just spent a year in Fiji. He worked his way north from Sydney to the Torres Strait Islands, changing jobs frequently, as his alien registration forms attest. He cut cane at Innisfail, and while in far north Queensland in October 1918 he volunteered to join the Australian Imperial Force but was rejected on medical grounds.[35] In the early 1920s he went to Papua and New Guinea where at various times he worked at Port Moresby, Yodda, the Waria River, Wau and Bulolo.[36] He was employed by the Bulolo Gold Dredging Company when, in January 1942, the Japanese invaded Rabaul and the call came for all able-bodied men to enlist in the New Guinea Volunteer Rifles or be sent south to Australia. According to the men he worked with, Hofstetter disappeared. In March when the Japanese landed in Lae, he joined them. Carlo Cavalieri, another Swiss who knew Hofstetter and worked with him at Bulolo, believed Hofstetter had some connection with Hans Schmidt Burgk, the NSDAP (Nazi Party) leader in the Wau–Bulolo area.[37]

The Australian New Guinea Administrative Unit (ANGAU) became interested in Hofstetter when, in early 1943, he was known to be helping the Japanese. A scribbled note in Gavin Long's papers for the Australian official history stated that Hofstetter was thought to be the white man seen guiding the Japanese advance on Wau in February 1943.[38] Those who knew him told ANGAU that Hofstetter's knowledge of the mining areas of the eastern coast of New Guinea was second to none. One of these, John Murphy, said that Hofstetter 'knows the Waria [River] backwards'.[39] There is no doubt he was indeed the man who aided the Japanese attack on Mubo and Lae. What has not been known until now is his connection with the earlier Kokoda campaign.

On Nankai Shitai maps Hofstetter is sometimes named, although it is misspelled Hoffstetter, and at other times he is referred to as 'the Swiss informant' or 'the Swiss miner [who] until last year had been a gold miner at Wau and Bulolo for about six years'.[40] Exactly how Hofstetter acquired his knowledge of the Kokoda Track is unclear, but it probably occurred when he worked at the Yodda goldfield in the 1930s. To get to Yodda he would have either come by sea to Buna, then along the Kokoda–Sanananda track, or come by air and landed at Kokoda, where miners often stopped for a day or two. It is unlikely that he had walked the Kokoda Track. According to those who mined in Papua before World War II, none of them would have ever considered doing that if there was an alternative.

A Japanese map note of 2 July 1942 explains: 'According to the statement of a Swiss in summarising the Mambare–Kokoda trail you can reach X [Moresby] by following the bank of the river from the river mouth by way of Tomoyaropa [Wiaropi], Kokoda, crossing a 2200m mountain SE of Mt Service though the line is being patrolled. Then going downstream to the Laloki river.' The Kokoda Track is described as '4 or 5 foot wide and can be travelled in 8 to 10 days'.[41] A post–Kokoda campaign Australian study of two Hofstetter maps noted that the Wau–Nadzab map 'carries a description of rivers (width, depth, rate of flow, composition of river bed), information on roads and trails (suitability for motor traffic, horse, foot, etc), details of size of airfields, bridges, anti British natives etc. From the description it appears that all particulars have been supplied by Hoffstetter and there is no indication that any of the information has been obtained by recce.' Of the second map was written 'same as above, but covers Lae, Buna, Moresby, Popondetta'.[42]

Aware of Hofstetter's contribution to what the Japanese knew about approaches to Wau and Port Moresby, ANGAU and CIB tried to locate him at the end of the war, although they thought he might have fled to Japan. Another line of inquiry confused him with a German from Finschhafen, and nothing definitive was learned of his whereabouts. Somehow ANGAU did not come across an Allied Translator and Interpreter Service (ATIS) item translated in 1944. It was a captured document, which stated: 'Josef Anton Hofstetter, a Swiss, was killed in action on February 6, 1943 by enemy automatic rifle fire one kilometre northwest of Wau stock farm.'[43] The writer, Hofstetter's Japanese superior, said Hofstetter had officer status in the Japanese army and that he made excellent maps and was a good guide.

What, then, was the quality of the maps produced as a result of the various forms of intelligence-gathering outlined thus far? As far as the standard of an army's intelligence operation can be judged by the maps it produces, it is possible to assess Japanese maps of Papua in 1942 by comparing them to Australian maps made at the same time, but it is first necessary to explain just what a militarily useful map might be. The largest-scale map the Australians captured from the Japanese during the Kokoda campaign was a map of Papua sold by the H.E.C. Robertson company in Sydney in the 1930s. At 1:1 000 000 scale it was of hardly any military use. The other commonly used scales were 1:500 000, 1:250 000, 1:100 000, 1:63 000 and 1:33 000. There are three general rules of a map's military utility. First, the smaller the scale, the more useful the map as small-scale maps will have more topographic detail.[44] Second, maps with accurate grids are much better than ones without and, third, the same goes for maps with contour lines, preferably with heights marked on them. Of course it is easy to produce a simple enlargement of several map squares, but this alone does not make for a better map as any errors will simply be magnified. By the standard of 1942 any map more than 1:300 000 might not be very useful, but 1:100 000 scale can be quite acceptable if accompanied by a passably accurate grid and contour lines. Colonel Tsuji Masanobu thought that the maps for southern operations were poor compared with the excellent 1:100 000 IJA maps of Siberia.[45]

For the Australians at the start of the Kokoda campaign there were 'practically no maps of military value for either the Australian Territory of Papua or the former German colony of New Guinea'.[46] The first Australian unit to cross the Owen Stanley Range, a company of 39th Battalion, was very poorly prepared. The company had a list of the villages in the order that they should be encountered and crude maps of 1:300 000 scale.[47] The maps used by 21st Brigade, which followed in August 1942, were not much better, its brigadier, Arnold Potts, having fruitlessly searched Port Moresby for decent maps.[48]

The best that could be found was a map derived from others collected by Captain Harold Jesser of the Papuan Infantry Battalion (PIB). Jesser began his first trip over the Kokoda Track on 19 February 1942. He collected plantation maps up to Sogeri and made his own map thereafter.[49] The 21st Brigade war diary recorded on 16 August that one aerial photograph and 'one inaccurate map' was all that was available.[50] One battalion Intelligence Section took a trace map of the track, two aerial photographs and a blank grid map to fill in as they advanced.[51] Another battalion, the 2/14th, had a 1:500 000 map and also made their own sketch maps as they went along.[52] The last battalion of the brigade to enter the mountains, the 2/27th, was just a little better off. They had a 1:70 000 map but with useless five-mile grid squares and no contour lines.[53]

In September 1942, the Australian 25th Brigade advanced into the Owen Stanley Range with a map that, from Ioribaiwa to Kagi at least, was an improvement on any used so far.[54] It had been made by Australian army surveyors in Port Moresby and adapted from a map made in the Dutch East Indies – another source also used by the Japanese. It was one-inch-to-a-mile scale (1:63 360) with a 1000-yard grid, and it had contour lines. Once 25th Brigade passed Kagi they returned to another map of the low standard that 21st Brigade had used in August. Its scale was two inches to the mile with no practical grid and no contour lines, and it was very inaccurate. On it a brigade staff member has crossed out the location of Templeton's Crossing and written it in again at the correct position. An account of a patrol commented that the map was in parts 'absolutely unreliable'.[55] The next brigade to arrive, 16th Brigade in October, had nothing better with which to fight the second Eora–Templeton's action, but at the very end of October, in time for the reoccupation of Kokoda, much better maps were in general use.[56] These were made by 2nd Australian Field Survey Section, New Guinea Force (NGF) in Port Moresby and were the best maps produced by either side in the Kokoda campaign. They were issued in October 1942 and were used during the fighting at Oivi–Gorari in November. They had a scale of one inch to the mile, a grid of one square to a thousand yards and reasonably accurate contour lines, but with no heights marked. With these maps the Australians became lost in the jungle less often, and they were better able to report their own position and call in air strikes against the enemy. There is no doubt that they were superior to anything the Japanese had, and by late October they gave the Australians a significant advantage.

Japanese maps can be divided into two types: those produced before additional information from prisoners and captured maps could be processed, and those made after. The first Australian prisoners were taken in late July, and the Deniki engagement on 14 August was the first time the Japanese captured Australian maps, although it will be apparent from the foregoing that some of these were not especially useful. An IJA 41st Regiment staff report advised on 17 August: 'During this operation there will be no printed precision maps, therefore map information must be gathered from the Yazawa intelligence report and the attached maps of this report.'[57] No Japanese maps produced before the end of August have any useful grid or contours. They often have 'form lines', which do give an indication of the countryside, but these are much inferior to contours. One of the Hofstetter maps is typical of those with which the Japanese landed in Papua. Note 38 on the map stated it was drawn from two sources, a 1:50 000 Australian Territory of Papua map, such as appeared in a *Papuan Annual Report*, and Kreigsmarine maps 857, 859 and 816.[58] The Hofstetter map does not have a grid, nor does it have contours. What it does have that makes it better than the early period Australian maps is Hofstetter's notes on terrain features.

A second advantage the Nankai Shitai had was maps produced after aerial reconnaissance. Captain Kanemoto went along on one reconnaissance flight and reported that the track from the coast to Kokoda was easily seen but after that it seemed to disappear into the jungle.[59] A dozen such flights, some from a new seaplane base at Lae, were made before the campaign began. Major Koiwai Mitsuo, commander of 2/41st Battalion, came ashore in Papua with a sheaf of aerial photographs and the maps made from them.[60] Those of Eora Gorge south of Kokoda were so good, wrote Koiwai, that when the mist lifted he looked up the valley and was easily able to establish his location and that of the key terrain features.[61] The Japanese maps made from aerial photographs were by far the best-quality maps available to either side in August, but they still lacked a practical grid or contours.

Japanese maps of Port Moresby and surrounds are much more detailed than those of the Kokoda Track. They are often gridded, contoured and accurate. Much of this detail came from aerial reconnaissance from early in 1942. One map recorded that a feature was 'seen from a/c [aircraft] over the northern aerodrome 1/5/42', but there are some items of interest unlikely to have been observed by aircrew: 'Troops stationed here – less than 50 men ... BP warehouse ... navy officers' mess ... army barracks ... club and hotel.'[62] Unusually, there is no mention where this information came from, but two likely sources are Toyufuku or Hofstetter.

A comparison of Japanese and Australian maps suggests that, up to the battle of Isurava in late August 1942, Japanese maps of the area of operations were superior, although not greatly so. By late October this had changed. Japanese maps did not improve much as a result of capturing Australian maps, but Australian maps did improve as a result of the work of army map-makers, and it may be that this was a contributing factor in the Australian victory at Oivi–Gorari. The Japanese response to the Australian flanking attack there via Baribe was limited by confusion as to which tracks led where. Nankai Shitai veterans were curious enough about this to try to sort it out on one of their postwar trips to collect the remains of their dead. In 1967 they established that their maps of November 1942 had led them to mistake Gorari for Ilimo throughout the fighting.

The Kokoda myth supposition that the Japanese were ignorant about the theatre of war is a simplistic and inaccurate assessment. Building on a long-term interest in intelligence-gathering in the south-west Pacific, the Japanese did obtain a great deal of useful information on eastern Papua in the late 1930s. By 1941 a narrowing of interest can be discerned, and intelligence work was done on potential landing sites on the coast about Giruwa, on routes in the Papuan interior and on Port Moresby itself. By early 1942 Japanese intelligence studies specifically on the Kokoda route were underway. They drew on prewar work by IJA and IJN officers, intelligence gained in Australia, German and Dutch sources, and local informants, among whom Hofstetter was the most important. The maps to which he contributed were, as Dr Vernon observed, better than those available to the Australians, but by the end of the Kokoda campaign this was no longer true.

CHAPTER 4

THE NANKAI SHITAI

Six Japanese infantry battalions formed the bulk of the fighting forces of the Nankai Shitai. The Kokoda myth requires that they were large battalions; otherwise it is hard to see how the Australians, who committed 12 infantry battalions to the Kokoda campaign, can have been much outnumbered. In fact the Japanese infantry battalions were under strength when they arrived in Papua. The weakest, and the first to arrive, was the first battalion of 144th Regiment (1/144th). Drawn from 55th Division, the battalion was under the command of Lieutenant-Colonel Tsukamoto Hatsuo, who a year later took over the regiment when Colonel Kusunose Masao left Papua owing to illness.[1] On 25 November 1941 the battalion, 878 strong as shown in table 4.1, left Japan to invade Guam.

Eight months later, the 1/144th arrived in Papua with 586 men.[2] How it was reduced requires some explanation. The 878 men in table 4.1 represent neither a normal Japanese infantry battalion nor the order of battle the Australians believed one had in mid-1942. It was not normal because the Japanese had, in a sense, no normal battalion. The Australians reduced the size of their battalions for war in the jungle. Of 1068 men in the Australian 39th Battalion in Port Moresby, for example, just over half of them were selected to form the 'jungle-type' battalion, a smaller, lighter battalion better suited to fighting in the tropics. AIF battalions from the Middle East were similarly reduced to 580 men in New Guinea. The Japanese took this approach much further, having six types of infantry battalion.[3] A Japanese battalion could be as large as 1431 men or as small as 750, depending on circumstances. In

Table 4.1: 1/144th Infantry Battalion

Battalion Headquarters	7 officers, 30 men
Battalion Train	110 all ranks
Gun Platoon	1 officer, 54 men
Machine Gun Company	4 officers, 129 men
Company Headquarters	1 officer, 13 men
Two Machine Gun Platoons, each with:	1 officer, 45 men
—Ammunition Platoon	1 officer, 22 men
Three Rifle Companies, each with:	4 officers, 177 men
—Company Headquarters	1 officer, 18 men
Three Rifle Platoons, each with	
—Platoon Headquarters	1 officer, 1 man
—Grenade Discharger Section	13 men
Three Rifle Sections, each with	13 men
Total strength	878

Source: 39th Battalion war diary, August–September 1942, captured documents appendix E, AWM52 8/3/78.

the southern area of operations 750 men was considered the desirable size, and battalions that arrived in Rabaul larger than this were trimmed down before proceeding to Guadalcanal and Papua.[4] The flexibility of Japanese organisation can also be observed above battalion level and is somewhat reminiscent of the German idea of a *Kampfgruppe* – a force put together with a particular task in mind. The Nankai Shitai and the Eastern Detachment, which took Ambon and Timor, were just such purpose-built forces. By 1944 the Allies had identified four different kinds of Japanese divisions. The Nankai Shitai was classified as a 'special division'; that is, a light division built around two regiments of infantry instead of the usual three.[5]

Stepping back down to battalion level, the adjustment made to the 1/144th as it left Japan was the reduction of its machine-gun company to two platoons. Other armies of World War II tended to increase the number of automatic weapons; the Australians in Papua, for instance, began to double the number of both light machine-guns and submachine-guns in their infantry battalions from September 1942. The IJA, which had no submachine-guns, found it could not obtain enough medium machine-guns and, to increase the size of the army, it was necessary to decrease the numbers of them in its infantry battalions.

The Allied pre-campaign estimates for a Japanese battalion in Papua hovered around the 1027 mark, and it was thought that Japanese regiments were from 2716 to 3397 strong.[6] In fact, depending on the theatre of war or the mission, one could be as large as 3854, but 144th Regiment at 'jungle' strength was 2300 strong. It is natural to assume that the enemy are at full strength, and the Japanese were also guilty of overestimating enemy battalion size, believing that the 580-man Australian battalions in Papua were double that.

The reduction of the 1/144th began with the invasion of Guam in December 1941 when the regiment lost 31 men in battle and others to disease. In January 1942, the 144th invaded Rabaul where it lost 16 killed and 49 wounded after which 1 Company of the 1/144th was 37 below establishment.[7] With the exception of the abortive Port Moresby invasion attempt in May, which resulted in the Battle of the Coral Sea, 1/144th Battalion was in Rabaul from the end of January to the middle of July, when it sailed to Papua with the vanguard of the Nankai Shitai. More were lost to Allied air attack in Rabaul, dengue fever and malaria, which hit the 1/144th hardest of all, reducing the battalion to 710 men.[8] The wasting away of units in unhealthy climes, even when not engaged with the enemy, was a problem for both sides. The Australian 49th Battalion, after almost a year in Port Moresby, sometimes bombed from the air but otherwise having seen no action, had 678 men on parade on 26 July 1942. The battalion was short of establishment by 70, and 127 were in hospital.[9]

Another curious aspect of the Japanese system was that little attention was paid to replacements. Replacements, as distinct from reinforcements, which are complete new units arriving at the battlefront, are individuals who are sent in batches to replace those wounded in battle or debilitated by disease. The fighting power of a unit can be maintained at a higher level for a longer period if it receives regular replacements. The Australians usually adhered to this system but not in the Papuan campaign when, owing to supply problems that limited the number of men who could be maintained in the front line, it was thought better to pull out entire worn units and replace them with fresh ones. The Japanese approach resembled that of the Soviet Union's Red Army in World War II in that it chose not to expend resources on maintaining a large replacement system of depots or training battalions as the Australians and other Western armies did. Rather, the IJA policy was to send replacements when it caused little inconvenience to the more important task of raising new units. Western armies viewed this as a dangerously short-sighted solution

Photo 3 144th Regiment landing at Rabaul, 23 January 1942. (Kochi New Guinea Association)

to the problem. Not one of the infantry battalions of the Nankai Shitai received any replacements until November 1942 by which time 144th Regiment had been on active service for 11 months. When the first batch of 280 replacements arrived the regiment actually required more than a thousand.[10] By way of contrast, there were few times when an Australian infantry battalion on active service during World War II went more than four months without receiving replacements.

In July and early August 1942, 144th Regiment prepared for the new campaign in Papua. The wagons of battalion trains were left in Rabaul and some of the personnel sent to battalion headquarters. The regiment weeded out the weak and unfit; in each company from five to 15 men were left behind.[11] Company commander Lieutenant Noda Hidetaka identified two schools of thought: 'Many commanders like to take into battle with them as many of their men as possible but I myself incline to leave behind any who are not really fit. Can it be I am not sufficiently ruthless?'[12] Battle casualties, air attack, sickness and leaving behind the unfit reduced the 1/144th by 292 from the time it left Japan to the 586 men with which it arrived in Papua.[13]

The first battalion of 144th Regiment was 150 men weaker than the other two battalions of the regiment. The 2nd Battalion fought at Guam and Rabaul and in March occupied Lae and Salamaua. There was no fighting on land there, but a strike by USN carrier-borne aircraft hit the Japanese

Table 4.2: 2/144th on board the *Ryoyo Maru*

Battalion Headquarters	79
4th Company	168
5th Company	–
6th Company	163
Machine Gun Company	130
Gun Platoon	71

Source: captured documents, ATIS current translations no 42,
p. 6, AWM55 3/4; ATIS bulletin no 9, p. 4, AWM 55 1/1.

invasion fleet. In this setback the 2/144th lost 9 killed and 24 wounded.[14] The number that boarded the *Ryoyo Maru* in Rabaul in August to sail to Papua appears in Nankai Shitai shipping records (see table 4.2).

The figure for 5th Company is not clear but, if its strength was midway between that of 4th and 6th Companies, then the battalion sailed for Papua with 776 men, just six more than an Australian post-campaign report estimated.[15] Less is known about the pre–Kokoda campaign losses of the 3/144th. On 13 June 1942, 9th Company 3/144th was reduced by 25 (nine had been returned to Japan) to 156 men of whom 24 were in hospital.[16] The battalion arrived in Papua 738 strong.[17] Shipping records also show the strength of other elements of the 144th. The Regimental Headquarters (RHQ) had 73 men, the Regimental Gun Company (RGC) 110 and the Regimental Signals Company (RSC) had 122 or 131 men.[18] The total strength of 144 Regiment as it arrived in Papua was close to 2270.

The other infantry element of the Nankai Shitai was 41st Regiment. Since 1937 this regiment's three battalions had served in China where it specialised in amphibious assault. It was about 2800 strong in Malaya in December 1941. One battalion fought at Jitra and the regiment fought at Gemas, although they were not involved in the Australian ambush of 14 January 1942 there. The regiment again engaged the Australians, and put its amphibious skills to good use, when it landed on Singapore Island in February. Casualties for 41st Regiment in Malaya are unclear but were light. Next the regiment went to the Philippines where it suffered 'considerable' casualties in May 1942.[19] The regiment had four smaller infantry companies per battalion instead of the three infantry companies per battalion of 144th Regiment, and it had about 750 men per battalion by the time it arrived in Papua. Like the 144th, it had had no replacements since November 1941. Coming by sea from Davao, it was in Rabaul for just a few days so it suffered little from medical problems attendant upon a stay there. The unfit – 103 men – were left in Rabaul, and the regiment went to Papua with 2396 men.[20] The 2nd Infantry Battalion of 41st Regiment (2/41st) landed 755 strong, but the other two battalions were much smaller as 710 men were taken to form a temporary supply-carrying group, leaving the 1/41st with 343 men and the 3/41st with 424. One officer wrote, 'It was a pity that the soldiers of the regiment with great wartime careers became transport soldiers similar to military labourers, however temporarily, and were assigned to duty in the rear, carrying rice instead of guns.'[21] Not until October were the men detached for transport duty returned to their battalions.

The list of the formation and equipment of the 41st Regiment, drawn up by the regiment (see table 4.3), omits the regimental headquarters, which had 58 men giving a total of 1773 with the regiment in Papua.[22]

The fighting units of the Nankai Shitai that remain to be dealt with are Nankai Shitai Headquarters (NSHQ), 55th Division Cavalry Company (55 DCC), the mountain artillery, the Special Naval Landing Parties (SNLP), combat engineers and an anti-aircraft battalion. The NSHQ, a detachment from 55th Division headquarters, had 104 men, and 55 DCC probably had 83 men.[23] The main bodies of two combat engineer regiments and detachments from others were sent to Papua. Japanese engineer regiments, one battalion strong, could be as large as 1020 men with three field companies, each of 290 men, one stores company of 100 and a headquarters of 50.[24] The 15th Independent Engineer Regiment (15 IER) left one company in Rabaul and brought 600 men.[25] The other major engineer unit, 55th Engineer Regiment (55 ER), brought 800.[26] 3rd Company and a platoon of 10th Independent Engineer Regiment (10 IER), a platoon of 4th Independent Engineer Regiment (4 IER), a company of 55th Shipping Engineer Regiment (55 SER), 3rd Company 15 ER and 1st Bridge Construction Company (1 BCC) were also present with around 960 men.[27] The total number of uniformed IJA and IJN engineers that served in the Kokoda campaign was about 2360 men.[28]

One battalion strong, 55th Mountain Artillery Regiment (55 MAR), possessed nine 75mm mountain guns, which were light, man-portable howitzers. Understanding that the terrain in Papua would be the worst they had yet faced, the battalion left behind all but four guns but took three-quarters of its strength – 420 men – to carry them. One gun was

Table 4.3: Formation and equipment of 41st Regiment

Commander of the regiment: Colonel Yazawa Kiyomi

Commander of the 1st Battalion: Major Miyamoto Kikumatsu

Headquarters of the battalion	58 men
1st Company	45 men, 5 light machine-guns, 4 mortars
2nd Company	45 men, 2 light machine-guns, 2 mortars
3rd Company	37 men, 2 light machine-guns, 2 mortars
4th Company	50 men, 3 light machine-guns, 3 mortars
1st Machine Gun Company	67 men, 4 heavy machine-guns
Battalion Gun Troop	41 men, 1 gun
Total personnel	343 men

Commander of the 2nd Battalion: Major Koiwai Mitsuo
5th, 6th, 7th and 8th Companies in full war-time formation
The Machine Gun Company has 6 machine-guns and the Battalion Gun
Troop has just 1 gun

Total personnel	755 men

Commander of the 3rd Battalion: Major Kobayashi Asao (transferred); Major
Murase Gohei [commanded after Kobayashi]

Headquarters of the battalion	48 men
9th Company	41 men, 2 light machine-guns
10th Company	117 men, 6 light machine-guns, 3 mortars
11th Company	38 men, 1 light machine-guns, 1 mortars
12th Company	125 men, 9 light machine-guns, 9 mortars
2nd Machine Gun Company	39 men, 3 [heavy] machine-guns
Regimental Gun Troop	26 men, 1 gun
Total personnel	434 men

Regimental Gun Company	88 men including the commander
	1 Type 41 mountain gun; 60 rounds of [first-line] ammunition
Rapid-fire Gun Company	55 men, including the commander
	1 Type 94 37mm gun; 150 rounds of [first-line] ammunition
Signals Company	109 men including the commander
	6 telephone sets; 8 Type 5 wireless telegraph sets; 8 Type 6 telegraph sets

Source: Koiwai, *Nyuginia Senki* [Battle history of New Guinea], p. 61.

taken into the mountains by each company, and one was left in reserve at Giruwa.[29]

A Japanese SNLP corresponded roughly to a reinforced United States Marine battalion. For a given task an SNLP could be from 1000 to 2000 strong. No full-strength SNLP served in Papua, but elements of 5th Yokosuka SNLP and 5th Sasebo SNLP were sent there. The SNLP were not elite troops as their task in Papua indicates for, instead of fighting on the Kokoda Track, they guarded the Giruwa base.[30] They patrolled the coast by land and sea, occasionally skirmishing with the PIB, as far north as the Waria River and south well beyond Oro Bay. One company of 5th Sasebo SNLP, comprising 236 men, landed with the Yokoyama force and formed the initial garrison of Giruwa.[31] Another company came with the main force in mid-August. Leaving behind two platoons, it left Giruwa to participate in the Milne Bay landing but was stranded on Goodenough Island.[32] The two platoons left behind, comprising 110 men, stayed at Giruwa until they were killed in battle in January 1943. On 18 September a 280-man company of 5th Yokosuka SNLP, under Captain Yasuda Yoshiatsu, arrived at Giruwa and also remained there until the end.[33] Two out of three companies of 47th Field Anti-Aircraft Artillery Battalion (47 FAAAB) were sent to Papua. With a headquarters and an ammunition company, there were about 400 men present.[34] As was the case with a quarter of all Japanese units in Papua in 1942, 47 FAAAB was split between Seventeenth Army's two major concerns, Papua and Guadalcanal. 1st and 2nd Companies served in Papua while 3rd Company went to Guadalcanal.

The largest civilian units administered by the IJN and IJA were the pioneers, a usually unarmed labour force with or without specialised training. They performed a wide variety of tasks: unloading and transporting supplies, improving and maintaining the supply line, and building installations, including the Buna airfield for 25 IJN Air Flotilla. The Takasago Taiwanese battalion of 15 Naval Pioneers (15NP) arrived with Yokoyama's force on 21 July, 500 strong. Two more battalions with 1218 men arrived later.[35] The other naval pioneer unit, 14 NP, brought 600 of its normal complement of 1083, the rest went to Lae.[36] Of those who went to Giruwa, 210 were withdrawn to Rabaul on 4 November. A small detachment of 11 NP might also have been sent to Papua.

Distinct from civilian pioneers were small uniformed labour units that specialised in supply and construction tasks for both the IJN and the IJA. As near as can be ascertained, their initial strength in Papua was as shown in table 4.4.

Table 4.4: Nankai Shitai supply and construction units

106th Land Duty Company	370
105th Sea Duty Company	176
120th Land Duty Company	475
40th Sea Duty Company	250
55th Transport Regiment, no. 2 Company	145
61st Construction Company	150

Source: ATIS current translations no. 42, p. 9, AWM55 3/4, ATIS bulletin no. 9, p. 4, AWM 55/1/1; ATIS current translations no. 21, pp. 24–32, AWM55 3/2; ATIS interrogation report no. 152, AWM55 6/3; ATIS spot report no. 15, AWM55 2/1; Gavin Long papers, AWM67 11/29.

Two companies of Sakigawa Butai, 212nd Independent Motor Transport Battalion (212 IMTB), were sent to Papua. Normally a Japanese motor transport company, of which there were three to a battalion, had three truck companies, each with a theoretical strength of 50 vehicles and 130 men. Sakigawa Butai brought to Papua 72 trucks, mostly six-wheeled Toyotas, and 300 men in two truck companies, a maintenance company and a headquarters. Later arrivals included Fords and Chevrolets captured on Guam, a few staff cars and one armoured car, which, on arrival at Giruwa, disappeared from the historical record. The total number of vehicles landed was not more than a hundred.[37]

It is usually stated that 1200 men from eastern New Britain, the 'Rabaul carriers', were brought to Giruwa, but this was only the number that arrived with Colonel Yokoyama's advanced detachment in July.[38] The next month another 800 came and were split among IJA and IJN units, each infantry battalion being allotted a hundred carriers. Another two or three hundred Orokaiva from the Buna area were also employed as carriers, guides and armed scouts.[39] Including the 710 men withdrawn from 41st Regiment, a total of 7000 were available for the variety of labouring and transport requirements of the Nankai Shitai. The most unusual feature of the transport arrangements was the lack of a transport regiment. When 144th Regiment went south its parent 55th Division went to Burma, taking with it the divisional transport. Even so, the proportion of labourers and engineers in the Nankai Shitai was high, approaching half of the total force. This is twice the proportion of similar units sent to Guadalcanal, which suggests a higher level of awareness on the part of Seventeenth Army of the transport problems in Papua than they are usually credited with.[40]

Table 4.5: Nankai Shitai medical units

67th Line of Communication Hospital	230
55th Division Field Hospital	140
55th Division medical detachment, including sanitary and dental sections	220
Patient Collecting Butai, comprising 53th and 54th Casualty Clearing Station	155
Water and Hygiene Butai, comprising 17th, 24th, 55th and 150th Platoons	230
Umeda Civilian Hospital	110

Source: War Department, *Handbook on Japanese Military Forces*, 1944, pp. 60–1; War Department, *Handbook on Japanese Military Forces*, July 1943, end pocket chart. ATIS bulletin no 14, p. 2, ATIS bulletin no 47, p. 2, ATIS bulletin no 9, p. 4, ATIS bulletin no 25, p. 1, AWM55 1/1; ATIS current translations no 44, p. 21, AWM55; 3/4 Bullard, *Japanese Army Operations in the South Pacific Area*, p. 244.

The Kokoda myth asserts that the Nankai Shitai was 'woefully equipped' as regards medical services.[41] However, the most common Japanese divisional order of battle contained a larger percentage of medical personnel than did any Australian division in New Guinea in 1942, and 6 per cent of the Nankai Shitai was in nine medical units: two field ambulances, or Patient Collecting Butai (PCB), a field hospital, a line of communication hospital, a civilian hospital for labourers, and four hygiene and water purification units. Table 4.5 shows their strength. The total number of medical personnel was 1090, which was 78 men below the standard number for a full Japanese division, a formation a third again as big as the Nankai Shitai.

Each battalion, regimental and divisional headquarters contained communications specialists who have been included in figures thus far. As Seventeenth Army suspected that communications between the Owen Stanley Range, the Giruwa base and Rabaul would be difficult, additional communications units were added to the force (see table 4.6). Establishing the strength of these small signals units is particularly difficult as they were often split between Papua and Guadalcanal. For example, 88th Independent Communications Company (88 ICC), with a strength of 180 men, sent 147 to Guadalcanal and 33 to Papua.[42] There is no record of 7th Independent Wireless Platoon and 8th Independent

Table 4.6: Nankai Shitai signals units

45th Permanent Wireless Platoon	25
44th Permanent Wireless Platoon	25
88th Independent Wireless Company, one platoon	33
55th Division Signals Company, detachment	30
Seventeenth Army Mobile Wireless Station, Signals Section	18
5th Shipping Signals Platoon	18
37th Fixed Radio Platoon	26
33rd Fixed Radio Platoon	24
7th Independent Wireless Platoon, one section	15
8th Independent Telegraph Platoon, one section	15

Source: Military Intelligence Service, *Order of Battle of the Japanese Army, December 1942*, p. 330.

Telegraph Platoon being sent to Papua at all, yet four men from these two units were treated for illness in Giruwa in September 1942.[43] It appears that only a section of each unit was sent, giving a total of about 246 communications personnel outside those in infantry regiments and force headquarters.

An omission from postwar estimates of the Nankai Shitai order of battle is the personnel of a detachment from the IJN's 25th Air Flotilla, who were at Buna airstrip from the end of July 1942. The strip handled one squadron of nine Mitsubishi A6M Zero fighters until most were destroyed by Allied air attack and the strip was rendered unserviceable by bombing. The ground unit, comprising two airfield battalion companies with 357 men, was maintained there in the hope that the field would become operational again.[44] However, in September the major Japanese air effort was switched to Guadalcanal. Aircrew and ground personnel were evacuated by October 1942.

Yet to be mentioned are veterinary and military police detachments and the anchorage command. The veterinary detachment was not the full company normal for a division. Its strength was about 90 men who cared for 2630 horses. The military police, the Kempei Tai, had a platoon of 30 at Giruwa from 6th Military Police Company (6 MPC) based at Rabaul.[45] A few other military police were attached to maintain discipline among civilian labourers. The anchorage command, an IJN unit, had a staff of 37 and administered the unloading and storage of supplies in warehouses in the Sanananda–Giruwa area.

The total number of men who landed in Papua with the Nankai Shitai up to the end of the Kokoda campaign in November 1942 is usually stated to be between 13 000 and 13 500, excluding Papuans and New Guineans.[46] This number is too low, and 16 700 arrivals to 1 November is a better estimation. Another 800 landed on 2 November, but they played no part in the Kokoda campaign phase of the war in Papua so they have not been included here. Peak strength was not reached until late September, and from this casualties and those withdrawn to Rabaul (1300) should be deducted, so it is probable that at no time was the Nankai Shitai larger than 14 000–15 000, or 16 000–17 000 if carriers and scouts from New Britain and Papua are included.[47]

It has also been thought that the Nankai Shitai included 10 000 fighting troops, but the figure was not that large.[48] Including the infantry, and those from 41st Regiment who served as carriers for most of the campaign, combat engineers and artillery, the total number of fighting troops was not greater than 7300 and, before the battle of Oivi–Gorari, only half of these men had participated in any fighting in Papua. A half-and-half split in the force between fighting troops and those providing logistic, administrative and other kinds of support is still impressive. The Australians were able to achieve this in North Africa, but the supply problems of Papua were such that they were not able to maintain it there. On 6 October 1942 the Australians and Americans had 60 712 men in Papua, less than a third of whom could be considered fighting troops.

Postwar studies of the campaign have tended to inflate the size of the Japanese infantry battalions to a thousand strong to support the Kokoda myth that the Japanese were in great strength in the early battles along the Kokoda Track. This can be done only if the evidence provided by NGF from November 1942 is ignored. By then NGF had captured and translated enough documents to see that their own earlier estimate of Japanese strength was too large. Although their numbers were not precise, they were broadly correct in determining that the four Japanese infantry battalions they investigated were 500, 630, 744 and 795 strong on arrival in Papua.[49]

The Nankai Shitai is best visualised as a light division with a stronger than usual proportion of engineering, labouring and medical support.[50] The infantry, who did the lion's share of the fighting in Papua, was about 4660 strong. The Australians placed almost twice this number, close to 9000 infantrymen, in harm's way along the Kokoda Track.

CHAPTER | 5

FROM THE LANDING
TO DENIKI

Under 15th Independent Engineer Regiment (IER) commander Colonel Yokoyama Yosuke, the advance party of the Nankai Shitai sailed from Rabaul to Basabua in two convoys, each of two transports with escorts. They disembarked on 21 and 29 July 1942 at the cost of one vessel, the *Ayatozan Maru*, sunk by air attack after it had unloaded most of its cargo. The strength and composition of Yokoyama Force was as shown in table 5.1.

Colonel Yokoyama had five tasks:

1. to prepare for the arrival of the IJN units building an airstrip at Buna[1]
2. to establish a base centred on Giruwa, north of Buna, including a hospital, jetty, and buildings for administration and storage
3. to establish and maintain a supply line to Kokoda, where the forward supply dump was to be placed
4. to investigate other supply route options, especially the navigability of the Mambare and Kumusi Rivers, and
5. to advance to the southern side of the Owen Stanley Range crest south of Templeton's Crossing.[2]

The fifth task was to be carried out by a force of 900 men, comprising Tsukamoto's 1/144th Battalion, the mountain gun company, small signals, engineer and medical detachments and a hundred Rabaul carriers, but this force did not fully assemble at the front until 14 August, after the Deniki engagement.[3]

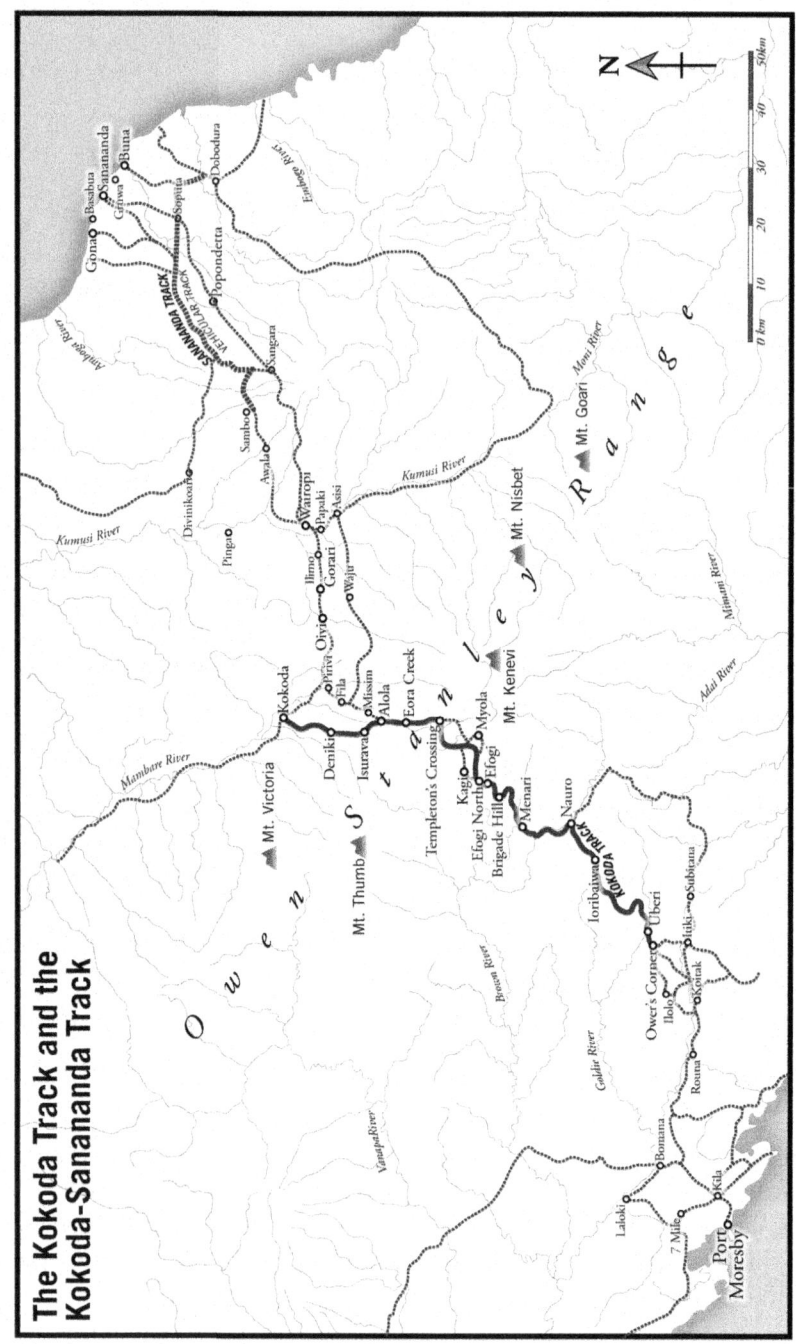

The Kokoda Track and the Kokoda–Sanananda Track

Map 3 The Kokoda Track and the Kokoda–Sananda track

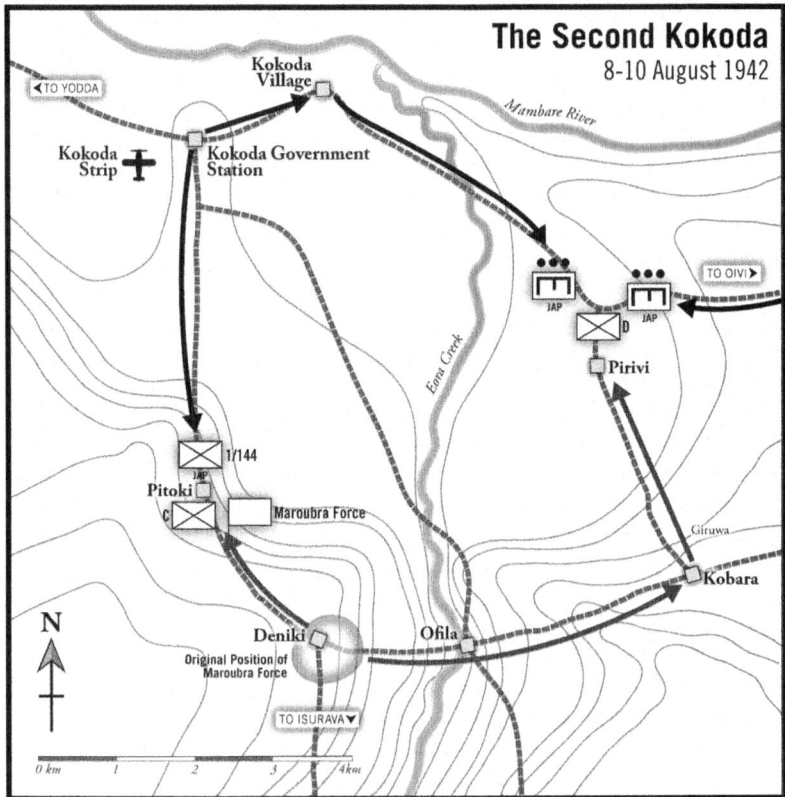

Map 4 Second Kokoda, 8–10 August 1942

The landing at Basabua was unopposed, and the Australians manning the Buna wireless station left as soon as they learned of the Japanese presence. 1st Company of the 1/144th, comprising 135 men under Captain Ogawa, was loaded onto trucks as soon as they were disembarked at 4.30 p.m. on 21 July. Ogawa took along bicycles, a platoon of the battalion gun company with one 70mm gun, a platoon of the battalion's machinegun company and one engineer platoon carrying rubber boats. He was accompanied by a few Orokaiva guides. They were seen by Australians scouting ahead of the Japanese advance, and it was Orokaiva who warned the Japanese that there were 60 Australians at Papaki (Wairopi).[4] One of them wounded Captain Harold Jesser of the PIB on 9 August.[5] It was 36 hours before any other part of Yokoyama's force left Giruwa, and the main body of the 1/144th, which arrived in the second convoy, did not leave until the evening of 29 July. Hence it was Ogawa's advance guard, about

Table 5.1: Yokoyama Force

Unit	Strength
1/144th Infantry Battalion	586
55th Mountain Artillery, 1st Company	121
47th Anti-Aircraft Artillery, 2nd Company	200
15th Naval Pioneers	500
55th Division Field Hospital, half strength	120
55th Division Signals Company, detachment	40
120th Land Duties Company, one platoon	50
Seventeenth Army Mobile Wireless Station, one section	18
45th Permanent Wireless Station	22
55th Division Medical Detachment: one platoon field ambulance, one platoon stretcher-bearers, two platoons water and hygiene	140
Carriers recruited in Rabaul	1200
Sakigawa Motor Truck Company	120
15th Independent Engineer Regiment, less one company	600
Yokoyama Force HQ, including 144th Regiment Signals Detachment	51
37th IJN Anchorage Command	44
5th Sasebo SNLP	236
Less casualties in bombing of Ayatozan Maru	9
Total arrivals	4057

Source: *Boeicho Boei Kenshujo Senshishitsu, Senshi Sosho: Minami Taiheiyo Rikugun sakusen*, vol. 1, *Poto Moresubi-Gashima shoko sakusen* [War history series; South Pacific Area army operations, vol. 1, Port Moresby–Guadalcanal first campaigns], p. 200; Yokoyama operational order no 1, spot report no 1, 16 July 1942, AWM55 2/1; ATIS current translations no. 4, pp. 24–5 & 40, AWM 55 3/1; ATIS current translations no. 266, p. 17, AWM55 3/2; ATIS current translations no. 62, pp. 13–27, AWM55 3/5; 39th Battalion war diary, captured documents, September 1942 appendix, AWM52 8/3/78.

230 men, that did all the fighting against the Papuans and Australians up to and including the first Kokoda engagement on 29 July 1942.

The advance was rapid as the road was suitable for motor vehicles as far as Sambo.[6] The next day a dozen of Ogawa's men appeared at the front gate of the Sangara Mission while Captain Tom Grahamslaw and Lieutenant John Chalk of the PIB were taking breakfast. The Australians fled out the back door so this cannot truly be considered the first encounter of the campaign. That occurred near Awala the following day when

38 men of the PIB under Major William Watson fired on the advancing Japanese. As described by Daera Ganiga, a PIB private, each man fired eight or nine rounds until Watson told them to run for their lives.[7] The skirmish went on long enough for the Japanese to set up and open fire with their 70mm battalion gun.[8] Later that day 11th Platoon of 39th Battalion engaged the Japanese further west along the Sanananda *dala*, the track from the north coast at Sanananda (near Giruwa) to Kokoda. The Australians demolished the bridge at Wairopi, and on 24 July fire was briefly exchanged across the Kumusi River, although no one was hit. As the Australians retreated Captain Jesser saw the Japanese engineers crossing in rubber boats.[9] The Australians and Papuans, by now a hundred strong, fell back to just east of Gorari where on 25 July they ambushed the Japanese once more and claimed 15 casualties. The actual Japanese casualties were two men killed from 1st Company 1/144th, the first fatal Japanese battle casualties in the land campaign in Papua.[10]

Oivi

Up to Oivi the Australian policy was, as Captain Sam Templeton told one of his platoon commanders, 'No do or die stunts'.[11] On 25 July Lieutenant-Colonel William Owen, the battalion commander, overruled Templeton, instructing him that he would, at Oivi, 'hold at all costs unless surrounded'.[12] Since the Japanese landing there had been an effort to mass the 300 men of the PIB, the Royal Papuan Constabulary (RPC) and 39th Battalion who were north of the Owen Stanley Range from the Waria River to Kokoda. At Oivi there were 60 PIB and RPC and 90 Australians, mainly B Company, 39th Battalion.[13] The defenders deployed across the track, less nine men with Jesser watching a parallel track to the south, which was to feature in the fighting here in November 1942. The Japanese attack, which included the engineer platoon, almost encircled the defenders, who fought on until the evening, then escaped to Deniki.[14]

During the fight, Templeton disappeared, and there has been some controversy about what happened to him. Japanese records make it plain that he was wounded, captured, interrogated and executed, as happened to a large number of Australians. This naturally occurred frequently during the Australian retreat and infrequently during their later advance. Australians seen by their comrades to have been killed in battle were so recorded. Others not actually seen to be dead were listed as 'death presumed'. Fifty-four deaths were presumed in the Australian retreat and seven more during the Australian advance from late September.[15] Japanese records show a larger number of captured Australians, about 110 for the whole campaign, so it would appear that the fate of many, both those officially killed in action and death presumed, was that they were captured, perhaps wounded, then killed. Between 25 July and 15 August the deaths of 18 men of 39th Battalion were presumed, but the Japanese captured 11 of them.[16] There is usually some mention in Japanese records of what information the prisoner gave when questioned and, although this is not stated, all were soon executed. If they were officers they were interrogated in greater detail and killed several days later, as happened to Templeton. Papuans of the PIB and RPC were also killed by the Japanese, but the number is unknown. No Australian soldier captured by the Japanese in Papua survived the war.

First Kokoda

After Oivi the scene of activity moved to an area around Kokoda where the front stabilised for two weeks. The area was triangular and bounded by Kokoda to the north-west, a track junction near the village of Pirivi to the north-east and the village of Deniki in the south on the main track to Port Moresby. Each side of the triangle was bordered by a track seven kilometres long. The most important feature in the Kokoda–Pirivi–Deniki triangle was the airstrip west of the steep-sided and flat-topped ridge on which sat Kokoda government station. Whichever army held the strip could fly in reinforcements and supplies while denying the same to the enemy. The Japanese planned to use the Kokoda strip for air supply as the Australians later did, but the loss of all air assets to the Guadalcanal campaign in August prevented this. As the only practical landing ground between Port Moresby and Buna, in the long run the army that held the Kokoda strip was best placed to win the mountain campaign. Small forces cannot defend large areas like airfields, but what can be done is to occupy a terrain feature nearby that overlooks it, thus at least preventing enemy aircraft using it. The obvious feature at Kokoda was the ridge beside the strip on which Kokoda government station stood. An old rubber plantation partly obscured the field of fire from Kokoda station in the direction of the strip, but it remained the best spot to make a stand.

The Kokoda Track is flat for the first several kilometres south of Kokoda and then rises steeply towards Deniki, which was of importance as it was the northern entrance to the Owen Stanley Range and because it offered a spectacular view of Kokoda. While other tracks from the Mambare valley led south into the mountains, the one via Deniki, the Kokoda Track, was the best and easiest, and no force holding Kokoda could be comfortable while all that they did was observed from Deniki. The north-east angle of the triangle was the track junction near Pirivi. Coming from the north coast and turning left at Pirivi provided a short cut to Deniki that avoided Kokoda. It made Kokoda strip hard to hold from either direction as an enemy could use this track to slip behind any force placed in Kokoda that did not also hold the track junction in its own rear. Owen had initially retreated from Oivi to Deniki, but decided to run this risk when he reoccupied Kokoda, leaving only a few men at Deniki. Ten days later, when Lieutenant-Colonel Alan Cameron attacked from Deniki towards Kokoda, in the Second Kokoda engagement, he sent a force from Deniki to threaten the Japanese rear at Pirivi.

The Japanese attacked Owen at Kokoda on the early morning of 29 July. The first Kokoda engagement has entered Australian folklore, where it serves as a prototype for the fighting that followed. The story runs that, outnumbered ten to one, with their commander mortally wounded, the Australians held out at Kokoda and, when they could not hold any more, stole away in the misty morning. Apparently during the battle '400 of Tsukamoto's 900-strong force charged up the short steep slope' of Kokoda plateau.[17] This did not happen. It is the Kokoda myth, for Tsukamoto, with the main body of the 1/144th, was still on the coast a hundred kilometres away and did not pass through Oivi until 6 August. One officer with Tsukamoto wrote that he heard 'our advanced force' had had a fight at Kokoda.[18]

There was another element of Yokoyama's force between Ogawa and Tsukamoto. It had left Giruwa 36 hours after Ogawa, and on the night of Kokoda it was camped 16 kilometres away at Oivi.[19] A signaller with this group complained that progress had been slow, the axle on his two-wheeled cart was broken, crossing the Kumusi had been a problem and it had taken six days to get from the coast to the west bank of the Kumusi, 50 kilometres from Kokoda.[20] The 'advanced force' that fought at Kokoda was Ogawa's alone, which, after casualties thus far, was about 200 strong. One of them, Private Watanabe Toshi, wrote that they were out on their own and feeling lonely.[21]

The number of defenders of Kokoda is usually stated to be 77 or 81.[22] These figures are only a little short for B Company, 39th Battalion alone, but far short of the total force of Papuans and Australians, now known as Maroubra Force, gathered at Kokoda. The battalion war diary

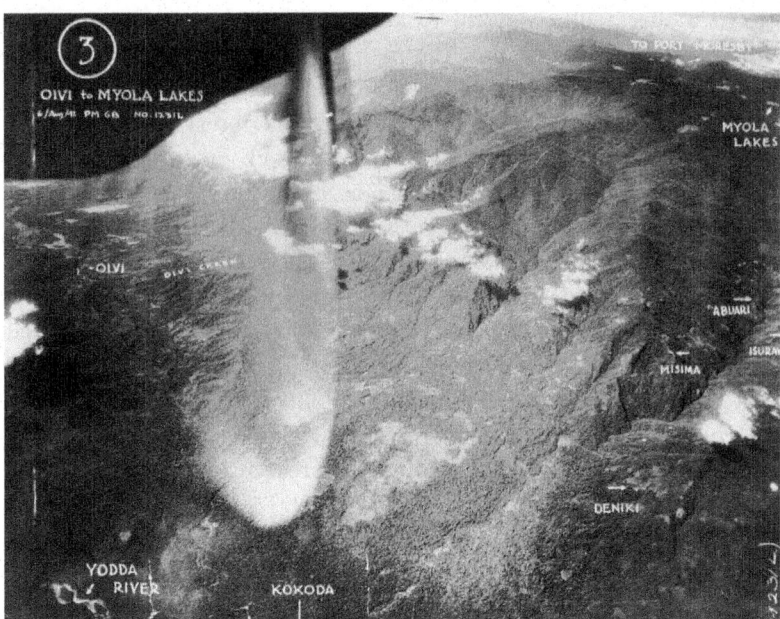

Photo 4 Aerial view looking south from Kokoda along Eora Creek Gorge towards Myola. (AWM 128150)

initially counted 72 men returned to Deniki after First Kokoda and 20 still missing, but a thorough check in a message of 2 August to NGF said there were now 12 missing believed killed and 27 missing believed deserted.[23] It appears that 39th Battalion assembled possibly as many as 111 men at Kokoda and to this should be added probably 20 PIB, four men from ANGAU, up to nine RPC and four signallers from 30th Brigade.[24] The total is 148, but there is some uncertainty here with 39th Battalion and RPC numbers, although it is safe to say that at least 130 Australians and Papuans defended Kokoda against 200 Japanese, which is nothing like the ten-to-one odds of Kokoda mythology.

The Australians were in a horseshoe-shaped line, around the northern end of the ridge. The Japanese attacked, mainly from the north, at 2.30 a.m. By 3.20 a.m., with Owen fatally wounded, the order to withdraw was given. At this point the 39th Battalion war diary records that artillery and mortar fire disrupted the rearward movement and 'our line then broke completely'. Ogawa's death at the moment of victory soured what was described by Major Toyufuku a few months later, in a lecture in Tokyo, as a successful company attack.[25]

Ogawa might have seen the two Australian aircraft that circled Kokoda on 28 July but did not land. They contained 30 men of D Company, 49th Battalion. The rest of the company was sitting by the runway at Seven Mile strip at Port Moresby, and the Australian plan was to send a company a day by air to Kokoda. Ogawa's attack forestalled this, and it has been argued that one extra company would not have made much difference against a Japanese battalion, and that might be so.[26] Against the one reinforced Japanese company that was actually present, however, it might well have made a great difference to the outcome.

SECOND KOKODA

After the first Kokoda engagement, the Australians retreated to Deniki. For a week the Japanese 1st Company 1/144th held Kokoda, awaiting the rest of the battalion. They scouted the Australian position and sent patrols to Yodda and into Hydrographers Range. A company of engineers from 15 IER arrived and began improving the track from Oivi to Kokoda, but the main body of the engineer regiment did not immediately come to Kokoda. Rather it concentrated on the most urgent task of all: improving and maintaining the motor road from Giruwa to Sambo. By mid-August 15 IER, along with 55 ER, was building the 17 major and many more minor bridges needed to upgrade the road from the sea to Kokoda. Japanese combat engineers played little part in the fighting because the task of building, maintaining and repairing after floods a 100-kilometre supply line from Giruwa to Kokoda fully occupied three-quarters of them for the entire campaign. By the end of October they had made 60 kilometres of motorable road from the sea to the Kumusi River and beyond that a serviceable packhorse track. Only three engineer companies ever entered the Owen Stanley Range.

Parties of Japanese 15th Naval Pioneers arrived at Kokoda carrying supplies for the planned dump. Sergeant Everson of 39th Battalion, while looking for an ambush site along the Oivi–Kokoda track on 6 August, counted 63 of them marching past.[27] The single mountain gun of the Yokoyama detachment had not arrived, and the 55th Division medical detachment was still at the Kumusi Crossing on 8 August, the day the second Kokoda engagement commenced. The full strength of the 1/144th was not assembled at Kokoda until 7 August, and Tsukamoto advanced up the main Kokoda–Deniki track the next day with a view to making a battalion attack on Deniki.[28] This did not occur as he bumped into Australians advancing in the other direction. On the same day Tsukamoto advanced on Deniki, Maroubra Force, under its new commander, Major Alan Cameron, launched a counter-attack to recapture Kokoda.

Deducting casualties thus far, Tsukamoto had about 522 men in the 1/144th and two platoons, 120 men of the engineer company of 15 IER. One engineer platoon was at Kokoda and the other near Pirivi; both became involved in the fight. Adding the small signals and medical detachments and a handful of Orokaiva, Tsukamoto had about 660 men engaged. Raymond Paull estimated that Maroubra Force had 480 men all ranks, including eight PIB and eight ANGAU, on 8 August.[29] This is too few as all infantry companies, plus the machine-gun company (serving as riflemen) and the headquarters company, had arrived and the PIB contingent had grown to 43 men.[30] Some PIB had returned to Deniki after being scattered at Oivi or Kokoda; others came in response to orders from their commander, Watson. There were also 12 men of 14th Field Ambulance, the 30th Brigade signallers, 14 RPC under Grahamslaw, probably eight ANGAU and five in Maroubra Force Headquarters (MFHQ).[31] With the 464 men of 39th Battalion, Cameron's total force was 550.[32] The 39th's B Company, which Cameron thought should be disbanded due to its poor behaviour at Kokoda, where 27 were thought to have deserted, was sent back to Eora. Warrant Officer John Wilkinson of ANGAU was also not impressed by B Company or the PIB. The following year he told the historian Gavin Long that 'the PIB went into action, fired one shot and ran, then B Company did the same'.[33] Also unengaged was Cameron's reserve, the fresh E Company. Neither B nor E Companies played any part in Second Kokoda so the force available to Cameron was approximately 430 men, or about two-thirds Tsukamoto's strength.[34]

Cameron's plan was to reoccupy Kokoda government station. If that could be done, supply and reinforcement by air could recommence from Kokoda strip. He sent four companies by various routes. One rifle company, with Cameron and his headquarters company, went directly down the main track towards Kokoda. These met Tsukamoto coming the other way. A third company took a side track to Kokoda out to Cameron's right, and a fourth went to the far Australian right, to the Kokoda–Oivi track junction near Pirivi at the top right corner of the triangle of tracks, to prevent Japanese reinforcements arriving at Kokoda. On the Australian right at Pirivi Captain Bidstrup's D Company, with 21 PIB attached, encountered two platoons of Japanese engineers of 15 IER engaged in bridge construction on the Oivi–Kokoda track.[35] One platoon of engineers attacked Bidstrup from his left, the direction of Kokoda, and the other came from Oivi. D Company fought with them all day, killing six and wounding 16.[36] When it was dark Bidstrup withdrew to Deniki.

In the Australian centre, A Company, under Captain Symington, entered Kokoda station by an unguarded track between the main track to Deniki and the one to Pirivi. Approaching Kokoda they saw a platoon of Japanese, who did not stay to fight but departed in the direction of Pirivi.[37] They were the Japanese engineers who an hour later hit the left flank of Bidstrup's force. Unmolested by any Japanese, A Company dug in at Kokoda government station. It was odd that the airstrip was not closely watched by the Japanese, although they had placed obstacles to ensure that landing there was impossible. The engineer platoon that left Kokoda heading east was probably intending to defend another vital place, the Japanese supply dump a kilometre or so east near Kokoda village. Surrounded by jungle, it was difficult to detect from the air. The Australians had no idea of the dump, instead directing their later air attacks on the station, which caught fire and burned down.

The leftmost of the Australian three-pronged attack, on the Kokoda Track, consisted of Captain Deane's C Company followed by 39th Battalion headquarters and the headquarters company. A Japanese advance guard from 2nd Company, 1/144th was encountered more than a kilometre from Deniki. It was driven back 400 metres until C Company found the main body of the 1/144th. Tsukamoto, unsure what this unexpected meeting portended, sparred with the Australians through the afternoon until the latter withdrew to Deniki. Tsukamoto followed up and was at Deniki on the evening of 8 August when he learned that Kokoda had been retaken by the Australians. It is curious that Tsukamoto did not leave anyone to protect Kokoda station and did not on this day show the competence for which he was known in China and would later see him chosen to command the regiment. The surprising explanation given by battalion veterans is that he was drunk on 8 August, another thing for which he had a reputation stretching back to his service in China.

Tsukamoto appears to have believed that there was one Australian platoon in Kokoda as he sent only 1st Company to retake it. This was his weakest company, although a platoon of the machine-gun company and the battalion gun went along with it. The company attacked that night and proved inadequate to the task. The explanation given by Lieutenant Hirano, who was present, was that a dark night made worse by heavy rain resulted in an uncoordinated attack.[38] The following day, 9 August, short of ammunition and food, and having heard nothing from Cameron, A Company, unmolested by the Japanese, evacuated Kokoda.

They headed west, then south through the jungle and emerged on the main track behind Deniki two days later. By then Maroubra Force was back where it began, holding Deniki, and Tsukamoto was able to continue with his delayed plan to attack it with his whole battalion.

The Second Kokoda engagement was the most interesting fight so far. Two battalion commanders, each far from support, were engaged in a battle of manoeuvre unlike any other in the campaign. Military forces can spend a lot of time stationary facing each other, scouting the other's position and preparing their next move. Usually one is looking to attack, and the other, not feeling strong enough to attack himself, plans to defend. It is uncommon, as occurred at Second Kokoda, for both to decide on the offensive and rare that both attempted it on the same day. The outcome was that Tsukamoto was wrong-footed by Cameron's completely unexpected move, and his attack on Deniki was delayed by four days.

DENIKI

Maroubra Force suffered 38 battle casualties, and a handful of sick men were sent away. The company in reserve at Isurava, E Company, was brought forward to Deniki, and the depleted A and B Companies replaced it. This left Cameron with C, D and E Companies, Headquarters Company, the RPC, ANGAU, 15 or 16 PIB and other minor detachments.[39] The reinforcement provided by E Company more than counterbalanced casualties and the withdrawal of two weak companies, so Cameron's engaged strength increased from to 430 to 470. No Japanese engineers were with the 1/144th at Deniki, giving Tsukamoto around 450 men.

For the first time the Australians and Papuans probably marginally outnumbered their enemy. From this point in the campaign numbers were usually about even until Ioribaiwa, and only at First Eora did the Japanese have a sizeable superiority. Of course, none of the participants in July and August had much idea about enemy numbers. In deciding to attack on 8 August Cameron estimated that there were from 300 to 500 Japanese in the vicinity when he was in fact outnumbered. When he decided to retreat from Deniki on 14 August it was, he said, 'because we were considerably outnumbered', when he was not.[40] The Japanese made the same mistake, estimating that up to a thousand Australians held Kokoda on the night of 28/29 July. In the Owen Stanley Range, the thickness of foliage is not as great as at sea level, and it is usually possible to see 20 metres and sometimes 50 metres, but this is not enough to tell

Photo 5 1st Battalion, 144th Regiment resting, probably near Kokoda, August 1942. (Kochi New Guinea Association)

the number of an enemy who did not wish to be seen, and it is remarkable how few enemy troops a veteran of jungle fighting actually saw. Judging by interviews with veterans, perhaps a third of Australian veterans of the campaign from front-line units never saw a live Japanese. The rest had only one or two glimpses of one or two enemy. It is much less common for a veteran to report that he ever saw a section or an entire platoon of Japanese – and lived to tell the tale. Japanese veterans make the same observation about the Australians, and *both* sides were equally convinced that the scarcity of enemy sightings was partly accounted for by the enemy's wonderful skill at camouflage.[41] It is almost axiomatic that in jungle war, even in daylight and when closely engaged, the two sides usually do not see much of each other, and most fire is directed at where the enemy are thought to be.

On 12 August Tsukamoto restarted his attack on Deniki with a bombardment by the battalion gun.[42] The Japanese scouted the Australian position on 13 August, by which time 1st Company had returned from Kokoda and was placed in reserve. The other two infantry companies attacked, but by nightfall little ground had been gained. This was not a charge with fixed bayonets as might be imagined – only two men were killed. The Japanese were wary of taking unnecessary casualties among, at this stage of the war, their well-trained infantry. They knew that the enemy could often be 'worried' out of his position by methodical and careful pressure. Tsukamoto regrouped and attacked again the next day to find that the pressure had worked, the Australians were gone and, as a sign of the hasty retreat to Isurava, they had left 100 000 rounds of ammunition, a map showing tracks to Port Moresby, food and blankets.[43]

CASUALTIES

We have seen that the number of Japanese engaged in the fighting up to Deniki has been considerably overestimated. Another aspect of the Kokoda myth is that Japanese casualties were great and many times those of the Australians. If Australian casualty claims are accepted at face value, as they have been, then a thousand Japanese casualties – more than were present near Kokoda up to 15 August – had been inflicted so far. While the actual figure was one-seventh of this, the phase of the campaign to Deniki was one where the Australians were able to inflict almost twice the number of casualties that they suffered. The Japanese battle casualty total, as appears in table 5.2, was 50 killed and about 87 wounded. Not including six members of ANGAU killed in the Buna area by the SNLP, the number of Australians listed killed in action, death in action presumed or died of wounds was 42, and 34 were wounded.[44]

Australian casualty claims for Japanese losses at Second Kokoda alone vary between 500 and 330.[45] The D Company fight on 8 August at the track junction near Pirivi was initially thought to have inflicted 182, which it was said were counted.[46] This was reduced in the 39th Battalion war diary to 40 or 50 killed and 50 wounded, but as table 5.2 shows, the Japanese 15 ER at Pirivi lost six killed and 16 wounded.[47] At First Kokoda the Japanese lost only 12 killed and 26 wounded, so we should be suspicious of descriptions of the engagement like this from the war correspondent George Johnston, who was not present at First Kokoda: 'The first wave fell, ripped to pieces by Australian mortars and machine-guns. The second wave climbed over the bodies of the fallen ... as fast as the Japanese were killed others scrabbled over the plateau to take their place.'[48] Suitable wartime propaganda it was, but 70 years later it still contributes to the mistaken idea that the Japanese suffered huge casualties in the Oivi–Kokoda–Deniki fighting.

Table 5.2: Japanese casualties*

25 July, Gorari	2 killed, about 6 wounded
26 July, Oivi	4 killed, 10 wounded
29 July, 1st Kokoda	9 killed and 18 wounded and 3 killed and 8 wounded from 15 ER
2 August	3 killed in a patrol encounter, possibly two wounded
5 August	1 Orokaiva scout killed
7 August	1 killed
8 August, 2nd Kokoda	6 killed and a few wounded from the 1/144th, and 6 killed and 16 wounded from 15 ER
9 August, 2nd Kokoda	2 killed, 18 wounded
10 August, 2nd Kokoda	6 killed, 10 wounded
12 August, Deniki	1 killed
13 August, Deniki	2 killed
15 August	3 killed, 1 wounded
Unknown date	2 killed

* From the 1/144th unless otherwise stated.

Source: *Hohei Dai 144 Rentai Senki* (Battle Records of the 144th Infantry Regiment), list of war dead. pp. 625–726. NIDS 302.9.H. This 101-page list shows the name, birthplace, place of death and day of death of all 5000 men who died while on active service with the regiment. As it is organised by name, the casualties for each battle are scattered across the entire document; Azuma Shigetoshi list of 144th Regiment casualties, p. 1. Azuma commanded the 144th Regimental Signals Company and compiled a list of regimental casualties in 1986; copy in author's collection. Lieutenant Hirano, diary, p. 1, current translations no. 23, AWM55 3/2; Private Watanabe Toshio, 1st Company 1/144th, diary, current translations no. 4, pp. 5–6, AWM55 3/1; Yazawa butai intelligence report 10 August 1942, AWM55 5/3/28; file of Yazawa butai orders, p. 50, AWM55 5/3, ATIS enemy publications no. 28, p. 25, AWM55 3/1; 39th Battalion war diary July–September, appendix A, copy of Japanese diary entry, 11 August 1942, AWM52 8/3/78.

CHAPTER 6

ISURAVA

Two weeks after Deniki the first major battle of the Kokoda campaign occurred at Isurava. Far from being Australia's Agincourt or Thermopylae, Isurava was a defeat with few redeeming features.[1] It is claimed that a vastly outnumbered Australian force inflicted many more casualties than it took and held the Japanese to a standstill for four vital days, upsetting their timetable and causing them later to run out of food. Apart from the fact that the Australians did inflict more casualties than they suffered, this account, the Kokoda myth version, is not an accurate description of events.

It is generally accepted that the Japanese had a numerical superiority that was at the very least three to one and was more likely five or six to one.[2] Subscribers to the Kokoda myth describe the Australian problem at Isurava as 'like trying to stem a tidal wave' or fighting against 'monumental odds'.[3] Lieutenant-Colonel Ralph Honner and Lieutenant-Colonel Arthur Key, two battalion commanders who fought there, were convinced that the Japanese were 'definitely in superior numbers', but in fact about 2300 were engaged on each side.[4] The Japanese did suffer almost twice the casualties they inflicted, but the delay imposed was of small importance for, as will be described in the following chapter, Seventeenth Army had already decided to postpone the Nankai Shitai's attack on Port Moresby.

THE AUSTRALIANS

By late 27 August, the forces of both sides were assembled. From this point, Maroubra Force is properly referred to as an Australian force

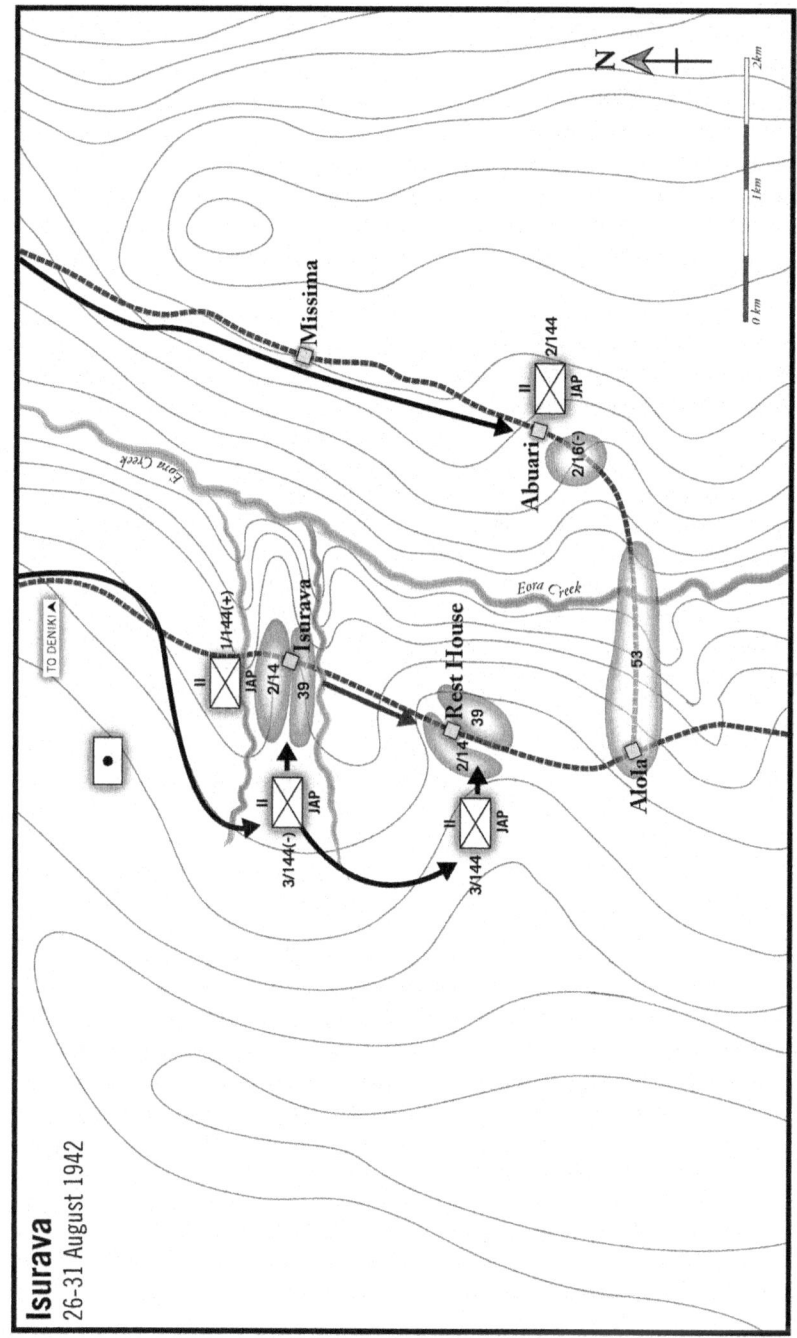

Map 5 Isurava, 26–31 August 1942

Table 6.1: Maroubra Force at Isurava

2/14th Infantry Battalion	542
2/16th Infantry Battalion	590
39th Infantry Battalion	410
53rd Infantry Battalion	550
Maroubra Force HQ inc. guard platoon, 21st Brigade HQ, detachment of 30th Brigade HQ, and K Section, 7th Division signals	122
Australian New Guinea Administrative Unit detachment	4
Papuan Infantry Battalion	20
Papuan Armed Police	14
2/6th Field Ambulance detachment	22
14th Field Ambulance detachment	18
Total	2292

Source: PIB war diary, 15, 19 & 29 August 1942, AWM52 8/4/4; 7th Division, messages dealing with Maroubra Force, messages 2 September 1942, 31 August 1942, AWM54 577/6/4; NGF General Staff war diary, AWM52 1/5/51; 21st Brigade report, pp. 29 & 52, AWM52 8/21/17; 14th Australian Field Ambulance, Papua, pp. 128–9, AWM54 481/12/68; 21st Brigade war diary, AWM52 8/2/21; 2/14th Battalion war diary AWM52 8/3/14; 2/16th Battalion war diary, AWM52 8/3/16; Maroubra Force battle casualties, messages, AWM54 171/2/20; Burns, *The Brown and Blue Diamond at War*, p. 132; Moremon, 'A triumph of improvisation', p. 163; Paull, *Retreat from Kokoda*, pp. 85, 103–4 & 138; McAuley, *Blood and Iron*, p. 70; Byrnes, *Green Shadows*, pp. 10–14; McCarthy, *South-West Pacific Area – First Year*, p. 212.

as the number of Papuans engaged was very small. There were four Australian infantry battalions, Maroubra Force Headquarters (MFHQ), detachments of ANGAU, PIB, RPC and a medical team drawn from 2/6th Field Ambulance and 14th Field Ambulance (see table 6.1).

The strength of the 53rd is usually thought to have been much lower. On 7 August the battalion was said to have sent 571 men forward. Between that date and Isurava it had battle casualties and en route had lost 37 men 'unfit to travel', 'exhausted' or 'collapsed'.[5] Most were evacuated but some rejoined within a few days. After Isurava the battalion was judged not to be fit for battle, and 358 men were marched back to Port Moresby. Another 120 were kept at Myola to carry supplies. Adding to this 39 battle casualties and 42 evacuated sick in the course of the fighting, a strength of 550 at Isurava seems right.[6]

THE JAPANESE

At Deniki and south of that point on 27 August there were four Japanese infantry battalions, two regimental headquarters, the NSHQ with the cavalry company attached, a company of engineers of 15 IER and a company from the Mountain Artillery Battalion. There was a second company of engineers improving the Kokoda Track north of Deniki, but they took no part in the battle. At the strength these units landed in Papua, the numbers present should have been as shown in table 6.2.

Three factors, readily apparent in Japanese sources, reduced the number engaged at Isurava from the 3555 listed in table 6.2 to about the same number the Australians had. As the Japanese strength at Isurava has long been unquestionably accepted to be very greatly superior to that of the Australians, it is necessary to go into some detail to establish why it was not so.

Table 6.2: Japanese forces in Isurava area

Nankai Shitai HQ, including signals, cavalry company and medical detachments	202
144th Regiment HQ	73
144th Regiment Signals Company	122
144th Regiment, 3 infantry battalions	2100
41st Regiment, including regimental HQ and one battalion	850
15th Independent Engineer Regiment, one reduced company	120
55th Mountain Artillery Battalion, one reduced company	88
Total	3555

Source: ATIS enemy publication, no 33, p. 8, AWM55 5/3; ATIS current translations no 4, p. 40, and current translations no 5, pp. 24–5, AWM55 3/1; Nankai Shitai operational order A, no 102, 24 August 1942, current translations no 42, p. 17, AWM55 3/4.

The first deduction concerns 41st Regiment, which did not fight at Isurava. The regimental headquarters of 41st Regiment did not go further forward than Deniki during the battle, and two of its battalions had yet to arrive in Papua. The one battalion available, the 2/41st, did not participate. The battalion commander complained that, during Isurava, 'Our battalion did not shoot a single bullet and no soldier was hurt.'[7] On 26 August the battalion was brought up to Deniki, six kilometres behind the front line. Horii expected to defeat the Australians with the

Photo 6 Major-General Horii Tomitaro, commander of the Nankai Shitai.
(Kochi New Guinea Association)

three battalions of 144 Regiment, keeping the 2/41st fresh for the pursuit. However, on 30 August at 1 p.m., Horii ordered the 2/41st to make a wide sweep up to the heights on the Australian left and cut the Kokoda Track deep in their rear. The battalion spent the next 15 hours lost in the jungle and emerged on the track north of Isurava rest house early in the morning of 31 August to discover that the Australians were long gone.

The second factor that reduced the Japanese numbers engaged was that Horii was anxious to attack the Australians before they withdrew further into the mountains. For this reason the main body of the Nankai Shitai, which landed from 19 to 21 August, forced marched from Giruwa to Isurava, and many men fell out along the way. One who finished the march was Sergeant Kawate Ryozo of 2/41, who wrote:

When we landed at Giruwa it was late afternoon. I was surprised that it was only jungle there. We all carried 30kg backpacks and started walking at night ... It was rainy and the path was very muddy and we could hardly move forward. Some of the newly recruited soldiers started saying, 'I cannot walk anymore. Kill me right here, please.' We had to beat them up and force them to walk. Even though we wanted to help them carry their bag, we all had heavy bags and couldn't help. We carried 7 *sho* [9.8kg] of rice because we didn't know when we could expect the next resupply. We walked and walked all night. But when the morning came, we realized that we only walked 16km from the beach.[8]

Some Japanese officers had expressed reservations as to whether their men could carry the 30–40-kilogram loads almost all were burdened with, and their fears were justified. As a result of the exercises carried out in Rabaul, where the men carried heavy loads up and down volcanic slopes, the medical staff recommended that, given the load, the heat and the difficult terrain, the troops should walk for 30 minutes then rest for 30 minutes. This advice was ignored in the forced march from the beach to Isurava, and hundreds fell out so they were not present for the battle.[9]

The first battalion of the 144th Regiment had been in Papua for a month, but the 2/144th and 3/144th marched a hundred kilometres to Kokoda in six days, arriving on 24 August. There they rested for a few hours before setting out again. The second battalion went to the east side of the Eora Creek gorge, which divides the battlefield into two, while the 3/144th went along the main track on the west side towards Isurava. The total distance covered in seven days was 120 kilometres for the 3/144 and 130 kilometres for the 2/144. Even carrying a more normal 20 kilograms, as the Australians did, 20 kilometres a day was excessive. A post-campaign Japanese study concluded that 10 kilometres a day was good going for large bodies of troops in Papua, and there is no other occasion in the campaign when either side attempted a similar forced march.

The records of 5th Company, 2/144th show that almost a third of the company dropped out due to exhaustion and injury on the march.[10] The company landed with 163 men, 14 below establishment, and two unfit men were immediately sent back to Rabaul. The first two-day march brought them to Sambo where two more men were sent back to Giruwa 'because of sprains'. The next day, 21 August, only 42 men completed the march to the Kumusi River at Wairopi on time, 117 falling behind. A short rest on 22 August enabled some to catch up, bringing company strength to 85. The next day the company commander returned to bring up stragglers and assembled 124 men and on 24 August 131 reached Kokoda. On 25 August they headed off east of Eora Gorge to flank the Australian position and on that day lost four men killed and four wounded in their first contact with the Australians. On 27 August two more men were killed and one wounded. On 30 August two men were sent away sick and on 2 September, after Isurava, a sergeant leading 27 stragglers rejoined the company, thus bringing company strength up to 150. Just 116 men of 5th Company fought at Isurava of the 161 who began the march. Similarly 3rd Machine Gun Company of the 3/144th had 112 men at Isurava, where it took several casualties, but a week later it was 20 men stronger.[11] One man from the 2/144th who completed the march from Giruwa to Missima thought a quarter of his company dropped out and that the battalion was 'terribly worn out after the march'. There was a plan to attack Missima as soon as they arrived there, but 'there was no more power mentally or physically', so no attack was made.[12]

A comparison with the Australians is illustrative. The 2/14th Battalion marched 80 kilometres to Isurava in seven days, each carrying an average of 20 kilograms, yet only two men fell out. In general, the Australian battalions marching up the track were carefully husbanded, covering short distances each day, with the result that fewer men were lost to exhaustion. The militia was less fit than the AIF battalions and, of A Company of the 53rd, which took six days to get to Isurava, only a quarter arrived on time.[13] In contrast, the Japanese 2/144th marched 120 kilometres in six days carrying twice the weight the Australians carried, and a quarter of one company and a third of another failed to arrive in time to participate in the battle. If the losses of 4th and 5th Companies of the 2/144th were representative of the rest of the battalion then it was 200 men under strength at Isurava. The case of the 3/144th was probably not so bad as the battalion's march was ten kilometres shorter and on a better track for the last day. Even so the gun platoon, 60 men strong, failed to arrive until the fighting was over.[14] Some 738 men of the battalion landed in Papua, but 135 men in the three rifle companies and the machine-gun company missed the battle.[15] If this same proportion was absent from the headquarters company, then the 3/144th had 540 men present at Isurava. In fact the proportion of headquarters personnel who failed to complete the march was almost certainly higher than average because they had not been ordered to climb the Rabaul volcanoes repeatedly with heavy packs so, according to battalion veterans, they were unfit and overweight when they arrived in Papua.[16] Major Horie Masao, a New Guinea veteran who has made a study of the Kokoda campaign, estimated that about a fifth of all Japanese who attempted the forced march did not rejoin the Nankai Shitai until after Isurava.[17]

The third reason to reduce Japanese numbers is the casualties already suffered by the 1/144th, which had been campaigning for a month and had had several sharp fights with the Australians and Papuans that cost it 125 casualties to 15 August. No more men from the battalion were killed until the fighting at Isurava began, but a small uncertain number were wounded.[18] If these are allowed to stand in the place of lightly wounded who returned to duty then it seems reasonable to deduct the full 125 men from the strength of the 1/144th to obtain the number likely to have been present at Isurava.

With the three battalions of 144th Regiment at 460, 500 and 540 men, the total Japanese force engaged late on 27 August was probably around 2130 against 2292 Australians. On 30 August, the last of four days fighting, the gun company of 144th Regiment and one more company of the Mountain Artillery Battalion arrived (260 men) bringing up the Japanese strength, not deducting for casualties, to 2400 men.[19] Even if the Nankai Shitai's loss on the forced march from Giruwa was not quite as high as has been estimated, there is enough here to show that the idea the Australians were greatly outnumbered at Isurava no longer has any veracity.

ISURAVA

Captain Frank Sublet of 2/16th Battalion thought Isurava a poor defensive position, yet he does not enlarge upon the point in his book on the campaign. The same view was expressed in the 21st Brigade report, but again it is not clear what the problem was.[20] Sublet probably had two things in mind: the ridge overlooking Isurava to the north provided the Japanese artillery with an opportunity for direct fire into the Australian position. Second, there was a track junction at Alola immediately to the rear of the Australians at Isurava on the west side of the gorge. This offered an alternative approach to the Australian rear via the track on the east side of Eora Gorge. Both of these features imposed significant disadvantages on the defenders, but none of the succession of commanders of Maroubra Force can be blamed as their orders from NGF in Port Moresby did not allow leeway for further retirement. Cameron, under an order to retake Kokoda, originally chose the position after his force was defeated at Deniki on 14 August. He had first retreated to Isurava rest house, a kilometre further south, but decided the rest house was too far back and 'lacked tactical advantages of Isurava area'. He was aware that the Japanese had at least one gun but presumably judged that the advantage of holding the top of a steep slope running parallel to his line at front creek, just forward of Isurava, more than compensated. It is hard to see why he thought this way, yet it is also true that he cannot have had any idea of the amount of artillery – six guns – that the Japanese would be able to place on the ridge overlooking Isurava from the north.[21] With a force of less than a full battalion he could not cover the east side of the gorge as well, although patrols were sent there to see whether the Japanese were interested in that approach.

Lieutenant-Colonel Ralph Honner took over Maroubra Force on 17 August, now with orders to prevent a Japanese advance, and Brigadier Selwyn Porter superseded Honner on 20 August with similar defensive orders.[22] Three days later, Brigadier Arnold Potts arrived with most of 21st Brigade, and by 27 August Potts had 39th and 2/14th Battalions on Front Creek west of Eora Gorge and 53rd Battalion east of the gorge. As the companies of the 2/16th came up they reinforced the 53rd. Potts had a new order, to retake Kokoda, but before he acted on it he was attacked at Isurava, and it was not until 29 August that he received by then redundant instructions from NGF: 'Your original role to capture Kokoda is postponed and you will endeavour to stabilise your position and maintain patrolling initiative.'[23]

Horii personally commanded the Nankai Shitai at Isurava but was not to do so again until Oivi–Gorari in November. The other actions and engagements of the campaign were fought by regiment-size forces and commanded by his regimental commanders, Colonel Kusunose Masao followed by Lieutenant-Colonel Tsukamoto Hatsuo, of 144th Regiment, and Colonel Yazawa Kiyomi of 41st Regiment. Horii was unaware that the Australians had been reinforced.[24] His plan was to make a major attack late on 27 August, then finish off the Australians the next day. Apart from the 2/144th's gun, which was east of the gorge with its battalion, the artillery was placed on the ridge north of and overlooking the Australians.[25] A measure of Horii's keenness to attack was that he did not wait for more artillery. The gun company of 144th Regiment with two 75mm and two 37mm guns, two more mountain guns and the battalion gun of the 3/144th had fallen behind in the forced march. In the event the mountain artillery arrived only in time to participate on the last day of the battle.

Horii attempted a double envelopment. The first battalion of the 144th was to pin the Australians on Front Creek (2/14th and 39th Battalions) while the 2/144th, on the eastern side of the gorge, went around the Australian right flank and attacked the Australians in their rear at Alola. After giving these two attacks time to develop and hopefully draw in any Australian reserve, the 3/144th would swing around the Australian left, thus trapping the Australians.[26] The plan did not work. Not only did the double envelopment fail but also an additional two days fighting was needed to dislodge the enemy. It might be said that the determination of the Australians accounts for one of these days and Japanese errors accounts for the other.

Looking first east of Eora Gorge, where the 2/144th was, there has been a view that this was essentially a diversion, but this is incorrect.[27] The battalion was tasked to 'Cut off the Australians and annihilate them'.[28] It failed for three reasons: first, on 26 August the 2/144th arrived too exhausted to advance on Missima. Their one achievement on this day was to find a position from which the battalion gun and the machine-gun company could fire on the far (western) side of the gorge to inflict casualties on Maroubra Force Headquarters (MFHQ) and 2/4th Field Ambulance.[29] The Australians mistook the artillery fire for mortar fire. The war correspondent Chester Wilmot was at MFHQ: 'They were lobbing 4 inch mortars on us this morning from that ridge on the right ... from that same ridge we can hear ... a heavy machine-gun ... they were shooting up Bde HQ with that this morning ... they put some in the RAP and the doc [Captain Hogan, 53rd Battalion] got hit in both legs ...'[30]

The second reason for the failure of the 2/144th was that, on 27 August, 53rd Battalion halted the Japanese advance towards Alola. The battalion has acquired a poor reputation as a result of its performance at Isurava, but on that day it did its job. Major Horie, commander of the 2/144th, was apparently convinced that his opponents were so strong that a frontal attack again the following day would not work and a flank march was called for. In attempting it on 28 August, the 2/144th became lost and failed to make contact with the Australians that day. The next day, 29 August, the 2/144th found the eastern track again and struck a major blow towards Abuari. At this point the Australian 53rd Battalion fell apart. One company 'appears to have dissolved soon after contact was made', and it is this failure for which the 53rd is remembered.[31] Not even the battalion history offers a defence.[32]

Two companies of the 2/16th arrived on the eastern side of the gorge and barely managed to stop the Japanese cutting in behind Maroubra Force by seizing the track junction at Alola. Japanese diaries, reports and histories written by campaign veterans often comment on Australian fighting prowess, usually but not always negatively. Of the period of fighting east of the gorge against the Australian 53rd and 2/16th, the typescript 'War History of 144 Regiment' made no distinction between the Australian militia and the AIF, relating that the 2/144th were up against Australians who fought stubbornly 'with lines changing hands several times' and 'little opportunity to make a speedy exploitation of the battle situation'.[33]

West of Eora Gorge the 1/144th patrols, at the cost of a few wounded, found the extent of the Australian position on Front Creek after they first located it on 15 August. This information was passed on to the artillery, and the Japanese attack on the west side of the gorge began with the artillery shelling the Australian 39th Battalion on 26 August.[34] This was to cover the move of the 1/144th as it advanced to contact with the Australians on a two-company front directly south along the Kokoda Track. One infantry company was held in reserve.

On 27 August, the 3/144th was brought up behind the 1/144th.[35] While the original plan called for the 1/144th to pin the Australians west of the gorge while the 3/144th went around the western flank a day later, 9th Company of the 3/144th was instead committed to the support of the 1/144th. This decreased the strength of the western flanking move, but Horii felt that the 1/144th's attack lacked vigour and was unlikely to force the commitment of Australian reserves. Some progress was made, with the Australian 2/14th giving ground near Lone House, the Japanese name for Isurava.[36]

On 28 August, the day the 2/144th became lost east of Eora Gorge, there was also a lull on the western side. Horii decided to give the 2/144th one more day to take Alola so he postponed the 3/144th's attack. He had the 2/41st six kilometres north at Deniki. He could have used it, but he wished to keep it fresh for the pursuit of the Australians after 144th Regiment won the battle. Now that he had discovered that the Australians were reinforced and putting up more opposition than expected, he still chose not to use this battalion in an attempt to finish off the fight a day or two earlier. This suggests that now he had achieved what he wanted – an opportunity to destroy the Australians – he did not feel so pressed for time as some accounts would have it.[37]

At 2 a.m. on 28 August, leaving 9th Company with the 1/144th, the rest of the 3/144th commenced its move to the high ground on the Australian left. As with the 2/144th across the valley, they soon became lost in thick jungle. In the dark the two Japanese infantry companies became separated from the machine-gun company and battalion headquarters. Both infantry companies bumped into the western flank of the Australians. The Japanese backed off and made a wider flanking move, aiming for the rear of the Australians along Front Creek, but disentangling the two companies took most of the night. At dawn on 29 August, 7th Company was where it wanted to be and, with artillery support, commenced its attack on Natsu, the Japanese objective, held by B Company of the Australian 2/14th Battalion.[38] While 7th Company was engaged, the rest of the Japanese battalion remained lost. The battalion headquarters did not arrive until midday and the machine-gun company not until 2.30 p.m.[39] An hour later Natsu fell to the Japanese, then a counter-attack, led by Lieutenant Lindsay Mason of the 2/14th, killed Lieutenant Kamiya, 7th Company's commander. The counter-attack was repulsed and almost all members of the Australian platoon were killed or wounded.[40] This was the end of the day's work for the 3/144th, which dug in. More Australian counter-attacks were expected but did not appear, and the caution of the 3/144th contributed to the ease of the later Australian withdrawal.[41] Meanwhile, 1/144 Battalion, assisted by 9th Company of the 3/144th, and facing Isurava from the north along Front Creek, briefly broke into the Australian position but was ejected by a counter-attack. At day's end the Japanese had made no progress there.

The events of 29 August west of Eora Gorge were listed by an officer at the 144th's Regimental Headquarters:

> The red roof and one house positions [Isurava] are stubbornly holding ... [there is] heavy fighting and casualties are increasing. Number 3 Battalion went around the [Japanese] right flank [and] is fighting a difficult battle and casualties are continuing to increase ... No 1 Company captured the red roof position but were nearly wiped out by an enemy counter-attack. Captain Takamori and his company are to go and recapture the position. It is an attack of certain death. The enveloping operations have been completed and the enemy has no way of retreating. Their counter-attacks are fierce. It is their final struggle.[42]

By last light on 29 August Horii had achieved his aim as all Australian reserves at Front Creek had been committed. During the night, accepting the view of the 2/14th's commander Lieutenant-Colonel Arthur Key that the Australians could not hold on another day, Potts ordered a withdrawal to the rest house, a kilometre south along the Kokoda Track. The withdrawal was completed without disruption from the Japanese, who were unaware of it and spent the night preparing to attack Front Creek again the next day.[43] Around this time Potts sent a succinct situation report to NGF: 'Enemy aggressive and successful to date.'[44]

There was no night withdrawal east of Eora Creek. On 30 August the formed bodies of Australians to the east of the gorge were two companies of the 2/16th and D Company and Headquarters Company of 53rd Battalion. Behind them, holding the Eora Creek crossing, were A and B Companies of the 53rd. A counter-attack was to be mounted by both companies of the 2/16th with the assistance of D Company, but the company did not arrive and the 2/16th attack failed. The Australians maintained a position just south of Abuari until ordered to withdraw in the afternoon. Many were unable to leave via Alola so they retreated south along the eastern side of Eora Creek.

By dawn on 30 August, the Australians west of the gorge were deployed at Isurava rest house. Two battalions, the 39th and 2/14th, blocked the track with two companies of the 2/16th behind them. In the course of the day they came under a strengthened bombardment. Before this, only the battalion gun of the Japanese 1/144th and one mountain gun had fired on them, but now two more 75mm guns of the mountain artillery arrived, together with the 144th Regimental Gun Company.[45] The battalion gun of the 3/144th arrived too late to participate, and the gun company of 41st Regiment did not arrive at all. By the afternoon of 30 August there were eight guns firing on the Australians. Six were concentrated at the ridge, one was east of the gorge with the 2/144th and one went forward in close support of the 1/144th.[46] The main battery supported the 3/144th's attack on the rest house position from the high ground to the west. For a while the Japanese guns also fired on the single Australian 3-inch mortar, the only weapon with the range to fire on the Japanese gunners on the ridge.[47]

During the night the 3/144th moved south again. 'Our mission is to deploy to … the south of Isurava, block the enemy's withdrawal, then annihilate them.'[48] With an engineer platoon leading, the battalion cut a track though the jungle along the high ground to the west of the rest house, this time with no loss of direction. Having found the Australians, the 3/144th's signallers contacted the guns to bring fire onto the rest house. The battalion's machine-gun company was placed overlooking it. The six-gun artillery bombardment falling on the rest house position, together with the machine-gun fire from the high ground to the west, contributed to Potts' decision that the rest house could not be held. At 3 p.m. he ordered a withdrawal. As it began, 8th Company of the 3/144th attacked down the hill towards the Australians. 7th Company, which had done most of the fighting the previous day, was in support. The Japanese battalion record stated that 'the enemy panicked and fled at our attack, leaving their wounded behind'. Around 4 p.m. there was an Australian counter-attack but '7 Company was thrown in and easily dispersed them'. The Japanese thought that this was not a properly organised counter-attack but a group of cut-off Australians attacking southwards to re-establish contact with their fellows.[49] This point must be kept in mind to make sense of what occurred next when the hitherto orderly withdrawal of the Australian 2/14th turned into a shambles.

The accepted explanation is that it was the 8th Company attack from the west that caused the sudden dispersal of much of the 2/14th, especially its headquarters company, which was formed up along the track, ready to retire to the south when the Japanese threatened it. Captain Harold Dickenson's C Company was ordered to put in a counter-attack to relieve the pressure. It has been thought that, as Dickenson's counter-attack was underway, the Japanese suddenly swept the track with fire, causing 2/14th Headquarters Company to scatter, most jumping over the side of the track down the precipitous slope to Eora Creek. Honner, who was present, told a different story to Gavin Long in Melbourne in September 1944:

> Key ordered Dickenson ... to relieve pressure on the battalion.
> Actually Dickenson's attack swung in towards [the] track and Key
> and his HQ were on the track and ... Key thought Dickenson's
> attack with blood curdling yells was a Jap attack. Suddenly Key went
> down over the edge of the track to cover. What were Dickenson's
> orders? ... Dickenson's charge caused [Australian] casualties and
> caused a stampede among the troops waiting on the track. Some
> 2/14th, as a result, disappeared way across the valley.[50]

The 39th Battalion war diary relates the same story: 'Captain Dickenson made a charge which carried all before it – not only the enemy but also BHQ and troops waiting on the track to withdraw. Lt. Col. Key, his adj, IO and RSM, disappeared over the side of the hill and the withdrawal was precipitated by the wall of fire coming down through the jungle with C Coy's charge.'[51] This version of events would explain why Dickenson, directed to attack westward against the 3/144th (but actually heading south), appeared to the Japanese to be an attack of a body of isolated Australians coming down from the north trying to cut their way through to the south.

From the moment the 2/14th headquarters was dispersed the reasonably orderly Australian withdrawal from the rest house position became the opposite. In the mid-afternoon of 30 August, a situation report from Maroubra Force to New Guinea Force explained that the enemy had 'penetrated both flanks, 2/14th infiltrated to rear, heavy fighting, 2/14th strongly pressed all sides, 1530 Bde commander decided to withdraw Eora'. Regarding events east of the gorge, it stated, 'A and B Coy [53rd Battalion] forced back to waterfall. Enemy encircled their rear ... Coy broke and scattered ... 1600 withdrawal commenced.'[52]

During the entire phase of the Japanese attack on the Isurava rest house position the Australians there were engaged only by the 3/144th, less one company still with the 1/144th, and by the Japanese artillery. No Japanese troops from the fighting along Front Creek came down the track to assist. When the Australians withdrew from Isurava village to the rest house on the morning of 30 August they did so unknown to their opponents at Front Creek, 1/144th Battalion and 9th Company of the 3/144th. At 7.30 a.m. these two units attacked the now-abandoned Australian position. The Japanese then advanced south along the main track encountering dispersed groups of Australians. The Australians must have delayed them considerably for it was not until 8 a.m, on 31 August, after Maroubra Force had left the battlefield, that 9th Company of the 3/144th was able to rejoin its parent battalion then at the rest house.

A few hours after the disarray caused by Dickenson's misdirected attack, the Australian withdrawal recovered a degree of order. The men still on the main Kokoda Track passed through a rearguard of two companies of the Australian 2/16th south of Alola, which did not withdraw until 1 a.m. on 31 August. Half an hour after this, two kilometres to the north, the leading Japanese troops settled into a position south of Isurava rest house. With them by 6 p.m. was Colonel Yazawa, looking for the battalion of his regiment that had made the wide flanking move to the west designed to cut the track in the Australian rear.[53] The lost battalion, the 2/41th, appeared on the track ten hours later, towards dawn, north of Isurava rest house, and well after the horse had already bolted via the stable door. The nearest formed bodies of Australians were then three kilometres away to the south, which was the closest the 2/41th came to the Australians at any time during the action.

CASUALTIES

The Nankai Shitai claimed to have killed a thousand Australians before the fighting ended, but immediately after the battle this was reduced to 300 Australians left dead on the field.[54] A week later a serious count found

105 Australian corpses, not too far from the actual figure.[55] Australian claims were similarly varied. On 2 September Potts' estimate was that his men had inflicted more than 700 casualties. This number grew after the war, in the manner of the Kokoda myth, to 550 Japanese dead and more than a thousand wounded.[56] Where a number is not given it has become customary to state that the Japanese suffered appalling losses.[57] Private Watanabe Toshio's diary, which laments that his company was reduced from '170–180 men to 50–60 men', is often quoted in support of the view that the Japanese suffered massive casualties at Isurava. It has been assumed that this applied to most Japanese infantry companies and that the losses occurred at Isurava.[58] Watanabe was a member of 1st Company of the 1/144th, which left Japan in November 1941 with 184 men and arrived in Papua with 135. It fought at Awala, Kumusi, Oivi, First and Second Kokoda, Deniki and Isurava. At Isurava 1st Company had the misfortune to be on the Japanese left at Front Creek where it faced, among other trials, the Australian counter-attack in which its company commander was killed and Private Bruce Kingsbury won his Victoria Cross. No Japanese company had done as much fighting and, after the diary extract quoted, Watanabe went on to say that his company had lost more men than any other.[59] In short, 1st Company 1/144th did not lose more than a hundred men at Isurava; rather it entered the action with 80 and lost 20 more there. The other companies of the 1/144th fought in the last three engagements listed above but, for all the other infantry companies of the Nankai Shitai, Isurava was their first encounter in Papua.

There is no difficulty with determining the number of Australians killed in action from 25 to 31 August. The official figure is 99 dead, and unofficial figures are within one or two either side of that. This includes any whose death occurred near but not on the battlefield or whose death was presumed within the period, as well as those who died of wounds. There were also 111 wounded. Although 31 August is considered the first day of the next engagement, First Eora, there was still fighting on the Isurava battlefield as small groups of Australians remained there. The 144th RHQ, advancing at midday down the Kokoda Track, blundered into one such group and took nine casualties.[60] A Japanese officer wrote, '... since none of our troops could be observed along the road [I said] it was too early to move forward but the recommendation was rejected. As [I] expected when we reached the ravine [just south of the postwar position of Alola village] Corporal Komatsu and five men were killed and Corporal Yamamoto and two men wounded.'[61]

Table 6.3: 144th Regiment dead at Isurava

West of Eora Gorge		East of Eora Gorge	
Unit	Number	Unit	Number
24/8	0	–	–
25/8	2	25/8	6 at Kaeri
26/8	3	26/8	0
27/8	7	27/8	6 at 'Muari', presumably Abuari; some possibly from the day before
28/8	16	28/8	0 (the day the 2/144th was lost)
29/8	48	29/8	10
30/8	14	30/8	8
31/8	9	31/8	1
Total	99	Total	31

Source: *Hohei Dai 144 Rentai Senki* (Battle Records of the 144th Infantry Regiment), list of war dead, pp. 625–726. NIDS 302.9.H.

An Australian infantry officer wounded in action at Isurava with 2/14th Battalion believed that 'we were killing them about one for one', but this is the minority view in Australia among both the veterans and postwar historians.[62] While more Japanese than Australians were killed in the action, it was much closer to one to one ratio than the five to one that has become accepted. After the war the 144th Regiment Association compiled a regimental history, which contains a list of all 5403 men who died during the war. It lists the man's name, the village he came from, the date and location of his death. There are a number of occasions in the regimental history – typically when a great defeat was suffered – when the date and location is unlikely to be accurate. At Isurava, with the leisure granted list-makers by a victory, the record, shown in table 6.3, is likely to be sound.

Adding about 226 wounded to 130 dead, the total casualty list for the 144th was 356.[63] One member of 15 IER was wounded, and the artillery suffered no loss.[64] As we have seen, 41st Regiment neither fired a shot nor took a casualty. Allowing for some uncertainty about the number of wounded, total Japanese casualties were certainly no more than 360. While this is a severe casualty rate, it is between a third and a quarter of what has been claimed. In the Second Eora engagement, which followed Isurava, the Japanese loss was similarly higher than that of the Australians, but after that it was not until Oivi–Gorari in November that

Table 6.4: 3/144 losses at Isurava

Unit	Killed in action	Wounded in action
Battalion Headquarters	2	2
7th Infantry Company	18	18
8th Infantry Company	15	36
9th Infantry Company	21	36
3th Machine Gun Company	2	5
3rd Battalion Gun Platoon*	–	–
Total	58	97

* 3rd Battalion Gun Platoon was not present at Isurava.

Source: *Hohei Dai 144 Rentai dai 3 daitai Sento Shoho* [Detailed battle records of 3rd Battalion, 144th Regiment], p. 25, NIDS, *Nanto zenpan* 174.

the Japanese again lost so great a proportion of casualties to those they inflicted. East of Eora Gorge both sides lost 31 killed in action and, in four days of trying, the Japanese failed to proceed far beyond Abuari. These casualty figures lend support to the view that the fighting east of the gorge was ultimately indecisive. On the west side of Eora Gorge, about Isurava village and rest house where the outcome of the battle was decided, the Japanese suffered more severely, losing 99 dead to 64 Australian dead.

The heaviest Japanese loss at Isurava was suffered by the companies that did the most fighting, those of the 3/144th, who fought the whole rest house phase of the fighting unaided against elements of three Australian battalions. The 3/144 battalion's losses are shown in table 6.4.

Potts' estimate of Japanese casualties was twice what his men inflicted, but this is not unusual as he made the estimate immediately after the battle when there was no way to know what the correct figure was. What is unusual, but entirely characteristic of the Kokoda myth, is that the accepted figure for Japanese battle casualties at Isurava has doubled again in the last few decades, to more than four times the true figure.

COMMAND AND CONCLUSIONS

The Japanese were surprised by the resistance offered by the Australians at Isurava. The majority of the Nankai Shitai were long-service veterans, more than half of 144 having served in China, but most of their

Photo 7 Japanese infantry with bayonets fixed climbing a hill in New Guinea. (Asahi Graph)

experience of war was against Chinese guerrillas. Even when they met Chinese regulars veterans thought 'a stand-up fight of any duration was a rarity'.[65] This is certainly true of the series of amphibious landings 144th Regiment made along the coast of China in the late 1930s. Only in the landing near Shanghai in 1937 and during the advance along the Yangtze to Nanking had 144th Regiment experienced the kind of determined resistance they faced at Isurava.

From December 1941, 144th Regiment had two easy victories, at Guam and Rabaul. Some soldiers complained that they did not get the chance to fire their weapons as the enemy surrendered too quickly.[66] In Malaya, 41st Regiment was generally successful and, when sent to the Philippines, the regiment saw action only against Philippine guerrillas.

Thus the average Nankai Shitai infantryman in Papua was probably confident of more easy victories to come. A 41st Regiment man told his commander that he knew how to deal with the Australians from his experience of them in Malaya and was looking forward to a second bout.[67] The shock of Isurava turned this thinking on its head. A 144th Regiment diarist wrote afterwards that these fellows at Isurava seemed a different kind of Australian from the ones he had fought in Rabaul. Isurava proved to be one fight too many for the 1/144th, which by the end had lost a third of the men with whom it had landed in Papua and was down to half the strength with which it had left Japan eight months earlier.

There is usually a connection between the casualties a unit suffers and its morale. After Isurava Lieutenant Noda Hidetaka commented in his diary that the 1/144th had 'lost its fighting spirit ... I hear that three officers of the number one daitai [battalion] have been killed and one wounded. The strength of this daitai is certainly becoming low.' Noda, who was a member of the 3/144th, then makes the connection between casualties and morale. 'I don't know whether it is because the number one battalion has had so many casualties but all ranks of commanders seem to have lost some of their offensive spirit.'[68] Horii saw that the battalion had performed poorly at Isurava and afterwards relegated it to transport duties, carrying wounded and supplies. It was not committed to battle again for two months until the Second Eora action at the end of October.

Horii expected a quick success at Isurava but did not get it. Although Isurava was still a convincing win for the Japanese, it was expected to be an annihilating one. The 2/144th was supposed to capture the track junction at Alola in the Australian rear, but this it failed to do. The 2/41st was supposed to be held out of battle, fresh for the pursuit. It became necessary to bring it forward, but it became lost while flanking the Australians and made no contribution at all to the victory. The third battalion of the 144th likewise lost a day trying to turn the Australian left. The first battalion of the 1/144th, flagging as a result of six weeks fighting against 39th Battalion and the PIB, failed to place enough pressure on the Australians along the line of Front Creek so it had to be reinforced by a company of the 3/144th. This reduced the 3/144th's strength for its hook around the Australian left flank on the night of 28/29 August, a hook that started a day late because the 2/144th had made no progress on the far side of the gorge.

Another criticism that could be levelled at Horii is that he exhausted and depleted his strength by force marching the main body of the Nankai

Shitai from Giruwa to Isurava. He feared another Australian attempt to retake Kokoda, but he was also worried that the Australians might withdraw beyond his reach, and for this he was willing to accept the temporary losses from the forced march. The same applies to his decision to begin the attack with just three instead of the ten guns he might have had. The decisive moves of the action were the attacks by 7th and 8th Companies of the 3/144th. On 29 August they broke into the left flank of the Australian first position along Front Creek at Isurava, causing the Australians to retreat, and on 30 August they struck again, down from the heights above the rest house into 2/14th Battalion.

The normal Australian explanation for failure at Isurava revolves around a Japanese superiority of numbers. 'Notes on Operations, Isurava Area', written on 10 September, is typical of the explanations for the defeat that have appeared since: 'Our troops appear to have been outfought and outmanoeuvred primarily because the enemy had superior numbers.'[69] This is the concluding comment after mention has been made of the failure of 53rd Battalion, uniforms not lending themselves to camouflage, and supply difficulties. Of 53rd Battalion in general, its poor fighting quality and in particular its early patrol failures, which allowed the Japanese to get into position unobserved, are mentioned. It is also said that supply difficulties delayed 21st Brigade's arrival. However, all the Australians were present by late on 27 August with the exception of two companies of the 2/16th, which arrived early the next day. In this same period, the Japanese had only two battalions committed and later an additional company of a third battalion arrived so, on 27 August, the Japanese were most probably slightly outnumbered by the Australians, which undercuts the view that delayed Australian arrivals contributed to the Australian defeat. The poor performance of 53rd Battalion, another explanation for defeat offered, also now seems less important as the 2/144th was so exhausted and reduced that 53rd Battalion, with the stiffening of two companies of 2/16th, was enough to hold them off for four days.

There is little if any criticism of Potts' handling of Isurava in postwar accounts, but that is because all have factored in a huge Japanese superiority in numbers. If it were so then comparisons between Isurava and Thermoplyae and Agincourt might be acceptable. But there were no more Japanese engaged than there were Australians so the battle, although a fascinating one, was not a wonderful defensive stand against overwhelming numbers as it has been depicted. Potts was also fortunate that his opponent Horii mishandled the action. Had the 2/144th been as adventurous and aggressive as the 3/144th and had they both, as well as the

2/41st, not become lost in the jungle on several occasions, it is difficult to see how Potts could have escaped with a less severe defeat than that administered to the Australians at Efogi a week later. At Isurava Horii defeated Maroubra Force but failed to destroy it, and the feeling among the senior Japanese officers who knew what had really happened was summed up by one: 'We missed a great prize.'[70]

CHAPTER 7

GUADALCANAL AND MILNE BAY

As Horii was making a mess of his opportunity to destroy the Australians at Isurava, an order arrived from Hyakutake on 28 August, the import of which can hardly be overestimated. Horii was told that the offensive against Port Moresby was off, certainly for six weeks and probably for longer.

On 7 August United States Marines had landed at Guadalcanal and taken from the Japanese an airfield they were constructing there. At Rabaul the Japanese Seventeenth Army found itself with an interesting problem. If the American force at Guadalcanal was large, a division or so, then it had to be dealt with using reinforcements earmarked for Papua. If it was small, then it need not affect Papua. Tokyo was consulted and assumed the worst. Imperial Headquarters directed the movement of air, land and sea assets towards Guadalcanal via Rabaul. By 16 August it was clear that Imperial Headquarters was right, the Guadalcanal problem was definitely a large one – in fact 11 000 United States Marines were already there – and Horii, still at Rabaul, was told that his attack on Port Moresby would be postponed.[1] The official order confirming this arrived during the battle of Isurava.[2]

Until 16 August Horii was planning his operation in Papua in accordance with an order of 18 July, which stated, 'The Nankai Shitai will land quickly in the vicinity of Buna, advance rapidly along the Buna–Kokoda road and will capture MO [Port Moresby] and the nearby airfields.'[3] Studies of the campaign have focused on this order, assuming it to be the order governing Horii's actions in the Owen Stanley Range.[4] What has not been properly understood is that the order that replaced it, and which forebade Horii from marching on Port Moresby, is in fact the key to an understanding of Japanese conduct during the Kokoda campaign.

Horii's new 28 August order was to 'advance to the southern slopes of the Owen Stanley Range and destroy the enemy troops there. Use a portion of your strength to secure the front but amass your main strength on the north side of the range in preparation for future operations.'[5] The order instructed Horii to secure an advanced location short of Port Moresby, but close enough to threaten it with a lesser force, and to keep his main body north of the Owen Stanley Range. This he did. Thus instead of sending at least 5000 fighting troops along the Kokoda Track to combine outside Port Moresby with an amphibious landing there (launched from Milne Bay) involving another 5000 or so, Horii now sent forward just four infantry battalions, two engineer companies and a reduced artillery regiment. These 3500 men advanced beyond Isurava to secure a position on the southern slopes of the mountains from which a future attack on Port Moresby could be mounted. This force, which did all the fighting until the last battle of the Kokoda campaign at Oivi–Gorari in November 1942, was of course far too small to make an attack on Port Moresby alone as the Japanese were aware that it contained 22 000 troops, half of them in combat units.[6] The troops who would have made an attack viable, by both reinforcing Horii and seizing Milne Bay – the Kawaguchi Detachment in the Palau Islands, the Aoba Detachment in the Philippines and the Ichiki Detachment at Guam – were to be split between Papua and the FS operation to capture Fiji and Samoa. With the cancellation of FS in July 1942 all were potentially available to go to Papua. All went to Guadalcanal instead. Moreover, the main body of the Nankai Shitai never entered the Owen Stanley Range, and at no time after Isurava was the Nankai Shitai advancing with orders to attack Port Moresby, as no order to that effect ever came.

The Chief of Army General Staff approved Hyakutake's proposal to limit Horii, stating, 'The offensive against Port Moresby, seen in the light of conditions in the Guadalcanal region ... was judged to require adequate preparations and a strengthening of troops numbers ... Consequently I must approve the appropriate restriction of the advance of the South Seas force to the south side of the Owen Stanley Range.'[7] IHQ concurred, declaring on 31 August that Guadalcanal was now Seventeenth Army's 'principal operational area' and issued Directive No. 127 confirming the postponement of the Port Moresby attack until 'after the development of Guadalcanal operations'.[8] There was now no need to rush combat units to Papua, but there was a still a requirement for non-combat troops to improve Giruwa to Kokoda communications, so one battalion of Horii's 41st Regiment was taken off the list of units to be sent immediately to Giruwa.[9] A thousand bridge building and road maintenance personnel took their place.

All this has consequences for the Kokoda myth. The quick dash to Port Moresby plan, which is myth shorthand for Japanese strategy, was in effect only from 18 July to 16 August, before the main body of the Nankai Shitai had even arrived in Papua, but it explains nothing about the Japanese plan thereafter. It follows that another pillar of the Kokoda myth is also without a foundation: that Horii had an 'ambitious timetable' and 'had to reach Port Moresby in around eight days' and that the Australians fell back in front of the Japanese, delaying them until they had no food left, inflicting such casualties that they ran out of steam on Ioribawa Ridge, so saving Port Moresby.[10] This cannot be true if it is also true that, from 16 August, the Japanese force that advanced down the Kokoda Track was too small to attempt to take Port Moresby alone, and was in any case forbidden to go that far – although its members hoped the advance would resume at a later date. It never did, and the next significant order Horii had after the postponement of the MO operation was to retreat from Ioribaiwa in mid-September. It is also likely that the 16 August informal notification to Horii of postponement influenced his battle plan for Isurava. A plausible explanation for his arguably rash forced march to Isurava is that he desired a battle as soon as possible, in case the formal order he knew was coming restricted his advance even more than he had been told it would.

A comparable case is the long-held view that the Japanese intended to invade Australia. It was argued that the Battle of the Coral Sea prevented invasion, but in recent years this has been shown to be in error because the Japanese did not plan to invade Australia.[11] Similarly the Australians on the Kokoda Track, although they understandably thought otherwise at the time, did not prevent the Japanese from taking Port Moresby because, after 16 August 1942, the Nankai Shitai was not trying to get there. Had there been no large Australian force blocking the Kokoda Track on Imita Ridge in September 1942 after the battle of Ioribaiwa, then it may have made no difference. The Nankai Shitai had brought forward a force adequate only to seize a position that threatened Port Moresby, and was denied by events at Guadalcanal the reinforcements that would have made it possible to take on the large Allied garrison of Port Moresby.

A favourite son of the Kokoda myth is Colonel Tsuji Masanobu who, it is said, went beyond his authority as liaison officer from IHQ and told Hyakutake to attack Port Moresby before IHQ had made a final decision.[12] Tsuji was certainly no respecter of authority and had made a career of making trouble, but this version of events looks like invention. The story is that Yokoyama's force, the advance guard of the Nankai Shitai, was sent off to Papua in July with instructions to investigate the practicality of an advance over the Owen Stanley Range, but on the very day Yokoyama landed it was decided to attack Port Moresby along the Kokoda Track without waiting for Yokoyama's appreciation. It is said that Tsuji, speaking on behalf of IHQ, lied in telling Hyakutake the decision had been taken when it had not been.[13]

There are two problems with this interpretation. The first is that it was a common procedure for senior headquarters to advise their subordinates that a certain order is about to be issued and to send the order officially later – as was done to Horii. At a higher level IJA Great Army order no. 596, concerning where Seventeenth Army units would land in New Guinea and the Solomon Islands, was sent unofficially from IJAHQ to Rabaul on 28 January 1942, and again officially five days later. It also sometimes happened that the unofficial order was conveyed by a liaison officer, like Tsuji, who on arrival could explain more fully the thinking of the senior headquarters. Second, on 14 July, the day before Tsuji arrived in Rabaul, Horii issued operational order no. 85 to Yokoyama.[14] The order directed that 166 tons of food and fodder be transported to Kokoda by the end of August. This required that a four-month ration for Yokoyama's force be transported a hundred kilometres inland from the landing place for a force that was, as yet, supposedly there only for reconnaissance. This appears to be far too large a stockpile in an advanced location exposed to enemy attack, unless it was already unofficially understood by all that the MO operation would soon commence.

It seems more likely, then, that the story of Tsuji's lie is an invention and that when Tsuji arrived in Rabaul from Tokyo he was confirming to Hyakutake what Hyakutake already knew: that Yokoyama's advance was to be more than a reconnaissance and that the MO operation was on.

In *South-West Pacific Area – First Year*, McCarthy, an Australian official historian, argued that the Japanese were tardy in making up their minds about Guadalcanal and that it was not until the destruction on 21 August of the Ichiki Detachment, which they sent to Guadalcanal, and the naval battle of the Eastern Solomons on 24/25 August confirmed that the Americans were in great strength there.[15] When on 7 August Seventeenth Army first learned of an American landing on Guadalcanal and Tulagi, the main force of the Nankai Shitai had yet to board their transports in Rabaul to go to Papua. There was an option to delay their departure but it was not taken, and it has been thought that this suggests the initial Japanese reaction to Guadalcanal was complacent. The Japanese did, however, have some grounds in the first few days after the American landing for thinking Guadalcanal was either a raid or a small-scale operation such that the airfield the Japanese had built there could easily be recaptured when convenient. Air reconnaissance reported the withdrawal of the USN and troop transports from the area the day after Admiral Mikawa Gunichi took seven cruisers to Guadalcanal and sank four out of five of Rear-Admiral Victor Crutchley's cruisers at the Battle of Savo Island on the night of 8 August. It appeared possible to the Japanese that the Americans were not present in great strength or were withdrawing.

Moreover the Japanese were convinced the Allied counter-offensive would come from Australia via New Guinea and that the Allies had not enough strength for two offensives. With this predisposition it was reasonable for them to consider that Guadalcanal could well be a feint to draw attention away from New Guinea.[16] This view is, however, misleading in that it might account for the Japanese reaction in the first 48 hours after the Americans landed at Guadalcanal, but by 10 August IHQ had determined that the American landing, and to an extent surprising events in Papua, required a major recasting of their plans.[17]

On the day after the Guadalcanal landing word came to Rabaul that Kokoda had been retaken by the Australians (at Second Kokoda). There had already been discussion at Seventeenth Army headquarters that because communications in Papua were proving so difficult it might be better to postpone the MO operation, and now there had appeared stronger than expected Australian opposition at Kokoda.[18] What seems to have occurred is that at the same moment as a delay to MO as a result of unanticipated Australian opposition was being discussed in Rabaul and Tokyo, new intelligence arrived indicating that the American landing at Guadalcanal was more significant than first thought so some or all 7000 reinforcements available to Seventeenth Army would be needed at Guadalcanal. On 10 August General Sugiyama Hajime, Chief of Army General Staff, and Admiral Nagano Osami, Chief of Navy General Staff, reached an agreement that directed Hyakutake to use the reinforcements to retake Guadalcanal.[19] Forewarned by earlier receipt of an informal order, the nearest available unit, Colonel Ichiki Kiyonao's 28th Regiment, was ready to sail from Guam for Rabaul on the same day. The Ichiki Detachment was to have been the landing force to capture Midway but,

Photo 8   Colonel Tsuji Masanobu, Imperial Headquarters liaison officer to Seventeenth Army. (Kochi New Guinea Association)

with the Japanese naval defeat there in June 1942, Ichiki was sent to Guam. Since July, he had been told that his force would be brought forward to Papua for the MO operation. He was now told that he was to go via Rabaul to Guadalcanal. The next day, 11 August, Vice-Admiral Kondo Nobutake and Vice-Admiral Nagumo Chuichi, with three carriers and 30 other ships under their command, were ordered to prepare for a major operation in the Solomons. Then on 16 August Horii was advised that MO was postponed for at least six weeks.[20]

Thus within several days of the American landing at Guadalcanal IHQ had responded by ordering its only IJA reserves in the region and all the carriers immediately available towards Guadalcanal. It would seem then that the Japanese did react with celerity, and this had consequences for Papua. The day Ichiki received his order to go south to Guadalcanal must also be the day it was clear to Seventeenth Army that there was now no reserve on hand in the South Pacific, no reinforcement for Papua and no large force available for the proposed attack on Milne Bay on which Horii's advance to Port Moresby depended. With the Kawaguchi and Aoba Detachments also to be committed to Guadalcanal if Ichiki failed, Hyakutake thought it prudent to retain a battalion of 41st Regiment for two weeks as a reserve in Rabaul.

That a six-week delay of MO might be too optimistic an assessment was underlined by the failure of Ichiki. His advance force of less than a thousand men landed on Guadalcanal on 19 August. Ichiki was told by Hyakutake that the American force was probably of divisional size and, if that was so, he should not attack but rather take up a position near his objective, the airfield, and await reinforcements.[21] Ichiki did not heed these words of caution and launched an attack that resulted in his death and the annihilation of the Ichiki Detachment on the Tenaru River, east of the Guadalcanal airstrip, on 21 August. Four days after Ichiki's destruction the Kawaguchi Detachment was to land at Guadalcanal. The IJN covering force of Nagumo and Kondo encountered American carriers at the Battle of the Eastern Solomons on 24–25 August 1942. The Japanese lost one transport, one light carrier and one destroyer against negligible USN losses. As a result, Kawaguchi's first attempt to land on Guadalcanal was abandoned. By the time Horii received the official order postponing MO on 28 August, during Isurava, further bad news from Milne Bay confirmed the wisdom of the postponement.

MILNE BAY

Before the landing of the Nankai Shitai in Papua, Seventeenth Army had considered that the island of Samarai, near Milne Bay, was a suitable location for an air base and intended to take it with an operation launched by the navy from Giruwa using either the Kawaguchi or the Aoba Detachments.[22] Then, as Horii approached Port Moresby, an amphibious force from Samarai would also land there. The landing was to be made with destroyers fast enough to sail along the south coast of Papua to Port Moresby overnight, thus avoiding air attack from north Queensland. On 7 August, the same day the Americans took Guadalcanal, the Japanese discovered that the Allies were building an air base at Milne Bay so they decided to take that instead and to launch the amphibious operation against Port Moresby from there.[23] An air base somewhere on the eastern tip of Papua was deemed a prerequisite for an assault on Port Moresby. Aircraft based there would be well placed to provide air cover over ships rounding the eastern tip of Papua, and air attacks could also be launched at Port Moresby and far north Queensland without flying over the Owen Stanley Range, which, with its notorious turbulence and low clouds, was an obstacle to air operations.

Once the Allied airfield at Milne Bay had been discovered, Seventeenth Army also expressed the view that unless it was taken, the shipping for the Nankai Shitai from Rabaul would be threatened by air attack from there. Mikawa's sinking of the Allied cruiser squadron off Savo Island persuaded IHQ that now was a good time to act regarding Milne Bay. Even if the USN attempted to stop Kawaguchi with an operation east of the Solomon Islands, which it in fact did, without cruiser cover the USN carriers were believed to be very unlikely to venture into the Coral Sea to interrupt the simultaneous Milne Bay landing.[24]

Although the IJA troops who were to have taken Milne Bay were unavailable, the moment seemed propitious, and the Japanese believed that there was less than one battalion of Allied troops there – in fact more than 9000 Australians and Americans were present, half of them infantry. Imperial Headquarters decided to allow the navy to go ahead without waiting for IJA infantry, as 2300 Special Naval Landing Party (SNLP) marines and navy pioneers should, they believed, be capable of doing the job. The SNLP was accompanied by two light tanks, two 37mm guns and two 70mm infantry guns.

Everything that could have gone wrong did. The supporting SNLP force from Giruwa, which was to have landed at Taupota to the north of Milne Bay, was stranded at Goodenough Island when No. 75 Squadron RAAF P40s sank their barges. With an escort of cruisers and destroyers, the first Japanese landing, 809 SNLP and 362 NP, took place between Waga Waga and Wandula on the northern shore of Milne Bay on the night of 25 August 1942. The landing was 10 kilometres east of the chosen spot at No. 3 strip, and the Japanese approach to the airfields, their objective, had to be along an easily defended narrow coastal strip between the mountains and the bay. The Australians had a battery of field guns, the weather was appalling and the two Japanese light tanks bogged, which was a good thing for the Australians as the same mud prevented them bringing forward their anti-tank guns. Communications with Giruwa and Rabaul failed and, as a result, the IJN did not know when there was enough of a break in the persistent low clouds and heavy rain for air support to be effective. Fourth Fleet later estimated that only one in every four sorties to Milne Bay from Buna, Lae and Gasmata were of any value. In contrast the RAAF, with an airstrip only minutes away, could attack Japanese ground troops when there was a short break in the weather.

The SNLP have been thought of as an elite force, but they had a poor reputation in the IJN and those sent to Milne Bay were known not to be of the best quality.[25] The United States War Department handbook on Japanese forces described the SNLP as having 'a surprising lack of ability in infantry combat'.[26] At Milne Bay they fully lived up to their reputation, making unsophisticated mass attacks at great expense and with little result. With the failure of the last charge against No 3 strip on 30 August the force was withdrawn to the east. A reinforcement of 800 SNLP had failed to help, and Mikawa decided not to send more. Having lost 625 men the Japanese invasion force was withdrawn from Milne Bay on the night of 5 September.

THE KOKODA FRONT

When Horii received the order of 28 August confirming that MO was off for the time being he was told it might be on again within six weeks; but within a week failure at Guadalcanal and Milne Bay made it clear that November was now the earliest time an advance on Port Moresby might be resumed. Hyakutake wrote, 'We shall endeavour to capture Port Moresby by the end of November at the latest. After the capture of Guadalcanal, the army, co operating with the navy, will quickly move to the key positions of eastern New Guinea and hasten preparations for the Port Moresby [attack].'[27] Hyakutake's November plan was the same as the August one in that he still intended a two-pronged move, along the Kokoda Track and via Milne Bay:

> By the end of November ... the operational group in the Buna
> area will be strengthened then [it will] press the advance towards
> Port Moresby with all possible haste. A detachment will carry out
> a landing operation at Rabi [Milne Bay] ... [then] as quickly as
> possible a powerful detachment with a mechanised unit will carry
> out an opposed landing in the sector east of Port Moresby. Against
> Port Moresby a combined land, sea and air attack will be prepared
> and with full strength capture Port Moresby at one blow.[28]

An additional consequence of Guadalcanal for the Nankai Shitai came on 1 September when all IJN air assets were withdrawn from Papua and committed to Guadalcanal. By mid-September, when the Tainan Air Group left Lae, there were almost no Japanese aircraft based in New Guinea. Apart from a few air raids on Port Moresby launched from Rabaul, fighter cover for supply convoys to Giruwa and the evacuation of Milne Bay, and several airdrops of supplies late in the campaign, there was no Japanese air activity over Papua until late November.

The most important consequence of the loss of air assets was that the Japanese air supply plan would not now go ahead. Hyakutake had expected to land supplies at Kokoda strip and to airdrop supplies in the Owen Stanley Range in much the same way as the Australians were to do. The first message sent after the capture of Kokoda announced to Rabaul that they had 'Captured airfield on 29th. Width 50m, length 750m, plenty of room for expansion.'[29] IJA aircraft had used airdrops in China and the Dutch East Indies and had in Rabaul a large supply of parachutes suitable for dropping food and ammunition. There was an air transport squadron in Rabaul but, with the loss of fighter cover over Papua, the transport aircraft were not risked until the supply crisis in late September. The second effect of the switch of Japanese air assets, especially fighters, to the Solomons was that the AAF was not interrupted in its work, except occasionally over the Giruwa anchorage. They could, and did, strafe and bomb Japanese troops and supplies at will. Fortunately for the Japanese, as chapter 17 illustrates, the effort was small and ineffective.

GUADALCANAL, MILNE BAY AND THE KOKODA MYTH

The Kokoda myths that Horii was marching down the Kokoda Track to attack Port Moresby, that the march was to be a rapid one adhering to a strict timetable and that the Australians, although defeated as they fell back, fatally delayed him, are all revealed to be incorrect. On 16 July Horii was ordered, once in Papua, to advance rapidly and take Port Moresby. Then the American landing at Guadalcanal on 7 August and Maroubra Force's brief retaking of Kokoda the following day gave the Japanese pause. Before the Nankai Shitai arrived in Papua the attack on Port Moresby was postponed so that the reinforcements, without which it could not go ahead, could be used instead at Guadalcanal. This was thought to require a six-week delay, and during that time Horii was to send a relatively small force along the Kokoda Track to seize a position past the crest of the Owen Stanley Range from where the offensive might later be launched. With the defeat of the Ichiki Detachment at Guadalcanal and the first unsuccessful attempt to land the Kawaguchi Detachment there, the six-week delay was extended. The failure at Milne Bay was one more nail in the coffin of the MO plan. If the Allies held Milne Bay, instead of the Japanese, the MO operation was thought to be impractical. Without Milne Bay, it was unlikely that the attack on Port Moresby would be revived, and it never was. The Battle of Milne Bay was also affected by Guadalcanal. A regiment of IJA infantry was to have been used there and, as the Kokoda campaign was to show, IJA infantry were a far more formidable opponent than an equivalent number of second-grade SNLP.

With hindsight it is clear that Milne Bay was one offensive too many. The decision to launch an amphibious assault there was taken on the day Ichiki's force was defeated and resulted in Seventeenth Army being thinly spread on three fronts: Kokoda, Guadalcanal and Milne Bay.[30] Of the three fronts Guadalcanal was the most important because Seventeenth Army chose to make it so. By July 1942 Seventeenth Army had 14 000 fighting troops under its command (although not all had as yet arrived), half of them destined for Papua in the Nankai Shitai.[31] The other half in three detachments – Kawaguchi, Aoba and Ichiki – was intended to assist the Nankai Shitai take Port Moresby, by land or by sea invasion. When Guadalcanal occurred all three were committed there instead, and Japanese strategy became wedded to the position that, until Guadalcanal was finished with, Port Moresby could not be restated. Thus the strict timetable to which the Kokoda myth supposes Horii adhering, and falling well behind, simply did not feature in Japanese planning after 16 August, before the main body of the Nankai Shitai had even landed in Papua.

Moreover, the reinforcement doubling the combat strength of the Japanese in Papua, a requirement for the MO plan, did not arrive there. It would make no sense to suppose that Horii was seriously attempting to take on 22 000 Allied troops in Port Moresby with the 3500 he had on the Kokoda Track even had he been allowed to do so. It is vital to an understanding of the campaign to realise that from the time Horii arrived in Papua he was under orders to wait for permission to attack Port Moresby and that this permission was never given to him. The reason, of course, was Guadalcanal. The connection between Guadalcanal and Kokoda was simply put by Lieutenant-Colonel Tanaka: 'There was originally a plan to assemble a large force at Kokoda and push it over the mountains but, because of Guadalcanal, the force never assembled.'[32]

CHAPTER 8

THE JAPANESE
BUILD-UP

The Kokoda myth's view of Japanese supply arrangements is a simplistic one. It stresses that Nankai Shitai supply was poorly organised and that their retreat and defeat was largely because the Japanese ran out of food. Those who subscribe to the myth imagine that the members of the Nankai Shitai were issued with between 15 and 20 days food and expected to be in Port Moresby by then, or risk starvation.[1] It is a startling claim that a 20th-century regular army such as the IJA would conduct operations in this way. And it is quite untrue. In fact the Japanese in Papua were supplied in the conventional manner of regular armies, but with certain important Japanese characteristics. The 15–20 days food supply each man carried on his back on arrival in Papua did not constitute the Japanese supply plan, but was rather a measure to allow time for a permanent supply system to be put in place.

By the beginning of September, as the First Eora engagement was fought, the Nankai Shitai had established a satisfactory level of supply for the force to hand, and had eased their supply problems by abandoning the plan to advance rapidly on Port Moresby along the Kokoda Track. The error of the myth in part arises because the IJA supply system was a great deal more streamlined than that of the Australians. The difference was that the IJA was a 'light' army and conducted operations on four tons of supplies of all kinds per thousand men per day (PTMD). It did so in successful wars in China and Korea in 1898, 1904–05, 1914 and from 1937. A faster tempo of operations was achievable if supply was reduced to a minimum and as much food as possible was taken

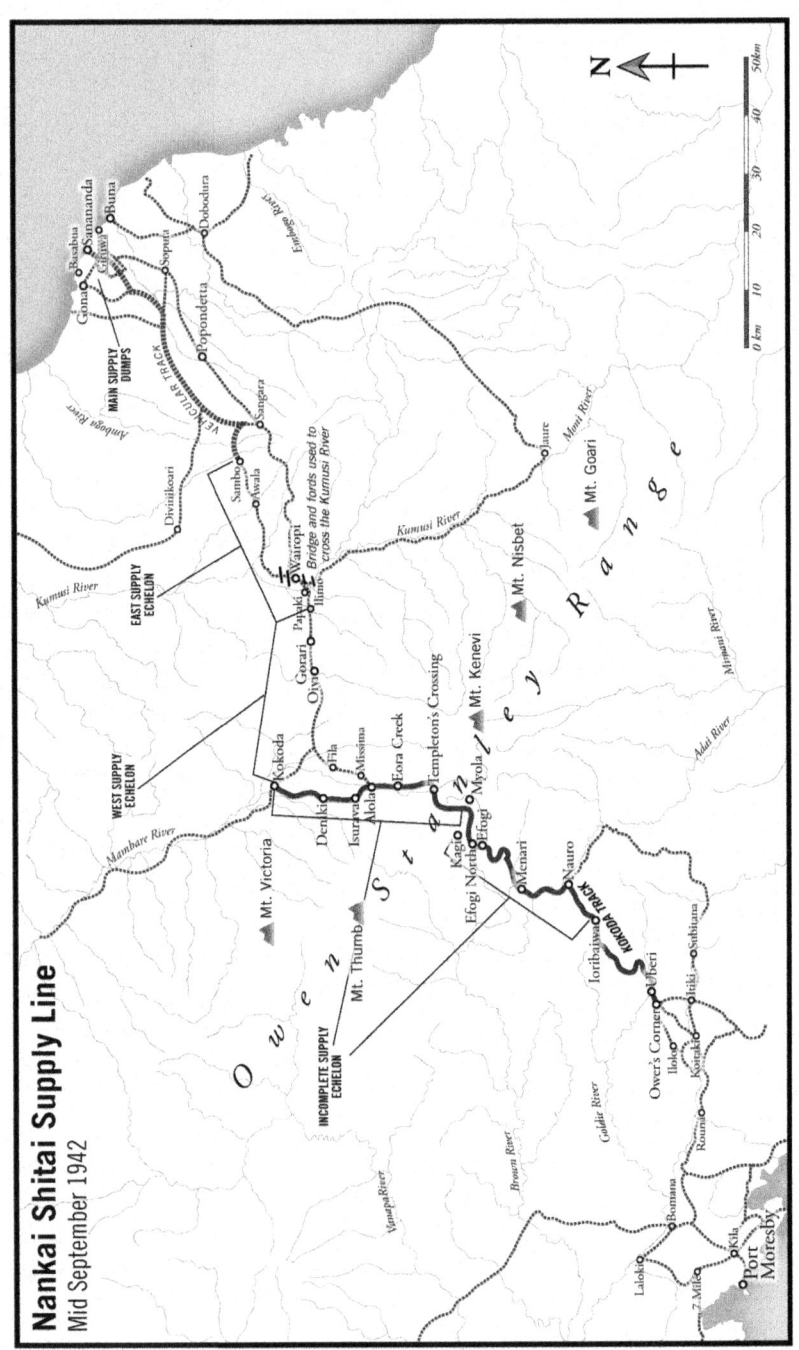

Map 6 Nankai Shitai supply line, mid-September 1942

locally. The Australian Army in Papua was a 'heavy', slower-moving force that required up to three times as much supply. To better understand the difference it is first necessary to explain some of the basics of supplying armies.

An indication of the bare subsistence level of supply required by mid-20th-century armies can be found at Stalingrad in early 1943. Three tons PTMD was the modest amount requested to be flown in to Stalingrad to maintain the surrounded and doomed German 6th Army.[2] More was needed when on the move, and Oberkommando der Wehrmacht calculated that the Germans on the eastern front in 1941 could get to Moscow on an average of six tons PTMD, provided that large parts of the army did not move for weeks at a time.[3] In Korea in 1950–53, the Chinese, whose army resembled the IJA in terms of supply, required six tons PTMD for an offensive. At the other end of the scale was the United States Army, for the past 150 years the best supplied in the world. Even American Civil War armies, when at the end of a rail network, received six tons of all kinds of supplies per thousand men each day.[4] By the Spanish–American War of 1898, 12 tons PTMD was being shipped to the theatre of war, and the United States Army in Europe in 1944 received 70 tons PTMD, the highest rate in World War II.[5] For geographical and topographical reasons this level of supply was not possible in the Pacific where the Americans were able to supply each thousand men with 22 tons per day.[6] The Australian system was similar. In 1942 they sent an average of 19 tons PTMD to Port Moresby, most of it allocated to the Kokoda front. The difference between the two systems was not quite as great as these numbers suggest. Australian supply was less efficient and more complicated. Their packaging was heavy, and Australian soldiers received a more varied diet requiring yet more packaging. In addition they needed more food as they were on average 10 kilograms heavier and more than 100mm taller than the Japanese.[7] Including packaging weight, one ton of food supplied 1600 Japanese in Papua for a day but only 1000 Australians. The Australians learned a lesson on the Kokoda Track and simplified their supply system. By the Huon Peninsula campaign of 1943 they had reduced requirements to 12 tons PTMD.

A soldier's food ration weighs between two-thirds of a kilogram and one kilogram.[8] While his requirement for a sustaining diet has not changed through the ages, modern armies require other items apart from food, and the heaviest of these is artillery ammunition. In World War II a single field-artillery piece might use two tons of ammunition in a day of firing. The mechanisation of armies also required a considerable volume of petrol, oil and lubricants (POL), and together, artillery ammunition and POL made up about three-quarters of supply needs. Food, water, small-arms ammunition, medical, engineering and administrative stores accounted for the remaining quarter. Where there are no roads, the proportions of supply requirements change. In the Owen Stanley Range there was no need for POL and without roads there was less artillery, and water was plentiful so overall tonnage PTMD was reduced and food, normally a small proportion of the total, rose to between a quarter and a third of all requirements.

The essential distinction here is between armies that try to supply their men with everything they can and armies that aim to get by on as little as necessary and assume that they will take much of what they need from the locality and the enemy. There is virtue in both approaches for the motorised army can move faster when there is a road network, and it diverts manpower to logistic tasks intended to increase the combat power and morale of its fighting forces. The advantages of light armies is that they can place a greater percentage of their men in the fighting formations and move faster in unfavourable terrain than heavier armies, which were accustomed to trucks delivering their considerable requirements to the front line. On Pacific islands, where there were often no roads, the light army was well suited and the heavy army was not.

In the Russo-Japanese War Captain Frederick Sedgewick saw the IJA on campaign and wrote that 'the Japanese soldier can live for days on rice and fish ... no European troops could march and fight on such a diet.'[9] By the end of 1942 the Australians were well aware of Japanese logistical advantages. In his report on the Kokoda campaign Lieutenant-General Sydney Rowell, echoing Sedgwick's words, said that 'we were behind the enemy who had reduced these matters [of supply] to extreme simplicity'.[10] While the IJA, founded in 1873, had taken much from the Western military tradition, it borrowed from China when it came to supplying its armies in the field. First tried experimentally in the 1877 Samurai Rebellion in Kyushu, this system, dangerously frugal by Western standards, had worked for them since, and they expected that it would suffice for the advance into South-East Asia and the south-west Pacific.

THE SUPPLY LINE FROM
RABAUL TO GIRUWA

By mid-1942 Rabaul was a vast supply base well on the way to holding the war materials for 120 000 men for six months in the 6 million square metres of storage space that it had attained by March 1943.[11] A *kaisenbun* was an IJA unit of supply, usually for a division for three, sometimes four months of operations, but they could vary considerably in their content. The Aoba Detachment, for instance, in leaving the Philippines to join Seventeenth Army at Rabaul, was directed to take a three-month allocation of fuel, four months of food and six months of medical supplies.[12] In May Seventeenth Army held six *kaisenbun* of the 108 available to the IJA at the start of the war; 25 more were produced in 1942. In June the head of the 1st Shipping Division of the Fourth Fleet, Major-General Ito Shinobu, set his staff to planning the delivery of supplies to Papua for the attack on Port Moresby. For the Nankai Shitai, a light division, 7500 tons was required in addition to that needed by the IJN to build an air base at Buna and what was carried by each soldier.[13] The *kaisenbun* contained about 2000 tons of food, with which we are primarily concerned, 2500 tons of artillery ammunition and about 3000 tons of other items. Beginning in October, a second *kaisenbun* was sent, although not all of it arrived in Papua before the end of the Kokoda campaign.[14]

An unusual feature of Japanese transportation practice was that they crammed far more men into a ship than their opponents. Infantry on short voyages were packed in at a rate of three men to an area measuring 1 by 2 metres, three times more closely than was practised by Western armies.[15] The Takumi Detachment, which landed at Kota Bharu in Malaya on 8 December 1941, required only three ships for 5300 men and their equipment. American and Australian practice used nine ships for a similar load.[16] The entire Japanese Malaya landing group in December 1941, a force of more than 50 000 men plus ammunition, vehicles, artillery, tanks and horses, filled only 20 ships averaging 6000 gross tons each.[17] The same standard was adhered to in the landing in Papua; two ships that carried the Nankai Shitai, the *Ryoyo Maru* (5973 tons) and *Kazuura Maru* (6804 tons), between them held 3400 men, 167 horses, half a dozen artillery pieces, 185 tons of fodder and other unspecified cargo.

Fourteen transport ships were available for the MO operation. They had a total deadweight tonnage – that is, the tonnage of cargo they could carry – of 55 000 tons. Twenty-three shiploads sailed for Giruwa to 1 November 1942.[18] Nine of these sufficed to transport all Nankai Shitai personnel, equipment and artillery, and one, the *Nankai Maru*, was entirely devoted to all the paraphernalia for building an IJN airfield there as well as the base administrative facilities. Another carried a bridge-building company with more than 2000 tons of construction material. Deducting one ship that turned back and two sunk before they had finished unloading, this left nine shiploads, or about 33 000 tons of cargo capacity, for the 15 000 tons (two *kaisenbun*) required to be shipped.[19] The appearance of surplus tonnage here is deceptive to a degree, as items that require a lot of space but are not especially heavy can distort a calculation of theoretical cargo capacity. For example, 10 tons of tents will take up much more space than 10 tons of artillery ammunition.

Apart from a shaky start, when the *Ayatozan Maru* from the first convoy was sunk by air attack, ships were able to proceed almost uninterrupted from Rabaul to Giruwa. They arrived at dark and left by dawn, which sometimes saw them leaving still partly loaded, but this was not an insurmountable problem.[20] Of the first *kaisenbun*, incomplete records show that at least 2000 tons of food arrived. This was probably the full allocation and, with the reduced scale adopted for the campaign, that was enough to feed the Nankai Shitai for three months. Of the second *kaisenbun* less is known but, as more than 90 per cent of all that the Japanese shipped to Giruwa in 1942 arrived there, it would be difficult to argue that insufficient food was sent from Rabaul to the Nankai Shitai in Papua.[21]

From Giruwa to Kokoda

A fleet of 50 barges, working from ship to jetty, brought the cargo ashore, initially at Basabua. By 20 August the anchorage was moved to Sanananda near the Japanese headquarters at Giruwa, where the barges could transport the cargo directly from the ships some distance upriver to the supply dumps along the present Popondetta-to-Sanananda road not far northeast of where the Huggins Road Block Monument now stands. From the dumps the Sanananda road was suitable for vehicles as far as Sambo, 40 kilometres inland. Anchorage command, an administrative unit with at times up to 2000 labourers, oversaw the landing and storage of all Nankai Shitai supplies. Tarpaulins and prefabricated huts were sent from Rabaul to protect supplies from the weather.[22] The Sanananda–Sambo road was found in good enough condition for troops to be driven along it on the day of the Yokoyama Force landing and, on 25 July, the first of two truck transport companies began to move supplies from Giruwa to Sambo. The average load was just over a ton per truck, and 51 trucks and 10 other vehicles were available. Forty bushels of rice per vehicle were transported on the first day of operations. In spite of the efforts of a permanent force of engineers and labourers, every now and again the road became useless when rain fell and the trucks churned it into mud.

On 4 August just 6.27 tons of food and fodder arrived at Sambo, but the next day 20 tons of rice arrived.[23] On 21 August rice was being carried forward by backpack, but the next day the road was drivable. In the first 13 days of regular transportation 92 tons of rice alone arrived at Sambo. As the campaign wore on many of the vehicles broke down, but in the first few months all went well, each truck making one trip a day when the road was usable.[24] Even if a third of the vehicles were non-operational on any given day there was no obstacle, apart from the weather, to delivering 50 tons of supplies per day to Sambo, enabling a reserve to be built up. Troops were also sometimes brought forward by truck, suggesting that the motor transport companies were not having any problem filling their daily quota. From early August to mid-November, when the Australians overran the Sambo dump, it seems to have always contained sufficient food and ammunition. On 2 September 300 tons of food was warehoused there, and on 1 November Private Kiyoichi Ishiguro reported that his whole battalion loaded up at Sambo with 9 kilograms of rations per man as they proceeded up the track to the front.[25]

From Rabaul to Sambo we have so far seen no insurmountable supply problem but, from Sambo onwards, all supplies had to be carried on the back of man or horse, or on a cart or bicycle. The Japanese were well practised in moving supplies and equipment over rough terrain. Their organisation of ponies, carriers and purpose-built light carts, as well as their habit of packaging supplies in man-portable size, was noted by Western officers in the operation to relieve the siege of the Peking Legations in 1900.[26] This same system was now used to establish a supply line to Kokoda with a dump there to meet the requirements of the force before it had used up the initial supply each man was carrying.

The idea that if each man could carry up to 20 days of food enough time would be allowed for permanent supply arrangements to be made was controversial in Rabaul. Second Lieutenant Kanemoto Rinzo was one of the supply officers tasked with assessing whether it could be done. 'The research ordered by the South Seas detachment shortly after I joined Seventeenth Army was to experiment how many *sho* [1.4 kilograms] of rice each soldier could carry and how to carry the rice. It was apparent ... that this experiment was the key to the overland advance on Port Moresby,' he wrote. A frame was made for carrying on the soldier's back, and rice sacks full of volcanic ash were used. As a result of the experiment Seventeenth Army decided that the average soldier could carry 8 *sho* (11.2 kilograms) of rice and still be able to fight. If the standard quantity of rice for a soldier was reduced from six *go* (840 grams) to four

Photo 9 One of 14 Nankai Shitai transport ships, the *Taiko Maru* arrived at Giruwa on 10 October 1942. Among its cargo was 180 tons of vegetables, 60 tons of meat, 25 tons of soy sauce, 9 tons of sugar, 100 tons of rice, 2 000 000 cigarettes, 200 000 bottles of soft drink, 20 000 bottles of beer and 5 tons of sweets. (AWM 303997)

go per day then the soldiers could advance for about 20 days without resupply from the rear.[27] Once a permanent supply line was established rations could return to normal. Kanemoto was somewhat sceptical that this would work as planned, but the consensus among the supply specialists was that it could be done.

Some men carried 14 kilograms of food with them. Most did not take this much as they were also carrying extra ammunition. The total weight carried was on average 40 kilograms, more for the machine-gunners, who were not supplied with horses to carry their weapons.[28] This seems an incredible amount, but the plan was that it was possible if the men rested half an hour, then walked half an hour. However, when the main body of the Nankai Shitai arrived in Papua in August Horii decided that it should force-march to Isurava, and the rest plan was ignored. Many men fell behind and were not present for the battle there.

Standard IJA procedure was to establish a supply echelon for each two days march.[29] A day's carry was set at 15 kilometres instead of the normal 20, a concession to the extremely heavy loads. The march from the roadhead at Sambo to Kokoda was to be done in four days. The east echelon, under Lieutenant-Colonel Tomita Yoshinobu, was responsible for forwarding supplies from the coast to Ilimo.[30] The west echelon, under Lieutenant-Colonel Hozumi, was based at Ilimo to cover the remaining distance to Kokoda. A depot was set up half way along each of these 30-kilometre segments where supplies were stored in huts or under tarpaulins.[31]

In August, each segment of the supply line had about 500 carriers from 15 NP and two horse-transport companies of 300 horses each. The Takasago volunteers from Taiwan were assigned to the west and the Koreans to the east echelon, and a thousand Rabaul carriers were split between the two.[32] Horses were to carry 80 kilograms, each Asian carrier 35 kilograms and each Rabaul carrier 25 kilograms.[33] Up to 40 kilograms was carried on bicycles, but bicycles were not a success and were returned to storage in Giruwa. The total carrying capacity of this force in ideal circumstances was 150 tons. Almost all the carrying capacity was devoted to building up the depots as battalion stores, first-line ammunition and other requirements were brought forward by each battalion, which had up to 140 two-wheeled carts.[34] As it was an eight-day round trip from Sambo to Kokoda, in theory one eighth of 150 tons – 18 tons per day – could have been delivered to Kokoda once the system was properly established. However, for various reasons this amount could not be delivered regularly. Neither the men nor the horses could work without a break, later there was sickness among both, and there were delays in September when bridges were washed away by floods. In addition, the men and horses themselves consumed some of their own load, which reduced the amount that went forward. Before we look at what supplies arrived at Kokoda, this last point calls for some examination.

The commander of the Nankai Shitai, Horii, did not at all like the 'fast' plan to take Port Moresby by a rapid march over the mountains. Not surprisingly, he wrote a negative appreciation of what he perceived as the impossibility of supplying such a march.[35] He calculated that a carrier would consume half what he carried on the round trip from the coast to the front line, so the huge number of carriers required would be unobtainable. However, Horii knew well that it was not done this way. What actually happened is that the carrier brought forward his load to a dump and went back to get more from the dump where he was based. The next echelon then picked up the load and carried it to the next dump and so on until slowly a large dump was built up at Kokoda. Once this was done, consideration could be given to repeating the process in the mountains along the Kokoda Track.

Both the carriers and the horses in each echelon would consume about 10 per cent of their own load per trip. As horses eat 10 times what a man eats yet carry only three times what a man might carry, there would be no profit in using horses at all unless they were better able to obtain food en route than men were.[36] There is probably no military campaign on record in which army horses have been completely supplied with fodder from the rear as it is next to impossible – the Nankai Shitai would have had to bring forward 24 tons of fodder every day. Instead the horses lived on grass available locally. At the end of several months, the horses would be in poor condition and many would be dead unless their intake was supplemented with high-protein concentrated fodder, about 10 per cent of their total intake, usually one kilogram of concentrated oats each day.[37] Even grass that is low in nutrition can keep a horse going for months despite continuous hard work as long as it gets 10 kilograms of grass a day and a supplement. Larger centres of population in Papua had more grass as jungle was cleared around villages, but the low population of the Owen Stanley Range meant that there was less suitable grass.[38] Without high-nutrition fodder, such as the concentrated oats the Japanese brought to Papua, a horse required much more green fodder, thus reducing the time it could be worked. The Japanese used nosebags to overcome this problem and expected 14 hours of work from a horse each day, provided it received its oats supplement.[39] The Nankai Shitai brought 2360 horses from the 5000 that Seventeenth Army had in Rabaul and 200 tons of concentrated fodder, enough for 90 days, as a 10 per cent supplement.[40] This was, unsurprisingly, the same proportion of fodder, one kilogram per horse per day, brought forward from Port Moresby to supply the animals of the Australian 1st Independent Light Horse working on the same task at the other end of the Kokoda Track.[41]

The Seventeenth Army Chief of Staff, Major-General Futami Akisaburo, expected a loss of 20 per cent for carrier consumption, wastage and delays, and his plan called for the delivery of 780 tons to Kokoda within 62 days of the first landing, by 23 September. As it took two weeks to set up the system, 15 tons per day of supplies, including 5 tons of food, should have been arriving daily at Kokoda from early August. The Kokoda dump began functioning on 2 August, but nothing like Futami's estimate was achieved. As explained elsewhere, in mid-August, the plan to attack Port Moresby was postponed due to events at Guadalcanal. One fortuitous result was that supply was reassessed and a more realistic plan made, cutting in half the daily tonnage expected to arrive at

Kokoda. The new plan called for the delivery of 3 tons of rations and 6 tons of other supplies per day, so as to have 33 tons of food at Kokoda by 23 August.[42] This was achieved and, with no requirement to supply a large force rapidly advancing on Port Moresby, the supply line was functioning satisfactorily. The 1st Battalion of 144th Regiment, at Deniki on 14 August, had run out of the food it landed with in late July, but men sent back to dumps in the rear were able to obtain more.[43] On 26 August a unit picked up 17 kilograms of rice per man from the Papaki and Ilimo dumps. After the arrival of the temporary transport unit in early September supply line capacity was lifted to the level of the original plan; that is, six tons of food per day.[44]

Should the supply line encounter further problems, air supply was to be used.[45] The first Japanese at Kokoda passed back information on the length and width of the airstrip, and later suitable locations for airdrops were noted at Oivi, Kokoda, Nauro and Kagi. An air transport squadron in Rabaul was available but, with the redeployment in September of all air assets to support Guadalcanal operations, this important part of the supply plan had to be dropped.[46] During the supply crisis from late September it was revived, and five missions were flown, dropping about 20 tons of food at Kokoda.[47]

LOCAL FOOD SOURCES

Until the advent of rail and motorised road transport, armies, unless operating along a navigable river, found it impossible to bring forward enough food for all their needs as they advanced. Local foraging for food was essential. Even the mainly horse-powered German Army of 1914, advancing with two million men into Belgium and France, was able to feed itself, both man and horse, off rich countryside in a favourable season.[48] By World War II motorised armies, including the Australians, had given up the idea that a large part of their food should be obtained by foraging locally – although, with their own supply problems in Papua, foraging was forced upon the Australians, too. The IJA had not abandoned the practice and foraged as a policy, not a temporary measure as the Kokoda myth presents it.[49] Japanese planning laid great stress on what could be obtained either from the enemy or from local produce because it greatly reduced the amount that had to be brought forward from the rear.[50] In heavily populated parts of China the IJA sometimes obtained all of its food locally, and a similar result was achieved in Malaya and the Philippines. It was expected that less food would be found in Papua, but in the event the men of the Nankai Shitai were surprised at how much was obtained there.[51]

As soon as the Japanese landed a foraging program began. A rectangle of land 40 kilometres in width and 120 kilometres long from Giruwa to Yodda, north-west of Kokoda, was divided into foraging areas. Taro was common everywhere but there was also sweet potato, pumpkin and coconut, mainly along the coast.[52] Before the campaign the soldiers were also told that pigs would be a valuable supplement to their diet. At an average of one pig per four inhabitants there were probably about 10 000 pigs in the region foraged. Even a quarter of these could supply 50 tons of meat, and Japanese diaries contain many references to taro-gathering and pig-shooting. On 8 September, a soldier of one of the transport units near Oivi recorded his delight when his adjutant shot two pigs, each of 30 kilos.[53]

Logisticians can calculate how much food an army might obtain passing through a given area. The starting point is population and harvest. If an isolated rural area has a permanent population of 1000 then it produces 1000 x 365 days supply of food and probably a small surplus for trading purposes. If it did not do that reliably, then fewer than 1000 people would live there permanently. If it had only one harvest a year and if the army arrived soon after the harvest there should be something like 365 000 rations on hand. Of course, the locals will then starve to death, but this does not always concern the interlopers. In New Guinea the staple crop, which in 1942 was taro, was planted and harvested constantly. Even now rarely more than a few days go by without harvesting from small village gardens.[54] As the crops were grown year-round, at any time 10 per cent of this produce might be taken without bringing about widespread starvation as this was the excess used for festivals or trade. The soil in the Mount Lamington area, within the region described, is considered among the most fertile in New Guinea, and it might well be more than 10 per cent of local food could have been taken without causing famine.[55]

Estimates of a population of 400 000 for Papua in 1942 are probably not far wide of the mark.[56] About 10 per cent of these lived between Yodda and the north coast 20 kilometres either side of the Kokoda–Sanananda track.[57] If 40 000 inhabitants were deprived of 10 per cent of their produce then 4000 Japanese could subsist there without causing the native population to starve. In practice what occurred was that the 14 000 or so Japanese who spent August to November in the region supplemented their rations by perhaps a quarter by using local produce, although

Photo 10 Between 100 and 140 two-wheeled carts per infantry battalion were used to transport battalion stores from the roadhead to Kokoda. (Kochi New Guinea Association)

consumption was far from orderly. The soldiers rapidly exhausted some areas by simply taking everything in the village garden, including the root of the taro plant, so nothing more would grow from it.[58] Nevertheless, it was not found necessary to forage as far as 20 kilometres north or south of Giruwa until October, and a program to grow vegetables at the base was begun in the same month.[59] The sometimes chaotic collection of local produce notwithstanding, taro and pig supplemented the supplies of the Japanese, in the Kokoda to Giruwa area, to a much greater degree than in the Owen Stanley Range where the population density was less than a quarter of what it was in the lowlands to the north. An additional problem was that taro and sweet potato was not easily transportable. A short time in a backpack in a hot climate reduced it to rotting mush, so it was impractical to carry it from the lowlands north of the Owen Stanley Range any distance into the mountains.

By 1 September there was a 40-ton reserve of food at the Kokoda dump. As the campaign ration was set at two-thirds of a kilogram per man per day this was enough to feed the Japanese force then forward of the Kumusi River – 4800 men – for about 12 days. It was being added to from the rear at about 3 tons a day, and work began to establish new dumps at Isurava, Eora and later Myola. The main supply line was shortened by using a track from Oivi to Fila and Eora, avoiding Kokoda. This route was also suitable for horses, some of which eventually went as far forward as Ioribawa.[60] The normal Japanese ration, 16 000 kilojoules per day (6 *go* of rice supplemented by bean soup, shoyu sauce and fish), was cut for the Owen Stanley operation to about 11 000 kilojoules per day (4 *go* of rice plus the same) on the assumption that the 5000 kilojoules would be made up with local food and captured rations. While it is impossible to be sure that this was achieved, it seems that it was. If so, the soldiers of the Nankai Shitai probably had, before their supply crisis, an adequate ration comparable to that of the Australians, and the Japanese supply plan, difficulties notwithstanding, was a success. The two-thirds ration was supplemented by local forage, and the food carried by each man lasted until permanent supply arrangements were in place. Although it was an unusual system to Western eyes, there was nothing hasty, poor or *ad hoc* about it as the Kokoda myth claims. On the contrary it was typical of those arrangements by which the spectacular Japanese offensive in Asia and the Pacific from December 1941 had been accomplished.

CHAPTER 9

FIRST
EORA–TEMPLETON'S

Dr Vernon wrote in his diary that the fighting in early September near Eora village 'seems to have been one of the major clashes in the retreat yet was largely passed over in silence in the Australian press'.[1] The five days of fighting rates a few lines in the Japanese official history, the *Senshi Sosho*, and a page in the Australian official history. In part this is because First Eora follows hard upon Isurava and is obscured by it, the Japanese referring to it as Second Isurava.

Weakened by Isurava, the Japanese 144th Regiment was rested while 41st Regiment pursued the defeated Australians. The problem was that 41st Regiment was incomplete. The decision to postpone until November the advance on Port Moresby resulted in a change in shipping priorities. Japanese infantry were no longer urgently required in Papua so part of of 41st Regiment was delayed while more labourers and bridging specialists were sent to improve the Giruwa–Kokoda supply line. The regiment had also lost 710 men to form a new temporary supply unit.[2] As a consequence, the whole of 41st Regiment was not assembled until it defended Oivi in early November 1942. Before November, the only elements of the regiment that did any fighting on the Kokoda Track were the headquarters, the gun company, the 2/41st and 12th Company of 3/41st Battalion. When the 1/41st, the delayed battalion, finally arrived in September, it advanced to Nauro and on arrival was ordered to return to Kokoda. The 3rd Battalion's commander, Lieutenant-Colonel Tomita Yoshinobu, was responsible for the

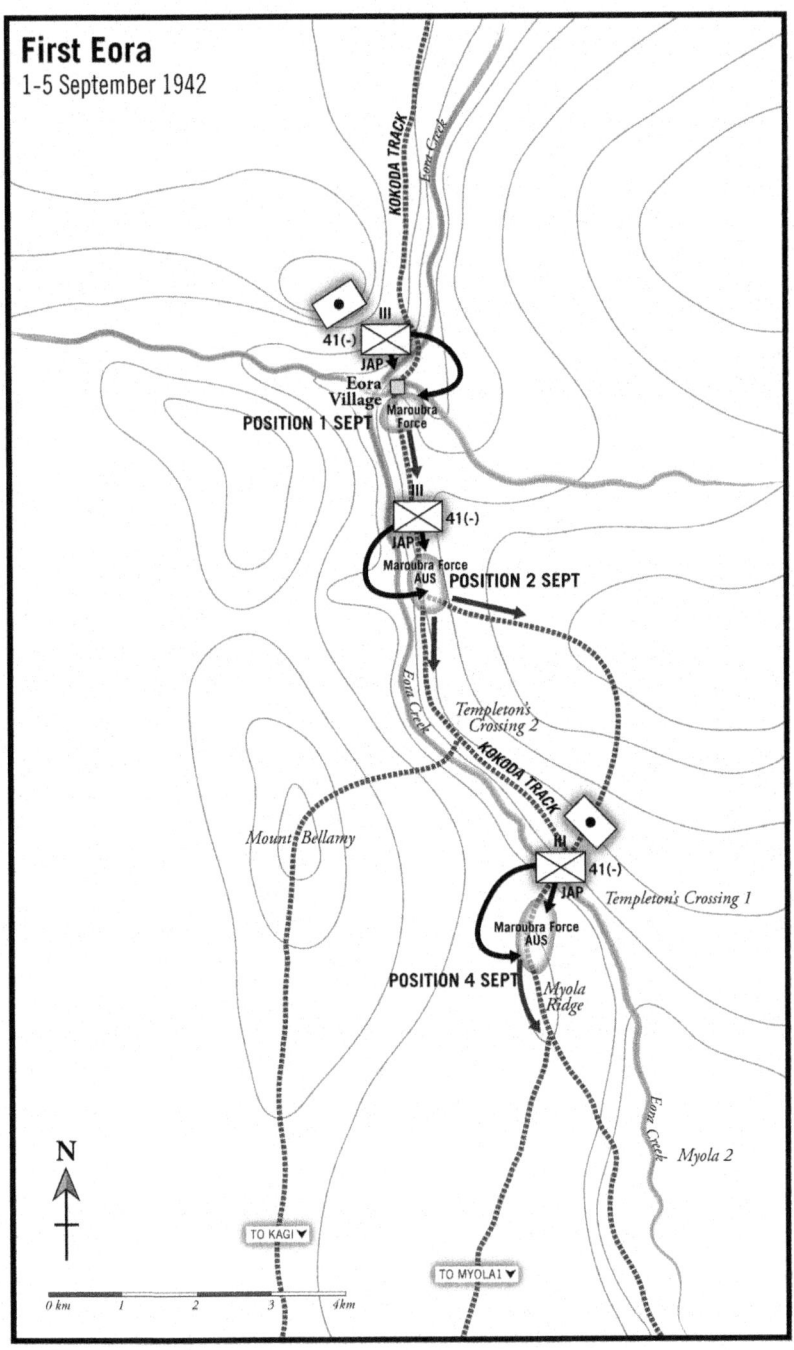

Map 7 First Eora, 1–5 September 1942

Table 9.1: Japanese engaged at First Eora–Templeton's

41st Regiment HQ	58
Regimental Signals Company	109
Regimental Gun Company	88
55th Mountain Artillery Regiment, 2nd Company	110
3/41st Battalion, 12th Company	130
2/41st Battalion	755
15th Independent Engineer Regiment, one platoon	55
Total	1305

Source: *Hohei dai 41 Rentai Nyuginea senkyo hokoku* [War records of 41st Infantry Regiment], p. 12, NIDS *Nanto higashi Nyuginia* 255; Battle report, 7th Company, 2/41st Battalion, current translations no. 25, pp. 11–13.

defence of Giruwa and for the eastern of the two supply echelons to Kokoda. His battalion did not leave the coast until it marched to fight at Oivi in November.

THE JAPANESE

Yazawa's 41st Regiment had a reduced headquarters and a small gun company with one 75mm mountain gun and one 37mm gun. All of the 2/41st (and its 70mm gun) was present, as was 12th Company from the 3/41st.[3] There was also a company of 15 IER and a mountain gun company with one gun.[4] This was the force that replaced 144th Regiment and became the pursuit group.

All the battalions in 41st Regiment were square battalions with four infantry companies as opposed to triangular battalions with three infantry companies, as in 144th Regiment. Reduced for South Seas operations, a square battalion had 760 men; a battalion headquarters of 60 men, a gun platoon of 35, four 140-man infantry companies and a machine-gun company of a hundred. A company of engineers was attached to the regiment, but only one of its platoons participated in the coming fight while the rest were employed to improve the track along the line of advance.

THE AUSTRALIANS

Apart from a detachment of 2/4th Field Ambulance and a few PIB, 2/14th and 2/16th Battalions, with one 3-inch mortar, were on their own. All other units from Isurava had retired south along the Kokoda Track and took no part in the engagement. First Eora was a desperate rearguard after a defeat, and there was no time to count heads, so we cannot be certain about Australian numbers but it is probable that about 710 Australians were present. First Eora was the last time in the campaign when the Australians were significantly outnumbered and, at close to two to one, it was the largest ratio by which the Japanese outnumbered the Australians in any battle in Papua. It is ironic that in the least-examined engagement of the campaign there is some merit in the myth of a significant Japanese numerical superiority.

A few days before First Eora, 2/16th Battalion had arrived at Isurava 590 strong. It lost 44 killed and wounded, and several groups were still making their way back to the track after having been cut off east of Eora Creek. The dysentery epidemic that was to reduce Australian numbers more than battle casualties had begun, and ten men per day were being evacuated, but it does not seem possible for the battalion assembled at Eora to have been as low as Sublet's estimate of 400.[5] He is certainly not counting Captain Dennis Goldsmith's C Company of the 2/16th, which marched down the eastern side of the gorge to rejoin at Eora on 1 September. About 450 all ranks present that day would be closer to the mark.

The other Australian infantry battalion, the 2/14th, was weaker as it had been scattered at Isurava. The battalion commander Key, together with his headquarters company, was lost in the jungle. Most of the company eventually rejoined their battalion, but Key was captured and executed. Other parties of the battalion rejoined over the next few days – Captain Stan Bisset brought in 13 men on 3 September. Some 230 men of the 2/14th were estimated by 21st Brigade to have been present at First Eora. The battalion lost 54 battle casualties thereafter, an average of seven a day to sickness, and 150 men were still present at the end of the engagement, so the brigade's estimate was probably correct.[6] There was in addition a detachment of signallers from 21st Brigade, a small group from 14th Field Ambulance and several men from ANGAU, bringing the total to about 710.

FIRST EORA

On the night of 31 August the Japanese were aware that the Australians had a blocking force on the track in front of Eora Creek. This was the

2/14th, but the battalion soon fell back through the 2/16th and, by 7 a.m. on 1 September, all the Australians had withdrawn to the heights south of and overlooking Eora Creek crossing. The stronger battalion, the 2/16th, held the line while the 2/14th was placed behind it to deal with any enemy flanking move. Yazawa, in his first fight in Papua, decided to slip his main infantry force, 2/41th Battalion less one company, around the Australian left on the night of 31 August while pinning the Australians to the front with 6th Company of the 2/41st and 12th Company of the 3/41st. Advancing along the track with Yazawa was the 2/41st's machine-gun company. The battalion gun and the RGC were in reserve near RHQ.

Although the 2/41st had missed the battle of Isurava by becoming lost on a flank march, the battalion tried it again on 31 August, with the same result. For a second consecutive night 2/41st Battalion wandered lost in the jungle looking for Australians but not finding any. The battalion commander, Major Koiwai Mitsuo, who had persuaded Yazawa to try the move, described his reasoning thus: 'If we attacked them from the front we would end up attacking from the lower position of a slope, with no cover from enemy fire. Obviously this would result in great losses on our side. Therefore, though it would take time, I decided to go around the forest and attack them from their rear.'[7] When he failed to find the Australians, because they had already withdrawn from their position north of Eora, Koiwai returned on his original compass bearing to his starting point. He emerged with his battalion, doubtless with a strong feeling of *déjà vu*, back on the Kokoda Track at 3.30 on the morning of 1 September, 12 hours after he had left. The frequency with which battalions went missing during the Kokoda campaign was a lesson not lost on the Japanese. Major Okamoto Takahisa, who commanded a battalion in New Guinea from 1943, said, 'One of the things the 1942 campaign taught us, is that large formations moving through the jungle in the dark always get lost. We learned the lesson and did not try it much later in the war.'[8]

Meanwhile the rest of 41st Regiment closed up to the Australians on the heights south of Eora village. Yazawa sent out scouts to find the limits of the Australian position while, assisted by the engineers, his artillery and machine-guns set up on the same heights north-west of the creek crossing that the Nankai Shitai were to use for the same purpose in the fighting that took place here in October during the Australian advance. They opened fire on the Australians, who could be seen digging in on the opposite heights, while Yazawa awaited news of his lost battalion.[9] Later in the day, when Koiwai caught up with Yazawa, the latter expressed his dissatisfaction. 'It was natural that the regiment commander got angry.

Photo 11 A USAAF aircraft making a supply drop at Myola, an area of dry lakes on a wide plateau 1500 metres above sea level. Although clouds often closed in around midday, the area provided an ideal site for the resupply by air of Australian forces on the Kokoda Track. (AWM P02424.071)

I had delayed the advance of the troops ... by a half-day; my fault was not light.'[10] Suitably chastised, Koiwai began preparations for his battalion's part in the attack. In the afternoon of 1 September Yazawa's infantry moved into position. 7th Company, with a platoon of 6th Company, worked their way under fire across Eora Creek. 5th Company and the rest of 6th Company crossed the creek further north and aimed for the Australian right flank. 8th and 12th Companies were held in reserve. The plan was to be in a position to attack at dark when the Australian front would be fixed by 7th Company's advance while 5th and 6th Companies would envelop the Australian right.

With the day to prepare, the Japanese attack still got off to a late start. There is a tendency in postwar accounts to imagine Japanese infantry attacks as massed assaults with 'sudden screaming charges'. In fact these were rare events. The typical Australian experience of night fighting in the jungle was not of repelling serried ranks but, more commonly, one of sitting in a fighting pit lobbing a grenade every now and again at where the enemy might be, all the time seeing nothing but hearing quite a bit. When questioned about infantry assaults, Japanese officer veterans stress two things, the first being that in their training great emphasis was laid on not squandering their high-quality infantry by charging if the object could be accomplished more slowly with fewer casualties. Such charges, when they did occur – and one did at First Eora – should be for finishing off an enemy whose powers of resistance had been worn down to the point where a bayonet charge should not cost many lives. Second, they point out that, after some fighting, it was difficult for even a section of a dozen men to gather to make a coordinated assault in darkness. The best that could be done – and what the three infantry companies of the 2/41st did at Eora – was to crawl carefully forward in small groups, each under an NCO or an officer, attempting to infiltrate the enemy line.

By 4 a.m. on 2 September the Japanese had broken into the Australian position at a number of points at about the same time as the Australians decided on a withdrawal. The commander of 7th Company, Lieutenant Ono Tetsuo, led one of these infiltrating groups and wrote afterwards in his report that he entered the Australian position at the cost of two killed and nine wounded. His men had expended 870 rounds, thrown nine grenades and captured a mortar, a light machine-gun, a Thompson submachine-gun, 25 rifles, clothes and rations.[11] On the Japanese left flank, 5th and 6th Companies failed to envelop the Australians, but there is no detailed record of what transpired there. Whatever it was, it was certainly more severe than the experience of 7th Company as the total losses to 41st Regiment for the day's preparations and night attack were 18 killed and 36 or 37 wounded, and four-fifths was sustained by 5th and 6th Companies.[12] The Australians lost 17 killed and 12 wounded.[13] Seven of those killed were in the category 'death presumed'. This, together with the low number of wounded compared to killed, indicates that the fighting at the end was close, the Australian withdrawal was executed under considerable pressure and that some wounded were not able to get away.

Contact between the two sides was broken before first light as the 2/16th withdrew through the 2/14th. The 2/16th deployed again just over a kilometre south on the track to Templeton's Crossing, then the 2/14th, in its turn, fell back through the 2/16th. By the evening of 2 September the Australian rearguard was placed as it had been the previous evening, with the 2/16th in front and the 2/14th immediately behind it. The Japanese were not aware of the Australian retreat until they advanced on the morning of 2 September. Koiwai thought it 'unusual for the hard working Australians to give up a position so quickly, but anyhow it was good news and took a load off my mind. Our loss [his own battalion] since yesterday amounted to 17 dead and 27 wounded. This day we buried the dead in the mountains for the first time since landing. I issued an order to start the pursuit at 7am.'[14]

7th Company, now the weakest, became the regimental reserve while 5th and 6th Companies rested in place and 8th and 12th Companies took up the pursuit. Smarting from his losses the previous night, Koiwai proceeded carefully, expecting to find that the Australians had not removed themselves far. He sent 12th Company along the track and 8th Company through the jungle on his left and placed his machine-guns on a knoll the Australians had occupied the night before. No enemy was encountered. Yazawa arrived and rebuked Koiwai for advancing slowly when there were no Australians about. 'Since yesterday's failed attack, he had not liked my cautious approach. He seemed to be anxious for a quick victory, but it was not easy to attack the enemy ... without knowing their situation. Being too eager for a victory could result in not only delaying the pursuit but increasing our losses. This is the last thing a commander should do.'[15] The disagreement between Koiwai and Yazawa touches on a problem faced by both sides. While a fast pursuit was preferable, it also costs more lives. A month later the Australian 7th Division faced the same dilemma during their advance. The divisional commander Major-General Athur Allen was believed by his seniors to be moving too slowly in an effort to minimise casualties when they required a quick advance, so he was removed from command.

Before dark on 2 September Koiwai's scouts had found the Australians again. 'The Japanese', wrote Sublet, 'were probing both flanks and in order to avoid what had happened in the last contact, when both flanks were threatened, an immediate withdrawal was decided on.'[16] Lieutenant-Colonel Albert Caro, in command of the force, thought the retreat would be quicker if two tracks were used. His 2/16th Battalion took a track to the east that rejoined the Kokoda Track further south, while the 2/14th retired down the main track. Neither had any contact with the Japanese, and by mid-morning on 3 September both battalions were back on the main track. They crossed to the west side of Eora Creek and took up a position at the north end of Myola Ridge where they were attacked on the night of 3/4 September.

Again the Japanese plan was to approach by day and attack at night, pinning the Australians with two companies while sending another two around a flank. Koiwai had 8th Company in hand but decided they had been worked hard since 1 September and were now tired: 'I could not push that company too much.'[17] Instead, he wanted to use 7th Company but had to wait until 5 a.m. for it to come up. 'I was looking forward to the arrival of 7th Company because of the quality of the command. Lieutenant Nakao, the company commander, had fought in China, and his warrant officer, Kaneshige, was also a superb fighter with lots of experience.' While 7th Company deployed on the Japanese right, Koiwai arranged for artillery support. Yazawa gave his assent, and the commander of 2nd Mountain Gun Company came to arrange the details:

> Though called a company they had only one gun and I was told that they were allowed to fire no more than ten rounds ... Even ten rounds would be enough. My goal was not to destroy the enemy position, but to scare them with the mountain gun. There can be no better tactics than to crush the enemy morale ... I wanted to fire it right before the night attack of 7 Company ... I assigned it a position and a target after closely observing the enemy with binoculars. It is usually considered wasteful [of ammunition] to fire an artillery gun in a night attack [but] human psychology in the front line was kind of beyond tactics. My plan was that, after firing shells at the position ... and terrifying the enemy out of their senses, we would charge with bayonets at them with the result they would be in fear of our attack in the darkness of the jungle.[18]

The 41st Regiment attack went according to plan. 8th Company was held in reserve as 6th and 12th Companies probed the Australian front to draw attention away from 7th and 5th Companies moving into position across Eora Creek. Then the mountain gun opened up as 7th and 5th Companies attacked the Australian left flank. The flank attack penetrated the 2/16th as far as the battalion's headquarters.[19] Caro reported to Potts that his left had been driven in and that it was neccessary to retreat.[20] Accounts from both sides stress the fierce nature of the fighting. Sublet described the Japanese penetration as having been achieved by '300 determined men', and one of them, Warrant Officer Utsumi, reported that Australian resistance was 'strenuous' and that Japanese casualties were considerable.[21] Lieutenant Araki of 5th Company remarked that the enemy sometimes stood up in their fighting pits and threw grenades.[22]

At 2.40 a.m. on 4 September, Koiwai received a report that his men were in the Australian position and were holding their ground.[23] They were told to dig in and expect a dawn counter-attack and that 8th Company would advance to join them. Koiwai's caution allowed the Australians to escape once more as, with Potts' permission, Caro was organising a retreat at the same time. Australian accounts record that the Japanese had cut the Kokoda Track in their rear and had to be ejected for the force to escape, but there is no mention of this in any Japanese record. In confused fighting in the jungle at night a unit would commonly not

Photo 12 The Australian supply dump at Eora Creek village on 28 August 1942. Carriers wait in the background while Royal Papuan Constabulary (in dark jackets) guard the supplies. (AWM 013250)

know where it was and whether a track it was on was the main Kokoda Track or some other. After cutting through the Japanese blocking the track in their rear, the Australian retreat to Efogi was unmolested.

CASUALTIES

Japanese casualties for the Eora–Templeton's engagement were heavy for the size of force involved, a fact that might have contributed to general criticism in the Nankai Shitai about the quality of 41st Regiment. As a general rule the better quality the officers and the soldiers, the more that is accomplished with fewer casualties. A counter to this, however, as Koiwai pointed out, is that if the task is rushed then even high-quality troops will take more casualties than they should. Japanese casualties from 1 September to 5 September were between 40 and 45 dead and from 53 to 62 wounded, but Japanese hospital records show that only 41 wounded from First Eora were treated.[24] The shortfall, if there is one, can be explained by lightly wounded men who were attended to by their own medics and did not require evacuation. As a rule of thumb, about 10 per cent of all Japanese wounded in the campaign fall into this category and another 10 per cent of the wounded died before they reached hospital. It seems likely, then, that 41st Regiment's casualties were close to 43 killed and 58 wounded. The pattern of Isurava was repeated in that, although defeated, the Australians, who lost 21 killed and 54 wounded, did inflict heavier casualties on their enemy than they incurred.[25]

THE ADVANCE TO EFOGI

Although Horii was not now marching on Port Moresby, but rather to as an yet ill-defined point on the 'southern slopes of the range', there was still reason for haste as he wished to catch and finish off the Australian force that had escaped him at Isurava. On 5 September Horii ordered 41st Regiment to cease the pursuit and for a two-battalion group of 144th Regiment to take over. This had not been the original plan, but Horii was highly dissatisfied with 41st Regiment's progress. They had neither advanced quickly nor destroyed the Australian rearguard. As they moved forward over the Australian dead it was also clear that they had taken the heavier losses. From 1 to 5 September 41st Regiment had advanced 10 kilometres, an average of 2 kilometres a day. When Kusunose's 144th Regiment replaced the 41st progress increased rapidly. Kusunose covered 40 kilometres in the next eight days, an average of 5 kilometres a day. As importantly, on 8 September, Kusunose's pursuit group defeated and dispersed the Australians at Efogi. Kusunose achieved there what Yazawa had thrice tried and failed: to pin the Australians to their front then, by putting a force around the Australian flank into their rear, to almost destroy them. Worse still – not that the Japanese would have been aware of it at the time – was that the Yazawa Regiment at First Eora had a significant superiority of numbers, close to two to one, an advantage that Horii did not have at Isurava nor Kusunose at Efogi.

There is a strong feeling, amounting to bitterness, between the surviving veterans of the two Japanese regiments. According to veterans of

Photo 13   Colonel Yazawa Kiyomi, commander of 41st Infantry Regiment.
(Kochi New Guinea Association)

the 144th, it was the failure of 41st Regiment at First Eora that gave
rise to accusations that 41st Regiment was not keeping its end up. As
144th veterans see it, they did the hard work at Isurava whereas 41st
Regiment made no contribution to that action and had only to pursue
and annihilate an already broken Australian force, and this they failed to
do. The slow rate of advance of 41st Regiment and the loss of contact
with the Australians, from the morning of 2 September to the evening of
3 September, suggests there could be something in this complaint.

CHAPTER | 10

EFOGI

After First Eora the Australians abandoned their source of air supply, the dropping zone at Myola, and fell back to Efogi. The engagement at Efogi (also called Mission Ridge and Brigade Hill) between Potts and Kusunose was fought because Potts was directed to make a stand with all his force. Potts, convinced he was heavily outnumbered, did not want to stop and fight, but Rowell told him to 'yield no repeat no more ground and regain initiative at earliest possible moment'.[1] Rowell judged that with the fresh 2/27th Battalion at Efogi, 3rd Battalion almost at Nauro and 2/1st Pioneer Battalion on Ioribaiwa Ridge, Potts was well placed for another attempt to stop the Nankai Shitai.

Rowell passed on to Allied Land Forces Headquarters in Melbourne Potts' claim that he was greatly outnumbered, but Potts was not believed. MacArthur was receiving patchy information via the interception and decoding of enemy communications, which suggested Japanese numbers were not as high as first thought.[2] By early September MacArthur had enough indicators to be convinced, correctly, that the Japanese force advancing along the track did not outnumber the Australians to any significant degree yet, even with the natural advantages of a defender over an attacker, the Australians were still being defeated. On 6 September MacArthur told General George Marshall, the US Army Chief of Staff, that the Australians were unable to match the Japanese in jungle fighting. The next day MacArthur asked Land Headquarters in Melbourne to explain why the Australians were falling back before a force that was not superior in numbers to them.[3] According to the Kokoda myth,

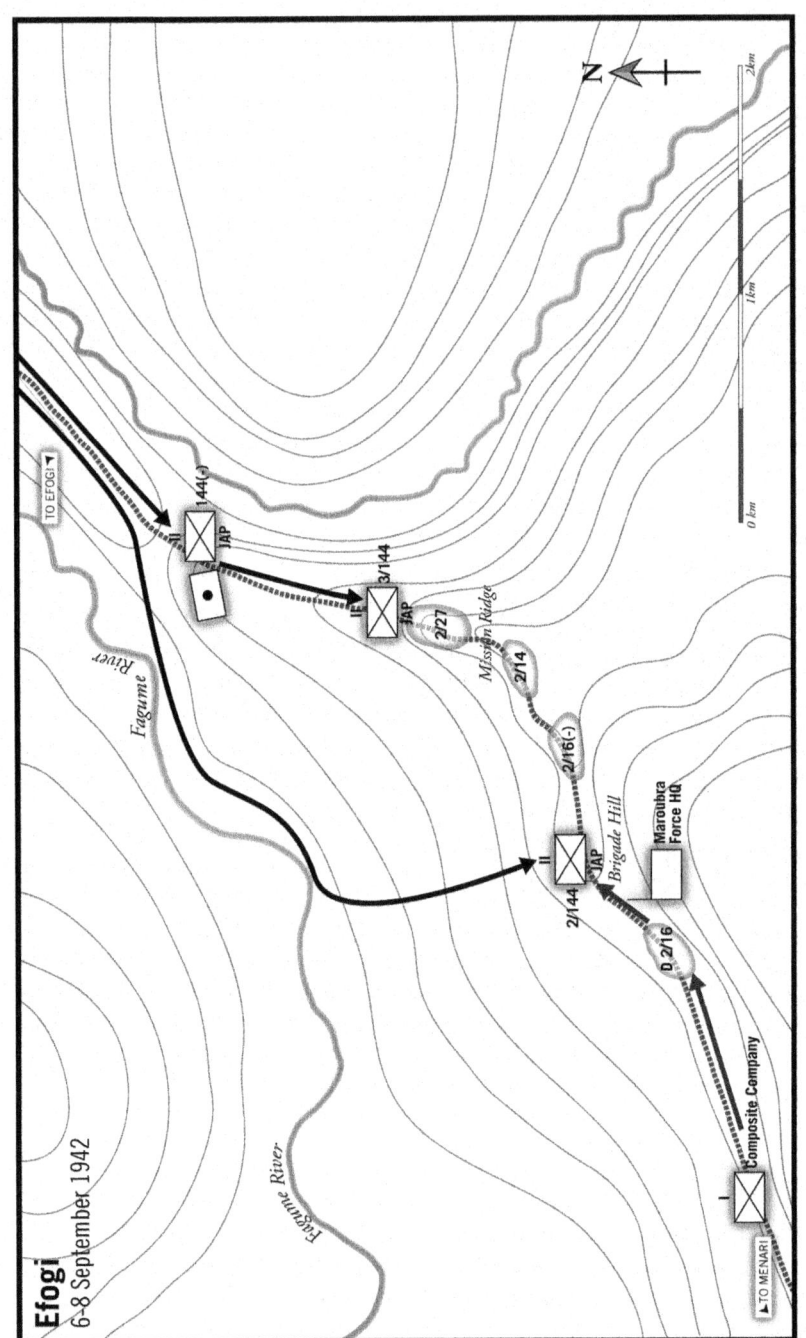

Map 8 Efogi, 6–8 September 1942

MacArthur was out of touch with the true situation, and the statements he made to Marshall, Blamey and others have been used as evidence. If the Australians were outnumbered then this criticism of MacArthur might be valid but, as they were not, MacArthur's position appears in a different light.

An interesting situation was developing among the Allies, involving two conflicting estimates of enemy strength. Those at the top saw intelligence that indicated lower Japanese numbers whereas those further down the chain of command were responding to the inaccurate intelligence coming in from the front line that exaggerated enemy strength. MacArthur's complaints have been dismissed by historians, who have tended to side with Potts.[4] But MacArthur and Blamey were right and it was Potts who had it wrong. Rowell was in the middle and, not privy to 'most secret sources', at first believed Potts' estimate of enemy strength but later changed his mind.

The argument was not confined to Australia. President Franklin Roosevelt complained to the US War Council that the Australians were not outnumbered yet the Japanese were well on the way to Port Moresby. In September American newspaper articles appeared stating that the reason the Japanese were able to assemble large forces against them at Guadalcanal was because the Australians in Papua were offering only light resistance to the Japanese advance.[5]

Ordered to fight, Potts selected a very good position. Mission Ridge and Brigade Hill form one high and wide feature offering excellent observation in the direction of the Japanese approach where there were large patches of open ground affording opportunities for the air strikes Potts requested. The forward part of the position, Mission Ridge, runs in a north–south line while Brigade Hill, a lower continuation of Mission Ridge, turns south-west so the whole is a boomerang shape. There was rough ground on both flanks. The high ground on the Australian right was so difficult that Kusunose decided not to go that way as his patrols there on 6 and 7 September reported that the terrain was 'too complicated'. The patrols were seen by 2/27th Battalion, giving rise to the idea that there was to be an attempt to turn the Australian right.[6] It was instead on the Australian left flank, along the low ground beside the Fagume River, that the Japanese chose to make their move.

Efogi was Kusunose's affair, and he was delighted that the Australians were making a stand. Unlike Yazawa in the period 1–5 September,

Photo 14 Left to right: Brigadier Arnold Potts DSO MC, his driver Corporal Ronald Simpson, Captain Keith Murdoch, Lieutenant A. Salom and Captain C. Thompson, September 1942. (AWM 026716)

Kusunose appreciated the importance of the opportunity – one that had been missed several times – to destroy the Australians, and his fast advance left the rest of the Nankai Shitai behind. Horii and the NSHQ had not moved with 41st Regiment during their five days as pursuit group and did not arrive at Efogi until after the battle. Yazawa's regiment rested at Templeton's Crossing after Kusunose took over, and the field ambulance (PCB) did not arrive at Efogi until the day after the battle. An order of 4 September had set up the new arrangement. The pursuit group from 5 September was to be 144th Regiment less the 1/144th.[7] During the Efogi engagement the main body of 1/144th was at Myola collecting Australian airdropped supplies, which were still scattered about the jungle there, while 180 men were detached to carry wounded back to Kokoda.[8] As supply carriers the battalion did not arrive at Efogi until 14 September.[9] Another absent unit was the 55th Mountain Artillery Regiment. One company was attached to 41st Regiment, and on 8

September, the decisive day at Efogi, the other two were 20 kilometres away at Templeton's Crossing.[10] The whole Japanese force in the mountains forward of Kokoda, including engineers working on the track and those carrying supplies, both Japanese and New Guinean, was about 4000. A force of this size, if all on the track at one time, would occupy at least 16 kilometres so, if there had been any idea of assembling all of it for a blow against the Australians at Efogi, a further two days delay was required to assemble it there.

FORCES ENGAGED

Kusunose had his RHQ, including the RGC and two infantry battalions, each with their battalion gun platoon.[11] He had also a platoon of 15 IER. After Isurava, Horii attached one company of engineers to each of his two infantry regiments. These two companies of engineers were the only ones to do any fighting for the remainder of the campaign in the Owen Stanley Range, but the change was not complete and only one engineer platoon had joined Kusunose. Neither of Kusunose's two infantry battalions had been involved in any fighting since 31 August, and sickness had not yet reduced the ranks by much. The strength of the 3/144th was 589. The battalion records show a loss of 144 killed and wounded at Isurava from the 738 who arrived in Papua, leaving five men unaccounted for.

The small numbers of sick and lightly wounded from both the 2/144th and 3/144th who had rejoined is unknown, but those who fell out on the forced march from Giruwa to Isurava had by now caught up. 5th Company 2/144th, for example, rose in strength from 116 at Isurava to 127 at Efogi.[12] Allowing for about a hundred casualties in the 2/144th at Isurava, and the rejoining of all those not present there, there cannot have been more than 650 men present, probably fewer. Adding to this the regimental units and the platoon of engineers, about 1570 Japanese fought at Efogi.

The important addition to Maroubra Force in early September was the South Australian 2/27th Infantry Battalion, the part of 21st Brigade that was originally left in reserve at Port Moresby. It had between 582 and 588 soldiers as it marched up the track.[13] Just two men fell out en route – a mark both of the fitness of the battalion and of a slow advance intended to husband its strength. In addition there were 2/14th and 2/16th Battalions, a composite company assembled from 21st Brigade elements, the various headquarters and small detachments of 2/6th and

Table 10.1: Maroubra Force, Efogi

2/27th Battalion	580
2/16th Battalion	350
2/14th Battalion	270
ANGAU detachment	10
RPC under Lieutenant T. Grahamslaw	12
2/6th Field Ambulance detachment	29
21st Brigade composite company	110
Maroubra Force headquarters, inc. 21st Brigade headquarters, a detachment of 30th Brigade headquarters and signals, the guard platoon and 7th Division signals detachment	135
14th Field Ambulance detachment	19
Total	1515

Source: New Guinea Force, general staff war diary, 5–10/9/42, AWM52 1/5/51; interview with Brigade Major G. Lyons, 15 August 1944, Gavin Long papers, AWM67 1/6; 14th Australian field ambulance, report on operations, AWM54 481/12/68, pp. 3–6; James, *Field Guide to the Kokoda Track*, p. 232.

14th Field Ambulances. The PIB had been withdrawn along with 39th and 53rd Battalions (see table 10.1).

There are lesser estimates than those shown in table 10.1: 150 men for the 2/14th and 250 for the 2/16th, but these must be too low.[14] At the end of 2 September 2/14th Battalion counted 244 present.[15] As the battalion had lost 89 battle casualties and 20 to sickness from the 542 it had at Isurava, it is apparent that about 190 men, scattered by the disorganised retreat from Isurava, were separated from it. The majority rejoined the battalion over the next several days. In this same period, 2–6 September, the battalion lost a further 52 battle casualties and 21 to illness. Captain Phillip Rhoden, now commanding the 2/14th, counted 200 men present at Ioribaiwa several days after Efogi. As the battalion lost 79 at Efogi and during the retreat over the Maguli Range, and certainly more sick, this suggests a battalion strength of at very least 270 men at Efogi.

At the end of 2 September 2/16th Battalion had 450 men and lost 21 battle casualties up to Efogi. It had the normal rate of loss to illness, and a few small groups of stragglers rejoined it. An estimate of 350 present for this battalion is a total that errs on the low side. Potts' signal to Port Moresby on 6 September seems to support this estimate. Potts said 2/27th Battalion had four companies, the 2/16th had three companies and the 2/14th two companies. As he is only talking of rifle companies, and four

Photo 15 Looking south-west towards Mission Ridge. The Australian 2/27th Battalion defended the top of the steep slope just to the right of the centre of the skyline. The Japanese 3/144th Battalion attacked along the crest of the same feature from right to left. (Photo: author's collection)

rifle companies was a full complement, he appears to have said that the 2/16th was at three-quarters strength and the 2/14th at half strength.[16] The Australian composite company that appears in table 10.1 did not arrive until towards the end of the fighting on 8 September (and might have been 50 fewer than shown), but 9th Company of the 3/144th was also a Japanese late arrival. The Kokoda myth, true to form, estimates that the Japanese outnumbered the Australians from between four and six to one at Efogi.[17] However, when the battle began, about 1420 Australians and 1450 Japanese were present, so there is no basis for believing that the Australians were outnumbered to any notable degree.

THE ATTACK

Kusunose divided his command into three parts, an artillery and machine-gun group and his two infantry battalions. His plan was to pin the Australian front with one battalion while another executed a flanking move around the Australian left. The artillery was located so as to support both of these attacks. A bamboo grove on a knoll was selected, 1500 metres from 2/27th Battalion and 3000 metres from the 2/14th and 2/16th's position.[18] The bend in the Mission Ridge–Brigade Hill feature permitted the Japanese guns placed on the knoll to fire both on the Australian 2/27th and on the Australian position further away on Brigade Hill. At the bamboo grove were massed the RGC of the Japanese 144th Regiment and the battalion guns of the 2/144th and 3/144th, a total of two 75mm guns, two 70mm guns and two 37mm guns.[19] The medium machine-gun company of the 3/144th, equipped with telescopic sights, was placed forward of the artillery about a thousand metres from the Australian 2/27th Battalion.[20]

On 6 and 7 September Allied aircraft bombed the Japanese assembling at Kagi. The first attack killed two and wounded two.[21] When the second attack came on 7 September, 144th Regiment was caught concentrated in just about the only large open area along the track from Owers' Corner to Kokoda. Eight B26 Marauders and four P40 Kittyhawks bombed and strafed the regiment, scattering the men and delaying the advance for several hours.[22] The air attack has been heralded as a great success that killed a hundred Japanese.[23] The actual losses, 11 killed and 20 wounded, are discussed in detail in chapter 17.

When the Japanese attack finally got underway, 7th Company, one of the two infantry companies of the 3/144th that were present, closed with the Australians on Mission Ridge, then 8th Company came forward on 7th Company's left. The task of the 3/144th was to pin the Australians. Without taking high casualties they were to locate targets for their artillery and try to draw forward Australian reserves, although Potts did not take the bait. On 7 September the Japanese artillery alternately supported the 3/144th on Mission Ridge and fired upon Brigade Hill where the 2/144th, about to execute its night flanking move, was expected to arrive on the morning of 8 September. On the night of 7/8 September the 3/144th made several platoon-size attacks and took some ground from the 2/27th. Kusunose decided not to push the advance past daylight of 8 September as the ground was too open and the Australians were well placed at the top of a steep slope.[24] At 4.30 a.m. on 8 September the last Japanese attack of the night was made. There was a degree of caution at this stage, Kusunose having committed all his available infantry as 9th Company had yet to arrive and the 2/41st, the next nearest force, was still two days away. During daylight on 8 September the 3/144th withdrew a little while 'a deluge of HMG [heavy machine-gun], mortar and mountain gun fire' fell on the Australian 2/27th.[25] The Japanese infantry's withdrawal to avoid being too close to their own artillery fire allowed the Australian battalion to retire without the Japanese being aware of it. In the late afternoon of 8 September, led by 7th Company, the 3/144th advanced to find the Australians were gone. Early in the evening, with little contact with the Australians, they linked up with the 2/144th on Brigade Hill.[26]

The events that brought about the withdrawal of the Australian 2/27th Battalion on 8 September began with the movement of the Japanese 2/144th Battalion to the Australian rear on Brigade Hill. The previous day a distinctive tree on the hill was pointed out to Major Horie, the 2/144th's commander. Kusunose ordered Horie to place his battalion near the tree.[27] The battalion began its march in the late afternoon of 7 September, and proceeded along the Fagume River to just east of the present day location of Enivilogo village, then it turned directly uphill to climb the steep slope, in part following a track towards the knoll: 'The march took a night and a bit. We left before sunset and arrived just as the sun was about to come up. 6th Company led and I was in 5th Company just behind. Leading 6th Company were friendly local natives. It was not difficult going along the track system but the last bit was difficult. Towards the end we went up a steep track.'[28] They arrived on top of Brigade Hill at dawn without contact with the Australians.

The route described is not the one normally accepted. Postwar maps tend to show the 2/144th making only a slight diversion from the line of the main track over Mission Ridge to Brigade Hill, just enough to pass clear of the left flank of the Australian 2/27th Battalion, but there are problems with this. First, the 2/144th did not know exactly where the left of the 2/27th was. To attempt to pass by close to the Australians was to risk bumping into them, as had happened to the 3/144th at Isurava. Second, Japanese maps, including one from a 2/144th signals sergeant showing where he laid the telephone line as he moved with the battalion, indicate a wider flanking move, first along the Fagume River then directly uphill.[29]

It was soon apparent to the Australians immediately on either side of the Japanese 2/144th (to the south MFHQ and to the north 2/16th Battalion) that the Kokoda Track had been cut. MFHQ was fired on, the telephone line to the battalions ceased to work and wireless communication was from then on intermittent.[30] What was not apparent was the size of the Japanese force that blocked the track. It was first described as a raiding party, but when 6th Company of the 2/144th advanced towards MFHQ Brigade Major Lyons decided that at least two Japanese companies must be present.[31] The Japanese battalion began directing artillery fire on an Australian position that could now be seen to the rear of Mission Ridge. This was B Company, 2/16th

Battalion, whose battalion history relates that they were bombarded all day on 6 September with little effect, but on 8 September, with Japanese artillery observers of the 2/144th on Brigade Hill looking at them, the fire became effective, and a short, accurate bombardment killed two Australians.[32] It was a risky tactic for the Japanese because any shells from their own artillery that carried too far might have landed among their own men of the 2/144th.

In one of the periods when Potts did have communication with his brigade he ordered a counter-attack from the north. Three hundred men, drawn from four companies of 2/14th and 2/16th Battalions, formed across the ridge on a front of 150 metres and assaulted south towards the 2/144th. This took some time to organise, and the attack did not go in until 3 p.m. The Japanese used the time to dig in, and the Australian attack was a complete failure, costing a hundred casualties. One or two platoons of 5th Company, in the path of the Australians, were overrun but only ten Australians, by working along the slope of the ridge, got through to MFHQ. A later attempt to attack in the other direction was made from MFHQ with the assistance of two platoons of D Company, 2/16th Battalion, which was with the headquarters. This also failed, and Potts decided to withdraw. Those with him followed the Kokoda Track directly to Menari. On the other side of the Japanese blocking battalion, Caro also decided to pull out. Potts had told Caro to take over the brigade and withdraw it if the counter-attacks failed. Two battalions, the 2/14th and 2/16th, headed east that night, then turned south and got to Menari before the Japanese. The third cut-off battalion, the 2/27th, left last and was forced to take a detour much further east. The battalion marched through the jungle for two weeks before it was able to rejoin Maroubra Force. On 9 September Kusunose, in light of the 2/144th's heavy casualties, directed the 3/144th to take up the pursuit and, with support from two 37mm guns from RGC, it advanced on Menari, forcing the Australians to evacuate. The Australian retreat continued through Nauro and over the Maguli Range until Ioribawa, where the next stand was made.

CASUALTIES

At Efogi 144th Regiment lost 56 killed in action.[33] There may have been a few more from the engineer platoon attached to the 2/144th but, as all the engineers of the Nankai Shitai lost two killed and four wounded for the month of September, they cannot have been many. In general Japanese engineers, while combat-trained, were too valuable to be put into close fighting in the mountains in large numbers. Such a thing did not occur until the catastrophe at Buna–Gona in January 1943 where, battalions at a time, they were expended in the role of infantry. Of the 56 Japanese deaths, the 3/144th lost 10 killed (and 45 wounded) in their two days in contact with 2/27th Battalion.[34] In the more serious affair on Brigade Hill the 2/144th lost 43 dead and about 40 wounded.[35] Three Australian 3-inch mortars, with 105 rounds, were airdropped at Myola and carried to Brigade Hill, and for the first time the Australians were able to respond effectively to Japanese long-range weapons, killing three and wounding 14 Japanese gunners.[36]

All but six of the 2/144th's dead were in 5th Company, which bore the brunt of the Australian charge on Brigade Hill.[37] To the south of the knoll, facing MFHQ, was 6th Company, which lost six men killed and 30 wounded.[38] The battalion headquarters, 4th Company and the machine-gun company, placed between 5th and 6th Companies, took no casualties.[39] Total Japanese losses at Efogi, excluding the air attacks of 6 and 7 September, were 60 dead (if the engineers lost their two dead here) and about 98 wounded.[40] The detachment of 55th Division's field hospital at Kokoda received 84 of the wounded nine days after Efogi.[41]

The usually reliable official list shows 87 Australians killed or died of wounds and 77 wounded between 6 September and 9 September, and this agrees with battalion figures for losses. Of the 87 dead, 31 died on Mission Ridge and 56 on Brigade Hill. The claims for enemy dead from both sides are much inflated. A Japanese report stated that 320 Australian bodies were counted while the Australians believed they killed at least 200 Japanese.[42] The reason for the low proportion of Australian wounded against killed, 77 to 87, compared to the Japanese, is likely to be that the Australians withdrew in haste. While the Japanese held the ground and the PCB arrived to tend to Japanese wounded the day after the battle, all Australians who were wounded and unable to leave the field were killed.

COMMAND

The outstanding feature of Efogi is the success of Kusunose's plan when compared to the unsatisfactory Japanese victories at Isurava and First Eora. With a force about equal to that of the dug-in Australians Kusunose threw them out of a good position and inflicted as many casualties as he lost. The Japanese artillery was a major contributor to this achievement; indeed Kusunose thought it was his artillery that had driven the Australian 2/27th out of its position. In addition, Kusunose soon realised that he had cut a large number of the defenders, 2/27th Battalion, from their line of communication. The battalion took no further part in the fighting in Papua until it was committed to the beachhead battles in November 1942. In effect the Japanese success at Efogi removed, in battle casualties and the absent 2/27th Battalion, 700 Australians from their order of battle – half the Australian force and a far better outcome for the Japanese than Isurava. Japanese diaries and official reports began to state that they believed they had broken the Australian 'fighting spirit'.

Kusunose's manoeuvre of Horie's battalion behind the Australians was the key event. The battalion had tried this once at Isurava and failed. It was to try it again at Ioribaiwa where the result was inconclusive, but at Efogi the movement worked exactly as desired. It might not have been so but for the Australian deployment. After Efogi there was criticism from his superiors of Potts' arrangements at Efogi, and his defeat there precipitated his relief from command of Maroubra Force.[43] In deploying his battalions one behind the other, with MFHQ well to the rear of it all and D Company of the 2/16th beyond that, he left gaps one of which the Japanese penetrated to cut him off from the force he was supposed to be commanding. His very deep deployment – more than 2 kilometres from the front of 2/27th Battalion to D Company, 2/16th in the rear – does not look like an arrangement to yield no more ground as he was ordered, but rather one to facilitate a retreat in the same way, as at First Eora, when the two Australian battalions deployed one behind another and fell back through each other. If Potts had deployed with a view to halting the Japanese advance then a more compact deployment might have been expected. It was not possible to prevent the Japanese once again cutting the track in the rear as they had attempted five times in the last two weeks. Another attempt must have been anticipated, and the correct response would have been to maintain a reserve with which to eject it. In addition 3rd Battalion was on its way to Potts and could assist by attacking north through the Japanese blocking force to reopen the track. In short, Potts' deployment does not look like one aligned with his order to yield no more ground. Potts' deployment did, however, serve to maximise the chance of extracting the force if required, and the placement of D Company behind his headquarters was either in expectation that the Japanese blocking of the track might occur very deep in the Australian rear, or D Company was so placed to act as the advance guard of the retreat Potts intended.

A second criticism is that Potts misused 2/27th Battalion. Rowell, who made this comment, implies that Blamey agreed with him.[44] Rowell meant that the 2/27th should not have been where it was: up front to face the first Japanese attack. As someone must do the job of holding a firm base around which the reserve might manoeuvre, Rowell was saying it should not have been the fresh 2/27th Battalion. The only other task Rowell can have had in mind for it was to hold it in reserve, with a view to a counter-attack and using the depleted 2/14th and 2/16th as the blocking force. Given that it was probable the Japanese would pin the forward-most battalion then throw another force around a flank, the best response would have been to hold out a powerful reserve with which to counter the Japanese flank move once it had revealed itself.

Why did Potts not do this? Soldiers who have had hard fighting and now find themselves retreating through newly arrived troops hope to be placed behind them for a rest. Alternatively, if the commander was confident that their morale was good, he might give them the job up front so as to keep his fresh battalion as a strong reserve with which to counter-attack once the enemy design was revealed. This is just what Honner did during his short period in command of Maroubra Force in the early stages of Isurava. When 2/14th Battalion arrived he decided to leave the tired 39th Battalion where it was in the front line and hold the 2/14th in the rear so as to 'keep a fresh uncommitted reserve'.[45] At Ioribaiwa a week after Efogi, Brigadier Kenneth Eather adopted the same solution as Honner. The force retiring after Efogi was placed to hold the enemy to their front while Eather's new 25th Brigade made a counter-attack. Potts, when he assumed command after Honner, faced this same dilemma but at Efogi came to the opposite conclusion. A possible reason for his decision was that he doubted 2/14th and 2/16th Battalions would hold the line so he felt obliged to commit his fresh formation. Either Potts was not confident that the 2/14th and 2/16th could hold the track, so he simply could not afford to put the 2/27th in reserve, or it may be he had no intention of risking a counter-attack at all if it could be avoided. It begins to look as if, having been ordered to make a stand, he did so reluctantly and with a view to retiring again on 8 September, but he was forestalled by the manoeuvre of 2/144th Battalion on to Brigade Hill.

Potts was relieved after Efogi. The 'front-line view', a part of the Kokoda myth, since adopted by most accounts of the campaign, was that Potts did a wonderful job and was unfairly dealt with. There can only be merit in this view if Potts was faced by an overwhelming enemy force, and he was not. The view from Port Moresby and Melbourne was that

Potts had been defeated several times and pushed back 40 kilometres by an enemy force of about the same number, so something was wrong either with the soldiers or with their commander.[46] In particular, Potts' performance at Efogi was criticised, and it was not unusual for a head to roll after a series of failures. Rowell's account, given after the war to historian Gavin Long, seems a reasonable explanation:

> 21st Bde had failed to hold the Japanese. We knew the terrain was most difficult and the Japs were very good jungle fighters, but the 21st Bde was sent to stop them and it didn't. The task set Potts was a most difficult one and it may be that many other brigadiers would have done no better. But I do suggest [to replace Potts and] bring Dougherty from Darwin to command 21st Bde was a very proper course. What appears [in an official history draft] is therefore not quite fair to TAB [Blamey] or me for that matter. Neither of us was looking for anyone's head ... but we wanted to make 21st Bde as efficient as possible ... it would have been wrong for us to allow ourselves to be influenced by Potts' feelings ... there was nothing vindictive about it.[47]

Whether or not Potts mishandled Efogi or intended to retreat, although ordered to stand, is arguable, but our view of the battle must take into account the forces present. If Potts was outnumbered five to one and his men killed Japanese at a rate of four to one, as Potts himself believed, then Efogi might be a part of 'a feat of Homeric proportions', as his biographer has described the period from Isurava to Efogi.[48] Sadly, it was not so. Potts was not outnumbered, nor, at Efogi, did his men inflict more casualties than were inflicted on them. As a consequence of the battle, his only fresh battalion was dispersed in the jungle, taking no further part in the Kokoda campaign. If Isurava was an Australian defeat redeemed in small part because the Japanese took heavy casualties, then Efogi was a defeat with no redeeming feature.

CHAPTER 11

IORIBAIWA

On 10 September 1942 Brigadier Selwyn Porter replaced Potts as commander of Maroubra Force. Porter brought reinforcements, 30th Brigade headquarters and 3rd Battalion. The Australian force defeated at Efogi retreated to join Porter. There was fighting near Menari and, their rearguard under attack as they crossed the Maguli Range, the Australians fell back to a blocking position on Ioribaiwa Ridge, where they were to be further reinforced by 25th Brigade. Something more than another defensive stand was planned. While Porter's force held the Kokoda Track, 25th Brigade was to leave the track south of Ioribaiwa and march to outflank the Japanese on both sides, as Horii had tried at Isurava. The move was in motion when Kusunose's pursuit group arrived in front of Ioribaiwa. While Kusunose waited for his guns to come up he probed the Australian position. This was vigorous enough for the Australian composite battalion, formed from the remnants of the 2/14th and 2/16th, to think they had repelled an assault. Unaware that the Australians were reinforced and intending an offensive, Kusunose launched his own attack on the afternoon of 14 September. It was to be his last battle in Papua. So ill that he ran the battle from his bed, he was evacuated soon after.

THE AUSTRALIANS

Brigadier Ken Eather's 25th Brigade had 1736 men in its three infantry battalions. Adding a brigade headquarters and a detachment from 2/4th Field Ambulance, there were 1861 in all. In Maroubra Force by now

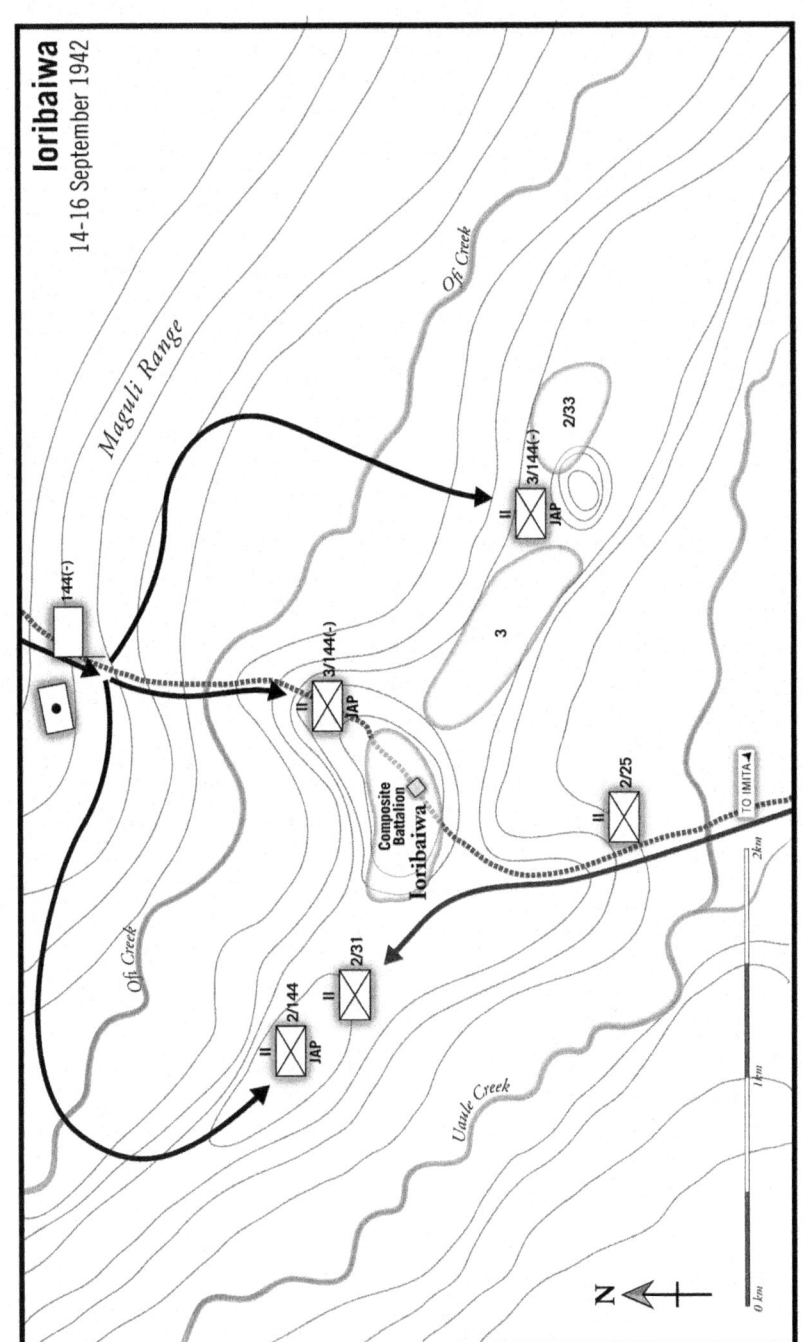

Map 9 Ioribaiwa, 14–16 September 1942

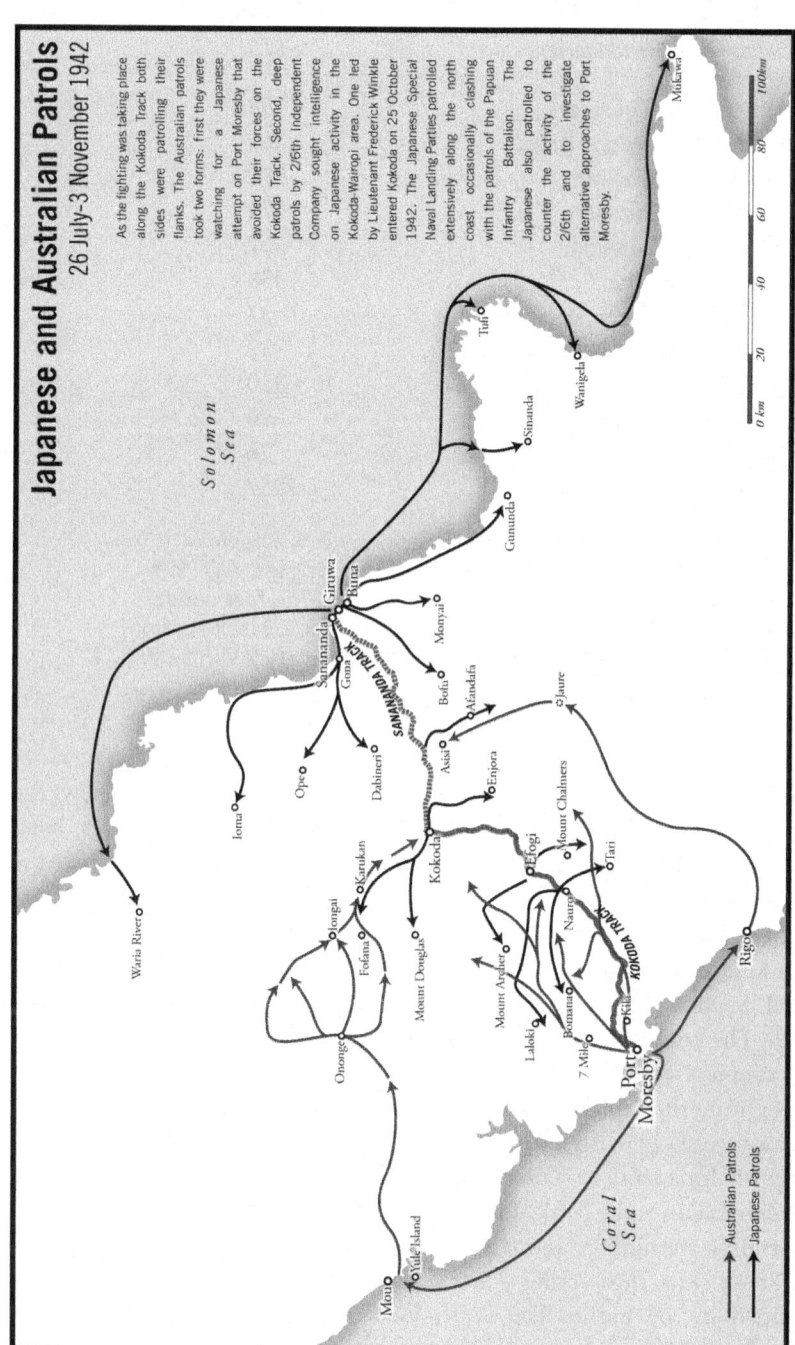

Japanese and Australian Patrols
26 July–3 November 1942

As the fighting was taking place along the Kokoda Track both sides were patrolling their flanks. The Australian patrols took two forms: first they were watching for a Japanese attempt on Port Moresby that avoided their forces on the Kokoda Track. Second, deep patrols by 2/6th Independent Company sought intelligence on Japanese activity in the Kokoda–Wairopi area. One led by Lieutenant Frederick Winkle entered Kokoda on 25 October 1942. The Japanese Special Naval Landing Parties patrolled extensively along the north coast occasionally clashing with the patrols of the Papuan Infantry Battalion. The Japanese also patrolled to counter the activity of the 2/6th and to investigate alternative approaches to Port Moresby.

Map 10 Patrols, 26 July – 3 November 1942

137

Table 11.1 Maroubra Force at Ioribaiwa

Maroubra Force Headquarters	175
25th Brigade headquarters	88
L Section, 7th Division signals	55
2/31st Infantry Battalion	590
2/33rd Infantry Battalion	579
2/25th Infantry Battalion	567
3rd Infantry Battalion	450
2/4th Field Ambulance, detachment	37
14th Field Ambulance, detachment	30
2/14th and 2/16th composite battalion	320
21st Brigade composite company	90
C Patrol, 2/6th Independent Company	26
Total, less 50 estimated sick	2957

Source: 7th Division operational instructions, no. 9, Appendix 1,
AWM52 8/2/21/17; Notes on operations, 25th Brigade, AWM54
577/7/8; Laffin, *Forever Forward*, pp. 80–1; Crooks, *The Footsoldiers*,
p. 145; 2/25th Battalion war diary, AWM52 8/3/25; 2/31st Battalion
war diary, AWM52 8/3/31; 2/33rd Battalion war diary, AWM52 8/3/33.

there was a constant high wastage to sickness, amounting to ten men per
battalion per day. It was not this bad for 25th Brigade as it was new; the
men were fit and had only been in the mountains for three days. Even
so it appears that about 50 men of the brigade were absent during the
battle. To 25th Brigade must be added those already on the ridge when
Eather arrived. Under Porter there was a combined Maroubra Force
Headquarters, including 21st and 30th Brigade headquarters, which now
had L Section of 7th Division signals attached, and was about 175 men
in all. The composite battalion had 320 men, and there was the composite company of 21st Brigade, which had arrived at Brigade Hill during
the fighting there.[1] Its strength was now about 90. 3rd Battalion (militia)
was also present with 450 men.[2] Last of all was the 26-strong C Patrol
of 2/6th Independent Company, who had just returned from scouting
the Australian right flank. They were placed with MFHQ, giving a total
Australian strength of about 2957 (see table 11.1).

There were three other Australian formations nearby that were not
engaged in the battle. The 2/5th Field Company was improving the
Kokoda Track on the south side of Ioribaiwa Ridge while 7th Field

Company and two companies of 2/1st Pioneer Battalion were on Imita Ridge just south of Ioribaiwa.[3] Their task was to patrol the flanks, and during the battle they lost a man in a skirmish several kilometres west of Ioribaiwa. For similar reasons a Japanese engineer company working along the track to the rear of Kusunose's pursuit group has not been included in the force engaged. The Australian force was the largest concentration for battle so far achieved on the track by either side. It was only possible to supply the force because the Australians were just 20 kilometres from their roadhead.

THE JAPANESE

Kusunose's pursuit group was essentially the force that fought at Efogi, less casualties and plus the mountain artillery and medical personnel. The battalion history of the 3/144th gives 539 present at Ioribaiwa.[4] For the 2/144th there can only be an estimate of strength. Its 5th Company, which had borne the brunt of the fighting at Efogi, was reduced to 88 men and the battalion was close to 525 strong.[5] There were then about 1064 in the two infantry battalions to be added to the same RHQ force that fought at Efogi. The company of 15 IER was about 150 strong. Two of its platoons were allocated, one each, to the infantry battalions, and the third platoon cut tracks to facilitate the deployment of the artillery. The 55th Division medical detachment and a detachment of the PCB was present as well as all three mountain guns and the 144th regimental gun company.[6] Kusunose had, in all, close to 1714 men.

The Nankai Shitai was, as yet, not much troubled by sickness. In the month of September 76 men from 144th Regiment were listed as sick out of 226 for the entire uniformed component of the Nankai Shitai in Papua.[7] One of the regiment's battalions, the 3/144th, had 182 battle casualties by the time it arrived at Ioribaiwa, but only 17 men had fallen sick so far. Kusunose's losses to illness since Brigade Hill can hardly have been more than 50.

A food shortage was looming, and several days before Ioribaiwa 1050 men, chosen from all units from Ioribaiwa to Nauro, were sent to Isurava for supplies. Non-combat troops and carriers were sent where possible, but some fighting troops also had to go. Kusunose's infantry regiment sent 200, mostly non-fighting personnel, but 30 of them were infantry from the 3/144th, who were absent from the front for ten days and missed the battle. If the other combat units had to send a quota similar to the 3/144th then 70 men were absent from the fighting elements of the pursuit group.[8] However, as we can only be sure about the 30 men from the 3/144th, and because some went from units not present at Ioribaiwa, like 41st Regiment, the total Japanese force engaged at Ioribaiwa should be estimated at 1650 men – a little more than half the number of Australians that opposed them.

In terms of firepower, the outstanding feature was that the Japanese had at least a dozen medium machine-guns and nine artillery pieces – the largest assembly of guns they managed until the Oivi–Gorari action in November. There were five 75mm mountain guns, two 70mm battalion guns and two 37mm light guns. The Australians had three Vickers medium machine-guns, used for the first time on the track, and three 3-inch mortars.[9] The infantry of 25th Brigade brought double the usual complement of Thompson submachine-guns, giving an average of two per section, a powerful addition for the close-range fighting that typified the campaign.

As the ratio of Japanese to Australians present at Ioribaiwa seems so far below the numbers of Japanese that have become accepted – about 5000 according to the Australian official history – it is necessary to be sure of the location of the other Japanese fighting units forward of Kokoda.[10] There are four to be accounted for: the NSHQ, including attached dismounted cavalry, 41st Regiment, 1/144th Battalion and the remainder of 15th Independent Engineer Regiment. The NSHQ and the 1/144th camped on the high ground just south-west of Nauro on 12 September and remained there until at least 16 September.[11] Yazawa's 41st Regiment had one battalion on the coast at Giruwa, one battalion less a company at Kokoda, and one battalion plus a company, RHQ and the gun company, at Nauro.[12] Apart from patrolling, there they stayed until the Japanese retreated from Ioribaiwa.

There were two reasons the Yazawa Regiment was placed as it was. First, the advance was to cease on Ioribaiwa Ridge, and Nauro was where Yazawa would leave the Kokoda Track to advance on Port Moresby when ordered. The few Japanese historians who have examined the Kokoda campaign believe that Horii advanced too far without permission and that this was the first misstep that brought him undone.[13] When Kusunose captured Ioribaiwa, Horii was accused of having 'gone beyond the strategic line indicated by 17th Army and [of having] dangerously extended [his] supply lines'.[14] The problem is that no definite line was ever indicated. Horii's superior, Hyakutake, quite rightly left it to Horii to choose the precise location to halt. Horii's chief of staff Tanaka thought Ioribaiwa was too far forward, and a rumour that the two had a blazing row about it spread through the Nankai Shitai.[15]

Horii still expected to be reinforced and to be given permission to go ahead with the Port Moresby attack by November, and Yazawa was assured of an important part in it. Consequently, while Kusunose's regiment pushed directly down the track, Yazawa's regiment was given the task of examining other approaches to Port Moresby.[16] Hofstetter, the Nankai Shitai's Swiss informant, claimed there was a suitable track branching west from Nauro.[17] It led down towards the Brown and Goldie Rivers, both of which offered approaches to the Allied airfield complex in the Laloki–Kila–Bomana area, just north of Port Moresby. Yazawa's patrols extended out to the west as far as the Brown River and into the Maguli Range around the sources of the Goldie River. New Guinea Force knew that the Japanese track south-west from Nauro was being improved and were watching for just such a move as Horii planned.[18] There were three or four skirmishes in the area between Japanese 41st Regiment patrols and the Australian 2/1st Pioneer Battalion and 2/6th Independent Company.[19] It was at this time that the commander of the Allied Air Force and US Fifth Army Air Force, Lieutenant-General George Kenney, informed NGF that if a single Japanese patrol crossed the Goldie River he intended to pull all his aircraft back to Queensland. In fact 41st Regiment patrols did get as far as the Goldie River but might not have crossed it.[20] By the time Yazawa reported that he had found no suitable route to Port Moresby, the Japanese retreat was being organised. On 14 September, the second day of fighting at Ioribaiwa, 41st Regiment was told that, in two days time, it would advance 'on the western side of Ioribaiwa'.[21] The next day, Hyakutake's order for 41st Regiment to withdraw was received and Yazawa was to take his force back to Kokoda and Giruwa.

The third reason for the deployment of Yazawa around Nauro was to protect the supply line. It was known that several large Australian groups, mainly from 2/27th Battalion, had been driven off the track at Efogi and were lurking to the east.[22] The main body of the 2/27th, 303 men, was east of Nauro working their way south to rejoin their brigade. They encountered 41st Regiment patrols extending east to the Nauro River and as far south as the Adai River. Yazawa was instructed to ensure that they did not interfere with the Nankai Shitai supply line. The story of the privations endured by the 2/27th in their retreat is well known, but not that they helped the Australian cause by creating Japanese anxiety for their communications along the Kokoda Track.[23]

Yokoyama's 15 IER HQ was also based at Nauro while it worked on the Nauro to Ioribaiwa section of the Kokoda Track. The earlier arrangement for the attachment of 15 IER engineers was maintained. One company was with Kusunose at Ioribaiwa, another was with Yazawa's patrols, a third (attached to Yokoyama from 55 ER) was working on the track from Kokoda to Menari.[24] The activity of the engineers in bringing the track up to packhorse standard also indicates that Horii expected to stay in the mountains for some time to come.

The reason previous researchers have been misled as to the number of Japanese engaged at Ioribaiwa could be because they have misinterpreted an order issued by Horii on 22 September for the withdrawal of the Nankai Shitai after Ioribaiwa. The order stated that 'adjutants [are] to attend an orders group from following units: Kusunose [Kusunose's two-battalion pursuit group], 1st battalion [Kusunose's other battalion of 144st Regiment], Koiwai [2/41st Battalion], Kawashima [55th Division cavalry detachment], Hozumi [mountain artillery], Takamori [15 IER], Akao [hygiene unit], and Banto [medical]'.[25] The order was captured later, and the 39th Battalion war diary, for instance, states that this order shows which Japanese units were at Ioribaiwa.[26] The order lists the times when each unit should withdraw and the places each should get to each day thereafter. What has not been noticed is that it would not be possible for the units listed to get to the places mentioned in the time allowed unless they were already well north of Ioribaiwa. The NSHQ, for example, was to leave at dawn on 24 September and spend that night at Kagi. This was difficult enough to do from Nauro, quite impossible from Ioribaiwa.[27]

IORIBAIWA

On 11 September Kusunose ordered his regiment, the 3/144th leading, to advance to find the enemy and for 55th Mountain Artillery Regiment to follow.[28] After two brief clashes with elements of the Australian 21st Brigade in the Maguli Range, Kusunose's force arrived in front of the Ioribaiwa position on 12 September. The regimental gun company was placed under Hozumi, the mountain artillery commander. He sent spotters out to locate targets for the artillery now massing in one body on the slope north of Ioribaiwa Ridge.[29] The next day, Kusunose ordered the infantry scouts out to locate the Australian front line, meanwhile sending all the 2/144th off to the west to swing around the Australian flank into their rear, as it had done twice before.

On 14 September Kusunose explained his plan to his subordinates:

> It appears that over 200 of the enemy have occupied a position in
> the Ioribaiwa area. 2nd Battalion's main force is making a flanking

attack to the W[est] ... and will be the right front line. 3rd Battalion [less detachments] will be the left front line and will attack the enemy position at Ioribaiwa parallel with the main road. The mountain artillery will stay at its present position and cooperate with the regiment and with the 3rd Battalion. The regimental gun company will establish itself with the mountain artillery and cooperate with 3rd Battalion. The communication unit will liaise between the front line battalions and regimental headquarters. I will advance at the rear of 3rd Battalion.[30]

Kusunose's estimate of Australian strength was revised upwards on the same day but only to two battalions, as he was still unaware that a fresh brigade of Australians was in the offing.[31] While the 2/144th went around the Australian left (without its battalion gun) the 3/144th, supported by eight guns including its battalion gun, pinned the Australians to the front. It was the Efogi plan again, but this time the appearance of Australian reinforcements was to thwart it.

Although Eather was not officially placed in command of Maroubra Force until 17 September, he exercised command at Ioribaiwa under the instructions of his divisional commander, Major-General Arthur Allen, and with the compliance of Porter.[32] Having consulted Porter, already on the ridge, Eather decided to leave Porter blocking the track while using his own brigade to swing around both flanks, a battalion on each side, to take Nauro in the Japanese rear. The first of his battalions to arrive, the 2/33rd, was to head east from Imita while the 2/31st marched west along Ioribaiwa Ridge, then turned north to approach Nauro from the south-west. The third battalion, the 2/25th, was to remain in reserve directly behind the composite battalion in the Australian centre. Once the 2/33rd left the track to make its way through the jungle its commander, Lieutenant-Colonel Arthur Buttrose, reported that progress was impossibly slow. With only five days rations his battalion would not get to Nauro any time soon. Eather revised the plan. Buttrose brought his battalion back to the Kokoda Track, then up to Ioribaiwa Ridge on the Australian right. From there it was to make a shorter right hook into Nauro. This brought Buttrose along the line of the present Kokoda Track, which runs east of the wartime track and through Ponoon village.

As the 2/33rd arrived on the right of 3rd Battalion on 13 September, the composite battalion was attacked by the Japanese. Eather responded cautiously, deciding to hold the 2/33rd in place to see how the advance of the 2/31st on his left progressed. Eather now had four battalions (counting the composite battalion as one) in line abreast along the ridge and one battalion in reserve. On the left was the 2/31st, next to the right was the composite battalion, then 3rd Battalion and last on the right was the 2/33rd. His line was not quite 2 kilometres long.

Kusunose's attack began on 14 September. On the Australian left flank 2/31st Battalion, advancing west along the narrow ridge crest, collided head on with the Japanese 2/144th. Both sides threw a company out to both of their steeply sloped flanks and butted against each other all afternoon, to no effect. Meanwhile, against the Australian centre, one and a half Japanese companies of the 3/144th, plus elements of engineers, advanced against the composite battalion. Seven Japanese guns fired in support from the north and the battalion gun of the 3/144th was brought up to within a hundred metres of the Australian position.[33]

Throughout the action Japanese artillery concentrated on the composite battalion. They inflicted a considerable number of casualties and forced the battalion to give ground. Even so, the progress made on 14 September did not please Kusunose. A 3/144th officer who lost five men wounded by Australian mortars thought the Australians were resisting unexpectedly well, and it was now clear that they had been strongly reinforced.[34] Kusunose still had half the 3/144th in reserve and decided to use it in a new attack around his left (east) while his centre and right pinned the Australians to their respective fronts. The reserve, built around 8th Company and reinforced by a platoon of engineers and half 9th Company, headed off east with the engineers leading. To lessen the frequency with which they became lost when they left a known track and entered the jungle, the Japanese had tried a new system at Efogi and used it again here. An engineer platoon's first section would cut the track, one behind that would escort the cutters while a third one navigated.

Late in the morning of 15 September this force approached the Australian right along the postwar Kokoda Track where it crosses Ofi Creek. They surprised a platoon of D Company of 3rd Battalion, which gave ground, thus allowing the Japanese to insert themselves between 3rd Battalion and 2/33rd Battalion.[35] The Australian reserve, 2/25th Battalion, sent two companies to eject them, while the 2/33rd sent one company to do the same from the other side of the Japanese. The counter-attack failed, partly because, as happened so often in the campaign to both sides, A Company of the 2/33rd got lost and failed to find any enemy to attack.[36]

In the Australian centre it was the same story as the day before. At 4 a.m. the Japanese attacked with 7th Company of the 3/144th, plus a platoon of 9th Company and one of engineers. They advanced on the Australian composite battalion while calling in an artillery bombardment on Australian positions further up the slope of the ridge. Again their battalion gun fired in close support and again progress was slow but steady. The IJA doctrine for the use of battalion guns stressed that in the attack their proper place was 800 metres or more behind the leading infantry.[37] Frequently in practice, as here, the gunners worked their pieces up much closer and suffered crew casualties to small-arms fire as a consequence. The 3/144th gun was now brought to within 50 metres of the Australians and began firing rapidly. 'In a moment the position of the enemy's Czech machine-gun [Bren light machine-gun] in front was blasted away and the nearby jungle was transformed into a forest with dead trees … The roar of the gun echoed in the valley creating an intense and heroic atmosphere. In accord with the battalion gun, the mountain gun unit and the infantry gun unit fired at any enemy positions which perturbed them.'[38]

On 15 September on the Australian left, the Australian 2/31st and Japanese 2/144th continued to spar tentatively with one another. Kusunose told Horie of the 2/144th to do no more than keep the Australians there busy while he awaited the outcome of the new thrust on the Japanese left. By the evening Kusunose's position was still unsatisfactory. He had committed all his infantry and in two days fighting had failed to drive the Australians off Ioribaiwa Ridge. If the Australians essayed a major counter-attack with their reserve he had nothing spare with which to meet it.

On the morning of 16 September, 8th Company of the 3/144th, on the Japanese left, enlarged its position by seizing 'Sankaku Yama', a striking pyramid-shaped hill just east of the modern Kokoda Track. This was potentially serious for the Australians as the crest of Sankaku Yama overlooked the spine of Ioribaiwa Ridge, and it would be possible to enfilade the Australian line with machine-guns placed there. The Japanese at Sankaku Yama also stood off an attack by B and D Companies of 2/33rd Battalion. With the failure of this effort, Eather contacted his divisional commander Allen in Port Moresby, and obtained permission to withdraw. The withdrawal commenced at midday, and by evening, apart from a battalion in a rearguard position, Maroubra Force was set up on the next ridge to the south, Imita Ridge. The Japanese, heavily outnumbered and fought to a standstill with no reserve in hand, were not in a position to interfere with the Australian withdrawal.

CASUALTIES

Australian casualties from 13 to 17 September 1942 were 49 dead and 121 wounded.[39] All but one, from the patrol clash between the Japanese 2/41st Regiment and 2/1st Pioneer Battalion well to the west, were incurred at Ioribaiwa. Apart from among the infantry there were few Japanese battle casualties. The 15 IER lost at most two killed and four wounded.[40] The massed Japanese artillery were not fired on by the Australian 3-inch mortars, the only weapons with the range to hit them, as they could not be located. Total Japanese casualties were 39 killed and about 120 wounded.[41] A week after the battle the Japanese hospital at Kokoda, after taking in only one or two casualties each day, suddenly admitted 122 in two days, mostly from Ioribaiwa.[42] The records of the 3/144th suggest that the ratio of killed to wounded was closer than 39 to 120, but this could be accounted for by the difference between killed in action and died of wounds.[43] The latter category is always problematic, and Australian records, especially during their retreat, are also likely to be in error in the number of killed in action against died of wounds.

According to the Kokoda myth, the series of Australian defeats up to Ioribaiwa, the furthest point of Japanese advance, was mitigated by the large number of battle casualties, in the several thousands, inflicted on the Japanese. As with the myth that the Japanese thought there was a road over the Owen Stanley Range, it is possible to find the odd Japanese diary entry that supports this. One Japanese diarist believed that a thousand of his countrymen were killed in August alone, but Japanese unit records do not support this. The myth owes a great deal to the sensational and unreliable Japanese newspaper reporter Okada Seizo, who accompanied the Nankai Shitai. Okada wrote that four-fifths of the Japanese force were casualties by Ioribaiwa, and studies of the campaign have accepted this as correct, assuming that a thousand Japanese had been killed in battle and that many thousands more were wounded or sick.[44]

In fact the Japanese lost no more than 900 killed and wounded from the start of the campaign to the end of Ioribaiwa.[45] By 4 October, two weeks after Ioribaiwa but before any further serious fighting, 405 men had been killed in battle and about 450 wounded were then in hospital.[46] In 144th Regiment it was estimated that casualties to 28 September were 300 killed and 400 wounded.[47] The other major unit, 41st Regiment, was the pursuit group for five days at the start of September and took 102 casualties. Just 11 battle casualties are recorded for all other units in September. The battle casualties for other units in August is unknown but must be small, so 900 would appear to be a reasonable estimate of Japanese battle casualties so far.[48]

Rowell reported 464 killed and 567 wounded Australians for the Kokoda front up to 4 October, and these figures are supported by AMF battle casualty graphs.[49] The lowest official number is 805 if daily casualty records from July to the end of September are added, but daily records are not likely to be as reliable as an end-of-campaign report.[50] Either way, not much credence can be given to the argument that while the Australians were being pushed back along the Kokoda Track they were exacting an extremely high price from the Japanese.

There was at Ioribaiwa an extreme example of the phenomenon of overestimating enemy casualties. On 17 September, the day after the battle, a Japanese patrol pushing down the main track towards Imita Ridge entered a clearing where it was ambushed by C Company of the Australian 2/33rd Battalion. The ambush entered Kokoda myth folklore. It is described in detail in the battalion war diary, the brigade war diary, the battalion history and almost all books on the campaign, and the story is a favourite among battalion veterans. The account runs thus: a few members of C Company showed themselves to a Japanese patrol, which came after them and fell into the ambush with the Australians opening up from three sides. Fifty Japanese were killed with no loss to C Company, who then withdrew to Imita Ridge.[51] The brigade account claims only 40 dead.[52] It is said that 3000 rounds were fired and that many Japanese must have been hit several times over. Paull in *Retreat from Kokoda* wrote that 40 Japanese from Kuwada Battalion (3/144th) were killed and 'none returned'.[53] There is no estimate of the number of Japanese wounded, but 50 killed is more than the Japanese lost in the three-day battle on Ioribaiwa Ridge.

The ambush can be checked against Japanese records. Those ambushed were from 9th Company, 3/144th and were led by Lieutenant Okabayashi Shintaro. His account of the event, which was given to the battalion historian, is at variance with the Australian one. On 17 September Okabayashi's patrol was advancing down the main track when they saw a few enemy and chased them, but they were then fired on from all sides. Support arrived, and the Japanese withdrew with two men wounded.[54] It is likely one of these men subsequently died as the regimental list of deaths records one man only for 17 September and the ambush of Okabayashi was the only fighting of the day. It was not only the Australians who were guilty of overestimating enemy dead. At Rabaul 144th Regiment claimed to have killed 300 Australians but actually killed 22, and on the Kokoda

Track 30 Australian corpses were apparently counted by the Japanese after a skirmish in the Maguli Range on 11 September, but Australian records show only two Australian dead.[55]

COMMAND

The Japanese at Ioribaiwa were outnumbered almost two to one and were attacking a naturally strong position against a dug-in enemy, half of whom were fresh veteran troops. Moreover Kusunose's plan was based on a great underestimate of the size of the enemy force he had to deal with and the length of front on which it might be deployed. Eather said afterwards, correctly, that he thought the Japanese did what they did because they initially had no idea of the presence of 25th Brigade. The result was that 2/144th Battalion failed to get behind the Australians as it had done at Efogi. Instead it bumped into the Australian 2/31st west of Ioribaiwa, and accomplished nothing other than to keep a larger force engaged. In the Japanese centre and left, the 3/144th, fighting in two parts, opposed elements of four Australian battalions. Although their artillery gave them an important advantage, the Japanese were too greatly outnumbered to drive off such a large Australian force. In their centre they were able to gain ground slowly against the composite battalion while on their left they were only able to hold the ground they had seized.

Just why the Australians retreated, not clearly defeated and with half their force as yet only lightly engaged, requires some explanation. Certainly Buttrose thought so. The feeling in his 2/33rd Battalion was that they had hardly had a battle and most of the battalion had never been engaged.

The first cause of the Australian defeat to eliminate is any general collapse of morale, as happened to 53rd Battalion at Isurava. There was no disordered retreat, and when the order came to go back to Imita, it was done in exemplary fashion. While a platoon (and possibly more) of 3rd Battalion was surprised, thus allowing the Japanese penetration of the Australian right, this was an isolated incident, although tactically important. Nor had the Australians suffered grievous casualties, having lost 6 per cent of their force by the end of the action. Why then did Eather retreat? The reasons usually given are those in his report, which was written a few days later. They are repeated in 7th Division's report on operations and are summarised here:

1   by continuing to hold the ridge, all units were committed to defensive tasks so freedom to adopt the offensive was lost

Photo 16 Looking east along Ioribaiwa Ridge to Sankaku Yama. The area
in the foreground and the hill was taken by the Japanese 3/144th Battalion,
attacking from left to right, on 15–16 September 1942. (Author's collection)

2   it was essential to keep the force intact for future offensive roles
3   supply was precarious
4   a withdrawal allowed a firm base at Imita from which patrols could
     regain the initiative
5   supporting artillery could be had from the Imita position but not the
     Ioribaiwa position, and
6   enemy supply problems would increase to breaking point.[56]

Most of this is plausible, but it is at variance with what was written in
the 25th Brigade war diary at 11 a.m. on 16 September at the time withdrawal was decided upon: 'Owing to enemy penetration on both flanks
of our position on Ioribaiwa Ridge Brig. Eather considered that enemy
could not be held in present position and ordered Bde to withdraw to
vicinity of Imita Ridge.'[57] Another similar explanation appeared in 2/25th
Battalion war diary: 'Brig. Eather ordered withdrawal of brig group to
Imita range owing to Jap encircling tactics on left and right flanks.'[58]

The 7th Division account explains a number of sensible reasons why
a withdrawal would be a good idea, but the war diary explanation gets
to the nub: in the opinion of the commander the position could not
be held, which in the end is the best reason of all, if correct. From the
afternoon of 15 September, the Japanese had made almost no forward

progress precisely because they were heavily outnumbered. Eather could not have known that he outnumbered the enemy by almost two to one so there was small chance of Kusunose's force driving him off the ridge, but this is not an excuse. Generals often do not know the enemy strength. Major General George Vasey, who later commanded 7th Division on the Kokoda Track, said that this was especially so in the jungle, but 'I don't see how we can overcome this, so [we should] make a well informed guess and get on with it'.[59] Nor did Eather know that both of Kusunose's battalions were stuck fast and that Kusunose had no reserve to hand. Had Eather hung on rather than retreated, Kusunose could have done nothing more. Had Eather counter-attacked with the 2/25th, which he still had in reserve, Kusunose had nothing to counter it with.

It may be that Eather thought the composite battalion was about to collapse. If that occurred he still had the 2/25th to fill the gap but would then be left with no reserve. The members of the composite battalion had seen hard service for three weeks now. They had been constantly defeated and retreating, and a week before Ioribaiwa Potts considered them unfit for further operations.[60] At the same time the enemy too had expressed the view that 'these troops are in a state of utter confusion, and to a great degree have lost the will to fight'.[61] For two days now the Australian composite battalion had fought under the fire of the largest concentration of Japanese artillery so far assembled in the campaign. The importance of the Japanese artillery was mentioned in a conversation on the ridge on 16 September between Dr Vernon and an AIF officer. The officer told Vernon that the withdrawal was because 'too many were picked off at long range from lack of skill in concealing themselves [and] the Jap mortars were firing with deadly precision and they had more powerful weapons with longer range than we had'.[62] The diarist of 2/14th Battalion is more specific: 'The strain was beginning to tell ... and some of the lads ... began to crack up. Enemy mortar, MG and field pieces continued to do deadly work on our forward positions all morning and our casualties mounted.'[63] Perhaps it was this that prompted Eather at 8.15 a.m. on 16 September to signal Allen 'enemy feeling whole front and both flanks. Do not consider can hold him here. Request permission to withdraw to Imita Ridge if necessary. Porter concurs.'[64]

It has been said that it is less important to defeat the enemy force than to convince their commander that he has lost the battle. A likely cause for the Australian defeat would seem to be that Eather became convinced he was defeated, and so he was. It is difficult to imagine Kusunose asking Horii for permission to withdraw in similar circumstances. Kusunose might have argued that he had attacked what he thought was a small force to find it greatly reinforced. His flanking attack, by the 2/144, had achieved nothing. He was aware by now that he was significantly outnumbered and that his plan had stalled. His left flank, having penetrated the enemy line, was trapped there. He had no reserve at all with which to hazard a new blow or to meet a counter-attack of the enemy, which might come at any time. The difference between Kusunose and Eather was that the former in parlous circumstances held grimly on, the latter withdrew. Pierre Bonnal's explanation for the defeat of the French under General Frossard at Spicheren in 1870 is apt. 'General Frossard, undefeated, thought he had been defeated and so he was. General von Zastrow was half defeated but refused to be and so was not.'[65]

CHAPTER | 12

JAPANESE ARTILLERY

The Kokoda myth explanation that the Australian defeats in the first half of the Kokoda campaign were a result of being greatly outnumbered has been shown to be untrue. An alternative might be that Japanese artillery had a lot to do with explaining the outcome of the battles on the Kokoda Track. The Nankai Shitai brought 16 artillery pieces to Papua. They took 13 of them into the mountains, although not all were used there, and employed 15 at Oivi–Gorari, the final battle of the campaign.[1] Artillery can determine the outcome of battles, especially where the opponent has none. The ability to concentrate artillery fire on a single point on a battle front can significantly affect the opposing infantry and lessen the advantage of prepared defensive positions. Even a few guns when used well can do so, but not much has been written about Japanese artillery during the Kokoda campaign.[2]

Postwar accounts have mentioned the effectiveness of Japanese mortar fire, and there has been an assumption that the main Japanese long-range weapon was, together with a mountain gun or a 37mm Quick Firing (QF) gun or two, the 81mm medium mortar.[3] But of the hundreds of Japanese rounds recovered during the campaign and since, not one mortar round of this size has been found on the Kokoda Track. In Melbourne in early 1942 a facility was established to test Japanese equipment, ammunition and weapons. As rapidly as possible samples were sent there from the battlefield, yet no Japanese medium-mortar rounds appeared in Melbourne until after 15 December 1942 simply because no Japanese medium mortars were used in the Owen Stanley Range.[4] The only ones used in Papua

152

were in the defence of Buna–Gona from late November 1942. It should be noted here that we are not talking about the 'knee mortar', a light mortar. There were three of these organic to each Japanese infantry platoon. These were short-range weapons incapable of filling the role of artillery as, to some extent, the medium mortar was.

The second reason Japanese artillery on the Kokoda Track is usually vaguely described as consisting of 'a mountain gun and several mortars' involves a translation error.[5] The Japanese called their 70mm battalion gun a 'gun-mortar'. The Allied Translator and Interpreter Service (ATIS) usually translated this as 'mortar'.[6] Australian Army technical reports, resulting from test-firing captured Japanese artillery, do not make the same error, but elsewhere it is a common mistake. Australians in battle also mistook artillery for medium mortars because the sound of the exploding shell of the 70mm gun was difficult to distinguish from that of a mortar. Both the Japanese 75mm mountain gun and 70mm infantry gun were high-angle weapons and, by definition, both were light howitzers. While artillerymen and sometimes experienced infantry could often tell from the sound what kind of weapon was fired, there was confusion among the Australians about this. Two situation reports sent from 21st Brigade at Efogi to NGF reported 'Japs using long range mortars' and 'heavy mortars' or 'enemy using two QF guns, [and] a heavy mortar'.[7] What the Japanese actually had there was two 75mm guns, two 70mm guns and two 37mm guns. Even the battle-experienced Japanese could be in error. At Efogi the Australians used a 3-inch mortar, but a Japanese report mentioned that 'it was the first time the enemy used the mountain gun'.[8] At Second Eora when the Australians also had 3-inch mortars, a Japanese officer reported that 'mountain guns opened fire at our troops'.[9]

The supposedly ubiquitous Japanese mortars have become a part of the Kokoda myth because that is what the front-line soldiers reported was firing at them, and the myth has always preferred evidence from the front line to that from elsewhere. NGF in Port Moresby did not make the same error. Information from signals interception, captured documents and prisoners gave NGF, over time, accurate information on the type – if not the number – of Japanese weapons. On 1 November NGF thought the Japanese had nine mountains guns and ten 70mm 'mortar-guns' on the Kokoda Track.[10] A mortar-gun is so called because it has been thought of as a highly portable, breech-loading mortar on wheels, but this is incorrect. As the gun's round is spin stabilised, not fin stabilised (and more accurate thereby), it is an artillery piece and not a mortar.

Photo 17 Barrel of a Type 41 mountain gun used by 55th Mountain Artillery Regiment. The mountain gun could be carried by 18 men. In Papua double crews were used to share the load. (Kochi New Guinea Association)

Medium or heavy mortars were not a standard Japanese divisional weapon, nor were they, as with the Australians, integral to an infantry battalion. Seventeenth Army had 81mm mortars in Rabaul in mid-1942, but it was decided to take the more effective light and mountain artillery to Papua.[11] Later most of the mortars were sent to Guadalcanal.

The Japanese embraced mountain artillery before the Russo-Japanese War and later used it in China. They learned that, in difficult country, all the artillery they would have was literally what they could carry on their backs. The 70mm infantry gun or battalion gun was actually the standard mountain artillery weapon of the time. In 1932, with the development of the 75mm mountain gun, the 70mm gun was handed over to the infantry as their close-support weapon. The Australians had no similar experience of mountain warfare or mountain artillery. They had fought in North Africa, Greece, Crete and Syria in 1940–41 and some of that experience was mountain fighting, but those mountains had at least a minimal road network, quite a different proposition from the Owen Stanley Range. In the Malayan campaign, too, Australian infantry were rarely far from a road and the possibility of field artillery support. It is noteworthy that after their Kokoda experience, at the battle of Buna–Gona, the Australians deployed mountain batteries with the vintage 3.7-inch pack howitzer, and later still they used the US 75mm pack howitzer.

Table 12.1: Nankai Shitai artillery in the Owen Stanley Range

55th Mountain Artillery Regiment (1 battalion)	3 x 75mm
144th Regiment gun company	2 x 75mm, 2 x 37mm
41st Regiment gun company	1 x 75mm, 1 x 37mm
1/144th Battalion gun platoon	1 x 70mm
2/144th Battalion gun platoon	1 x 70mm
3/144th Battalion gun platoon	1 x 70mm
2/41st Battalion gun platoon	1 x 70mm

Source: *Nankai Shitai Efogi minamigawa ni okeru sento* [Nankai Shitai battles south of Efogi], npn, NIDS, Nanto, Soromon Bisumaruku 130; list of cargo, *Teiyo Maru* no. 474, AWM55 3/ 4; *Hohei Dai 144 Rentai Senki* [Battle records of 144th Infantry Regiment], p. 44, NIDS, 302.9.H; Yazawa to Tomita, 2 August 1942, current translations no. 33, pp. 16–17, AWM55 3/3; Bullard, *Japanese Army Operations in the South Pacific area*, p. 157.

The Japanese left one spare mountain gun at Giruwa, and the infantry guns of two battalions of 41st Regiment also stayed there. The part of the Nankai Shitai that went forward into the mountains was built around four infantry battalions, a mountain artillery battalion and two engineer companies, the whole being initially 3500 fighting men and 13 guns. Thirteen guns, or four guns per thousand men, was a standard ratio for the IJA in the Pacific, although it was exceeded by the proportion of guns taken to Guadalcanal – five guns per thousand men as well as 19 medium mortars up to 20 October 1942 – where the coastal strip on which much of the fighting took place was easier ground on which to move artillery. The artillery that went along the Kokoda Track was organised as shown in table 12.1.

It required a huge effort in manpower to carry the guns and their ammunition along the Kokoda Track. Was it worth it? To answer this question first the effort must be quantified, then the battlefield results examined. Normally a Japanese mountain artillery battalion had 12 guns and 610 men. If the terrain was expected to be difficult the number of guns was reduced to nine. In the Owen Stanley Range the terrain was expected to be near impossible, so each of the three gun companies took only one gun. 55th Mountain Artillery Regiment was also slimmed down to 420 men. A mountain gun battalion would normally have had a horse transport company of 230 horses.[12] This too was reduced to 45 horses, just enough to carry the guns and first-line ammunition as far as Kokoda.[13] From Kokoda on, everything was carried on the backs of the men. The battalion's three guns served together as a unit only at Isurava, Ioribawa and Oivi–Gorari, but individual guns were often in action elsewhere.

The 144th Regiment Gun Company (144 RGC) was at full establishment: 122 men, while the reduced gun company of 41st Regiment had 88 men.[14] The infantry battalion gun platoons began with 55 men, but all the gun platoons in the Nankai Shitai were stronger than this because, while the medium mortars were left in Rabaul, some of their crews were added to gun platoons as ammunition carriers.[15] Lieutenant Sakamoto Mitsuri's gun platoon had 87 men and that of the 3/144th had 72.[16] Together the mountain, regimental and battalion artillerymen totalled about 940, or a quarter of the uniformed portion of the Nankai Shitai that entered the Owen Stanley Range.

The 75mm gun weighed 540 kilograms, the other two types about a half that. In good going, the average weight carried by each man when the gun was man-ported was 30 kilograms; heavier parts were shared between two men in addition to carrying personal rations, weapons and equipment. The total weight of the 13 guns was 5 tons, and 160 men were required to carry them. The reason for the reorganisation of both mountain gunners and infantry gunners in Rabaul was so that two crews of gunners could share the load.[17]

With 320 men devoted to carrying the guns 620 were left to carry first-line ammunition and other stores, sometimes assisted by Rabaul carriers. An ammunition box for the 75mm gun contained three shells each weighing 8 kilograms.[18] A man carried one box, and each 75mm gun company had at least 120 rounds in its gun train, excluding the 20 rounds always carried with the gun itself.[19] The 70mm ammunition was lighter – 5 kilograms per round – and five rounds were carried in a box. In this case 200 men were available to carry ammunition, giving 1000 rounds for six pieces, or about 167 rounds per barrel. The third artillery piece was the type 94 37mm gun. It was an anti-tank gun that was also capable of firing high-explosive rounds. Both types of rounds were quite small, weighing only 650 grams.[20] One horse or three men carried its first-line ammunition.

Australian and Japanese accounts point out that the effect of the Japanese 'mortars' was much reduced in the Kokoda campaign as they had only 150–200 rounds per piece, but this is an error as it only takes account of first-line ammunition, not the full allocation of artillery ammunition for a kaisenbun.[21] The ammunition in a divisional kaisenbun was for 20 firing days in a four-month campaign and weighed between 2500 and 3000 tons. Normally, each regimental or mountain gun had 1300 rounds of which 10 per cent was carried, roughly in accord with what was calculated in the previous paragraph: another 10 per cent was in an ammunition train and 80 per cent was in a depot. A 70mm battalion gun had 1500 rounds of which 20 per cent was carried, 10 per cent was in a supply train and 70 per cent was in the depot, and a 37mm gun had 1200 rounds with the same proportions carried, in train and in depot.[22]

Actual practice in Papua varied from the norm. Half the total allocation of shells was brought forward as soon as possible, 2nd Mountain Gun Company loading 600 rounds for its single gun onto the *Ryoko Maru* on 26 July.[23] On arrival in Papua two-thirds of this was left at the Giruwa depot. As first-line ammunition was expended the reserve was brought forward along the supply line from the depot, but there was no proper ammunition train so first-line ammunition was increased. One gun arrived at Isurava with 261 rounds, and another had 300 rounds of first-line and reserve ammunition with it.[24] A further shipment of 150–300 rounds per gun, depending on the gun type, arrived by 2 September, and by October the first *kaisenbun* had been delivered to Papua and a second was beginning to arrive.[25] As an artillery officer of 41st Regiment said, there was little or no artillery ammunition problem in the Nankai Shitai, and those on the receiving end concurred: The war diary of the Australian 2/16th, among others, recorded that the Japanese guns 'seemed to have no shortage of ammunition'.[26]

It is clear that the Nankai Shitai expected results commensurate with the enormous effort involved in bringing so large an amount of artillery to Papua that a quarter of the force was required to service it. Was the effort justified by battlefield success? The main role of artillery is to neutralise the enemy – that is, inhibiting enemy movement and firepower – so that friendly infantry can defeat them. The casualties inflicted in the process of course contribute to the aim. Often infantry under artillery fire cannot be persuaded to move at all and their morale decreases, just as the morale of infantry whose own artillery is doing the damage is boosted. This does not matter quite so much in defence as in attack, but it is still important. Moving troops are far more vulnerable than stationary troops to all fire, including artillery fire, and the attacker might want to move most of his forces as the attack progresses, but the defender might only need to move his reserve – although he might not even be able to do that if the attacker's artillery has it under fire. A bombardment in support of an attack, although it must lift when the attacking infantry gets close to the defenders, will also significantly diminish the defender's fire against the attacker's infantry as some defenders will stay low in their fighting pits rather than expose themselves to use their weapon. A smoke-shell bombardment, which the Japanese also used on the Kokoda Track, also diminishes the effectiveness of the defender's fire by screening the attacking infantry from view.

When the Australians were on the offensive in October and November 1942 they were even more exposed to artillery fire than when they defended from July to September. At Templeton's Crossing and Eora some accounts suggest that the slow advance of Allen's 7th Division – which drew the ire of Herring, Blamey and MacArthur – was in part due to Japanese artillery fire. In the opinion of one of the Australian battalion commanders who faced it there, the Japanese artillery was the major problem for the Australians in their counter-offensive over the mountains.[27] Major-General Paul Cullen (then battalion commander of 2/1st Battalion) has pointed out that the Japanese artillery was sometimes powerful enough able to halt Australian manoeuvres at Second Eora. On 22 October 16th Brigade was pinned down by the artillery on the ridge north of Eora village for most of the day.[28] In November 1942 at Oivi, the seven Japanese guns on the heights above Oivi village were probably the main factor stopping dead the Australian attack there. Japanese artillery especially sought to neutralise the Australians' major source of firepower, their automatic weapons. In the earlier fighting along the track this was usually the Australian Bren light machine-gun. When Vickers medium machine-guns were used they became the priority target. Overnight on 24/25 October, an Australian Vickers gun, overlooking Eora Creek, was carefully camouflaged. At first light it was spotted by the Japanese artillery, which destroyed it and its crew with one shot.[29]

The Japanese artillery on the Kokoda Track inflicted casualties and curtailed Australian manoeuvre in three roles. The first was indirect fire where the gunners could not see the target. If the gunners are not in contact with their own forward observer who can see the target and direct fire on to it, then indirect fire is of little use. The 75mm and the 70mm howitzers were both capable of high-angle fire and suitable for the role, but mostly it was the 75mm guns that were used in this manner. At Efogi, the guns of the Japanese 144th Regiment had their fire directed into the Australian rear on Brigade Hill, and at Second Eora the mountain artillery made use of an observer overlooking Templeton's Crossing where artillery inhibited all Australian movement near the creek crossing and the smoke of cooking fires by day drew fire.[30]

The second role of the artillery was direct fire, with the gunners able to observe the target at ranges between 1000 and 2000 metres, out of effective range of Australian weapons with the exception of the 3-inch mortar. Before the Australian medium mortars arrived in numbers, Japanese artillerymen were usually safe a little beyond 1000 metres from the Australian infantry. At Isurava, 70mm guns were used in the direct-fire role. The battalion gun of the Japanese 2/144th fired across Eora Gorge from the eastern side at MFHQ, which was on the west side less than 2000 metres away. At Efogi, 70mm guns fired at the Australian 2/27th Battalion from 1500 metres.[31]

The third role for the Japanese artillery was in very close support of the infantry. The 37mm gun and sometimes the 70mm gun were used in this way.[32] Both were lighter and had a lower profile than the 75mm and were dragged forward by ropes drawn by their crawling crew. In this role, the preferred tactic, as prescribed in Japanese doctrine, was 'to seize the initiative and open fire unexpectedly and get good results within a short period'. The gun should be used 'close up behind the infantry and [should] fire on enemy heavy weapons'. The crew 'should avoid firing on targets within 150m of friendly infantry unless they are prone'.[33] A British officer in Burma described how artillery was used against him in this role: 'One of the weapons the Japs used most adroitly was a … field piece, an infantry gun which could be man-handled easily in forward positions and fired over open sights at point blank range. We nicknamed the shells from these guns "whizz-bangs" – you would never have time to hear the one that hit you.'[34] At Ioribaiwa a 37mm gun was brought to within a hundred metres of the Australians, and the gunners lost several men to rifle fire. An IJA pamphlet stated that it was important to be able to generate a great deal of fire suddenly in such circumstances. The 'urgent fire' rate was used when the weapon was first revealed, 10–12 rounds a minute for two minutes. The rate normally used in long-range fire was two rounds per minute.[35]

A US study of which weapons inflicted casualties on their own troops in Papua from November 1942 to January 1943 found that 38 per cent of all casualties were to shrapnel, but this included grenades and light mortars.[36] Another estimate was 33 per cent, but it was not always clear what weapon inflicted a wound, although a blown-off hand or foot was believed to be a clear indicator that artillery was the cause.[37] An Australian surgical team in the Kokoda campaign reported that there were generally two kinds of wounds: gunshot wounds and fragments of shells, grenades and mortars, and that the latter was the larger class.[38] In two instances in the Kokoda campaign there is sufficient evidence to calculate the proportion of casualties inflicted by the Japanese artillery

Photo 18 A captured Type 41 75mm mountain gun. Assembled, the gun weighed 540 kilograms. (AWM 057968)

as against fire from other weapons. At Efogi, 2/27th Battalion was under fire from Japanese artillery and attacked by 3/144th Battalion over three days from 6 September 1942. The 2/27th had 38 casualties, and between 16 and 19 of them were from Japanese artillery fire.[39] It was at its worst on 7 September when between seven and ten men of C Company were hit and the company's position was 'rendered untenable by mountain gun fire'. The next day 'the whole battalion was deluged with HMG, mortar and mountain gun fire'.[40]

A second example was Ioribawa where the Australians were under the heaviest bombardment until Oivi. One of the nine Japanese guns fired 160 rounds, but it is not known how many the others fired.[41] In addition to one killed and seven wounded among 21st Brigade headquarters by a combined artillery, medium machine-gun and knee-mortar barrage, the composite battalion lost six killed and 11 wounded in a short period to artillery fire alone, more than half the losses of the battalion at Ioribaiwa.[42] Private Eric Williams was present: 'Unfortunately these blokes had their head against this tree and I suppose the Japs must have seen us from over there and the next thing we knew was this mountain gun was fired and exploded in this tree just above our head. And it killed the three blokes with their head on the tree, because the percussion went straight down, split their skulls open ... I could see they were dead.'[43]

Japanese artillery played an important, perhaps decisive, role on the battlefields of the Kokoda Track. Except for a few days after Ioribaiwa, when two Australian 25lb field guns fired from Owers' Corner at the Japanese holding Ioribaiwa Ridge, the Australians had no artillery support. It was contrary to doctrine for infantry to fight without artillery, but the Australians had none of a type that could be carried into the Owen Stanley Range. Australian light mortars and Brens could not touch the Japanese artillery beyond a thousand metres and, before the arrival of numbers of 3-inch mortars, with three times the range and three times the explosive power, the Australians had nothing with which to counter Japanese artillery.

Carl von Clausewitz made two observations about artillery that are relevant to the Kokoda campaign. He said that there is a correct proportion of artillery for every campaign and that too much will become a logistical inconvenience.[44] The artillery the Nankai Shitai brought into the mountains certainly imposed a huge burden upon it, but it was probably justified. Clausewitz's second point, taken to heart by the Australians after the Kokoda campaign at Buna, Gona and Sanananda, was that artillery is the one arm an army can least do without.

CHAPTER 13

MALARIA AND DYSENTERY

Hans Zissner has written that epidemics get the blame for defeat while generals get the credit for victory.[1] The final defeat of the Nankai Shitai in Papua in January 1943 can in large part be blamed on sickness. Before this, during the Kokoda campaign, it was the Australians who suffered more from illness than did the Japanese. By the Japanese retreat after Ioribaiwa, at the end of September 1942, the Australians had evacuated 1752 sick from the front line while the Japanese had lost only 343, and this disparity no doubt contributed to the Australian defeats in August and September. The main problem for the Australians was dysentery; for the Japanese it was malaria. In the second half of the mountain campaign, sickness among the Japanese began to rise, exacerbated by the supply crisis, but it was not until mid-November, as the Kokoda campaign concluded, that Japanese medical problems became as bad as those of the Australians.

The Kokoda myth has it in reverse – that on the Kokoda Track Japanese medical casualties were much worse than those of the Australians and that even in early September the condition of the Japanese troops was 'rapidly deteriorating'.[2] The origin of this error may be an Australian Army report from the first few days of October 1942. As the Australians advanced they found Japanese dead on the track, somewhere between Ioribaiwa and Nauro. The corpses were reported to have no discernible wounds, and it is implied that illness, not starvation, was the cause of death.[3] From this time there appeared in Australian reports frequent mention of Japanese debilitation due to disease. The view that Japanese losses to illness were enormous, even in the early stages of the campaign, was given a boost after the war with the translation of Okada Siezo's eye-witness account of the trials of the Nankai Shitai. The ever-sensational journalism of Okada suggested there had been ten times the actual num-ber of Japanese medical casualties up to the latter half of September 1942 and that four-fifths of the Japanese force on the Kokoda Track was by then ineffective owing to illness and wounds.[4] Okada's account is a staple of the Kokoda myth, but it is unreliable and exaggerated.

Sickness will increase in all armies as soon as they leave their barracks. In healthy environments the decline is slow, but New Guinea was not a healthy environment. As soon as thousands of soldiers are camped in close proximity in a tropical climate disease prevention becomes a major con-sideration. The Australian 49th Battalion, for instance, in garrison in Port Moresby, supposedly one of the healthier places in Papua, usually had more than a hundred men in hospital at any time.[5] An Australian medical officer thought three months in New Guinea brought about a noticeable decrease in effectiveness in a unit even if it was not engaged with the enemy, and by six months the unit would be worn down to uselessness by the health hazards of the environment. US studies of Guadalcanal came to the same conclusion, and a 1943 Japanese investigation of the Papuan campaign concurred, stating that after three months there troops were only fit for static defence.[6] Critics of Allied command, who argue that more Australian Imperial Force infantry could easily have been sent to New Guinea earlier in 1942, forget that maintaining the health of the troops was a good reason to hold them back as long as possible.

If the health of both armies rapidly deteriorated in New Guinea the question becomes which army dealt with this best and became disabled the slowest, but before looking at medical records, something should be said about malaria and dysentery. The Japanese base at Giruwa was a hyperen-demic malarial area. The Australian base, Port Moresby, was malarial but to a lesser degree.[7] Half the Nankai Shitai line of communications, from Giruwa to Kokoda, was malarial but, owing to a thinner population, it was not as bad as at Giruwa. Malaria is predominantly a human disease, dependent on a population of infected human hosts. Consequently, low population densities inhibit the spread of the disease and troops suffer far more in heavily populated areas. The second necessary factor is the female anopheles mosquito, which bites an infected human, becoming the primary host of the parasite and the vector for transmission of the disease to the uninfected. Anopheles mosquitoes usually bite at night so a soldier taking maximum precautions might live in a hyperendemic area for many months without contracting the disease.

Once malaria is contracted, if it is not cured and provided it is not the potentially fatal falciparum version, then recurrent attacks can occur from two to six months apart for many years.[8] The members of the Nankai Shitai, most of whom had had malaria before in China, Indo-China, the Philippines or Rabaul, used a high dose of quinine and had no problem until supplies ran out. Milne Bay, where the Australians had 5000 cases of malaria in 1942, is at sea level in a populated area and few anti-malarial precautions were taken. In contrast the Kokoda campaign was largely fought above a thousand metres, where malaria was then absent. It is no surprise that of a party of 14 men of the Australian 2/27th Battalion, lost in the mountains for a month without quinine, none caught malaria.

Dysentery is a bacterial disease. It is necessary to swallow the micro-organism to contract it. Oro-faecal contamination occurs most commonly when contaminated food is eaten or water drunk or the bacteria is picked up on the hand, which then touches the mouth. Healthy troops moving into an area after others have contaminated it can quickly become infected. This occurred to the Japanese as they advanced south to Ioribaiwa and to the Australians as they later advanced north to Eora Creek. A Japanese post-campaign analysis reported: 'Dysentery was a major problem in a country where very heavy rain washed infection into the myriad of streams which intersected the broken terrain … as a waterborne disease it was almost impossible to control.'[9]

Many benefits accrue to a regular army with much practical experience of war. One of these is an understanding of the importance of maintaining a high standard of hygiene discipline lest the army wither away. The Japanese had this approach, as did the Australians in the Middle East, where malaria and dysentery had been encountered and defeated. There is a general impression that the Japanese were not prepared for war in the tropics, but this is doubtful. The Japanese medical services had been admired by Western specialists since the Russo-Japanese war, and in ten years in China the Japanese had fielded large armies and dealt with both malaria and dysentery. When 11th Division returned to Japan from Shanghai in 1938, 500 men came down with malaria, and in 1940 it was estimated that 47 per cent of the men returning from Korea were malaria carriers – but only 7 per cent showed symptoms owing to a regimen of prophylactics.[10] Realising that they would encounter similar problems in the south-west Pacific, the IJA established a new medical branch at their school of tropical research in Formosa in 1940, and some of the students and teaching staff served in the Nankai Shitai.[11] The equivalent Australian Army Medical Research Unit was not established until 1943.[12]

Members of the Nankai Shitai were inoculated for cholera, plague and typhus.[13] A post-campaign Australian study of the IJA noted, 'No army has ever been as frequently and diversely inoculated as the Japanese are today.'[14] Smallpox, typhoid, plague, cholera, food poisoning and dysentery were routinely inoculated against, although there was doubt as to the efficacy of the last two. Refresher doses were given at 'astonishingly short intervals by our standards':

> Laboratory work in the field on infectious diseases is carried out
> by the hygiene and water purifying units – they are equipped to
> carry out pathological and bacteriological work. They used animals
> for experimental work ... It would appear the Japanese are keen
> pathologists and a great deal of work is done ... blood is examined
> for malarial parasites ... this was frequently, if not regularly
> performed on whole units with a view to determining the number of
> infected men ... Amoebic dysentery was diagnosed by culture when
> at all possible.

Another indicator that the Nankai Shitai was initially better prepared for medical problems than the Australians is the numbers of medical personnel each had. For the Nankai Shitai in August 1942 it was 6 per cent; for the Australians it was less than 4 per cent early in the campaign and 5 per cent later.[15] Among the Japanese medical units were specialists not found in the Australian force. The 230 Japanese in water purification and hygiene units were tasked with the prevention of dysentery and other waterborne diseases. In contrast, when Colonel Frank Kingsley Norris, senior medical officer of the Australian 7th Division, arrived in Port Moresby in August 1942 he was surprised to find that he had no specialist hygiene personnel at all in Papua.[16]

Australian medical reports written after the Japanese were evicted from Papua did not make a distinction between conditions in the mountains during the Kokoda phase of the fighting and those on the coast at Buna–Gona in January 1943. One study said Japanese losses to malaria were high because the Buna area is hyperendemic and that the advance into the Owen Stanley Range was made with infected men.[17] This is not quite right. It takes a lot of mosquito bites at night to stand a good chance of contracting malaria, because malaria-carrying mosquitoes are rare among mosquitoes in general. Most Japanese who fought in the mountains spent a very short time on the coast, usually disembarking at Giruwa and marching off within a few hours and entering the mountains within a week. They would have been very unlucky to contract malaria in such a short period.[18]

What the Australian report ignored is that half of the Japanese had spent six months in hyperendemic Rabaul. The rest had most likely had malaria during the earlier southern China, Malaya and Philippine campaigns. Almost all had already had one bout of malaria, in some cases many more, and were taking anti-malaria medicine. Sometimes this cures malaria, and sometimes it suppresses it. Few long-service veterans of the IJA would never have had malaria, and all the members of Colonel Yazawa's 41st Regiment, according to him, had had it before.[19] When atebrin and quinine, in common with other supplies, stopped arriving at the front line in mid-September as a result of the supply crisis, men whose malaria was suppressed relapsed. One 144th Regiment soldier said there was no malaria at all until the quinine stopped arriving.[20] A large number of Japanese did die from cerebral malaria, but this occurred in December 1942 and January 1943 during the Battle of Buna–Gona.

The Australian report went on to say that 'widespread bacilliary dysentery ... swept though their force'.[21] Again, this is true, but it did not begin until towards the end of the Japanese advance in the mountains when the Japanese took the ground where the Australians were suffering a dysentery outbreak of epidemic proportions. This can be traced to dysentery among carriers at Ioribaiwa in July. As all Australian troops had to pass by on the way to the front or the rear, dysentery spread up and down the track from Ioribaiwa, arriving at Isurava as the fighting there ended.

Japanese casualties to all causes in Papua to 31 July 1942 were 110, of which 30 were sick. Lieutenant Hirano, who usually noted his company's health in his diary, wrote on 16 August that 'a few cases of diarrhoea and malaria have broken out', but there was no general problem and no general concern about the troops' health until September.[22] Even then, at Ioribaiwa at the end of September, 3/144th Battalion reported only 17 medical evacuations so far.[23] Evacuation from Giruwa to Rabaul of the seriously ill did not occur until 17 September when 124 patients left.[24] The Japanese arrangements for evacuation of medical cases were similar to those of the Australians. The general hospital 67 LOCH arrived with the main force at Giruwa. It then split into two parts, one staying in place and one going to Kokoda, where it was operational on 1 September.

Table 13.1: Nankai Shitai sick and wounded, September 1942

Unit	Sick	Wounded
55th Engineer Regiment	1	4
144th Regiment	76	219
15th Independent Engineer Regiment	72	1
15th Naval Pioneers	50	2
120th Land Duty Company	25	0
106th Land Duty Company	38	1
41st Regiment	23	41
9th Division Bridge Construction Company	8	0
24th Water Purification Unit	1	0
55th Transport Regiment	2	0
47th Anti Aircraft Artillery	8	0
55th Division Medical Unit (67 LOC)	3	0
55th Division Field Hospital	12	0
7th Independent Wireless Platoon	3	0
8th Independent Telegraph Company	1	1
Seventeenth Army headquarters	2	0
5th Shipping Engineer Regiment	3	0
Emergency Transport Company	5	1
55th Division Water Purification	4	0
55th Division Infantry Group HQ	2	1
45th Fixed Radio Unit	1	0
55th Mountain Artillery Regiment	2	0
2nd Independent Mountain Artillery Regiment	0	1
40th Sea Duty Company	5	0
Subtotal	347	273
Total	620	

Note: includes all Nankai Shitai casualties except outpatients and patients of a civilian hospital run by Umeda Tai for Korean, Taiwanese and other civilians.
Source: Records of 67 LOCH, enemy publications no. 24, pp. 32 and 62, AWM55 5/2.

In advance of 67 LOCH was a casualty clearing station run by 55th Division's field hospital.[25] This unit set up in various locations as far forward as Nauro.[26] Forward of this was the PCB, a field ambulance. The total number of Japanese sick and wounded these units recorded for September is given in table 13.1.

Note that this is the number collected for treatment through the month, not the number in the hospital at month's end. Also the figures are for the whole of the Nankai Shitai, not just the force that went into the mountains; hence the number sick is comparable to New Guinea Force figures but not to the Australians on the Kokoda Track – Maroubra Force. To obtain a correct comparison with Maroubra Force men evacuated from the mountains, 93 Japanese cases, from units that never went beyond the Kumusi River, should be deducted. This leaves 227 evacuated sick from the Nankai Shitai on the Kokoda Track by the end of September. This was about 6 per cent of the force and a small fraction of Maroubra Force losses to sickness in the same month.

For the Australians on the Kokoda Track dysentery was by far the major problem. The precise number of medical evacuations from Maroubra Force before the arrival of 2/4th Field Ambulance and 14th Field Ambulance is difficult to come by. An incomplete report gives 74 evacuated sick from 29 July to 29 August.[27] The 39th Battalion war diary on 26 August recorded: 'Bn [was] greatly weakened by dysentery, malaria and lack of food, sleep and shelter.'[28] Dysentery struck Maroubra Force at the end of August, and from the beginning of September 50 to 80 men a day were evacuated and the total was either 493 or 530 by 12 September.[29] At one point in September 80 men per day had passed though the 2/6th Field Ambulance post at Ilola. Captain Lionel Joseph was there and recorded 1200 men evacuated (sick and wounded) through the post, 'mostly with dysentery', in the first three weeks of September.[30] Another report gave 883 sick for the period 6 August to 19 September. As the average strength of Maroubra Force was 2000 then, one man in 30 was being evacuated each day. On 4 September 33 men from 2/16th Battalion were sent away sick, and 2/25th Battalion lost 92 sick and 14 battle casualties in 21 days from 26 September.[31] After 38 days in the Owen Stanley Range 25th Brigade had lost 771 sick to 203 battle casualties, a platoon a day from the brigade's fighting strength.[32]

The cause of the epidemic was investigated and found to be poor field hygiene resulting in fouled ground.[33] Captain John Oldham of 2/6th Field Ambulance thought field hygiene was 'amazingly bad for a two year old army'. Elementary hygiene precautions were ignored: inefficient latrines, poor garbage disposal and unboiled water. Oldham concluded: 'The hygiene of the march and campaign was generally a disgrace for a modern army and dysentery figures support this remark.'[34] Vernon saw that 'the whole length of track from Ioribawia to Uberi is seriously fouled and undoubtedly a dysentery focus. During the retreat in darkness the

Table 13.2: Stanley Shitai, current casualties, all causes, 3 October 1942

Unit	Size	Malaria	Stomach	Beriberi	Wounds	Other	Total
2/144 HQ	66	5	2	8	0	0	15
1/144, 2 Coy	85	19	16	1	0	2	38
2/144, 4 Coy	86	5	0	4	0	0	9
2/144, 5 Coy	46	5	2	3	0	4	14
2/144, 6 Coy	5	8	4	12	0	5	29
1 MG Coy	18	0	0	0	0	0	0
2 MG Coy	91	4	14	4	0	11	33
1 BIA*	26	5	2	7	0	3	17
2 BIA	55	1	2	6	0	0	9
ITL*	28	6	2	6	0	0	14
Unknown	25	20	0	0	5	0	25
BA*	107	8	2	4	2	1	17
P*	120	29	9	30	0	15	83
S*	179	11	0	5	0	0	16
Total	937	126	55	90	7	41	319

*The meaning of these initials in the original Japanese record is not clear.
Source: ATIS bulletin no. 24, p. 7, AWM55 1/1.

men were compelled to relieve themselves anywhere and the whole route literally stank. By this means the dysentery which had established itself at Ioribaiwa was spread ...'[35]

The total Australian medical evacuations from Maroubra Force from the start of the campaign to the end of September was about 1752 against about 343 Japanese.[36] On both sides sick expected to recover soon were not evacuated, but there is little doubt the Japanese number should be higher as more Japanese were held longer in forward areas before evacuation, as is evident in a record of the Stanley Detachment, the foremost unit of the Nankai Shitai in early October.

The sick from the Stanley Detachment, almost a third of the force, were evacuated over the next few days. The Australians were losing about 35 a day in the first week of October so, even if all 312 sick in table 13.2 were added to the end of September numbers, the Japanese evacuated sick figure was still a third of the Australian figure by the end of the first week in October 1942. The Stanley Detachment suffered greatly from starvation, as chapter 14 shows, but there is less overlap between starvation and illness than may be imagined. Malaria and dysentery are no more likely to be contracted while starving, although the chance of survival is decreased and the length of recovery time is increased.

The effect of the dysentery epidemic on Australian fighting power can be imagined when it is seen that in the month from Isurava to Ioribaiwa 2/14th Battalion had 243 battle casualties and 210 sick while 2/16th had 163 battle casualties and 284 sick. By comparison the Japanese 3/144th Battalion had 145 medical evacuees (to the end of October) after spending twice as much time in the mountains as the 2/14th and 2/16th. In October, during the Second Eora action, the numbers of sick on both sides began to draw closer together. After the extremes of September the Australian rate of medical evacuations settled to about 35 per day. By 31 October the Australians and the Japanese had evacuated from the front line for medical reasons approximately 2800 and 1400 respectively.[37] The Japanese decline became marked when a one-month supply of medical requirements that arrived on the *Yamaura Maru* on 3 October was consumed and some time passed before it was replaced.[38] As a consequence the end of October Japanese daily evacuations jumped to 90 a day, and by 16 November, after the Kokoda campaign concluded with the battle of Oivi–Gorari, both sides had evacuated about 3500 sick men.[39]

These numbers make it hard to sustain the Kokoda myth that illness was a major cause of the Japanese defeat in the fighting in the Owen Stanley Range. On the contrary, it probably made an important contribution to the Australian defeats up to and including Ioribaiwa. Only in December, during the battle of Buna–Gona, does the myth begin to correspond to the reality. By 27 December 1942 Australian medical casualty evacuations from the Kokoda Track and the beachhead battles totalled about 4860 whereas Japanese losses in the same category exceeded 6000.[40]

CHAPTER 14

THE JAPANESE
SUPPLY CRISIS

According to the Kokoda myth, the Japanese turned back at Ioribaiwa because they ran out of food, and for the remainder of the Kokoda campaign they were starving. The myth explains that the Japanese did not bring enough food with them as they intended a rapid advance to Port Moresby. When the advance was slowed by Australian resistance they went hungry. We have already seen that this is incorrect. Enough food was brought to Papua where a regular, although less than generous, supply system was put in place, and the plan for a rapid advance to take Port Moresby was abandoned at Isurava. There was, however, a Japanese supply crisis that began in mid-September and was at its height during the battle of Second Eora. It had little to do with supposedly inadequate preparation, lasted for less than six weeks before the problem was solved and was catastrophic for only a small portion of the Nankai Shitai: the Stanley Detachment, fewer than a thousand men of the 15 000-strong force. What happened to the Stanley Detachment has been thought to apply to the whole of the Nankai Shitai, or at least to the part of it that went south past Kokoda. A typical example appears in Ham's *Kokoda*: 'Captured diaries and documents dated towards the end of September portray an army slowly starving to death.'[1]

The cause of the supply crisis was flooding along the supply line, and when the water receded supply resumed. On average 277.5mm of rain falls each September in the Kokoda–Buna region, and over the past hundred years it has varied from 440.1mm to 124.7mm in that month.[2] The rainfall charts the Japanese brought to Papua showed that rainfall increased after August to an average of 27 days of rain in September, 25 in October and 27 in November.[3] Unfortunately for the Japanese, September 1942 was a month with exceptionally high rainfall. It cannot be known how much rain fell as the rainfall gauges were not manned in the areas the Japanese held, but both armies saw it as an usually wet month, and the Papua New Guinea Bureau of Meteorology has estimated that 400mm of rain fell into the tributaries of the Kumusi River, the major river on the route between Kokoda and the north coast, in September 1942, causing massive flooding.[4] It was not unprecedented. In 1905 all bridges from Kokoda to the north coast were destroyed and 5 kilometres of track disappeared; in 1922 the entire Sanananda–Kokoda track was washed away; and in 1925, 33 kilometres of track was 'obliterated'.[5] Something similar occurred in September 1942, and in 2007 it happened again. The rain tends to fall heavily for several days, then there will be light rain or no rain for a period. The transition from low to high water is accomplished in moments as a wall of wild water arrives, sweeping everything before it. The day after the rain ends the Kumusi is typically calmer, and within several days it will be fordable again. When the Kumusi is high it is also wider, 120 metres when unfordable and about 60 metres when fordable. Over the period of the Kokoda campaign the Kumusi was fordable, on and off, about half of the time.

Heavy rain fell from 9 to 13 September 1942 and swept away the Japanese supply system from Kokoda to the north coast.[6] On this route today there are 17 large bridges, about the same number of bridging tasks that were presented to the Nankai Shitai when they arrived in July. In addition there were dozens of smaller bridges across streams easily fordable at low water but small torrents when it rained. The September flood destroyed the Kumusi bridges, the three bridges to the west between Ilimo and Oivi, which was the watershed between the west-flowing Mambare and the north-east-flowing Kumusi, and all bridges east to the sea.[7] On the coast at Giruwa it was reported that 'heavy rains fell in the mountains [and] the Giruwa River overflowed'.[8] The banks of streams and rivers were inundated, sweeping away the Kokoda–Giruwa track as far as Oivi and leaving a lake of mud a hundred kilometres long. For two weeks, from Giruwa to Oivi, there was very little military movement of any kind, and the supply line ceased to function. It was this natural disaster that was the cause of Japanese supply problems, not their own shortcomings. Japanese engineers thought that two weeks was required to rebuild just the main bridges.[9] By and large this was achieved, the supply system began to function again and the AAF Intelligence summary, drawing on aerial observation of Japanese activity, noted with admiration that the Japanese rate of bridge construction was unequalled.[10]

Lesser floods occurred twice again up to November. A 41st Regiment report stated simply that 'when the Papaki [Wairopi] bridge floods, supply stops'.[11] An artilleryman wrote that, with the bridges washed out, 'we can't get provisions through so they must be dropped by aeroplanes'.[12] The first Japanese airdrop of supplies took place at Kokoda on 23 September. On 15 October, during one of the periods the river was in flood due to rain, Horii recorded:

the quality of Shitai supplies will depend entirely on the equipment available for crossing the river … the Shitai will improve the equipment for … river crossing. The Yokoyama Independent Engineer Regiment will, according to requirements, strengthen the personnel employed at the [Kumusi] river crossing, and apart from ropes and boats for crossing the river, separate provisions will be made in case the above equipment is damaged. [They] will prepare river crossings by bridges and fords in wide areas both upstream and downstream [of Wairopi]. Colonel Yokoyama … will be situated in the vicinity of Papaki to encourage the foregoing arrangements.[13]

The IJA's 1943 report *Lessons from Operations*, written by engineers who had served in Papua, stressed that rain was the major factor in halting supply and movement. It recommended that in future similar operations twice the proportion of engineers would be needed to maintain any similar line of communications. The general problem of fast-rising rivers was enlarged upon:

Estimation of width and velocity of a river is apt to be inaccurate [and] precautions must be taken with rivers which flow out from a mountain range. Such rivers cannot be crossed except by cable … As the rivers shown on aerial photographs were narrow it was estimated that they would be easily crossed. However, the mountainous areas have steep inclines and … the velocity of the stream is surprisingly great. In the future it is necessary for the engineers to make a study of the method of crossing rivers with very rapid currents.[14]

What was the effect of the flood? In a rapid advance on foot and without motor transport, no supply system can keep up with the forward troops.[15] After Isurava the element of the Nankai Shitai that had the task of seizing a location forward of the mountain range crest advanced 80 kilometres in 11 days. Seven kilometres a day was fast going for a body of troops in inhospitable terrain while fighting their way forward. It was too fast for supplies coming up from the rear to keep up, but when the Nankai Shitai halted on Ioribaiwa Ridge in mid-September, supplies could be expected to catch up, but they did not. Food ran out in the front line ten days after the bridges were washed away, but would not have lasted even this long but for supplies captured from the Australians. The Japanese overran supply dumps at Alola, Eora, Templeton's, Myola, Kagi, Efogi, Brigade Hill, Menari and Nauro. Australian reports greatly underestimate the amount of food captured.

CAPTURED FOOD

After Isurava the first Japanese unit to come upon the Australia dump at Alola was the 2/41st. 'We captured unexpectedly a great amount of ammunition and food (hardtack biscuit and canned food) and some clothes. They were indeed a gift from heaven ... We had as much food as we could possibly carry. The supply of food was so abundant that our regiment could not carry it all and the rest was handed to the main force ... Everyone was as excited as a child with their gorgeous breakfast of hardtack and butter.'[16] At Alola the Australians had seven days' reserve of food for 2000 soldiers and 80 carriers. The Australian 21st Brigade report stated, 'Time and circumstances did not permit destruction of stocks to any great extent', but goes on to say that the estimated loss was only 2000 rations, which could be a considerable underestimate.[17]

The next occasion when the Japanese captured food was at Eora Creek: 'It is impossible ... to state with any accuracy the amount of stores destroyed but it is estimated that approximately 1000 unbalanced rations were not destroyed.'[18] The Japanese disagree and claim that two and a half tons of food was taken here.[19] At the Australian supply dump at Templeton's Crossing on 24 August there was one and a third tons of food. The 21 Brigade report said, '... once again it is impossible to accurately estimate quantity of stocks destroyed however all ration stocks not evacuated were completely destroyed.'[20] This is untrue. What destruction was achieved was done by 70 carriers in 90 minutes before the Australians retreated. Most of the food was rice or tinned beef, and fires were not used for fear of advertising the location to Japanese artillery. The normal system was to scatter the rice and puncture the tins. This was probably not completely effective as the Japanese arrived half an hour after the Australians left.

Photo 19 Japanese engineers repairing a bridge. During the Kokoda campaign more than 2300 combat trained engineers maintained the supply line of the Nankai Shitai. (Asahi Graph)

The airdrop zone at Myola, the major source of Australian supply, was the next place taken by the Japanese.[21] 'No carriers were available for evacuating supplies from Myola ... consequently stocks on hand at Myola had to be prepared for immediate destruction.' The claim was that 10 000 rations were destroyed by the time Myola was evacuated at 7 a.m. on 5 September.[22] The interesting thing at Myola is that at least 110 000 rations were airdropped there by the Australians, and the fact that a third of the quantity was mistakenly dropped into the jungle around Myola was the subject of acrimonious signals at the time between New Guinea Force and Potts.[23] Almost none was recovered by the Australians, who lacked spare carriers or troops to go looking for it. The Japanese held Myola for a month, and the 1/144th was camped there. The Japanese battalion scoured the jungle and collected many thousands of rations, enough to convince Australian aircrew who overflew Myola that the Japanese were building a supply dump there.[24] On the same day the Australians abandoned Myola an order was given to evacuate Efogi dump. A few days notice was enough, and all stocks in the Efogi–Kagi area should have been moved or destroyed. Some was moved, but not all, as the Allied air strike of 6 September hit 144th Regiment as they were assembled for the distribution of captured Australian food.[25]

The sudden defeat of the Australians at Efogi meant no rations from their dump could be withdrawn: 'Owing to darkness and confusion ... many native bearers left without being loaded ... circumstances did not permit the destruction of ration stocks ... [and] 1500 rations were left.'[26] At Menari there was no demolition or firing of dumps and 3000 rations were left there and another thousand at Nauro. Vernon saw 'quantities of tobacco, chocolate, boots and clothing dropped from the air spread out in the village square for anyone to take'.[27] At the last Australian dump captured by the Japanese at Ioribaiwa it is unclear whether any food was obtained.

The amount of Australian food captured must have been significant as, advancing faster than their resupply, the foremost Japanese had only the 15 or 20 days food they carried. For the Nankai Shitai main body, which landed on 19 August, this can hardly have lasted past the first week of September. Perhaps it did not last even that long as carelessness, pilfering and wastage were serious problems. A 41st Regiment veteran said, 'To tell you the truth, old soldiers like us learned from experience, I think we carried only half of the food ... that we were supposed to bring ... but it was still heavy. We believed if we win like in China, the Philippines, and Malaya, we can have the enemy's food.'[28] It is hard to say how much of this went on. In an effort to avoid it officers were told to inspect their men to ensure that they carried all they were issued with.[29]

An order of 28 August tried to limit wastage: '... while on the march, some stragglers have thrown away ammunition [and] used clean rice in excess of their ration ... In view of the special nature of the present operation, in which replenishment of munitions and provisions is extremely difficult, those of all ranks who hold authority must exercise the greatest caution, control and supervision.'[30] Another report stated that large amounts of half-cooked rice were left by the side of the track to Kokoda. There was also pilfering: 'Last August 13th while a boat was being unloaded at Basabua, about 60 cases of beer disappeared and no one knows where. A box of condensed milk was guarded but disappeared at night. It was for the hospital patients. There are among soldiers some who are not worthy of the name.'[31] A report of 6 October noted that bags had food removed from them by the time they arrived at the front line and boxes had bayonet holes punched in them. Food was stolen and some was spoiled. Of 33 tins of beef five still contained it; the rest were filled with stones.[32]

The Australians estimated that 8500 rations were abandoned to the enemy and another 39 500 were destroyed, but this seems overoptimistic and possibly as much as 10 per cent of all food carried or flown into the mountains by the Australians up to mid-September, about 11 tons, fell into Japanese hands.[33] It appears likely that what food the Japanese ate for a period before 20 September, perhaps 10 or 15 days depending on the level of wastage and pilfering, was substantially Australian.[34]

THE EFFECT OF THE SUPPLY CRISIS

When the news reached Horii on 10 September that the supply line had been washed away it was apparent that a halt to allow supplies to catch up would not suffice and some time must pass before the supply line was re-established. Meanwhile the Nankai Shitai would have to rely on supplies already forward of the flood at Kokoda. Some food was still en route from Kokoda to the front line, but it was not enough, and the following day Horii ordered 1050 personnel to go back to the nearest dump and return with food.[35] While they were away the ration was reduced to two then one *go* (140 grams) of rice per day, and foraging parties were sent out to collect 'an abundance of potatoes' north of Ioribaiwa.[36] Food was less easily found in the Owen Stanley Range than in the lowlands, but it was not negligible there. Even after the Japanese had scoured the mountains for a month, on 8 October during the Australian advance, the Australian 2/25th Battalion 'augmented [rations] by food from native gardens and wild pigs'.[37]

The 1050 Japanese arrived at the new dump at Isurava to find it empty and had to proceed to Kokoda where each was loaded with 20 kilograms, 90 per cent of which was rice.[38] Their return to the front lines with 21 tons of food coincided with an urgent request for an airdrop of food at Kokoda, although the dump there was not yet empty. Four days later, on 22 September, 9th Company of the 3/144th was given the task of picking up 20 days food per man from Kokoda and taking it forward to a new dump at Eora village.[39] Bad weather delayed the airdrop for several days, but on 23 September eight medium bombers dropped 10 tons of food near Kokoda.

The front-line troops ran entirely out of food at Ioribaiwa on 20 September. On that day a medic wrote in his diary 'had no meals today', and it seems to have been the first time this occurred.[40] The next day the 1050 men returned: '21 September. Long awaited rice for two days was issued, 2 go of rice with miso and soy bean sauce. Though ration is only 1 go a day life is tenacious.' This diarist mentioned food again the next day when a day's ration of dried bread was issued. On 25 September two days' rations were issued, one pack of dried bread and 7 shaku (100 grams) of rice.[41]

Four days after the front line ran out of food, the Japanese withdrew from Ioribaiwa. From this time it is necessary to consider the supply problem of each of the three groups into which the Nankai Shitai was now divided. The 986 men who became the Stanley Detachment withdrew only as far as Templeton's Crossing and stayed there until the Japanese defeat at Second Eora at the end of October. For five weeks from 20 September they had little food, none on some days. Depending on their access to food, various units rationed rice at 3 go, 2 go or 1 go.[42]

Second, there was the main body of the force in the mountains, which immediately retreated to the Kokoda–Kumusi area. They began to leave on 16 September, four days before food ran out at the front line, and they never ran out of food themselves. The men of the Japanese 41st Regiment, at Nauro when the withdrawal began, took 18 go (2.52 kilograms) of rice each from a dump there when they left.[43] This dump did not exist earlier when the 1050 men went back looking for food as the supplies in it were those brought forward from the airdrop at Kokoda, which had occurred a week after they were there. As other units retreated through Eora they found a 'considerable quantity' of rice, also from the airdrop.[44] A medical officer based at Eora wrote that rations were 4 go per day in mid-September, although he was expecting it to be cut to 3 go.[45] Over the period of the supply crisis the second group always had at least half a ration. The third group was the remaining two-thirds of the Nankai Shitai, 10 000 men who had always remained north of the mountains. Some experienced two-thirds or half rations for several weeks; others had no food shortage at all.

Only the first of these three groups, the Stanley Detachment, experienced all the terrible privation recorded in the Kokoda myth, a debilitating and sometimes fatal food shortage usually credited to the Nankai

Shitai as a whole. Some died of starvation, some resorted to cannibalism. The emaciated, dead or near-dead Japanese overtaken by the Australians during the advance from Ioribaiwa to Eora were widely publicized in Australia. The *Argus* in Melbourne reported that Japanese bodies found on Ioribaiwa Ridge 'were gaunt and thin, these men were hungry when they died'.[46] The *West Australian* newspaper's special correspondent wrote on 8 October that the Japanese diaries, with their unburied bodies, were found between Ioribaiwa and Nauro and that 'Diaries are one of the possessions that soldiers cling to longest'.[47]

We know so much about these men because, as they fell behind, died of hunger or were killed in battle, their dairies were captured and translated by Australians eager for military intelligence. The stories of cannibalism and starvation, which it was assumed affected the whole of the Nankai Shitai, were then passed to reporters and comforted the Australian public eager for news of the enemy in distress. After the war this version of events was incorporated into the Kokoda myth, which requires a selective use of sources to sustain itself. For example, in accord with the myth was a 7th Division report that said the majority of the Japanese killed on the night of 28/29 October were thin and carried no food except for a small amount of fish paste. But there is plenty of other evidence that does not fit the myth so well. One Australian patrol who must have heard the story that the Japanese had no food were at pains to point out that 'Jap killed by 2/33rd Battalion did NOT appear starved or exhausted'.[48] Lieutenant-Colonel Dice, who from his location can only be describing the original Stanley Detachment, which held positions south of Templeton's Crossing on both the main and Kagi tracks, recorded: 'Japanese troops encountered along Kagi and Myola tracks forward of Templeton's Crossing appeared fresh and well equipped, with plentiful supplies of food.'[49] No doubt the majority of the Stanley Detachment (not the Nankai Shitai) was starving but, inconveniently for the Kokoda myth, some were not.

The original Stanley Detachment was reinforced during the Second Eora action by troops who brought ten days rations with them. These men, who had rested between Kokoda and Oivi for several weeks and were returning to the front, or had never been as far forward as Ioribaiwa, had not run out of food. While resting they had been on a two-thirds ration as they waited for the flood to recede. Koiwai's battalion, for instance, returned from Nauro to Oivi on 4 October. There 'the battalion, was spending very careless days. As we had retreated this far the transport of provisions seemed to be working effectively and we could eat almost four *go* [560 grams] of rice a day and sometimes even canned fish was delivered to us ... there was no shortage of cigarettes ... we were leading an easy life.'[50]

For the third group, the bulk of the Nankai Shitai, which never went past Kokoda, the supply problem was even less. Some were never reduced from the standard 6 *go* ration, none east of the Kumusi complained about any shortage at all until late September and it was 9 October before the several thousand civilian labourers at Giruwa found it essential to forage for food to supplement rations. Apart from a brief period on half rations, the 67th Line of Communication Hospital (67 LOCH) at Giruwa received a two-thirds ration all through October. Hospital staff and patients were given 7000 cigarettes and 21 600 litres of wine.[51] Lieutenant Sawatori Zengoro, from the provisional transport unit that worked between Kokoda and the coast, was captured later in the campaign and told his interrogators that food had been plentiful in his unit until December.[52] On 28 November Private Miyaji Chikara of the infantry gun platoon of the 1/144th also fell into Australian hands. He had been in Papua with his battalion since the very start of the campaign in July. The interrogating officer wrote that 'this prisoner, by his own admission, [was] quite healthy when captured'.[53] One of the reasons the supply problem was never so great north of the Owen Stanley Range is that local supplies were still available. At Kokoda early in November an Australian 2/6th Independent Company officer shot pigs and obtained pawpaw, taro and pineapples, and Dr Vernon dug up potatoes when he arrived there.[54] When 2/4th Field Ambulance was at Kokoda '12 native boys delivered ... loads of sweet potatoes, taros [and] pawpaws'.[55]

By early October, for those not in the Stanley Detachment, the supply crisis was over. The floods had receded and the bridges were rebuilt. Equally important, the road from Sanananda, which had been drivable 40 kilometres to Sambo, was now suitable for trucks as far as the Kumusi River, more than half way to Kokoda. With less requirement for manpower on the supply line Horii agreed to Yazawa's request that those of his 41st Regiment men who were still in the provisional transport unit be returned to their battalions.[56] Several hundred Korean labourers were also taken from supply duties and returned to Giruwa.[57] This reduced the number of men engaged in carrying supplies by almost a thousand, and it was done even though fewer Rabaul carriers and horses were engaged in supply work. Of the 2000 carriers brought from Rabaul 800 were still working for the Japanese. A few had died, the rest had deserted.[58] Of 2360 horses, a quarter was sick or dead but, with a shorter supply line and a longer motor road, fewer men and horses were needed.[59] The supply line from the coast to Kokoda was, with breaks due to rain, working satisfactorily in late October, and even the dump at Isurava began functioning properly just before the Australians captured it. Passing through Isurava with the Australian advance Vernon saw 'cities of accommodation and supply dumps, abandoned gear' and 'ammo left by the road, food, even biscuits very like our own ... dried fish and barrels of a fermented sauce, a first class preventative of beri-beri'.[60]

Entering the Kokoda–Kumusi region in early November the Australians found Japanese dumps still full of food. These dumps at Papaki, Ilimo, Gorari and Oivi had never been empty; rather they had been isolated by the flood for two weeks, and a considerable amount of their contents was ruined by water, but when the flood receded they became accessible once again. The troops sent to Eora Creek to reinforce the Stanley detachment in late October obtained additional food from them to take to the front line. When the Australian 2/25th Battalion entered the area 'captured rice supplemented our depleted rations and helped considerably'. And 'much rice and biscuits had been left by the enemy in what was apparently a large ... dump'. The battalion's end-of-month report added that 'the [supply] position was ... greatly relieved by the use of foods left by the retreating enemy. Rice became the staple diet.'[61] A Japanese taken by 2/2nd Battalion had five days rice on him when captured and said that rice was plentiful, and the battalion historian wrote that the Japanese they encountered at Oivi (from the 41st Regiment) in early November 'had plenty of food'.[62]

The Japanese supply crisis lasted three or four weeks for the majority, longer for the Stanley Detachment, and most were on short rations before this and some for periods afterwards. What effect did the poor diet have on fighting ability? An average sedentary male adult uses around 9000 kilojoules per day.[63] Light activity requires 12 000 and daily heavy work or long marches up to 16 000, which was the Japanese field ration of 1942. The ration was cut to 12 000 at the start of the campaign on the assumption that the remainder would be made up locally. Those of the Nankai Shitai in the lowlands north of the Owen Stanley Range achieved this, but those in the mountains did not. From 11 September the Japanese along the Kokoda Track had their ration cut to about 4000 kilojoules a day, and nine days later many of them had no food at all for varying periods. The Stanley Detachment existed in this manner for at least four weeks, but the other two-thirds of the force in the Owen Stanley Range had returned to rest in the Kokoda–Ilimo area where they were placed on a ration of about 10 000–12 000 kilojoules (4 *go* of rice and tinned fish) and whatever could be obtained locally.

A modern United States Army study found that men on half rations for 30 days, but not doing strenuous work, could still perform their duties and were still capable soldiers, although there was a small slow deterioration over the whole period. An Australian study placed volunteers on half rations and worked them hard for 12 days, and found there were no special problems at the end of this period.[64] Another American study showed that soldiers can perform effectively for ten days on 5000 kilojoules with no loss of performance.[65] The Australian Defence Nutrition Research Centre holds that a soldier can operate effectively, although not at 100 per cent efficiency, for two months on 8000 kilojoules per day. The most extreme example is a British Army nutritionist of the World War I era who believed that well-nourished soldiers with 8 kilograms of fat can stand a fast of 20 to 30 days.[66] The Stanley Detachment of October 1942 cannot be described as well nourished, and these studies have more relevance to the second Japanese group, those who retreated to Kokoda by 4 October, in that the studies show soldiers can still be effective, although not fully, after an extended period on half rations. As the third Japanese group – those always north of the Owen Stanley Range – suffered even less than the second group, it is apparent that the supply crisis was a catastrophic event only for the Stanley Detachment.

The difficulties of the second Japanese group, those who retreated from the mountains leaving behind the Stanley Detachment, might not have been very much worse than the Australian 21st Brigade. When the supplies delivered to Maroubra Force fell as low as 3.5 tons per thousand men per day for several weeks, it was seen as 'hopelessly inadequate'.[67] Another example was 2/27th Battalion after it was forced off the Kokoda Track as a result of the Australian defeat at Efogi. The main body of the battalion existed on very little food, often nothing at all for several days at a time, for 17 days until it regained Australian lines. By then average loss of weight was 12 kilograms, yet only a third required hospital treatment at the end of the ordeal. The 2/27th Battalion history explained that 'apart from the loss of weight, digestive complaints and sores due to scratches on the legs and arms, the men were still fit, though weakened, and their morale was high'.[68] Within 20 days of returning, two-fifths of the men set off into the mountains again as members of Chaforce and Jawforce. A third example was 2/14th Battalion, which engaged in hard fighting and marching while on approximately half rations, or 8000 kilojoules, for five weeks from Isurava. The medical report on the battalion's health at the end of the ordeal said more than two-thirds would be fit for operations within two weeks.[69] Further afield there is a comparison that might be closer to what was experienced over an extended period by the majority of the Nankai Shitai. The 111th Brigade of the Chindits, which operated in Burma in 1944, was poorly supplied throughout their campaign. Over 110 days with a great deal of hard marching they carried out their assignment on an average of 12 000 kilojoules per day.[70] Average weight loss was 15 kilograms.

In early November, when the supply crisis was past, there was still friction in the supply system. There were periods of food shortage, rationing and disorganisation resulting in some units not receiving food for a few days at a time, although it was still possible to find fields of sweet potato and fruit along the banks of the Kumusi.[71] The replacements who arrived on 2 November received 14 days full rations, but on the same day others were reduced to a two-thirds ration and one other unit went without food for several days.[72] Considerable difficulties notwithstanding, the Japanese supply system recovered from crisis and continued to function until a larger supply disaster hit the Nankai Shitai at the end of December while defending the Buna–Gona beachhead.

The death by starvation of a large number of Japanese soldiers in the Buna–Gona area in January 1943 has helped to create the impression that hunger was also an enormous problem in the prior Kokoda campaign. After the Allied victories at Gona, Buna and Sanananda in December 1942 and January 1943, when the enemy lay dead all around them, the Australians might have obtained a more representative sampling of diaries and documents that would have made it clear that the earlier Japanese supply crisis was temporary but, as the enemy had now been destroyed, there was not the same urgency to do so. It is easy to see how the small number of diaries obtained during October from the dead of the Stanley Detachment conveyed the impression that an extremely serious food shortage among the Nankai Shitai was long term, widespread and frequently resulted in starvation or near starvation.

This explanation ties in nicely with another part of the Kokoda myth, which seeks to excuse the series of Australian defeats from July to September 1942 by arguing that the Australians can be credited with starving the Japanese by delaying their advance until they ran out of food. This was not the case. It was, rather, that a sometimes struggling, but adequate supply line in July and August broke down as a result of the flood in September. Had the flood not occurred the supply problem that arose from a rapid advance to Ioribaiwa would have been solved by the arrival of food from the rear.

Photo 20 An Australian officer buying fruit and vegetables near Kokoda in November 1942. That food could still be purchased in an area occupied by the Japanese for five months suggests that the Japanese supply crisis has been overstated. (AWM 013613)

The experience of the great majority of the Nankai Shitai was not that of facing starvation during the Kokoda campaign. Rather there was a long and gradual deterioration in health resulting from, on average, a two-thirds ration over three months that might have had something to do with the unusually poor performance of the Nankai Shitai at the battle of Oivi–Gorari in November. A much smaller group, the original Stanley Detachment, did suffer all the appalling conditions described in the Kokoda myth.

CHAPTER | 15

SECOND
EORA–TEMPLETON'S

On 14 September, as the battle at Ioribaiwa commenced, Horii was at Nauro working on a plan for the attack on Port Moresby, due to take place in November provided Guadalcanal was taken first and reinforcements were forthcoming. The part to be played by the expected reinforcements is unclear, but Horii anticipated that 144th Regiment would pin the Australians, now on Imita Ridge to his front, while 41st Regiment, most of which would have to be brought up from the rear, would march west then south and take Port Moresby's airfields via the Goldie and Brown Rivers.[1] Two days later, as Ioribaiwa concluded, all had changed. Horii received an order from Seventeenth Army to send the elements of 41st Regiment then in the mountains back to Giruwa – a clear sign that there would not be an attack on Port Moresby any time soon. A week later Horii was ordered to withdraw his whole force: 'The commander of the South Seas Force will assemble his main strength in the Isurava and Kokoda areas and secure these as a base for future offensives. In addition the defences in the Buna area will be strengthened.'[2]

Horii also learned that reinforcements for Seventeenth Army were coming to Rabaul from the Kwantung Army in Korea, the first time major forces had been taken from operations in Asia to assist those in the South Pacific. The reason for retreat, as General Tanaka explained after the war, had nothing to do with supply, as the Kokoda myth supposes.[3] Again, events at Guadalcanal and Milne Bay were the cause of change. Kawaguchi's second attempt to land on Guadalcanal was successful, but his attack on 13 September to take Henderson field had been badly

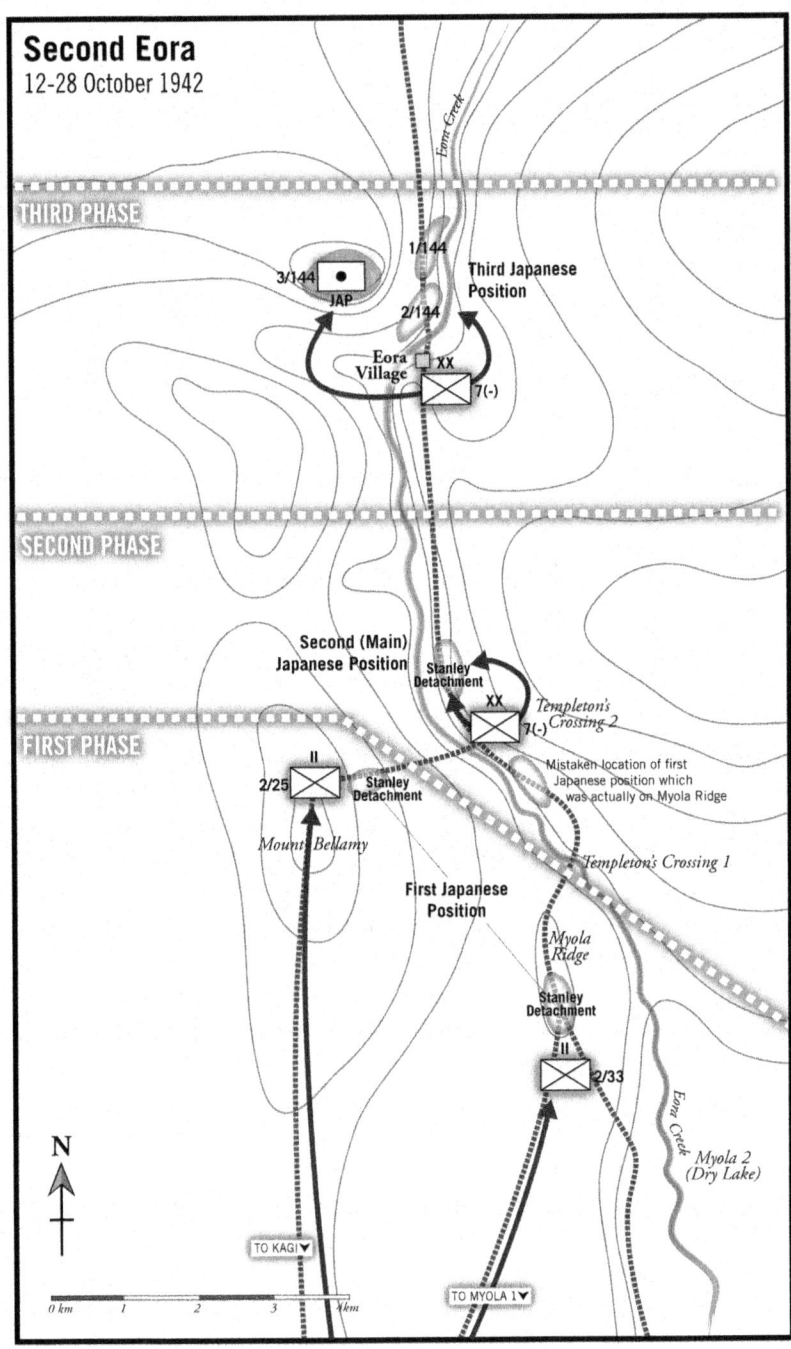

Map 11 Second Eora, 12–28 October 1942

defeated at the Battle of Edson's Ridge. Hence the new troops from Asia would first be required at Guadalcanal. If they could retake Guadalcanal then Hyakutake, commander of Seventeenth Army, still planned to send some of them to reinforce Horii for an attack on Port Moresby in November. Until then Hyakutake wanted the Nankai Shitai to withdraw to a less exposed position further north along the Kokoda Track.

With larger forces coming, another level of command was required. Guadalcanal was to become Seventeenth Army's sole responsibility, the new Eighteenth Army would now run New Guinea and Papua, and a new Eighth Area Army headquarters in Rabaul, the equivalent of an Allied corps headquarters, would control both. While the restructing was taking place there was a noticeable loss of interest in Papua on the part of those in Rabaul. On 10 October Hyakutake arrived on Guadalcanal to take command. From then until 18 November, when Eighteenth Army under General Adachi Hatazo took over as New Guinea/Papua commander, Hyakutake commanded Horii from Guadalcanal, leaving his chief of staff Tanaka to mind the shop in Rabaul.[4]

The connection between Milne Bay and the orders to retreat concerned 41st Regiment. The regiment was recalled towards Giruwa because the Japanese had learned that the Allies were about to advance from Milne Bay towards the base of the Nankai Shitai at Giruwa.[5] Captain Tomita Yoshinobu, the senior IJN officer at Giruwa, was told to expect an Allied landing from the sea, and the next day the false rumour spread that the Allies had come ashore at Basabua. Giruwa remained tense for the rest of the month, although no attack came.[6]

In July Lieutenant-General George Kenney, commanding the AAF, had proposed an advance from Milne Bay to Giruwa. The following month American engineers at Milne Bay investigated the possibility of using an old airstrip at Wanigela, south of Giruwa. MacArthur gave the go-ahead, and by 11 September a plan was ready for an air and sea move along the coast north from Milne Bay via Wanigela and Pongani to Giruwa.[7] On 25 September Blamey flew to Milne Bay to discuss details with Major-General Cyril Clowes. The Japanese believed, incorrectly, that the attack was imminent and would take the form of a direct amphibious attack on their Papua base. In fact it was to be a cautious advance, without an amphibious assault, and it did not start until 5 October.

The Japanese learned of the plan from several sources: from USN signals traffic, from New Caledonia and from Australia. Seventeenth Army monitored Australian broadcasts and received reports on the contents of newspapers; both were remarkably informative. On 24 September

Australian politician Billy Hughes, member of the Advisory War Council and United Australia Party leader, stated in the *Daily Telegraph* that he advocated a 'flank move on the Japanese supply line ... well behind their forward forces in the Owen Stanleys'.[8] On 5 October, when the Japanese were falling back and unaware of how far behind them was the Australian pursuit, the *Sydney Morning Herald* divulged that the Australians had just reached Efogi. It appears this was repeated in a broadcast, for two days later Nankai Shitai intelligence reports stated, 'According to broadcasts from Australia on 5 October enemy occupied Efogi.'[9] Australian broadcasts were so useful that Seventeenth Army doubled the number of English-language specialists listening to them. Chester Wilmot, for one, unintentionally provided valuable and timely information to the Japanese. In mid-July, at the time the Japanese had lost communication with their own Yokoyama Force then advancing on Kokoda, Wilmot told the Japanese its location in his broadcast from 4QG in Brisbane. In August Wilmot reported that clouds in the Owen Stanley Range were inhibiting the airdropping of supplies at Myola, and this comment appears in Japanese intelligence reports several days later. No wonder Blamey was irritated and told Wilmot: 'We should give thousands of pounds to have someone in your position in Japan trying to undermine the C-in-C there.'[10] Nankai Shitai intelligence bulletins also credit the Spanish and Chinese consulates in Australia as sources. On 17 September 'the resident attaché for Chunking in Australia' sent word to the Japanese of current Allied troop strength in Port Moresby and Guadalcanal.[11]

THE JAPANESE RETREAT FROM IORIBAIWA

On 24 September the Japanese main body withdrew from Ioribaiwa. A clean break was made, and the rearguard concealed the fact that a retreat was occurring, thus delaying pursuit. On 26 September the Australian advance from Imita Ridge began, and on 28 September the Australians, who had artillery support, assaulted empty trenches on Ioribaiwa Ridge. The Nankai Shitai retreated rapidly, and the Australians, who advanced slowly, did not see it again for two weeks.

Horii reorganised the Nankai Shitai into three parts to meet the requirements of his new instructions. On the coast to protect against the expected Allied landing he placed the 1/41st with the 3/41st, already at Sanananda.[12] Between the Kokoda Track and the north coast, to act as a reserve for both, to rest as many men as possible in the better-supplied lowlands between Kokoda and Oivi, and to guard against enemy coming out of the Owen Stanley Range there, he placed the 2/41st and the main body of the 144th except for the 2/144th, which formed the Stanley Detachment.[13] Living quarters were constructed in expectation of a long stay, and a convalescent camp was set up for those in special need of rest and more food but not weak enough to require hospitalisation.

The Stanley Detachment was the third formation Horii created. Their task was to hold a forward position until conditions again favoured the Emperor's cause. Seventy kilometres from the Allied airfields north of Port Moresby, the Stanley Detachment served as a useful threat. At any time it might be reinforced and advance on Port Moresby, so the Allies had to keep a large force there, large enough to guarantee that Port Moresby would not fall. In early October the thousand men of the detachment contributed to keeping over 20 000 Australians and Americans defending Port Moresby and not available for operations elsewhere. Far from marching into a strategic dead-end, a relatively small Japanese force on the Kokoda Track rendered a valuable service by helping to pin a far larger Allied force in place. MacArthur took note of this apparent threat and insisted that the coastal advance from Milne Bay could not draw on troops from Port Moresby and could not commence until additional forces arrived.[14]

The intent of Hyakutake's order for the Nankai Shitai to retire to Isurava was that Horii should hold a blocking position within the Owen Stanley Range from which a future advance might be made. Yet Isurava was too far back to threaten Port Moresby as strongly as a position further forward, and it was too close to the northern exits of the mountains. Should the Allies advance from Port Moresby along the Kokoda Track it was too easy for them, from the vicinity of Isurava, to find a flanking track into the Japanese rear at Oivi. Consequently Horii decided that the Stanley Detachment should dig in near Myola. The three Australian attacks on the three successive lines held by the Stanley Detachment in October, the Japanese reinforcement of the detachment and the subsequent Japanese defeat, is called the Second Eora–Templeton's action.

SECOND EORA

The three stages of Second Eora were the Australian attack on the first Japanese position south and west of Templeton's 2 (the original Templeton's Crossing) in mid-October; the Australian attack on the main Templeton's 2 position; and third the attack on the Eora Creek village position at the end of October.

Second Eora has not been well understood. Beginning with the official history, accounts have concentrated on the third period of fighting at Eora village. This focus misses the point that the main Japanese defences were at Templeton's 2 and they were captured when the Australian 2/2nd Battalion, at considerable cost, broke into the Japanese position on 20 October, forcing on the Japanese a rapid withdrawal to Eora village and creating an opportunity there that the Australians failed to exploit.

The neglect of the earlier phases of Second Eora extends to some of the fighting being wrongly located. One of the two Japanese outlying positions in their first line of defences has mistakenly been placed 3 kilometres from where it actually was. There were two routes from Efogi to Templeton's 2. One Japanese force blocked the Efogi–Templeton's track 2.5 kilometres west of Templeton's 2, and another blocked the Kokoda Track from Efogi to Templeton's 2 via Myola and Templeton's 1.[15] This second position has been wrongly located in postwar accounts and maps, where it appears a kilometre south of Templeton's 2 on the track to Templeton's 1 on the eastern side of Eora Creek.[16] In fact it was 3 kilometres south of there on the other side of the creek, and no fighting took place in the usually accepted location. To 2/33rd Battalion, which fought there, the 12–14 October fighting took place at 'Myola Ridge', which immediately suggests that it might be much closer to Myola dry lake than has been thought. Also known to 3rd Battalion as Bamboo Ridge, the ridge is long, steep-sided and narrow, nothing like the terrain to be found 3 kilometres north.[17] However, there is just such a long, steep-sided ridge, with a battalion's worth of Japanese fighting pits still visible along it, on the track 2 kilometres north-east of Propeller Track junction where the main Kokoda Track intersects one going directly to Myola 2. Here, where the side track to Myola leaves the main track, is where the Australian 7th Division's 1942 report correctly places the action.[18]

Further evidence that the outermost Japanese position of the Nankai Shitai's deployment has been mislocated comes from the 2/33rd Battalion history. After the Japanese withdrew from Myola Ridge on 15 October the battalion marched north for two and a half hours until it reached 'the first crossing of Eora Creek', now Templeton's 1.[19] The following day, the battalion marched for five hours with no enemy contact, through the supposed site of the Japanese position, now with Eora Creek flowing north on its left to Templeton's 2.

Placing the first line of the Stanley Detachment on Myola Ridge, 2 kilometres north-west of the northern tip of the dry lake called Myola 2, served a useful purpose. Myola itself offered no reasonable defensive position, but holding Myola Ridge threatened the Australians' ability to use Myola once again to drop supplies from the air close to their forward troops. There was little point in withdrawing far enough into the mountains to cause the Australians a supply headache if they solved it at one stroke by free use of Myola. It is easy to imagine the negative effect upon the regularity of supply dropping if Japanese patrols appeared at the edge of the lake and fired on Australian aircraft. Worse still, the lake was longest on a north–south axis, the one the Allied aircraft used to increase the accuracy of dropping. So either the aircraft had to fly near enough to the Japanese on Myola Ridge to take fire from them in approaching or leaving the lake, or they flew in on an east–west axis and accepted a greater loss of supplies falling into the jungle. Firing on aircraft did occur from Myola Ridge and from Japanese patrols sent out from there for just this purpose. On 11 October, the first day of airdropping, a pilot reported that he 'had been fired on by LMG [light machine-gun] using tracer from a high point SE of hut on W side of Myola lake'.[20] A patrol from 16th Brigade was sent to look for the machine-gun but failed to find it.

FORCES ENGAGED

The Japanese Stanley Detachment's strength on 3 October is shown in table 15.1. Almost a third were sick enough to be evacuated, and evacuation of the sick commenced the following day, leaving 667 men.[21] The 2/144th Battalion, around which the detachment was built and whose commander, Major Horie, also commanded the detachment, was down to about 300 effectives.[22] On the Kagi track was a 92-man company of the 2/144th, a platoon of the machine-gun company, an engineer platoon and a medical section, no more than 150 men.[23] The main force of 520 was on Myola Ridge with all three of the Stanley Detachment's guns (one mountain gun and the battalion guns of the 1/144th and 2/144th). In their rear, and not a part of the Stanley Detachment, was another company of the 1/144th. On 29 September, with the assistance of an engineer company, they began constructing the second and main line of defences north of and overlooking the Templeton's 2 crossing of Eora Creek.[24]

Allied Land Force Headquarters in Melbourne estimated that there were 4600 Australian soldiers and 2000 carriers forward of the Uberi roadhead on 15 October.[25] The majority was in seven infantry battalions and one pioneer battalion but, in the first period of fighting at Eora, when the two Japanese outer positions were attacked, half of this force, now called 7th Australian Division rather than Maroubra Force,

Table 15.1: Stanley Detachment order of battle

2/144th headquarters, three infantry companies, one machine-gun company and one gun platoon	398
2nd Company of 1/144th Battalion	85
1st Machine Gun Company of 1/144th, detachment	18
1/144th Battalion, gun platoon	26
55th Mountain Artillery Regiment, 2nd Company	107
144th Regiment signals company, detachment	28
144th Regiment, medical detachment	25
55th Engineer Regiment, 1st Company	120
Unidentified infantry unit of 144th Regiment	179
Total strength	986

Source: *Hiho to Tomoni-Sanpohei dai 55 Rentai senshi* (With fire: the war history of 55th Mountain Artillery Regiment), p. 40, NIDS 302. 9.S; ATIS bulletin no. 24, p.7, AWM55 1/1.

was well to the rear. The force in contact with the Japanese was under Brigadier Eather of 25th Brigade. Eather's divisional commander was Major-General Arthur Allen, but Allen's superior was no longer Rowell. Blamey had flown to Port Moresby at MacArthur's insistence to 'energise the situation'. He did so by replacing Rowell, New Guinea Force commander, with Lieutenant-General Edmund Herring.

The 25th Brigade Group had been depleted by battle casualties and by sickness to the strengths shown in table 15.2. The 2/31st Battalion was held at Kagi. From here another track led north, an approach Allen feared the Japanese might use. Two battalions, the 2/33rd and 3rd, went forward past Myola and another, the 2/25th, marched along the alternative Kagi track. On both lines of advance were detachments of signallers and field ambulance. At the start of the engagement 1400 Australians opposed 670 Japanese.

THE FIRST PERIOD OF FIGHTING

On 12 October, 2/25th Battalion advanced on the Kagi–Templeton's track towards Templeton's 2 with orders to take it. They had no contact with the enemy that day. The next day the Japanese position was found when Australian scouts were fired on. Two companies, B and C, attempted to flank the position. They lost eight men wounded but did not, in the words of the battalion war diary, 'take much ground'.[26] On 14 October

Table 15.2: Australian 25th Brigade Group, 12 October 1942

25th Brigade Headquarters	75
2/33rd Battalion	449
3rd Battalion	372
2/25th Battalion	426
2/31st Battalion	450
2/4th Field Ambulance	110
Total force	1882

Source: 2/33rd Battalion war diary, 1 October 1942, AWM52 8/3/33; Crooks, *The Footsoldiers*, pp. 189–90.

A Company relieved C Company, two 3-inch mortars were brought up and there was 'active patrolling' during which one man was killed. The next day there was a 100-metre advance at first light, then C Company took over the attack again and reached a barricade of wood and wire thrown up by the Japanese. They 'failed to advance further and withdrew to former position'. One man was killed and two were wounded. In three days the battalion lost 13 casualties from 426 men and made no impression on a force a third their size. The following morning the Japanese were gone, and the battalion advanced to Templeton's Crossing.

It does seem that, in the period 12–15 October, little attempt was made by the 2/25th to obey the order to take Templeton's 2. It was a small example of the lack of results MacArthur, Blamey and Herring were soon to complain to Allen about. Eather several times urged the battalion on, stressing that as the 2/33rd was making progress on the other track, the 2/25th might be able to get through to the Templeton's 2 track junction and cut off the Japanese on Myola Ridge. These messages had no effect. The battalion had been through two commanding officers in less than a month and lost a third to artillery fire on 15 October. Three days later another 2/25th officer was relieved of his command for failing to attack. All was not well within the battalion.[27]

On the main track near Myola no such problems beset the 2/33rd opposing the main body of the Stanley Detachment, 520 men placed on the long, narrow north–south Myola Ridge, each company behind the other in all-round defence. The Australian attack on Myola Ridge commenced when the 2/33rd, with its 3-inch mortar in support for the first time, made a company attack along the spine of the ridge, then put a company around its left, then another around its right, all taking fire from Japanese artillery as they manoeuvred. None of this dented the Japanese position, so 3rd Battalion was brought up to swing further out around the Japanese right while patrols penetrated the gaps between the Japanese companies. Aware that the Australians were reinforced and threatening to cut them off from Templeton's 2, the Stanley Detachment was gone by the morning of 15 October, the same moment as the Japanese in front of the 2/25th withdrew. Total Japanese casualties were 30 dead with the same number wounded, against 15 Australians killed and 49 wounded, 13 on the Kagi track and 51 at Myola Ridge.[28]

Sublet's view, in *Kokoda to the Sea*, was that: 'With minor forces, the enemy had parried Buttrose (2/33rd) and Marson (2/25th) for four days, which gave Horii time to progressively feed his rested men from the more moderate climes of Kokoda into their positions in the mountains.'[29] This was correct in that those Japanese who later reinforced the Stanley Detachment had had up to three weeks rest in the lowlands north of the mountains. It was also true that the 2/25th, who faced a third their number of Japanese, for some reason had not made a wholehearted effort. But it was incorrect at Myola Ridge, where 800 Australians faced 500 Japanese with three guns. It is unlikely that the Australians would have succeeded at these odds, but neither side knew the strength of the other. This time it was the Stanley Detachment's commander, Major Horie, who decided that he was significantly outnumbered and obtained Horii's permission to retreat.

It was Horie's last fight in Papua. He had the good fortune, at this difficult moment, to receive a positive response to his application to return to Japan to take an examination for promotion at the IJA University at Ichigaya, Tokyo. When Tsukamoto heard that Horie was leaving, he said he never wanted to see his face again. A few days later soldiers resting at Kokoda were surprised to see Horie galloping through on his horse on his way to the coast.

THE SECOND PERIOD OF FIGHTING

Lieutenant-Colonel Tsukamoto, who had commanded the 1/144th, replaced Horie as Stanley Detachment commander. The detachment now occupied the second line of Japanese defences, a well-sited position 500 metres deep along the Kokoda Track north of Templeton's 2. Horii regarded the first Japanese position as an outpost line he was willing to give up if indeed the Australians began a counter-offensive along the Kokoda Track, but Templeton's 2 he considered the main position and he was determined that Tsukamoto hold it. The third line, at Eora village, was an insurance policy against failure at Templeton's 2. Horii also ordered 41st Regiment to relieve the Stanley Detachment.[30] This redeployment, replacing the tired and hungry soldiers in the mountains with those who had now had several weeks rest on increased rations, would take more than a week to complete as 41st Regiment was spread between Oivi and Giruwa. As a stopgap, when Tsukamoto went forward to assume command he took the main body of his own battalion, his RHQ and one 37mm gun.[31] 41st Regiment was to be at Templeton's not later than 25 October, as Horii anticipated that Templeton's 2 could safely be held by Tsukamoto until then.[32]

The Templeton's 2 position was a good one as the creek crossing was overlooked, and the two battalion guns and one 37mm gun present could fire down along the line of the Australian approach from the south.[33] A Japanese mountain gun was also placed a kilometre north so as to fire down the gorge of Eora Creek. When the Australians arrived on 16 October, 2/33rd Battalion leading, this gun dropped 49 shells on the battalion in 20 minutes, inflicting one casualty.[34] The one weakness of the Japanese Templeton's 2 position was that it was itself overlooked from high ground running north along the Japanese left (east). An Australian attack coming from this high ground was to be the deciding movement in this phase of the fighting.

Deducting 60 battle casualties and about 20 evacuated sick each day and adding 300 men with Tsukamoto, the Templeton's 2 position was held by about 800 Japanese.[35] The Australians were reinforced to a much greater degree. The newly arrived 16th Brigade under Brigadier John Lloyd was now at the front, and Allen's plan was to use them to replace the worn out 25th Brigade, but as each new battalion was fed into the fight the one it was to replace was not always withdrawn. Seven battalions were available – in itself testimony to the advantage conferred by airdropping supplies at Myola, which was now possible as the Japanese had been forced from Myola Ridge. There were 1850 men in 16th Brigade and 1520 in the four battalions of 25th Brigade. Fighting power was further enhanced by eight 3-inch mortars and four Vickers medium machine-guns, although ammunition was limited. Now, as the Japanese had been doing to the Australians, the Australians could bombard with mortars and lay down suppressing fire with machine-guns before the infantry assaulted. On 18 October three Japanese were killed and seven wounded by Australian mortar fire.[36] The next day the 144th's headquarters was hit, and several more Japanese troops were wounded.

In the period 17–20 October, five of Allen's seven battalions were involved in the fighting, giving the Australians a four-to-one superiority. Handled passably well, this was more than enough to break the Japanese position. From 17 to 19 October the 2/33rd and 3rd Battalions bore the brunt of the effort, although the 2/25th and 2/2nd were also involved. Two Japanese counter-attacks were beaten off on 17 and 19 October. Then, on 20 October, 2/2nd Battalion drove into the centre of the Japanese position, cutting the track and causing a Japanese withdrawal to Eora village. The attack of the 2/2nd was a result of gradually working around to the high ground on the Japanese left. From here, the battalion attacked downhill as 2/1st Battalion attacked north directly along the Kokoda Track.[37] Tsukamoto saw that the position was lost and ordered a retreat without consulting Horii. The retreat was disorderly, but all the Japanese guns were safely brought out. The second period of fighting cost the Japanese 36 dead and 35 wounded against the Australian loss of 54 dead and 68 wounded.[38] For the first time in the campaign the Australian infantry had closed with a well-defended Japanese position and captured it outright.

The successful Australian assault marks a turning point in the Kokoda campaign. The Japanese at Templeton's seem to have panicked. For the first time since the controversy over the morale of the 1/144th at Isurava, there appeared mentions in Japanese diaries of a similar problem elsewhere in the regiment. Of 5 Company of the 2/144th, another company commander observed that it 'lacks fighting spirit'.[39] This company had suffered more casualties than any other in the battalion, having lost half of its men in one day at Efogi. Another officer thought that 'men under the rank of NCO, especially orderlies, are getting disrespectful' and that this was a sign of falling morale.[40] The regimental history stated that when the announcement was made that reinforcements were arriving and that the regiment would soon be on its way towards Port Moresby 'the situation improved immediately, and the desire to take Port Moresby blazed up and there were many shouts of joy and exultation'. Then, a week later, when they found that the reinforcements were going to Guadalcanal instead because of the Japanese defeat at Edson's Ridge, 'the morale of the Stanley Detachment dropped alarmingly'.[41] As the Australians had recently learned, defeat and retreat under enemy pressure by itself lowers morale just as advancing while driving the enemy back raises it. A deterioration of Australian morale was seen after the stand at Isurava, certainly by Efogi and Ioribaiwa. From the middle of October the Stanley Detachment was suffering from the same problem.

THE THIRD PERIOD OF FIGHTING

On the night of 20 October, when Horii learned of the sudden collapse at Templeton's a rush of orders went out from NSHQ. Horii ordered

Table 15.3: Stanley Detachment reinforcements

Date of arrival	Unit	Strength
22 October	3/144th detachment	120
25 October	3/144th detachment	70
26 October	2/41st detachment	92
26 October	55th Engineer Regiment, platoon	30
26 October	2nd Wireless Section	24
26 October	55th Division Field Ambulance, platoon	22
26 October	55th Mountain Artillery Regiment, 1 Company	120
27 October	Lieutenant Okamoto's detachment	10

Source: ATIS current translations, no 29, p. 67, AWM55 3/3; *Hohei dai 41 Rentai New Guinea Senkyo Houkou* [War reports of 41st Regiment in New Guinea], pp. 20–1, NIDS Nanto higashi New Guinea, 225; Japanese order, messages, sitreps relating to the period 1 October – 10 November 1942, Owen Stanleys, AWM54 577/7/9; *Hohei Dai 144 Rentai dai 3 daitai Sento Shoho* [Detailed battle records of 3rd Battalion, 144th Regiment], p. 82. NIDS, Nanto zenpan 174.

everyone he could lay his hands on to march immediately to the Eora village position, the third line of defence he had not expected to need. The complete dislocation of Japanese plans can be seen in table 15.3. The reinforcements were drawn from units resting dispersed along the Mambare Valley and at Oivi Creek. There was no time to gather formations properly; rather the fit men in any location were placed under any officer available and marched off. Some 495 men were fed into the battle as they arrived in the period 22–27 October.

On 22 October there were, including 120 Japanese who arrived that day, close to 700 within the Eora village position. By 27 October an additional 375 had arrived. Against this the Australians had the same seven battalions in two brigades. Of these, the strongest and most recently arrived was 16th Brigade. The battalions, the 2/1st, 2/2nd and 2/3rd, were the first battalions raised in the Second Australian Imperial Force in 1939. They also had the greatest experience of battle and the benefit of several months jungle training in Ceylon on the way back from the Middle East. They were probably the highest quality Australian infantry encountered by the Japanese thus far, and the fight at Eora village was to be their show. Lloyd had detachments from a field company, divisional and medical units, 1770 infantry and about 2100 troops in all in the fight. This was three times the number of the defenders as this phase of the fighting began and closer to twice the defender's number as it ended.[42]

Eora was a well-prepared position, in a way too well prepared, for it was designed for a force twice the size of the one available to defend it. Horii had assumed that, if he ever needed to use Eora, he would have plenty of time to bring up sufficient units to fill it. However, the attack of the Australian 2/2nd Battalion at Templeton's 2 resulted in a desperate effort to rush Japanese reinforcements to hold Eora. Horii had been forced to cash in his insurance policy, and it did not pay as well as he expected.

Tsukamoto placed the 2/144th in the centre at Eora, covering the creek crossing. On its flanks were the other two battalions: the 1/144th holding the Japanese left, close in behind the 2/144th, and the 3/144th was some distance behind the 2/144th to the Japanese right, holding the high ground where the Japanese artillery was deployed; a 37mm gun, two battalion guns and one, later two, mountain guns.[43] This high ground was the key to the position as artillery there could place direct fire on the possible Australian approaches. Unfortunately, in order to benefit from the advantages offered by the artillery position, hold the creek crossings and prevent the Australians gaining access to the Kokoda Track by turning the Japanese left, there had to be a gap somewhere. It was 600 metres wide in the Japanese right centre, between the 2/144th and 3/144th.[44]

From 22 to 24 October, Lloyd's 16th Brigade, spurred on by Allen who was hearing threatening noises from Blamey about the slow Australian advance, made a frontal assault on the Eora crossing position: 'Our attack [was] maintained in the face of tenacious enemy resistance and heavy persistent fire arty, mortars, MMGs.'[45] Cullen's 2/1st Battalion got across Eora Creek and penetrated a short way into the ground held by the Japanese 2/144th, but was then stopped.[46] Nor did the Australians find the gap in the Japanese lines. On 24 October the 3/144th reported that an Australian patrol had entered the gap but was driven out without the Australians having realised a gap existed.[47] Towards the end of Second Eora a 92-man detachment of the 2/41st arrived to fill the hole, which it could do only by holding a position in the centre and sending out regular patrols to its right and left. A second time, on the last day, an Australian patrol approached the gap and was again driven off.[48] Lloyd never learned of the potential opportunity created by the hole in the Japanese right-centre, but his brigade had been halted in its frontal attack, so he sought another solution. He brought the 2/2nd to the right of the 2/1st, where it encountered the Japanese 1/144th, and committed the 2/3rd around the Australian left. The attack of 2/3rd Battalion on 28 October broke into the lines of the 3/144th on the high ground north of the crossing where the Japanese artillery had been massed.

According to Australian accounts, the 2/3rd's attack demolished the Japanese defences, and they fled the field. From the Japanese perspective the story was somewhat different, and it is necessary to look at a broader picture to understand this difference. Again, the long shadow of Guadalcanal lay over Papua. With every Japanese defeat at Guadalcanal the prospect of an advance on Port Moresby receded. The Japanese failed on land at Guadalcanal again on the night of 24/25 October in the Battle of Lunga Point. Hyakutake consequently withdrew all his promises of reinforcements to Horii and ordered him to withdraw the Stanley Detachment to the Kumusi River. Horii, then at Kokoda, walked to Eora on 25 October to see Tsukamoto. Horii ordered him to withdraw from Eora on 28 October, the same day as the final Australian attack took place.[49] The necessity for retreat in Papua in response to events at Guadalcanal was underlined by the IJN's defeat at the sea battle of Santa Cruz on 26/27 October.

At Eora Japanese wounded, sick and the non-combat units were withdrawn on 27 October. The next day, the artillery left early and by 8 p.m. all infantry were to have begun to leave.[50] The withdrawal of the battalions by the creek, the 1/144th and 2/144th, was successful, although they were under renewed pressure from the Australian 2/1st and 2/2nd Battalions, but the 3/144th on the high ground was caught in the act by the Australian 2/3rd Battalion. Preliminary moves were begun by the 3/144th around midday and, when the Australians developed their attack in the afternoon, 3/144th was caught out of position and dispersed. Australian accounts that the Japanese battalion was routed are likely to be correct, but naturally the battalion history of the 3/144th does not concede this. It claims that the battalion was caught badly disposed, part of it already on its way down the hill to the rendezvous point. Although at one time it was almost surrounded, the battalion's story is that it fought off the Australian attack, then continued its retreat. The facts do not support this interpretation as only Kuwada, the battalion commander, his headquarters and the machine-gun company made the rendezvous at the foot of the hill on the Kokoda Track.[51] Kuwada's three infantry companies were scattered, and survivors found their way out by moving through the jungle to the north.[52] The battalion was reunited at Isurava, 7 kilometres away, having lost 44 killed and 15 wounded out of 190 men present.[53]

CASUALTIES

From 22 to 29 October, in the third phase of the Second Eora–Templeton's action, the Australians lost 72 killed and 154 wounded.[54] The Japanese lost close to 64 killed and 70 wounded.[55] That half of the Japanese dead were lost on the last day of fighting, against seven Australian dead, indicates that, caught amid a withdrawal, the Japanese suffered accordingly. That 43 Australians were killed in the first frontal attack period, 22–24 October, against 23 Japanese, also says something about the lack of success in this phase of the Australian attack. The battalion commanders involved in the frontal attack, Cullen and Stevenson, in the words of the official history, 'did not like the plan much'.[56] Cullen's much later version paints a grimmer picture than this, one in which insubordinate and heated words were exchanged with Lloyd, but the attack went ahead anyway.[57] The total cost to Australia of all three phases of the Second Eora–Templeton's action was 412 battle casualties against 244 Japanese.[58]

THE RELIEF OF GENERAL ALLEN

Second Eora was an Australian victory, the first in the Kokoda campaign, but the degree of success should not be exaggerated. Strategically it was important as the Allies could now exit the Owen Stanley Range and the Kokoda airstrip would soon be in their hands. Tactically it was less successful. The Japanese at Eora recovered from the dangerous situation that developed at Templeton's on 20 October and held firm for six days from the first Australian attack on 22 October. When we consider the celerity with which the Japanese sought to turn the Australians' flanks at Isurava, First Eora, Efogi and Ioribaiwa, the six days that elapsed between 22 October and 2/3rd Battalion's successful attack on 28 October at Eora does not reflect well on Lloyd or Allen. Blamey noticed this. On 26 October he signalled to Allen that since 21 October 'progress has been negligible against an opponent much fewer in number'.[59] This was quite correct. When the Japanese position was finally taken no Japanese guns were lost, the mass of the Japanese force managed to get away and it was the Australians who lost by far the larger number of men.[60] If the standard of Japanese successes from Isurava to Ioribaiwa is applied to the Australians here, then Second Eora was an Isurava, not an Efogi; an expensive victory that defeated the enemy force but did not destroy it.

Allen, having won the battle, was relieved of command. He is a hero of the Kokoda myth, as is Potts, and the myth holds that he was most unfairly dealt with.[61] The justice of Allen's relief should be reconsidered. On 17 October Allen was informed by Blamey, who was quoting MacArthur, that Allen's light casualties indicated that no serious effort was being made to advance. Allen replied to Blamey that 25th Brigade, since first contact with the Japanese, had taken 183 battle casualties. This was deceptive as half of these were from 25th Brigade's part in the Australian defeat at Ioribaiwa in mid-September.[62] Since Allen's advance commenced, just 87 casualties had resulted to 17 October. Allen also said that casualties alone were not a measure of success. This is true by itself but, together with a slow rate of advance, it might well indicate that 'no serious effort [has] yet [been] made to displace enemy'.[63]

What is missing from the discussion of the rights and wrongs of Allen's departure is that his advance was very slow *before* he had any contact with the Japanese. For 17 days from 26 September when the advance commenced from Imita Ridge, to 12 and 13 October, when the Japanese were contacted again by the 2/25th on the Kagi track and the 2/33rd on the Kokoda Track, Allen's men had advanced 40 kilometres, a little better than 2 kilometres a day, all unopposed. Comparing this to the prior Japanese advance, Allen's men went forward at the same rate achieved by Yazawa in early September, but Yazawa was fighting all the way. On 5 September Yazawa was replaced with Kusunose, who advanced 8 kilometres a day over the next eight days and administered a defeat to the Australians at Efogi along the way. Against this Allen's 2 kilometres a day, against no opposition and with better supply was, as MacArthur said to Blamey on 21 October, 'NOT repeat NOT satisfactory'.[64]

A second criticism of Allen came on 26 October when Blamey said, '... progress has been negligible against an enemy much fewer in number ... in spite of your superior strength enemy appears to be able to delay advance at will.'[65] This point also has some validity. Allen was able to place not less than two and sometimes four Australians into the fight for every one Japanese defender. The Australians could have had more men engaged, and this touches on the third criticism. Allen had seven battalions available, but at Eora village he used only one brigade at the sharp end. His defence was that no greater force could be supplied that far forward of Myola and that he wanted a reserve of 21 days of food built up there before he would push more battalions forward. If the Australians were to be husbanded rather than pushed to their limits then Allen's point about supply was reasonable. It was, however, the opposite of what his superiors wanted. Blamey said that the Australians were fresher than the Japanese and that the Australian supply problem could hardly be worse than the Japanese. This is the core of the argument. Herring, Blamey and MacArthur wanted the Australians pushed harder, even if it meant short rations and heavy casualties. Allen apparently lost his temper and considered replying directly to MacArthur that if he thought they could do better they could come up the track and try.

This is reminiscent of the strange complaint of Kokoda mythologisers that MacArthur never set foot on the Kokoda Track. In the normal way of armed forces commanders properly have only occasional direct contact with subordinates more than two echelons below them. Allen was three echelons below MacArthur via Blamey and Herring. It was not MacArthur's business to be looking over the shoulder of a front-line commander when MacArthur had the entire south-west Pacific theatre to oversee. Second, commanders should be where they can best influence the action of their subordinates. Senior commanders should sometimes be seen by the troops at the front, mainly for the positive morale effect provided, when it is convenient and can be done quickly without interfering with other tasks. They will also have the chance to obtain an impression of their front-line commander. However, this was not an option on the Kokoda Track. Taking a ten-day round trip half way up the track, with uncertain communications with the outside, was the worst place to be to exercise the wide command responsibilities of a theatre commander.

It is true, however, that it was unusual to relieve a divisional commander without his corps commander first seeing the situation himself, but again the Kokoda Track was an exceptional case. Herring was responsible for forces confronting the Japanese at Wau, the advance from Milne Bay, the attack on Goodenough Island and the Kokoda Track. He flew to Milne Bay several times, but a ten-day walk up and back from Allen's headquarters was more time than he could afford with the responsibilities of his position. It was rather the job of liaison officers to go forward from senior to subordinate commanders, and this was done. Herring sent Lieutenant-Colonel Minogue, who arrived at Allen's headquarters at Myola on 22 October.

Nor is Allen's point, one that is echoed loudly in the Kokoda myth, that MacArthur did not appreciate conditions in the mountains quite as straightforward as it appears. In the Philippines MacArthur had arguably gained as much practical experience of mountain war as any senior Australian officer except perhaps Herring, who served in Macedonia in World War I and Greece in World War II. As Commander US Army

Forces Far East MacArthur had waged a four-month campaign defending the Philippines from December 1941, most of it fought in the mountainous Bataan Province.

Another complaint from Allen was that he wanted the advance from Milne Bay along the coast to Giruwa to be pressed harder so that, with their base threatened, the Japanese on the Kokoda Track would be forced to withdraw. The Milne Bay advance was led by Hatforce, mainly 2/10th Battalion, which flew into Wanigela on 5 October. By 16 October the US 128th Regiment was also moving by air, sea and land towards Pongani, which its advanced elements reached on 21 October. Between 22 and 24 October the Australian 2/12th Battalion cleaned up a Japanese force on Goodenough Island. From that point, however, the advance slowed and no assistance to Allen was provided by pressure being placed on Giruwa. Oddly, the Japanese were completely unaware of the Allied forces in the Wanigela–Pongani region until 15 November.

Allen's complaint about Milne Bay was not received favourably by Herring and Blamey because Allen's advance was the major offensive and resources had been devoted to it in the expectation that Allen would obtain results – the advance from Milne Bay was a much smaller affair. On 5 October Blamey wrote to MacArthur that supply capacity forbade advances on all fronts so priority would be given to Allen's 7th Division.[66] Also, as the Guadalcanal campaign naval battles of Savo Island, the Solomon Islands, Cape Esperance and Santa Cruz demonstrated, the IJN was still a powerful force that could intervene against a coastal advance from Milne Bay by entering the Solomon Sea. The Allies were right to be cautious advancing along the Papuan coast. On 7 October Blamey assured MacArthur that no undue risk would be run: 'We are pressing on with two strings to our bow, one over the hills via Kokoda and one along the coast via Wanigela, and we will use every possible means to get to Buna in the shortest time that conditions permit ... A larger force [at Wanigela is] unwise owing to the difficulties of supply and the possibility of isolation should the enemy carry out a successful operation against Milne Bay ... I don't intend to make foolhardy advances.'[67]

The view of Allen's superiors was that the outnumbered Japanese on the Kokoda Track, already in worse circumstances than the Australians, would succumb first if pressure was applied. A quick advance was essential. While the Japanese were devoting all their resources to Guadalcanal, it was important to extract as much advantage from this on the Kokoda Track as was possible. If there was a chance to get to Giruwa via Kokoda before the Japanese could reinforce it, then Allen's superiors were prepared to take risks they were not prepared to take, for good reason, in the coastal advance. In such a circumstance a subordinate running the battle who is unwilling to take those risks becomes a liability.

The explanation offered by Rowell in a letter to Gavin Long covers most of these points and concludes that the relief of Allen was the correct thing to do:

> The rate of progress of 7th Division was a matter of concern to TAB [Blamey] and me ... Allen wouldn't go forward until he had 21 Days supply in reserve ... but he just would not see that owing to the terrain and the shortage of carriers, the building up of reserves at any one spot tended to hamper the advance we all wanted and not expedite it ... It took some time to build up the reserves and then after they had been built up, they could only be of use if carried forwards as the troops advanced. Left behind they were of course useless. And with the shortage of carriers they could only be carried forwards by the troops themselves. What NGF wanted to do was to keep dropping as far forwards as possible, so as to reduce the problem of carrying and making as many of the fighting troops available for battle as possible. NGF did not want the supply situation to enforce the siting of one bde defensively in the rear and yet it was just this very thing that Allen [did]. This prevented full pressure being exerted on the enemy and necessarily slowed down the progress of the advance ...[68]

Allen's desire to maintain a battalion covering the Kagi track junction was 'significant, it shows the type of commander he was. Not only was he saying that he could not press on without reserves, but he was worrying about a counterthrust by the Japs ... Progress had been slow when everyone agreed the greatest possible speed was necessary. This being so, something had to be done about it by TAB [Blamey] or NGF [Herring]. It was our business to speed things up if we could. Pressure clearly had to be put on to the responsible commander and that was Allen ...'[69] Herring agreed and had on 7 October expressed the view that Allen was not the right man for the job.[70]

That the real reason for the relief of Allen was he was not acting aggressively enough or pushing his men as hard as his superiors wanted is summed up in the conclusion of Rowell's letter. 'It is so easy to ... worry about all the things that might go wrong, to exaggerate ones own weaknesses and the enemy's strength, to take counsel of one's fears in

Photo 21 MacArthur's first visit to Papua, 3 October 1942 (left to right): US General Douglas MacArthur, Commander-in-Chief, South-West Pacific Area; General Sir Thomas Blamey, Commander Allied Land Forces, and Major-General Arthur Allen, Commander 7th Division AIF, at Owers' Corner. (AWM 150818)

other words. This way lays timidity, bold action is almost necessarily stultified ... and may I add that it's a poor compliment to the Australian fighting man that he can't be pushed beyond a certain limit ...'[71] Herring, Blamey and MacArthur thought Allen should be replaced. Rowell, although no longer in command of New Guinea Force, thought so, too. The Kokoda myth, however, gives more weight to Allen's opinion and holds that the others were all wrong.

Evidence from Japanese sources makes Allen's handling of the battle look even worse than it did to his superiors at the time and raises the question whether or not it was fully 'a remarkable victory', as Allen's biographer describes it.[72] The sudden Japanese collapse at Templeton's Crossing, in the second phase of the fighting, created an opportunity for the Australians to push hard at Eora village from 22 to 25 October while fewer than 600 Japanese were present. The gap in the Japanese defences provided a favourable line of approach, but the Australians never found it. Horii had been caught out and rushed a further 500 men to Eora, stabilising the position. Koiwai, who had an opinion about everything, wrote that when he arrived at Eora on 26 October the Japanese crisis was past: 'Considering the enemy's movements the situation at the front did not seem to be as pressing as reported ... I thought we could hold on without any problem ...'[73] However, Hyakutake had ordered a retreat, so when the Australians attacked on 28 October the Japanese guns were gone and their infantry were caught out of their defences. It could be that, had the Japanese stood on 28 October, Allen's men would have failed, and it is far from certain that he would have had a victory had events at Guadalcanal not dictated that the Japanese retreat from Eora.

CHAPTER 16

OIVI–GORARI

At the Oivi–Gorari action in early November 1942 the Kokoda myth that the Australians inflicted huge losses on the Japanese was at last partially correct. Something had changed, and Japanese generalship and fighting power were no longer what they had been, while those of the Australians had improved. One clear marker that a serious defeat has been suffered is the loss of artillery pieces to the enemy. In no battle so far had this occurred to the Japanese, but at Oivi–Gorari the Nankai Shitai lost every one of the 15 guns assembled there. The Japanese were also tossed out of their position and driven in disorder to the coast, which, with the loss of the guns, marks the battle as a very great disaster for the Nankai Shitai, on a par with Kawaguchi's defeat at Edson's Ridge on Guadalcanal. Even for the optimists in the Nankai Shitai and in Rabaul, Oivi–Gorari clearly marked the end of Japanese prospects for taking Port Moresby.

After the Japanese defeat at Eora at the end of October the question became: where would the Nankai Shitai next make a stand? The most important piece of ground was the Kokoda airstrip, which would solve Australian supply problems at a stroke, but another Japanese stand could not be made until reinforcements arrived from Giruwa. By the time this occurred the Australians would have already taken Kokoda. The next position the Japanese might use, which traded space for the time needed for the reinforcements to arrive, was at Oivi. Fifteen kilometres east of Oivi was the Kumusi River, the next possible choice. There has been confusion as to why Horii stood at Oivi instead of behind the Kumusi River, but the reason is not hard to fathom.[1] On 25 October Hyakutake ordered

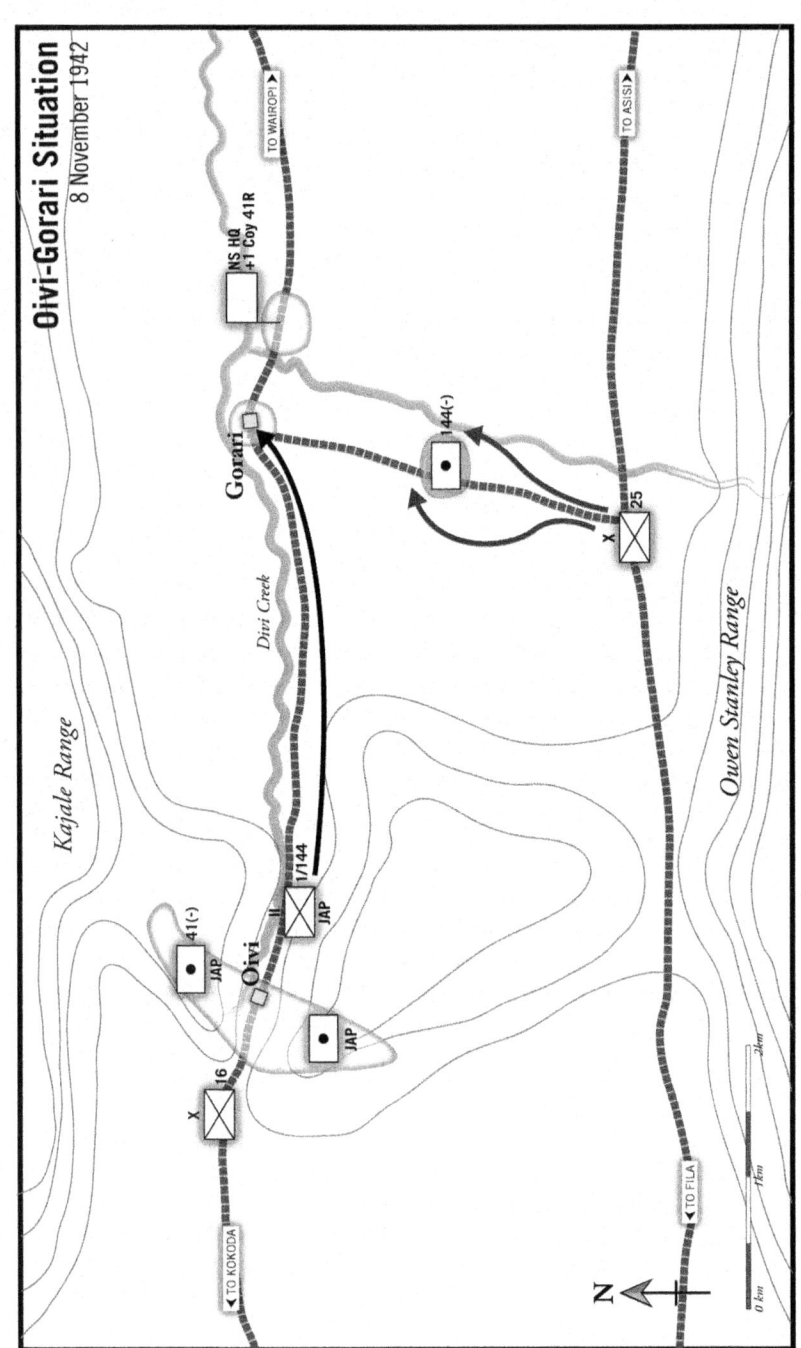

Map 12 Oivi–Gorari, 8 November 1942

the Nankai Shitai, then at Eora, to take up a new position east of Kokoda but as far forward as was reasonable.[2] The Seventeenth Army head-quarters was moving to Guadalcanal as a part of a command reshuffle. Hyakutake had already gone, but Lieutanant General Miyazaki Chuichi, his chief of staff, did not leave until 29 October. Miyazaki told Horii to stand in the Papaki (Wairopi) area forward of the Kumusi River.[3] Papaki was on the west bank, a kilometre from the river in a central position in relation to all the crossings. Three kilometres north-west of Papaki was Ilimo, an important supply dump. The reluctance to abandon food and ammunition accumulated in the Gorari–Ilimo area played a part in the decision about where to stand, and Horii specifically ordered that the contents of the dumps were not to be moved to the rear.[4] In order to cover the supply dumps it was necessary to hold a position forward of them, and the heights above Oivi village was the obvious choice.

In any case the Kumusi was a poor defensive position. The problem defending a river for an inferior force is that the defender must extend his front or the enemy will simply cross the obstacle up or down river from him – especially so at the Kumusi, which was often fordable. The cost of extracting a benefit from the obstacle is then the dispersal of the defend-ing force along the obstacle, a bad state to be in if a concentrated enemy forced a crossing at some point. Defending a river line also decreases the prospects for a future offensive as the river then becomes an obs-tacle to the defender's renewed advance, which the Nankai Shitai still intended. To hold a bridgehead after a retreat – and the Oivi–Gorari position can be considered a bridgehead west of the Kumusi – signals intent to renew the offensive at some future point, or at the very least a determination to retain the option to do so. At the end of October, the Japanese plan was still what it had been in early September: throw everything at Guadalcanal, solve that problem, then reinforce Papua and attack Port Moresby.

Major Koiwai summed up the situation to a fellow officer: 'The plan is to hold out here until the situation improves.' He was cognisant of the risk of a bridgehead, too, as he also said that, if things did not work out, they would be caught like rats in a trap.[5] Koiwai described the heights above Oivi as offering 'all the desirable defensive advantages'. There were steep slopes facing Kokoda and suitable gun positions. Proceeding along the route from Kokoda to the sea, the Ajule Kajali Range runs parallel to the road to the north, and Hydrographers Range runs parallel to the south of the road. The Oivi area is a link of high ground between the two. It is also a watershed; the Mambare River runs away from it west through

Kokoda, and Oivi Creek runs east from it to feed the Kumusi. East of the Kumusi, the northern range curves away to the north-east, widening the gap between the ranges. Oivi was the location with the shortest distance (5 kilometres) between the ranges that can be found between Kokoda and the sea. Another advantage of the Oivi heights was that thick timber and jungle there concealed observers while thinner coverage on the lower ground in front of the heights aided their observations.[6]

Oivi did have two weaknesses. The northern and southern ranges were too far apart, and the whole distance could not be closely defended. As the Oivi heights are closer to the northern range there is a gap of lower ground on the southern side, easier to cross than the mountains and with a track leading into the Japanese rear. The second weakness was that Oivi was further from the Kumusi crossing than would have been desirable. It was a Potts at Efogi dilemma. The position was the best available but still too large for the force holding it.

Despite these limitations, the choice of Oivi–Gorari was a fair one. No one in the Nankai Shitai was as yet aware that the Allies had advanced from Milne Bay north-west along the coast towards Giruwa, which they were soon to threaten, thus rendering any Japanese position outside the Buna–Giruwa–Sanananda–Gona defences strategically redundant. That the Allies were at Pongani, closer to Giruwa than Oivi, was not discovered by the Japanese until 15 November, five days after the retreat from Oivi–Gorari began.[7]

Within the defences, which had been prepared in late October in case of need, Horii placed his freshest troops, Yazawa's 41st Regiment, on the Oivi heights.[8] As the rearguard of the whole force, the 1/144th was west of Oivi and was to fall back through the Oivi defences, thus delaying the Australian advance from Kokoda. As it arrived within 41st Regiment's position the 1/144th came under Yazawa's command. Five kilometres east of Oivi was the main body of 144th Regiment, in reserve at Gorari. It could march west and reinforce 41st Regiment, or south-west to block the track that ran parallel to the main Kokoda–Sanananda track and led to the Kumusi. This southern track was well known to the Japanese, who had considered it as an alternative supply route but rejected it as being too rough for that purpose.

THE JAPANESE

By 2 November the Nankai Shitai was reorganised. The 144th Regiment was no longer known as Kusunose Butai as a new regimental commander arrived from Rabaul. He was Colonel Yamamoto Shigekagi. At the time the Australians believed the 'Yamamoto Butai' indicated that fresh troops had arrived at Oivi, and this confusion has sometimes been repeated post-war. In fact, reinforcements – the first replacements either the 144th or the 41st Infantry Regiments had seen for a year – did arrive on 2 November but neither they nor Yamamoto took part in the action at Oivi–Gorari.[9] Under Colonel Murase the 700 arrivals were placed well to the east of the Kumusi in case the Australians attempted to cross the river. The Stanley Detachment and the temporary transport unit were dissolved. All the men taken from 41st Regiment to carry supplies in August were returned to their regiment but not necessarily to their own battalions. The only battalion of the regiment that had been in battle, the 2/41st, was weaker than the other two with 300 men. The battalion that had spent all its time in Papua defending Giruwa, the 3/41st, had 400 men.[10] The remaining battalion, the 1/41st, had 385 men.

Twelve days before the fighting at Oivi, Colonel Yazawa sent to Lieutenant-Colonel Tomita his own estimate of his regiment's strength. He had with him on the coast RHQ, the RSC, five infantry compan-ies from the 2/41st and 3/41st, one machine-gun company, a battalion gun platoon and one attached engineer company. The total strength of this force was 1100 men.[11] Adding the 385 men of the 1/41st and the now 91-man detachment of the 2/41st, which had fought at Eora (where it lost one man) and rejoined the regiment at Oivi, 1377 members of 41st Regiment were present. The 80 men in 11th Company of the 3/41st stayed to guard the beach at Giruwa but the rest, with an attached engin-eer company about 200 strong, advanced towards the Kumusi.[12] Once there, an infantry company was placed immediately on the eastern bank to cover the main Kumusi crossing, and another was sent to Ilimo to pro-vide protection for Horii's headquarters. The rest went forward to Oivi to the prepared trenches on the heights west of the village.[13]

The first battalion of the 144th, the other Nankai Shitai infantry regi-ment, had 182 men, the 2/144th had 180 and the 3/144th had 275.[14] Adding RHQ, the gun company, signals company and medical detach-ment, the regiment was 891 strong. For the first time in the campaign, all six infantry battalions of the Nankai Shitai were assembled on one battlefield. Also present was the whole of the mountain artillery and a second company of engineers attached to 144th Regiment. Adding Nankai Shitai Headquarters with the usual accompaniment of minor elements, the Japanese force engaged at Oivi–Gorari was close to 2800 men. At last the Nankai Shitai was able to do what the Kokoda myth

Table 16.1: Australian infantry battalions at Oivi–Gorari

2/33rd Battalion	449
2/31st Battalion	450
2/25th Battalion	426
3rd Battalion	372
2/1st Battalion	425
2/2nd Battalion	450
2/3rd Battalion	437

Source: Report on operations in New Guinea, serial 16, AWM54 577/7/29; Walker, *The Island Campaigns* (medical), p. 73; 3rd Battalion war diary, 6 November 1942, AWM52 8/3/39; 2/33rd Battalion war diary, 2–11 November 1942, AWM52 8/3/33; Wick, *Purple over Green*, p. 232; Giveney, *The First at War*, p. 306.

imagines it was doing all along: bring the majority of its fighting troops to the battle.

THE AUSTRALIANS

The Australian 7th Division had seven infantry battalions available. All Australian battalions had been in the mountains for one to two months and had been reduced by a third. The strengths as Oivi–Gorari began are shown in table 16.1. There was a total of 3009 men in the infantry battalions against 1800 Japanese infantry. Adding 7th Division staff and signals, brigade staffs, guard platoons, detachments of 14th Field Ambulance and 2/4th Field Ambulance and a field company, there were about 3700 Australians at Oivi–Gorari against the 2800 Japanese.[15] Major-General George Vasey, who took over 7th Division at the end of October, was about to attack a strong enemy position without much superiority in numbers.

Against the 15 Japanese guns and 30 heavy machine-guns, the Australians now had some reasonable fire support with ten Vickers medium machine-guns and ten 3-inch mortars whose capabilities were much enhanced by the proximity of Kokoda strip.[16] In the mountains the mortars rarely had more than 24 rounds each but now, with ammunition supplied by air, the Australians were able to deliver sustained mortar bombardments. The 2/33rd Battalion history recorded that 'as ammunition for our mortars was now in plentiful supply from Kokoda airstrip, and the Japanese were actually fighting on the sites of their own dumps, the sounds of exploding bombs never stopped'.[17]

OIVI–GORARI

When the Australians occupied Kokoda, Vasey's orders were to advance to the sea, and it was not known that the Japanese intended to make a stand at Oivi. At Alola Vasey had, following Allen's plan, split his force. His 16th Brigade advanced by the most direct route: across to the east side of Eora Gorge, then towards Kobara via Missima and Fila. Simultaneously 25th Brigade advanced on Kokoda. On 2 November patrols from the 2/31st entered Kokoda unopposed and on the eastern track the 2/3rd advanced beyond Kobara. The two Australian axes of advance resulted in two separate but related combats. One was along the main track from Kokoda to Oivi against the Japanese 41st Regiment on Oivi heights. The other occurred east of Oivi about Baribe and Gorari where the Australians fought the 144th Regiment.

On 3 November the Japanese rearguard, the 1/144th with a mountain gun, was encountered west of Oivi. The Japanese withdrew after contact and the next day stood again briefly, then retired into the main Oivi defences. On 5 November the Australian attack on Oivi heights began. The 2/3rd Battalion went in and was stopped cold. On 6 November the 2/2nd, 2/3rd and two companies of 3rd Battalion attacked again, searching for the flanks of the Oivi position. On the Japanese right the 2/41st had all its four infantry companies in a line extending as far north as possible. Attacking where they believed the flank to be, the Australians instead hit the centre of the 2/41st's line. The Japanese company commander there reported that the attack was not delivered skilfully and was easily repulsed.[18]

On the Japanese southern flank at Oivi the Australians had more success. They threatened to get around the left of Major Miyamoto Saburo's 1/41st Battalion. It was his battalion's first fight since arriving in Papua and, according to Koiwai, Miyamoto was nervous about it. Unlike 2/41st Battalion, he held out one infantry company as a reserve. The company counter-attacked on 6 November, checking the Australian threat to the southern flank of the Oivi line. The company was to have been supported by the attached company of engineers from 55 ER, the first time in the campaign the Japanese committed a whole engineer company in the role of infantry. In another clear sign of the deterioration of the Nankai Shitai, it appears that the company refused to advance.[19]

Fighting on the Australian right at Oivi continued on 7 November, then settled down to a stalemate. As no headway could be made against Oivi, Vasey decided to throw his main weight against the Japanese rear at Gorari via the southern track parallel to the main track.[20] Once this decision was taken, it was only necessary that the Japanese at Oivi were kept engaged at minimum cost. The Australian mortar bombardment continued, at regular times twice a day according to the Japanese, and the AAF dropped 8 tons of bombs inflicting a handful of casualties. Then on 11 November the Australians found the Japanese trenches deserted as a result of events at Gorari.[21] It will be necessary to go back a few days to explain how Vasey's change of plan came to pass and why the Japanese abandoned Oivi.

Leading the advance down the other track, which ran parallel to the Kokoda–Sanananda track and south of it, was 2/1st Battalion. Their task was to find a way into the Japanese rear at Ilimo. Orokaiva scouts working for the Japanese informed Horii that there were Australians on this track as early as 3 November but that the number was unknown.[22] On the night of 5/6 November, the 2/1st camped at Leaney's Corner, close to Waju at the track junction. To the west the track they had just come along went back to Deniki; to the east it led to Asisi on the Kumusi River. The north-easterly track from the junction led to Gorari. A patrol up the Gorari track encountered a Japanese post, further alerting them to the Australian presence. Leaving a company at the track junction, Cullen took the rest of his battalion east on 6 November but missed the next track junction, the one he was looking for that led north to Ilimo. When he realised he was almost at the Kumusi he retraced his steps and brought the battalion back to Leaney's Corner on 7 November.

As Cullen was getting lost, at 6.00 p.m. on 6 November, Vasey made his decision. He believed there was enough promise in Cullen's advance and enough evidence, in the form of casualties without result, to show that the Oivi approach was a dead end. He decided to commit three more battalions along Cullen's route. Vasey explained later that he felt confident putting in his entire reserve. With Kokoda airstrip not far behind him he could count on a flow of food, ammunition – and reinforcement should he require it.[23] Eather was to take the three battalions of 25th Brigade, follow up the 2/1st and take that battalion under command. With four battalions he was to cut into the Japanese rear by seizing the main Kokoda–Sanananda track between Oivi and Ilimo.

While Horii was negligent in leaving the southern track almost undefended, he responded promptly when he learned that Australians were probing that way. He had most of 144th Regiment in reserve for just such an eventuality and moved first a company, then the whole of the 3/144, then the remainder of the regiment (except 1/144th, which was still with 41st Regiment) to Baribe, two-thirds of the way from Gorari to the track junction at Leaney's Corner.[24] To 144th Regiment the Oivi–Gorari fighting is known as the Baribe action, and there the regiment dug in, blocking the Australian route to the Kokoda–Sanananda track. Horii, aware that the Australian pressure on Oivi was easing off, also ordered the 1/144th to leave 41st Regiment and head east to hold the track junction at Gorari.[25]

Thus on 8 November, when the 2/31st led the advance of four Australian battalions north-east from Leaney's Corner towards Gorari, they encountered over 700 Japanese troops of 144th Regiment at Baribe. Here the Australians acted with a boldness not seen so far in the Kokoda campaign. Cutting through the jungle to one side of the Japanese, the 2/25th came out on the Waju–Gorari track behind the Japanese at Baribe and surrounded them with the help of the 2/31st. The other two Australian battalions continued towards Gorari. There on 9 November 2/33rd Battalion attacked the 1/144th and drove it off the track junction, taking Gorari village by evening. With the 2/33rd was the 2/1st, which turned east from Gorari and found Horii's headquarters and the 41st Regiment's infantry company protecting it. Horii personally organised a counter-attack, which appears not to have been vigorously carried out.

With the Australians now on the main Kokoda–Sanananda track, communications between NSHQ and the several parts of the Nankai Shitai were cut. Horii did not know whether the main body of the 144th at Baribe was still holding on, had been destroyed, or had retreated to the Kumusi. There was a suspicion in NSHQ that Tsukamoto, in command of the 144th at Baribe, was an independent-minded fellow who might have pulled out east towards the Kumusi without orders. At Oivi Yazawa's 41st Regiment had heard nothing from Horii since 8 November, and he did not know that the 1/144th no longer held Gorari. Still, Yazawa could see something was amiss and considered sending his reserve battalion back to reopen communications. There is again a parallel with Efogi. There, the placing of a Japanese force between Potts' headquarters and his main body had severed communications and led to confusion and retreat. The same thing happened to Horii here.

On 9 November Seventeenth Army, out of touch with the disaster unfolding, decided that Horii should make a measured retreat across the Kumusi, to be completed by 16 November.[26] By the morning of 10 November Horii realised that little time was available, and ordered an immediate retreat lest the Nankai Shitai be destroyed. Having lost signals communications, Horii sent out runners to inform the 144th and 41st

Photo 22 The crew of a Japanese heavy machine-gun in action. The Type 3 Juki heavy machine-gun was more robust and had a larger calibre round than the Vickers gun. It was fitted with a telescopic sight and could fire accurately to 1000 metres. As the Juki used a 30-round strip magazine it could not produce as high a rate of fire as the belt-fed Vickers. (Kochi New Guinea Association)

Regiments. Something more resembling a rush to the rear than a retreat now took place.

The runner for Yazawa found him, and 41st Regiment pulled out of Oivi unseen on the night of 10/11 November. The regiment's new order was to provide a rearguard at the crossings of the Kumusi and cover the retreat of the 144th. What actually occurred was that, with little contact with the Australians, 41st Regiment marched east then north along the west bank of the Kumusi until they found a crossing place. Abandoning all their guns, three infantry guns, the two regimental guns and two mountain guns, they crossed the Kumusi well north of Papaki at Pinga on 14 November. The Australian 3rd Battalion was in pursuit and found Japanese dead, including wounded who had committed suicide. About 900 Japanese reached the far side of the Kumusi, half of them having abandoned their rifles or lost them in the crossing, but almost all of these men arrived on the coast on 19 November.[27] The failure of 41st Regiment to perform its rearguard role, or even to attempt to do so, is yet another black mark held against it by 144th Regiment veterans.

The messenger from Horii to 144th Regiment did not get through but Tsukamoto, as Horii suspected, had decided on retreat. On the same night 41st Regiment retreated, Tsukamoto abandoned his six guns and cut his way through the Australians on the front of 2/25th Battalion, and crossed the Kumusi near Asisi.[28] Fortunately for the Japanese, the Kumusi was low and no one was lost in the crossing. There is nothing in Japanese accounts to support the oft-repeated story that many Japanese drowned in the river.[29] The last of the four parts into which the Nankai Shitai was now split was the 1/144th, which also abandoned its two guns and escaped across the river. In the confusion Horii was separated from his headquarters and headed downriver. Several days later at the mouth of the Kumusi, he and one other found a canoe to paddle along the coast towards Giruwa. The canoe was upset in rough water, and Horii drowned. In varying degrees of disarray, but with better fortune than attended Horii, the Japanese survivors of Oivi–Gorari made their way to the coast.

CASUALTIES

The Japanese claimed to have killed 416 Australians at Oivi–Gorari, a number still accepted in Japan.[30] Official Australian records show the correct figures to be 121 killed and 225 wounded.[31] On the Oivi front the Australians lost 33 killed in action or died of wounds and 81 wounded from 4 November to 11 November. Many of these were doubtless caused by the seven guns dug into the Japanese position overlooking the Australians. Almost all of the casualties occurred on 5 and 6 November when the 2/2nd and 2/3rd each made unsuccessful attacks. On the Gorari front the Australians lost 88 killed and 144 wounded.

Less easy to sort out is Australian claims of Japanese dead. After the battle it was said there were 500 to 580 of them. In the usual Kokoda myth fashion the number grew after the war to a thousand Japanese dead.[32] At Baribe, where the main body of the 144th fought, an Australian count of 143 Japanese dead seems about right as Japanese sources, not as reliable as in other Papua battles, give between 132 and 152 dead there.[33] The first battalion of the 144th lost 53 dead at Oivi–Gorari, and this indicates a total of 196 dead for 144th Regiment, which is close to the figure of 188 in the regimental history.[34] Six men from the regiment were captured.[35] When 144th Regiment was gathered together after Oivi–Gorari to garrison Buna, it had 700 men including wounded, confirming that the regiment lost about 200 dead at Oivi–Gorari. Oddly, after Oivi–Gorari, the replacements that arrived on 2 November did not join their regiment but were placed elsewhere at the beachhead, possibly to avoid infecting the new troops with the declining morale of 144th Regiment.[36]

The other major unit, 41st Regiment, did not lose heavily while at Oivi but lost many in the retreat, and the 41st Regiment company defending Horii's headquarters was surrounded and wiped out by 2/1st Battalion.[37] Of 1293 who left the coast before the battle, 180 did not return.[38] The other major units – mountain gunners, engineers and NSHQ – appear to have lost about 60 dead, which suggests that the total number of Japanese dead was about 440. Many wounded could not be got away and chose to stay to die, but about 380 wounded did escape.[39] Nearly a third of the Japanese force that fought became casualties, something not seen in the campaign so far.

REASONS FOR THE JAPANESE DEFEAT

Sun Tzu argued that mountain fighting is rarely decisive. To reach the deciding moment in a campaign it is usually necessary to push the enemy out of the mountains and beat them on better ground where there is more opportunity to manoeuvre and achieve a decisive result. Oivi–Gorari is a good example. For all their victories in the mountains, the Japanese did not obtain a decision there. Nor did the Australian attacks from Myola Ridge to Eora decide the campaign. The Oivi–Gorari action, outside the Owen Stanley Range, did decide the campaign by inflicting heavy casualties, capturing guns and supply dumps, and driving the Japanese in complete disarray to the coast.[40]

Three major factors gave victory to the Australians. First, they held Kokoda. Having an airstrip just 16 kilometres west of Oivi increased their supply capacity many times over, and increased supply enhances fighting power. Second, the Australians were fitter and healthier than their enemy, the opposite of the situation in August and September. By Oivi–Gorari there were signs that the cumulative effect of an extended period in a hostile climate on short rations was having a serious effect on the Japanese. The Australians at Oivi–Gorari were not the same men who had fought through August and September. None present at Oivi–Gorari, except 3rd Battalion, had been forward of Port Moresby for more than two months; half had been there just a month. On the Japanese side, most had been in Papua for three months, some closer to four months, and the daily sickness rate for the Japanese was approaching a hundred whereas the Australian rate was now half that.

The third factor was generalship. The boldness of Vasey's move, in thrusting an entire brigade into the rear of a Japanese force, was something the Allies had not dared so far in the Pacific War and is comparable to the aggressive generalship of Kusunose at Efogi or Ioribaiwa.[41] That it should work, against a force Vasey did not much outnumber, further supports the view that the quality of the Nankai Shitai had deteriorated seriously after an extended time in Papua. From the Japanese perspective, the action was very poorly fought. A defender dug in with 2800 men and 15 guns was defeated by an attacker with fewer than 4000 men and no artillery, although a dozen 3-inch mortars and air support was available. The reason this occurred was that Horii was outmanoeuvred and Vasey was able to bring more fighting power to bear at the decisive point. While three Australian battalions kept 41st Regiment busy at Oivi, Vasey threw four more battalions – three-fifths of his fighting strength – against the weakened 144th Regiment at Gorari. There, from Baribe to Gorari, the Australians had a local superiority of more than two to one.

Horii exercised battlefield command just twice during the Kokoda campaign, at Isurava and Oivi–Gorari. Isurava was a mismanaged victory and Oivi–Gorari a crushing defeat. His regimental commander Kusunose, if not Tsukamoto and Yazawa, had a better record. At Oivi–Gorari Horii did not expect the Australians to send a large force into his rear. Had he anticipated this he probably would have placed a strong force blocking the track at Leaney's Corner. The unadventurous moves of Allen at Second Eora during October might well have contributed to Horii's expectation that the Australians would not be so bold in attack as they proved to be at Oivi–Gorari. What occurred was the Australian riposte to Efogi: a pinning attack to occupy the enemy to the front followed by a deep thrust into their vitals.

THE END OF THE PORT MORESBY PLAN

As Oivi–Gorari began, the plan to take Port Moresby had still not officially been abandoned, but Hyakutake's opinion, absorbed as he was by the fighting at Guadalcanal, was conspicuously absent from the discussion. Tsuji, who had returned to Seventeenth Army as its IHQ liaison officer, told Lieutenant-General Hattori Takuhiro on 3 November that Guadalcanal was lost and that the main effort should be switched to Papua.[42] Tsuji's view did not prevail. A stronger current in Rabaul, recommending abandonment of a Port Moresby attack and led by the new

Seventeenth Army Chief of Staff, Major-General Akisaburo Futami, was more persuasive to IHQ. In response to requests to consider a future course, Colonel Nishimura Susumu of the Army Ministry in Tokyo wrote a paper entitled 'Is it essential to take Port Moresby?' The thrust of his argument was that shipping demands would be too great to continue with that operation.[43] Next, liaison officer Major Iwakoshi flew in to Rabaul from Tokyo to explain that, in addition to a shortage of shipping, no air reinforcements were forthcoming. This seems to have brought Tsuji around to the majority view. A week after he told Hattori that Guadalcanal must be abandoned in favour of Papua he wrote that 'as a result [of no new air assets] we hold absolutely no hope for success in the Port Moresby campaign'.[44]

By 16 November the results of the first and second battles of Guadalcanal (12/13 November and 14/15 November) were understood in Rabaul and Tokyo. These naval and air battles were defeats for the IJN, and most of the transports containing the army reinforcements from Asia and supplies for 'starvation island' (as the Japanese soldiers now called Guadalcanal) were lost. This underlined the decision that had been made. If Guadalcanal was to be persevered with, then nothing could be done at the same time in Papua. The position was formalised on 18 November by orders from IHQ for the new Eighth Area Army that it would do no more in Papua than hold the Giruwa base while it made yet another attempt to take back Guadalcanal. Within weeks, the strategic argument would further shift to whether Papua should be abandoned.

CHAPTER 17

THE WAR IN THE AIR

To what degree did the American and Australian tactical air offensive contribute to the Japanese defeat in the mountain campaign in the Owen Stanley Range? At the time Allied propaganda claimed that air attacks killed and wounded many Japanese and crippled their supply line, and this claim has been unquestioningly adopted by the Kokoda myth.[1] If it was so, then it might be considered an important factor in any explanation of the outcome of the campaign. On the face of it this does not appear likely, as both the Allied ground support and air interdiction effort was feeble in terms of tonnage of bombs dropped. Moreover, the Allied Air Force (AAF) was dropping most of its bombs on Japanese shipping (which it usually failed to hit), not in an interdiction role along the Japanese supply line in Papua nor in a battlefield support role – now known as close air support.[2] The result of the anti-shipping attacks on the Rabaul-to-Giruwa route was that two Japanese ships were sunk and two damaged, but 90 per cent of Japanese supplies got through to Papua up to the end of the Kokoda campaign in mid-November 1942. On land the Japanese were more concerned about the effect of heavy rain on their supply line than any problem caused by air attack, and far more bridges along the Giruwa-to-Kokoda supply line were destroyed by flood than by bombs.

The AAF was formed from all United States Army Air Force (USAAF), Royal Australian Air Force (RAAF) and Royal Netherlands East Indies Army Air Force units in Australia on 20 April 1942. Its north-eastern command exercised operational control in north Queensland and eastern

New Guinea. Here 'AAF' is used to denote both it and the US Fifth Air Force, which was formed on 3 September 1942. General Kenney retained command of both organisations, and until the Nankai Shitai landing in Papua the major effort of the AAF was directed towards distant targets.[3] Briefly, in late July, the attack was redirected against the ships of Yokoyama's advanced force, then the heavy bombers switched their effort to supporting the Guadalcanal campaign by bombing Rabaul, Buka, Buin, the Shortland Islands and shipping to the west of the Solomon Islands.

The medium and light aircraft of the AAF – the B26 Marauder or B25 Mitchell medium bombers and the P40 Kittyhawk or P39 Airacobra fighters – began a serious interdiction and battlefield support effort in September in Papua and, excluding Milne Bay and the Japanese air raids on Port Moresby, it is on this that we will focus. It is not necessary to compare the air strengths of the Allies and the Japanese for by 1 September, with the shift of Japanese attention to Guadalcanal, there was a near-complete absence of air opposition to Allied aircraft over the Kokoda Track and the Kokoda-to-Sanananda route. From September on this front, only when resupply convoys approached the Giruwa anchorage did Allied aircraft meet IJN fighters escorting the transports. The AAF operational survey, in summarising events through to January 1943, concluded: '... air superiority over the area was retained by the AAF throughout the campaign. Australian ground forces were molested by enemy air attacks in only a few isolated instances.' Japanese air activity 'was negligible, allied air forces retained overwhelming superiority'.[4] What was being described was closer to air supremacy than air superiority. The most telling number is that, of 2000 AAF sorties flown along the Kokoda Track and the Sanananda track, but not out to sea, from August to November, only a handful encountered any opposition in the air.[5] On one of these occasions, 26 August, the Japanese Zeros that operated for a short period from Buna strip were caught taking off. Four were shot down and others damaged.

Putting aside the four-engined bombers, which had returned to bombing strategic targets, the AAF air campaign was conducted by medium and light bombers, fighters and fighter bombers, in two roles, interdiction and battlefield support. Interdiction has been defined as 'the employment of airpower to destroy enemy troops, supplies and equipment before they reach the battlefield, or otherwise to hinder rear area movement so as to delay or prevent the arrival of troops and supplies at the front'.[6] The battlefield-support role was an attempt to hinder or destroy enemy forces on or very near the battlefield.

General Kenney provided a useful explanation of the special problems of tactical air power in the unusual environment of the South Pacific:

Tanks and heavy artillery can be reserved for the battlefields of Europe and Africa. They have no place in jungle war. The artillery in this theatre flies ... In the Pacific theatre we have a number of islands garrisoned by small forces. These islands are nothing more or less than aerodromes ... from which modern firepower is launched. Sometimes they are true islands like Midway, sometimes they are localities on large land masses. Port Moresby, Lae and Buna are all on the island of New Guinea but the only practicable way to get from one to the other is by air or by water; they are islands as far as warfare is concerned ... every time one of these islands is taken the rear is better secured and the emplacements for the flying artillery are advanced closer and closer to Japan itself.[7]

There might be a tendency to imagine that uninhibited control of the air over Papua resembled the scale of bombing and strafing achieved by the Allied tactical air forces over France in 1944, or the destruction wrought by tactical bombers and fighters of the USN and USAAF on Japan and nearby islands in 1945. In fact, early in the war, it was nothing like this. The massive increase in size of the Allied air offensive, from 1942 to the end of the war, can be gauged from fuel consumption and bomb tonnage dropped. In 1942 (May to December) the USAAF in the Pacific consumed 2 009 000 gallons of fuel. In 1943 it used 12 903 000 gallons and in 1944, 41 396 000 gallons.[8] The figures for bomb tonnage show that for every ton dropped in 1942, 16 tons was dropped in 1944. The USAAF air effort in 1942 was a small fraction, around 6 per cent, of what it was in 1944. The RAAF flew only 10 per cent of the interdiction and ground attack sorties along the Kokoda Track, so its absence from the fuel and ordnance figures above does not materially alter the point that the Allied air offensive over the Kokoda Track, like the tactical air offensive elsewhere in the Pacific in 1942, was small.

From Queensland and Port Moresby, the AAF dropped 1484 tons of bombs from July to November 1942 – about what Allied tactical air power alone in France dropped in two busy days in 1944. Of this, 842 tons was dropped on land targets in New Guinea and of this 842 tons, 307 tons was dropped along the Kokoda Track and the Kokoda-to-Sanananda track (see table 17.1).

What effect did this air offensive have on the Nankai Shitai? The question can be answered by counting the number of Nankai Shitai casualties

Table 17.1: AAF bomb tonnage, July–November 1942

	July	August	September	October	November
AAF total tonnage dropped	180	212	240	340	512
Of above tonnage dropped:					
—On land targets	0	200	170	170	302
—On sea targets	0	12	70	170	210
Of land targets total dropped:					
—In Papua on Kokoda front either in direct supply or supply line interdict	0	44	101	42	120
—Of land targets total on bridges	0	11	12	6	0

Source: RAAF War History Section, AAF situation reports and reconnaissance reports, AWM66 2/1/1–2/4/1; AAF operations, reports, AWM66 2/2/2.

caused and by assessing the effect on the Japanese supply system in Papua. Evidence for the casualties inflicted by AAF interdiction can be found in Nankai Shitai medical records. If fighting units are put aside and only units that did not go near the front, or went near it only as carriers of supplies, are considered, then presumably the majority of the wounded in those units would have been as a result of air attack. Table 17.2 shows the wounded for this category of Japanese units for September 1942.

Of some 2500 men in these units, just five are recorded as wounded in September. For the month of October the number is 20.[9] There were some killed as well, and there were a few casualties from civilian labour units not recorded in table 17.2, but the obvious point is that casualties to air attack along the supply line were amazingly low. A medical sergeant in a hospital well behind the front recorded undergoing 15 air attacks in six weeks, which had an effect only once, killing two men and wounding two.[10] The log of 2nd Company 47th Field Anti Aircraft Artillery at Giruwa recorded that an average of two air attacks per day occurred there in October and that the battery was the target of many of them. The battery lost one killed and one wounded for the month.[11] Also at Giruwa was 5 Yokosuka SNLP. The unit log recorded 25 air attacks in 11 days, which wounded two men.[12] It would be reasonable to assume that in the rear areas of the Nankai Shitai air attack caused insignificant casualties; less than one a day in September and perhaps one a day in October.

Table 17.2: Japanese casualties to Allied air attack, September 1942

Unit	Number wounded
15th Navy Pioneer	2
120th Land Duty Company	0
106th Land Duty Company	1
9th Division Bridge Construction Company	0
24th Water Purifying Unit	0
55th Transport Regiment, detachment	0
47th Anti Aircraft Artillery Regiment	0
55th Division Field Hospital	0
7th Independent Wireless Platoon	0
8th Independent Telegraph Company	1
Seventeenth Army headquarters, detachment	0
5th Company, Shipping Engineer Regiment	0
Temporary transport company	0
55th Division Water Purification Platoon	0
55th Division infantry group headquarters, detachment	1
45th Fixed Radio Platoon	0
40th Land Duty Company	0

Source: Records of 67 LOCH, enemy publications no. 24, p. 61, AWM55 5/2.

Given these low casualty numbers it is perhaps fortunate for the AAF that the main objective of interdiction is not to inflict casualties but to disrupt enemy movement of troops and supplies. Then, as now, the theoreticians warn that not much can be expected from interdiction unless it is used in massive amounts. A study of interdiction from World War II to Vietnam concluded that a small interdiction effort was not valuable.[13] The problem was that there can be a lot of unused capacity in a supply system.[14] In Papua the AAF's interdiction campaign persuaded the Japanese to move more often at night to avoid air attack. If moving mostly at night cuts the time supplies can be moved from 24 hours a day to 12 hours a day, but 12 hours activity per day is enough to keep the force supplied, then there is 50 per cent slack in the supply system. Thus the effect of enforced night movement may not be much. The 4000 Japanese, combat troops and supply troops, forward of the Kumusi River in September and October functioned on 16 tons of supplies of all kinds per day. This required the arrival each day at Kokoda of 100 horse loads and 200 man loads. As a day's march was 15 kilometres over four days from the Sambo roadhead to Kokoda, only six hours marching was needed each day – perhaps longer, allowing for slower movement in the dark. Had the Japanese been trying to maintain a much larger force beyond Kokoda such that they needed to use their supply line 24 hours a day, or had the interdiction effort been several times stronger, it may have had a large effect. As things were, air interdiction appears to have achieved little. According to General Tanaka Kengoro, the system functioned adequately and disruption caused by air attack was manageable: 'Enemy bombing did not so seriously interfere because the land movement of supply was carried out during the night or [during] intervals of the bombing.'[15]

The AAF interdiction was not spread evenly all along the line of communication and supply. General Kenney's analysts advised that the AAF concentrate on a natural choke point, where the Japanese supply line crossed the Kumusi River.[16] This place was generally spoken of by the Australians as Wairopi and by the Japanese as Papaki. There, or rather over a 7-kilometre stretch of the Kumusi River in this vicinity, the Japanese at various times used numerous bridge sites, or fords when the river was low. On 29 August, the Kumusi attack began. There was some fanfare at the time, but the bomb tonnage shown in table 17.1 reveals that not much changed. In August 11 tons of bombs was dropped on bridges, almost entirely at the Kumusi. In September 12 tons was dropped and 6 in October. These low numbers undercut the grand claims made for this series of attacks.

The AAF did, however, manage to twice destroy a large wooden bridge over the Kumusi. The reason Kenney thought the Kumusi was a choke point has to do with this bridge. It was a part of an upgrade of Japanese communications, to provide a vehicular road all the way from Giruwa to Kokoda. For this task the Japanese 1st Bridge Construction Company was detached from 9th Division in China. It arrived in Papua on the *Kinai Maru* on 13 August. The company brought 1650 tons of lumber and 220 tons of cement for bridge building.[17] With the assistance of 4th Independent Engineer Regiment, a bridge capable of bearing vehicles over the Kumusi was completed on 7 September. It was washed away in the great flood of 10 September and rebuilt. On 25 September the bridge was first knocked down by the AAF, but by 28 September Japanese engineers had rebuilt it. On 3 October it was destroyed again and not rebuilt. Nothing was done to protect the Kumusi bridges from air attack until 22 October when a machine-gun company was moved there.[18]

Why was the bridge not rebuilt a third time, and why were anti-aircraft guns not placed there? The answer is that the Japanese judged it unnecessary because, as we have seen when examining the supply crisis, flooding rain was a far greater concern, and because the Kumusi crossing was, in the absence of rain, not the choke point Kenney imagined. Over the period of the Kokoda campaign the Kumusi was in flood and uncrossable about 10 per cent of the time. Until wooden bridges were built, suspension bridges were used, and about half the time even these were unnecessary as the Kumusi was so low that it was easily fordable.

The AAF was aware that several fords and bridges were in use across the Kumusi, but they were not certain of how many. In fact the Nankai Shitai used least five sites for bridges and six for fords. On 17 September and 3 October RAAF air crew reported rope bridges in several places, and a report of 6 October said that the old suspension bridge at Wairopi had been destroyed but that there was bridge-building activity between the old and new bridges. Another pilot saw a bridge about 5 kilometres south of Wairopi, but the report was unclear about which of the several known Japanese bridges it was.[19] It was probably the suspension bridge near Asisi, which was the Nankai Shitai's preferred crossing of the Kumusi. The river was seen to be fordable on 25 and 28 September and 10 October.[20] On 20 and 24 October the river was low again, and an Australian 2/6th Independent Company observer hidden on high ground near Asisi watched Japanese troops crossing the river at a ford.[21]

Drawing together the threads of the discussion so far, three points stand out. First, the Kumusi offered many crossings on a 7-kilometre front so it was impossible to cut Japanese supply there. When it was cut, it was the weather's doing, not the AAF's. Second, the wooden bridge built by 1 BCC was not an essential feature of the Japanese supply line but rather an improvement to allow trucks to proceed to Kokoda. That trucks could now carry supplies more than half way from the coast to Kokoda already significantly enhanced the capacity of the supply line. The loss of the bridge built to carry trucks across the Kumusi river limited further improvement but was not a fatal blow. General Tanaka, who was quoted earlier saying that bombing and strafing was not a serious problem for supply, did point to one occasion when for a period a suspension bridge was knocked out, causing inconvenience. Notably, he did not think the destruction of the wooden vehicular bridge by bombing was as serious as the loss of the suspension bridge nor was it as worrying as the problem of the floods.[22] The third point that stands out concerns the date the wooden bridge was first knocked down by the AAF, which shows that this event was unrelated to the supply crisis. The bridge was not destroyed by air attack until 25 September, which was ten days *after* severe supply shortages first occurred at the front line in the mountains.

Turning to battlefield support missions, an American study of tactical air power in World War II stated that the USAAF's April 1942 ground support manual 'went out the window' when the aircrews encountered the difficulties of spotting a target in the jungles of New Guinea and the Solomon Islands.[23] Friendly troops were bombed by mistake increasing the reluctance of ground units to call in air attacks on enemy close by. The result was battlefield support missions were rarely executed in Papua because the jungle hid both the target and nearby friendly troops. An IJA post campaign study concluded that 'the force nearest the enemy suffered least damage from bombing.'[24]

Like interdiction, aerial bombing had to be truly massive in scale to cause many casualties. From June 1942, the USAAF began a bombing campaign against the Japanese-held islands in the Aleutian chain in Alaska. After the war it was discovered that 4300 tons of bombs killed 450 Japanese, or 10 tons of bombs per fatality. Other studies confirmed that this was an average result.[25] If this ratio is applied to Papua then the 307 tons of bombs dropped on land from the Owen Stanley Range to Giruwa from July to November might be expected to have killed 30 Japanese and wounded perhaps double that.

The United States Strategic Bombing Survey study of the effect of their air attack over the whole Pacific War concluded that about one in nine of all IJA killed and wounded were caused by air attack.[26] As Allied air power increased twenty-fold from 1942 to 1944, presumably the proportion of IJA killed and wounded by air attack was a great deal smaller in 1942. Another study of the effects of aerial bombs and artillery on troops argued that the key factor was not how well dug in the target was but how well dispersed the soldiers were.[27] A given amount of bombs was found to kill or injure twice the number of men within the target area if they were concentrated in half the space. The degree to which they were entrenched was a factor, but a lesser factor than how concentrated they were. The study did not address the added difficulty of determining the location of the target in jungle foliage. The target in the Aleutians was well dug in whereas Japanese attacked on the Kokoda Track were usually not dug in, but this was counter-balanced by the fact that the targets were, in many cases, dispersed in a single marching column over great distances along a track. In short, mountainous terrain will of itself disperse the target.

On one notable occasion the Japanese were concentrated when attacked from the air. This was 7 September as they prepared to attack

Photo 23 A suspension bridge built by the Australians using the remains of a more substantial Japanese bridge at Wairopi (known to the Japanese as Papaki), November 1942. Several kilometres either side of Wairopi along the Kumusi the Japanese used half a dozen bridges, and fords when the river was low. From September 1942 the Allied Air Force began attacking the Kumusi bridges in an attempt to disrupt the Japanese supply line. (AWM P02423.033)

the Australians at Efogi. The evidence usually cited for the number of men lost comes from Lieutenant Hayashi Hiroyuki, who wrote in his diary, 'Our losses from the bombing attack today totalled 100.'[28] If this were true it was a feather in the cap for battlefield support from the air. Unfortunately Hayashi was not present; he was with 1/144th Battalion 20 kilometres away, and was repeating the first alarming reports coming from the front. Nankai Shitai commander Horii also took the report at face value and passed it on to Rabaul the same day, before he could have known that it was overblown. A day or two later Horii discovered that the casualties were much less, but it appears to have suited him at the time not to point this out to his superiors. Horii lost all his air support at the start of September, coincidentally at the same moment the AAF embarked on its air offensive, and complained about it frequently to Hyakutake. In the same message he followed up mention of the Efogi air attack with: 'The lack of Japanese fighter activity means that enemy planes have complete control of the air ... I wish for steps to be taken to dispatch Japanese planes.'[29]

The true figure for the Japanese loss to bombs from aircraft for 7 September is 11 killed and about 20 wounded. The Japanese force bombed by 22nd Bombardment Group aircraft was entirely from 144th Regiment, and all the bombs fell on its third battalion. The 144th Regiment's list of its war dead cites 11 men killed by air attack on 7 September.[30] The battalion history of the 3/144th, somewhat unkindly, says that 'Lieutenant Kazue, the unpopular 3/144 pay officer, and ten others were killed'.[31] The number of wounded is less certain but was between 18 and 21.[32] For 16 tons of bombs dropped from 16 USAAF Marauders on 6 and 7 September to kill 13 (two on 6 September) and wound about twice that was still an impressive tally, but one not repeated in the campaign. The same USAAF unit a week earlier, in the same location, accidentally dropped six tons of bombs on the Australian 39th Battalion and hit no one.

The Kokoda myth has always been more concerned with the doings of Australian infantry in the front line and less concerned with other aspects of the fighting, so the war in the air has never been a strong feature of it. The air attack at Efogi is an exception, and an interesting one, as it tells us something about how the Kokoda myth has been constructed. No great claims were made by the Australians at the time of Efogi for huge casualties inflicted by an air attack they could plainly see from Mission Ridge. The 7 September attack is merely described in war diaries as 'heartening' or a 'great job'. In the 1957 official history the air attack is reported but with no claim about its effect, and in Colonel Keogh's 1965 *South-West Pacific 1941–1945* it was 'without any apparent effect'.[33] Raymond Paull's 1958 *Retreat from Kokoda* comes to a different conclusion. Paull had examined the Allied Translator and Interpreter Service translations and found Hayashi's diary entry reporting a hundred casualties.[34] Some authors since have followed Keogh and McCarthy, saying that the result of the air strike was never ascertained, while others have followed Paull and improved on him: in Paul Ham's *Kokoda* the hundred casualties have become a hundred dead, presumably with many more wounded, although this is not stated.[35] The myth has always been convinced that large numbers of Japanese were present at the series of battles on the Kokoda Track from July to September 1942, so it has been natural to assume that the whole of the Nankai Shitai, including diarist Hayashi and General Horii, were present to witness the air attack, but they were not.

The evidence should make us doubtful that air interdiction or ground support played anything approaching a decisive role in the campaign. This was also the view of the Japanese senior officers interviewed in Rabaul at the end of the war. They described casualties to air attack in the Kokoda campaign as light.[36] This is not to say that it was completely ineffective.

Samuel Marshall's study of World War II combat effectiveness, *Men Against Fire*, concluded that while air attack was far from being the main killer of infantry it was the most feared item in the enemy's arsenal. The Australian Army, after 1942, also looked into what weapon was most feared by the Japanese and came up with a result similar to Marshall. The report quotes Japanese diaries and prisoner interrogations: 'September 6 1942. Enemy air attacks have struck terror into our hearts. The morale of the ground troops is low',[37] or: '[Prisoner] stated he joined the army prepared to die for his country but when he thought of the bombing and the strafing [when] they got caught in the open in New Guinea, he still got the cold shivers ...'[38]

While terrifying the Japanese by air attack was a desirable outcome, MacArthur's claims for the air offensive along the Kokoda Track do not stand up: 'The outstanding military lesson of this campaign was the continuous calculated application of air power ... employed in the most intimate tactical and logistical union with ground troops.'[39] Nothing in this chapter concerning the period from July to November 1942 substantiates MacArthur's assertion, and a more circumspect conclusion was reached by the 1944 USAAF study of AAF air power in New Guinea in 1942 in which MacArthur's statement appeared. The study conceded that the performance of the AAF was hard to judge and did not seem to have been very successful:

> It is difficult to assess the contribution of the allied air forces during
> the first months of the Papuan campaign ... little evidence exists
> to support the glowing claims as to the damage done to the enemy
> along the Kokoda Track. Over much of it jungle foliage made
> possible effective concealment ... even the bombing and strafing of
> villages did not necessarily result in the wholesale destruction of
> stores since it is doubtful trained soldiers would have conveniently
> concentrated supplies in such obvious targets [and] in spite of losses
> the Japanese navy was able to reinforce the New Guinea invaders
> almost at will ... In spite of Allied [air] efforts during the first phase
> of the campaign the Japanese had had almost complete success.[40]

The Japanese official history is of the opinion that Allied air power had a major influence on events along the Kokoda Track, and Lieutenant-General Miyazaki Shuichi at IHQ in Tokyo agreed, but this was not the view of IJA and IJN officers who experienced it.[41] The size of the AAF offensive against the Japanese supply line was tiny compared to later in the war and was a classic case of a small interdiction effort not being worth the cost. Papua cost the AAF 344 aircraft and 540 American and Australian aircrew to January 1943. Half were lost, almost entirely to ground fire and accident, in the air offensive of the Kokoda campaign phase of the fighting in Papua. Against this, few Japanese were killed, nor did the AAF much interrupt Japanese supply, although it might have exacerbated what the rain initiated. When it is considered that all the bridges and all of the road from Giruwa to Oivi was washed away in the flood of 10 September, leaving a 100-kilometre mud lake in its place, this is clearly an achievement of the weather of an order of magnitude unapproachable by tactical air power.

CHAPTER | 18

CONCLUSION

The monument known as the Lion of Macedon on the battlefield of Chaeronea marks the victory of Phillip II of Macedon over the Greeks in 338 BC. In the ancient world a trophy was raised on the battlefield by the victor – never the vanquished. Now the vanquished do the same, and in 2002, at Isurava, Australia erected four granite pillars to a defeat. The sentiment, however, is different. One of the pillars has 'sacrifice' carved on it, and the Isurava monument conveys something of the feeling of the earth mound containing the remains of Spartan, Beotian and Theban dead at the Greek defeat of Thermopylae in 480 BC – a battle to which Isurava has been compared. An important part of the Thermopylae tradition, however, is that the Greeks were defeated fighting against overwhelming odds, which was not the case for the Australians at Isurava, nor elsewhere on the Kokoda Track.

The heart of the Kokoda myth is that the Australians were defeated on the Kokoda Track from July to September 1942 because they were greatly outnumbered. Japanese records show that this is untrue. The Papuans and Australians were outnumbered by one and a half to one up to First Kokoda. At Second Kokoda and Deniki they were slightly outnumbered, and at Isurava there was one Australian for each Japanese engaged. During the retreat from Eora to Efogi the Japanese superiority was at its highest, at close to two to one for five days from 1 September. At Efogi the two sides were about equal strength, and at the last Australian defeat at Ioribawa it was the Australians who outnumbered the Japanese almost two to one.

Photo 24 The Isurava Memorial was constructed in 2002 in remembrance of Australians and Papua New Guineans who died on the Kokoda Track in 1942. The memorial is said to be adjacent to where Private Bruce Kingsbury performed an act of valour for which he was posthumously awarded the Victoria Cross. The memorial features four Australian black granite pillars each inscribed with a single word – 'courage', 'endurance', 'mateship' and 'sacrifice' – representing the values and qualities of those Australian soldiers who fought along the Kokoda Track. The view looks toward Kokoda in the direction from which the Japanese approached the Australian position at Isurava. (Author's collection)

Why did Australians become convinced that there was a huge Japanese force advancing along the Kokoda Track in 1942? There is enough contrary evidence in Australian records alone, especially the translated documents in the Allied Translator and Interpreter Service held at the Australian War Memorial. The evidence might have been overlooked for three reasons. First, Australian military history tends not to be comparative. The focus of study is usually on the Australians, not their enemy. That said, a positive aspect of the writing about Kokoda by Paull, Ham, McAulay, Collie and Marutani is that they have used some Japanese sources and brought to the fore some aspects of the Japanese story. Second, the Japanese strength was roughly known at the top of the Allied chain of command by September 1942, while contrary information – that the Japanese were in great strength – was coming from battalion and brigade sources. It is the latter whose view had been accepted, not the former. Interestingly, in jungle war more than a few enemy at a time are rarely seen, so the view that there was a huge number of Japanese present was some kind of conviction, without hard evidence to underpin it – Japanese soldiers often thought they were outnumbered too.

There is an implicit prejudice in many postwar accounts against generals, especially MacArthur and Blamey at the top. In the middle were the corps commanders, Rowell then Herring, who escape without much criticism and, lower down, Allen, a divisional commander, and Brigadiers Potts and Eather and battalion commanders Honner, Cameron and Owen, who are favoured by postwar writers. The Kokoda myth gives their opinion far greater weight than that of the higher ranks. In short, when Potts incorrectly said he was outnumbered he was, and is, believed by the mythmakers. When MacArthur correctly said Potts was not outnumbered he is chastised. Even McCarthy, the author of official history volume on the campaign, normally not much given to exaggeration, said, '... MacArthur (completely disregarding the facts) told General Marshall in America: "The Australians have proven themselves unable to match the enemy in jungle fighting."'[1] The third reason evidence contrary to the myth has been set aside is that it is palatable to read of victories; almost as acceptable are defeats against overwhelming numbers. It is quite the opposite to read of battles lost fairly and squarely, and it is hard to make a myth from it.

Nor is the Kokoda myth correct to state that Japanese losses, especially in their advance, were many times heavier than those of the Australians and that this mitigates the series of defeats suffered in the first half of the campaign. The origin of the error is in overclaiming at the time by both sides. Australian post-battle estimates of huge Japanese losses have often been accepted and decades on have become cemented into the Kokoda myth. In fact total battle casualties to the end of Ioribaiwa (including minor skirmishes that have not been discussed in this book) were equal. Both sides lost about 900 men. To the end of Second Eora–Templeton's battle casualties rose to 1380 Australians against 1220 Japanese. This was overturned at Oivi–Gorari, and total battle casualties for the Kokoda campaign, from the first fight at Awala to Oivi–Gorari, were about 2050 Japanese and 1760 Australians.

Presumably Japanese casualties would have been much heavier had they often engaged in the 'banzai charge', descriptions of which makes frequent appearances in books that cultivate the Kokoda myth. In fact waves of massed Japanese were never seen during the Kokoda campaign, although there were occasions when sections and platoons did so. The army Japan possessed in 1942 was highly skilled after years of war in China. Japanese doctrine laid stress on winning by cunning and with as few casualties as possible. Japanese officers were told that their good-quality infantry was not to be thoughtlessly squandered when manoeuvre, firepower and time might obtain a better result at less cost. The bayonet charge was to be used sparingly, to finish off an enemy whose powers were so reduced that it could be done without much loss. The massed banzai charge was mainly, although not exclusively, a late-war tactic used when the quality of the Japanese infantry was in decline and it was less well able to perform complex manoeuvres on the battlefield.

Guadalcanal has loomed large in the examination of Japanese strategy as it concerned the campaign in Papua. Because of the American landing at Guadalcanal on 7 August 1942, Horii's march on Port Moresby was put on hold almost before it had begun. One after another the Ichiki, Kawaguchi and Aoba Detachments, more than 7000 troops who might have reinforced Giruwa or ensured victory at Milne Bay, were sent to Guadalcanal instead. As the MO operation was never reactivated it follows that the Australians on the Kokoda Track did not save Port Moresby nor did the Japanese plan fall 'fatally behind schedule' as there was no longer a schedule to keep.[2] Indeed, a better argument could be made that it was the Americans at Guadalcanal who saved Port Moresby. As General Tanaka said, there was a plan to assemble a large force and march along the Kokoda Track to take Port Moresby but, because of Guadalcanal, the force never assembled.

Japan had long contemplated a southward advance so New Guinea received a share of attention in the intelligence work done in the 1930s. By 1941 the Japanese, always more interested in a landward approach to Port Moresby, were examining the route via Kokoda. A series of studies was conducted, and Japanese knowledge about the route of advance over the Owen Stanley Range was quite good. Among their sources of information the names Chinnery, Hofstetter, Cheesman and Toyofuku are important. The decision to send less artillery and more engineers to Papua than to Guadalcanal is evidence that the Japanese were well apprised of the extreme difficulties of an advance over the Owen Stanley Range.

Turning now to the actions and engagements of the campaign, First Kokoda was a fight of an hour's duration where the legend of overwhelming Japanese numbers first appears. Second Kokoda was the more interesting affair both tactically and strategically. Cameron's counter-attack took Tsukamoto by surprise, and the repercussions were felt in Rabaul where strong and unanticipated Australian resistance had Hyakutake considering postponing the MO operation just as news of the Guadalcanal landing arrived. Deniki was important to both sides. As Second Kokoda had demonstrated, the Australians threatened both Kokoda and Oivi from Deniki. Tsukamoto's objective in attacking Deniki was to deny this option to the Australians, as well as denying them the view from Deniki overlooking Japanese activity in the Kokoda–Pirivi area.

Most of the Japanese 144th Regiment's extensive experience of war was against second-class Chinese troops, and they themselves did not think they were really tested at Guam and Rabaul. Isurava was the first time since the 1937 Battle of Shanghai that someone had stood up to the 144th, and they expressed surprise at the toughness of the Australian defence. At the same time the Australian stand presented an opportunity for Horii to wipe out Maroubra Force. He failed to do so as he mishandled the attack. A defeat was inflicted on the Australians, but Maroubra Force was not destroyed. First Eora, following Isurava, was a well-executed rearguard action on the part of the Australians. Yazawa's 41st Regiment took over the pursuit there and three times failed to cut off and annihilate the Australians. At both Isurava and First Eora entire Japanese battalions became lost in the jungle and failed to participate in the fighting.

At Efogi, at last, the Japanese hit their stride. Kusunose showed himself to be a better commander than either Horii or Yazawa. Whether Potts could have avoided defeat at Efogi is debatable, but at the next action, Ioribaiwa, there is a clearer case of Australian command failure. Kusunose frightened Eather into retreat by aggressive use of a force half the size of that which Eather commanded. Eather did well later in the campaign, but the defence that he did not know how many enemy there were at Ioribaiwa – and the same might be said of Potts at Efogi – does not hold up. It is a normal condition of warfare for commanders not to know the strength of the enemy. When the standard of generalship shown by an individual is measured, only small allowance is made for ignorance of enemy strength. The American Civil War Union Generals George McClellan, in 1862, and Joseph Hooker, in 1863, are well-known examples. They outnumbered their enemy but believed themselves heavily outnumbered, so they retreated. The verdict of historians on these two men is that their generalship was at fault and that ignorance of enemy strength is not an excuse for defeat.

In the second half of the Kokoda campaign, during the Australian advance from Ioribaiwa, it is well known that the Australians outnumbered the Japanese, but here too there is a little myth-making as the Australian offensive does not look so impressive when compared to the earlier Japanese advance. With no numerical superiority, except for a short period at First Eora, the Japanese, from their first attack at Isurava on 26 August took 22 days to take Ioribaiwa and push the Australians back to Imita Ridge. The subsequent Australian advance from Imita Ridge commenced on 26 September and, with a superiority varying between two and four to one, with better supply and fresh troops (and Vickers medium machine-guns and medium mortars that to some extent counter-balanced the Japanese advantage in long-range weapons), still took 36 days to fight their way back to Isurava. This is the reason Allen was relieved: he advanced too slowly with a force that was strong enough to advance quickly.

Because the Kokoda myth concentrates on the front line it misses the broad picture. The Japanese had committed themselves to win Guadalcanal and keep Papua on hold until then. Allen's superiors rightly believed that if he could put pressure on Giruwa by a rapid advance along the Kokoda Track then the Japanese would have had to reinforce Giruwa, thus easing the American difficulties at Guadalcanal, or abandon it. The sooner Allen could do this the better. Sometimes in war speed is required even at the cost of heavy casualties. The Australian advance along the Kokoda Track from late September 1942 was one of those occasions. Evidence from Japanese sources also suggests that Allen's opportunity at Second Eora was greater than has been suspected. On 20 October his men had broken the back of the main Japanese defences at Templeton's Crossing, but Allen did not realise it. Horii was caught with an inadequate force to defend Eora village in the third phase of fighting, and there was a gap in his line that the Australians failed to find. There were a few days before the Japanese reinforced Eora when Allen might have taken the position. But Allen was cautious and the chance passed.

The last action of the campaign, Oivi–Gorari, was the Australian Efogi. To November a certain man-for-man superiority of the Japanese over the Australians could be argued for, but it seems to be absent at Oivi–Gorari. There the Australians were well commanded and well supplied, whereas the Nankai Shitai, again fighting under Horii's direction, was not well handled and had been slowly worn down by three months in the jungle. Australian, American and Japanese studies all concluded that three months at war in an environment like Papua brought about a noticeable deterioration in any military force. By Oivi–Gorari the Japanese had had their three months in the jungle, whereas none of the Australians they faced had been there as long.

To point out the problems with the Kokoda myth is to make an argument that, until the Australian victory at Oivi–Gorari, the Australians in the Kokoda campaign did not do as well as has been portrayed. Their retreat was a series of defeats without any counter-balancing advantages, and their subsequent advance was slow. American criticism that the Australians on the Kokoda Track did not do well enough to take pressure off Guadalcanal has merit.

Some factors that might explain the outcome of the battles of the Kokoda campaign have been identified here and others dismissed. According to the Kokoda myth, the Japanese supply problem was an important reason for their defeat, but this is not correct. At the beginning, the Japanese were fairly well prepared in terms of supply and planned to do, with some modification, what had worked well for them for decades, and worked extremely well since December 1941. Airdropping of supplies was expected to supplement what could be carried, but Guadalcanal removed this option by taking IJN aircraft away from Papua. The Japanese supply crisis has been overstated. When it arose, in late September, the Nankai Shitai was in retreat but, it must be emphasised, not because of the supply difficulties. When the main body of the combat troops returned to the Kokoda–Kumusi area, supply improved. It was a smaller force, the Stanley Detachment, which stayed in the mountains, that came close to starvation. The larger picture of a starving Nankai Shitai is inaccurate.

Allied air superiority did not have much effect on the outcome of the fighting. Studies of air interdiction have shown that very large numbers of aircraft are necessary to have a serious effect, but the AAF campaign was a small one unlikely to achieve results. Airpower neither prevented the movement of troops and supplies along the Japanese line of communications nor killed or wounded many Japanese. Its effect on Japanese supply was nowhere near as large as the exceptionally heavy rain in September that washed away the supply line from Giruwa to Kokoda. Losses to disease is another factor thought to have caused Japanese defeat, but it is more likely to have disadvantaged the Australians, especially up to September when Australian losses to sickness were several times greater than those of the Japanese.

In his book *Kokoda*, Peter Fitzsimons is half right about one thing. He says, while criticising MacArthur, that he sent the Australians against 'an enemy overwhelming in its numbers and its firepower'.[3] The Japanese were not overwhelming in numbers, but perhaps they were in firepower. The light guns and howitzers they employed in all of the engagements might have been the deciding factor accounting for Japanese success in attack and stubbornness in defence. It may be that the Nankai Shitai artillery gave them such an advantage, especially against an enemy without any, that artillery is the single most important element explaining the outcome of the Australian defensive battles. During the Japanese retreat, too, it was an important factor in delaying the Australians. It is difficult to imagine the great Australian victory at Oivi–Gorari occurring at all if the Australians had had no choice but to attack straight into the eight Japanese guns on the Oivi heights. It seems, then, that the Japanese did obtain value from the immense effort they put into carrying a dozen guns into the mountains.

If artillery was not the decisive factor, then another possibility is morale. The majority of Japanese on the Kokoda Track believed in the warriors' code, bushido. Bushido, the way of the warrior, is described in an old Japanese saying as the soldier's search for a place to die. Their diaries reveal that most of the fighting soldiers of the Nankai Shitai believed that once they left Japan their lives belonged to the Emperor to dispose of as he desired and that they did not expect to return to Japan. The cult of bushido is of course alien to the Western way of thinking, although Western military theorists were aware of its advantages. Prussian General Gerhard von Scharnhorst, influential in remaking the Prussian army during the Napoleonic Wars, said, 'Victory is won by teaching soldiers how to die, not how to avoid dying.'[4] The Australians did not think this way. They wanted to survive the war if at all possible. To the Japanese this attitude appeared to show a lack of 'fighting spirit'; to the Australians it was common sense.

Morale is also built from training, experience and confidence in leaders. Morale is impossible to quantify, but it seems a reasonable view that at the start of the Kokoda campaign, Japanese superiority in training and experience of war, together with bushido, resulted in higher morale than the Australians had. Australian morale declined after Isurava, where the Japanese thought the Australians fought well, and rose again when the Australians, with fresh troops, commenced their advance from Imita Ridge. The panicked withdrawal of the Japanese at Templeton's Crossing on 20 October 1942 marks a turning point. That the Australians were now on the plus side of the morale ledger was confirmed at Oivi–Gorari. Even so, the conclusion of General Sir Thomas Blamey's report on the campaign may be open to doubt: 'The chief reason for our success in this campaign was our ground troops proved to be better led, better equipped and better trained than those of the enemy and were, man for man, better fighters.'[5]

The other seven elements of the Kokoda myth that have been identified are none of them as important as the central myth: that the eight-week-long series of Australian defeats from First Kokoda to Ioribaiwa can correctly be characterised as a feat of Homeric proportions, a David and Goliath struggle, or like trying to stem a tidal wave. This is what Professor Hank Nelson meant when he said the campaign was burdened with exaggeration – all these comparisons rely on the Nankai Shitai having had an enormous advantage in numbers. They did not, so the campaign does not deserve the epic descriptions it has attracted, and any explanation for the battles the Australians lost can no longer rely on this excuse. The Kokoda campaign, however, did end in an Australian victory and set the scene for the eviction of the Japanese from Papua at the Battle of Buna–Gona, fought from the end of November 1942 to January 1943. The main reason for the Australian victory in the Kokoda campaign was superior numbers – more than twice as many Australians than Japanese fought on the Kokoda Track.

NOTE ON SOURCES

The Japanese equivalent of the Australian War Memorial (AWM) in Canberra is the Military Archive at the National Institute for Defense Studies (NIDS). NIDS in Tokyo is the nation's official repository of historical military documents related to the Imperial Army and Navy. The NIDS holdings on the Kokoda campaign are collections of unit records and more general theatre and campaign records. Unit records, often assembled by the veterans, are in the main collations of original documents with little supporting narrative or analysis. For Kokoda, those of 144th Regiment, 41st Regiment and 55th Mountain Artillery Regiment are of outstanding importance.[1] One type of unit record that can sometimes be found at NIDS that has no Australian counterpart is a company history. NIDS holds several company histories for infantry, signals and artillery companies that fought in the Kokoda campaign.[2]

In Tokyo there are two other key locations for researching World War II in New Guinea: the Yasukuni Shrine and the National Diet Library. The Kaiko Bunkyo, an archive attached to the Yasukuni Shrine to the war dead, houses a large collection of books written about the war. It has no Australian equivalent in that the collection is devoted only to Japanese authored accounts, whether technical, analytical or reminiscent. The East New Guinea Comrades Association, which has its office nearby, is the starting point for contacting veterans associations. These meet annually in the cities where the regiment was raised. The depot of 144th Regiment was in the Shikoku city of Kochi. The region is wholly mountainous, at least as rugged if not as tree-covered as the Owen Stanley Range. Japanese veterans will often comment that it is no surprise that the men of Shikoku excelled in mountain warfare. The most useful items in the regimental collection in Kochi are a detailed account of the regiment's doings from 1941 to 1945 and a list of those who died while serving in the regiment. The list is especially important as it records day and place of death. Copies are held at NIDS.

The other infantry regiment that participated in the Kokoda campaign was 41st Regiment, from Fukuyama near Hiroshima. There is tension, amounting to bitterness, between the survivors of the two regiments. The veterans of the 144th accuse those of the 41st of letting them down on a number of occasions during the campaign. Veterans of 41st Regiment, citing a Japanese proverb that defeated soldiers should not talk about their battles, only reluctantly give access to their collection or grant interviews.

The National Diet Library in Tokyo bears comparison with the National Library of Australia (NLA). It holds a complete collection of the magazine *Maru*, which began in 1925. The magazine is devoted to Japanese military history since the Meiji era and contains more than a thousand personal accounts of Japanese soldiers, sailors and airmen who served during World War II. The remaining Japanese sources for the Kokoda campaign can be found in Australia. By far the most important primary source, and second only to NIDS overall, is the Allied Translation and Interpreter Service (ATIS) collection in the AWM. Then follows the Australia–Japan Research Project (AJRP) collection, and third the Japanese monographs at the NLA. The importance of the ATIS collection is recognised at NIDS, which has, via the AJRP, obtained copies of ATIS documents to fill gaps in its own records. ATIS was established in September 1942 with a view to gaining an intelligence advantage by collecting and translating captured Japanese documents and interrogating prisoners of war. Only a small proportion of all documents obtained were deemed worthy of translation into English. Even so, the incomplete AWM collection of ATIS has more than 100 000 translated pages in 55 volumes. Perhaps 5000 pages relate directly to the Kokoda campaign.[3] In addition, ATIS has a large number of translated Japanese personal diaries. Those of officers often contain a daily account of the strength of their unit as well as casualties to sickness and battle. Some of these are the only surviving source of information on Japanese unit strengths and casualties for particular days of the campaign.

Since 1997, and from 2002 with Dr Steven Bullard as project manager, the AJRP has provided access to Japanese records for Australians as well as introducing Japanese scholars to Australian military history collections. Although the AJRP no longer exists, it has left a valuable online database of translated accounts, documents and research by Dr Bullard, Dr Tamura Keiko and other scholars. There are also essays on Australian and Japanese collections that relate to the war in New Guinea, and the AJRP has translated a number of captured Japanese documents held by the Australian War Memorial.

The Japanese monographs, held at the National Library of Australia, is a series of accounts commissioned by the United States War Department and written by former Imperial Japanese Navy (IJN) and Imperial Japanese Army (IJA) officers.[4] Fifteen monographs discuss the Kokoda campaign. Their reliability varies as they were not always composed by those with intimate knowledge of the events they describe. The War Investigation Branch of the IJA Headquarters, under US direction, collected documents and private papers where it could not interview senior officers who participated in the campaign. Two especially useful ones were written by Lieutenant-Colonel Sadashima Noriyuki, who was a staff officer in Rabaul with Seventeenth Army in 1942.[5]

The main secondary Japanese source used is the *Senshi Sosho*, the Japanese official history. In 1955 NIDS took over the collection of the Office of War Studies and from 1966 to 1980 published the Japanese official history of World War II in 102 volumes. This series, known as the *Senshi Sosho*, is not an official history either in the traditional British style or in the Australian style. The focus is on the higher levels of war and emphasises command and strategy at the expense of front-line accounts. In contrast, the World War I and World War II Australian official histories are written in what might be called the Charles Bean style, in placing greater emphasis on the front-line experience but without neglecting the broader aspects of command and control.

The *Senshi Sosho* is neither fish nor fowl. Its authors, former senior officers of the IJN and IJA, were not trained historians, and the lack of an investigative approach is noticeable. The *Senshi Sosho* suffers from gaps in primary documentation, occasioned either by, as in the case of the Nankai Shitai, the near entire destruction of the force with attendant loss of documents in January 1943, or by the 'great incineration' of documents begun in Japan just before the end of the war. This was designed to destroy evidence that otherwise might be used in war crimes trials, but much that was irrelevant to those trials was also destroyed. As a consequence, a few parts of the *Senshi Sosho* were written from nothing but recollections of surviving officers twenty or thirty years after the event. Even this was a problem. While many Australian commanders, junior and senior, made themselves available to postwar researchers, the same cannot be said for the Nankai Shitai as 80 per cent of its members did not survive the war. As an example of the gaps in the *Senshi Sosho*, it skates so lightly over the fighting at Efogi in early September 1942 that it is not at all clear from the text that one of the most successful Japanese victories occurred there. That said, the *Senshi Sosho* does contain verbatim copies of a large number of important documents relevant to the Kokoda campaign, and these, which can also be found in the ATIS collection, can be relied upon. NIDS staff describe the *Senshi Sosho* as an accurate but disjointed account, and this is a fair assessment. Fortunately for Australian scholars, Dr Steven Bullard has translated the part of the *Senshi Sosho* concerned with events in Papua up to the end of the fighting in January 1943.[6]

Japanese accounts of the Kokoda campaign have contributed to the Kokoda myth. Two examples are Ienaga Saburo's *Pacific War 1931–45* and Tanaka Kengoro's *Operations of the Imperial Japanese Armed Forces in Papua New Guinea During WWII*. These are available in English translation and have repeated the error concerning the numbers of Japanese in the Owen Stanley Range in 1942 in assuming that the main body of the Nankai Shitai advanced south beyond Isurava. Very rarely a Japanese account appears in translation in an Australian journal. Moda's article 'From the other side: Success then death on the Kokoda Track' is one of a handful. One Japanese account, by Okada Seizo, should be avoided, although it is a favourite of the Kokoda mythologisers. As a newspaper reporter he covered the Japanese advance on Port Moresby and wrote an account in 1944, then an uncensored version called *Lost Soldiers* in 1946. It is so riddled with errors that it is hard to accept Okada was there. He was, but it appears he was never at the front line. For instance, he seems to have been in the middle of the Maguli Range, 50 kilometres from Port Moresby and where there is no prospect of a view of the sea when, on 12 September 1942, he witnessed the Japanese soldiers go 'wild with joy' as they saw the sea and soon expected to be in Port Moresby.[7] He claimed that the Nankai Shitai had already sustained 80 per cent losses in battle casualties and sickness by September, although it is easy to show that losses were no more than 10 per cent. Apparently during the retreat from Ioribaiwa the Japanese 'fled for dear life ... discipline completely forgotten'. But as Okada left the front before the retreat commenced it is hard to see how he can have known this, and it is in any case untrue.[8]

Foremost among English-language primary sources available in Australia is the AWM collection. In general, Australian battalion, brigade, division and corps war diaries are of a high standard and extremely useful to the researcher, and the post-campaign intelligence and research reports often contain analysis that is not observable to the same degree in comparable Japanese documents. The National Archives of Australia (NAA) holds documents relating to prewar Japanese espionage in Australia and New Guinea. These are an important source for an assessment of pre–Kokoda campaign Japanese intelligence efforts in eastern New Guinea.

At the end of the war the United States Army Air Force began a project to assess bomb damage in the two strategic air offensives in Europe and against Japan. The United States Strategic Bombing Survey grew into much more than this, and its 33 000 pages contain detailed research papers on a wide range of aspects of the Pacific War.[10] The survey also includes interviews with Japanese officers, including several Seventeenth Army and IJN Fourth Fleet officers who were involved in the 1942 campaign. More recently, American researchers – Eric Bergerud, James Dunnigan and Rafael Steinberg for example – have dealt thematically with the problems of land and air warfare in the Pacific War. They frequently have illuminating things to say about events in Papua in 1942.[11]

Australian secondary sources fall into four categories: unit histories; personal accounts; postwar analytical works; and postwar popular narratives. All infantry battalions that participated in the Kokoda campaign have published a unit history. There are also histories of some of the other units, pioneer battalions, Royal Australian Engineer field companies and the like. Australian unit histories do not much resemble the Japanese ones as Australian histories prefer a coherent narrative to an assembly of unit documents. Even so, Australian unit histories vary widely in their usefulness. Those of 2/3rd and 2/31st Battalions are not very useful while those of 2/27th, 2/33rd and 2/1st Battalions repay close reading as they contain a great deal of accurate detail and insightful comment.[12] Personal accounts such as those of Lieutenant-General Sir Sydney Rowell and Colonel Frank Kingsley Norris do not tend to mythologise the campaign, but nor do they aid demythologising. Frank Sublet's *Kokoda to the Sea* is probably the best postwar general account by a participant. Of postwar analytical work there is very little – a gap that this book in part hopes to fill. In *Armed and Ready* Andrew Ross compared the fighting strength of Australian and Japanese divisions by looking at weapons and supply.[13] A handful of Australian theses analyse aspects of the campaign; some include evidence from the Japanese side.

Robertson's and Richmond's analyses of Japanese supply problems in New Guinea are useful, and John Moremon's work on Australian supply enables some comparison to be made with Japanese supply problems. A useful thesis that examines the character of a Japanese soldier is Linda Zeitz's 'No half-hearted soldiers'.[14]

Notes

1 Introduction

1 'Kokoda Track' is the term used in this book, but 'Kokoda Trail' is the official term.
2 Three examples are Fitzsimons, *Kokoda*; Brune, *A Bastard of a Place*; and Ham, *Kokoda*.
3 'Nanke-Shetei', New Guinea war diary of 144th Regiment, papers of Lieutenant A. Salmon, AWM PR00297, items 13–15.
4 McCarthy, *South-West Pacific Area*, pp. 144–6.
5 Ham, *Kokoda*, p. 45.
6 Horner, *Crisis of Command* and *High Command*.
7 McAulay, *Blood and Iron*, p. 20.
8 Ibid., p. 72.
9 Dornan, *The Silent Men*, p. 139; Ham, *Kokoda*, p. 178.
10 *Rikugun tsushin no Gaikan* [Overview of Army correspondence], npn, NIDS, Bunko Jiku, 469; *Azuma Shigetoshio* [List of war dead of 144th Regiment], author's collection, p. 1; *Hohei Dai 144 Rentai dai 3 daitai Sento Shoho* [Detailed battle records of 3rd Battalion, 144th Regiment], p. 25, NIDS, *Nanto zenpan* 174; ATIS current translations no 15, p. 17, AWM55 3/1/193; ATIS enemy publications no 24, p. 32, AWM55 5/2.
11 Lindsay Mason, interview, Plenty, Tasmania, 17 December 2005.
12 Ham, *Kokoda*, p. 523.
13 Note on US War Council meeting, AWM54 577/7/32.
14 McCarthy, *South-West Pacific Area*, p. 234; Milner, *Victory in Papua*, p. 96.
15 Scott, *The Knights of Kokoda*.
16 Pratten, *Australian Battalion Commanders in the Second World War*, p. 12.
17 Edgar, *Warrior of Kokoda*, p. 164.
18 Professor Hank Nelson, 'Tracking Kokoda', Adventure Kokoda blog, <http://blog.kokodatreks.com/2009/12/01/tracking-kokoda-by-professor-hank-nelson>
19 Stocking (ed.), *Zombie Myths of Australian Military History*.

2 Strategy

1 Paull, *Retreat from Kokoda*, p. 90; Ham, *Kokoda*, pp. 12–15.
2 General Adachi, report on eastern New Guinea, November 1941, p. 1, AWM55 3/6/817, item 7.

3 Japanese monograph no 37, p. 18, NLA, mfm 1383.
4 Japanese monograph no 111, p. 20, NLA mfm 1383.
5 Colonel Hattori Takushiro, interview, AWM55 17/7.
6 Bullard, *Japanese Army Operations in the South Pacific Area*, p. 151.
7 Ibid., p. 57.
8 Japanese monograph, no 120, p. 48; no 122, p. 4, NLA, mfm 1383; Toyoda & Nelson, *The Pacific War in Papua New Guinea*, p. 224.
9 Bullard, *Japanese Army Operations in the South Pacific Area*, p. 56.
10 Rear-Admiral Tomioka Sadatoshi, statement, AWM55 17/7, npn; Toyoda & Nelson, *The Pacific War in Papua New Guinea*, p. 176. Rear-Admiral Tomioka was IJN Chief of Operations (1940–43), and Admiral Yamamoto Isoroku was Commander in Chief Combined Fleet.
11 Boeicho Boei Kenshujo Senshishitsu (ed.), *Senshi Sosho: Minami Taiheiyo Rikugun sakusen <1> Poto Moresubi–Gashima shoko sakusen* [War history series; South Pacific Area army operations (vol. 1), Port Moresby–Guadalcanal first campaigns], p. 225.
12 Franks, *Guadalcanal*, p. 22.
13 Hayashi, *Taiheiyo senso rikusen gaishi* [The Japanese army in the Pacific War], p. 51.
14 Bullard, *Japanese Army Operations in the South Pacific Area*, p. 36.
15 Papers attached to Yokoyama operational order, no 449, no 1, sheet 9, AWM55 3/4.
16 Bullard, *Japanese Army Operations in the South Pacific Area*, p. 56.
17 Ibid., p. 120.
18 General Adachi, report on eastern New Guinea, November 1941, p. 1, AWM55/3/6/817, item 7.
19 Toyoda & Nelson, *The Pacific War in Papua New Guinea*, p. 180.
20 Bullard, *Japanese Army Operations in the South Pacific Area*, p. 57.
21 Evans, *The Japanese Navy in WWII in the Words of Former Japanese Naval Officers*, p. 216.
22 Bullard, *Japanese Army Operations in the South Pacific Area*, p. 58.
23 Ibid., p. 59.
24 Ibid., pp. 100–1, 109.
25 Translation of OKI group [Seventeenth Army] order A, part 8, item 1167, no 10, 18 June 1942, and order C, no 15, 14 July 1942, AWM54 423/4/41.

3 MILITARY INTELLIGENCE

1 McCarthy, *South-West Pacific Area*, p. 144; Scott, *Knights of Kokoda*, p. 18; Brune, *A Bastard of a Place*, p. 99.
2 McAulay, *Blood and Iron*, p. 20.
3 File of Yazawa Butai orders, enemy publications no 28, p. 63, AWM55 5/3.
4 Ibid., pp. 48 & 63; Oki group operational order B, no 8, 1 July 1942, in Bullard, *Japanese Army Operations in the South Pacific Area*, pp. 114–15; signals to HQNGF from LHQ, 7th Division messages and signals dealing with Maroubra Force operations, 1 July 1942 & 25 June 1942, AWM54 577/6/4.

5 Major Tetsuo Toyufuku, translation of captured Japanese documents, report March 1941, pt 15, item 539, p. 19, AWM54 423/4/41.
6 Kanemoto, *Nyuginia senki, Taiheiyô Senki* [Account of the New Guinea campaign, Pacific War], p. 92.
7 Ibid., p. 97.
8 Vernon, war diary, July–November 1942, pt 1, AWM54 253/5/8.
9 Toyoda & Nelson, *The Pacific War in Papua New Guinea*, p. 175.
10 Matthews, *Shadows Dancing*, p. 47.
11 Japanese interests in Papua and New Guinea, report, pt 1, p. 13, NAA: A981/4, Jap 18.
12 Franks, *Guadalcanal*, pp. 153–4.
13 Department of Defence, 'Japanese preparations for war and plans for Australia', p. 11, AWM54 423/6/1.
14 Commonwealth of Australia, *Territory of Papua Annual Report, 1940–1941*, p. 30.
15 Japanese activities in New Guinea, report, p. 3, NAA: A518/1, FI 112/1.
16 Commonwealth of Australia, *Territory of Papua Annual Report, 1940–41*, p. 31.
17 Commonwealth Investigation Branch (CIB), 'Japanese interests in Papua and New Guinea and Japanese citizens resident in Australian New Guinea in 1939', report, NAA: A816/1, 19/304/188.
18 Nakamura Kokichi, 66 Infantry Regiment, interview, Tokyo, 6 March 2004.
19 Japanese activities in Papua, report, p. 12, NAA: A981, Jap 31.
20 CIB, 'Japanese interests in Papua and New Guinea and Japanese citizens resident in Australian New Guinea in 1939', report, NAA: A816/1, 19/304/188.
21 Combat Intelligence Centre, SPAC force US Pacific Fleet, report, pt 15, AWM54 423/4/41.
22 CIB, 'Pro German activity east New Guinea', p. 8, AWM55 16/2; inventory of maps, no 2, AWM54 883/4/12.
23 Outline of the work of German missionaries, evidence of pro-German and pro-Nazi activities, report, pp. 8 & 15, AWM54 883/4/12; file of correspondence in connection with the Japanese occupation of Dutch and Australian New Guinea, p. 10, AWM54 423/9/27.
24 General Adachi, report, 29 December 1941, AWM55 3/6/817, item 7.
25 Japanese summary of provisions available in Papua, March 1942, translation, p. 6, AWM55 5/14.
26 Japanese rainfall charts, enemy publications, no 162, pp. 4–5, AWM55 5/14.
27 Department of Defence, 'Japanese preparations for war and plans for Australia', p. 220, AWM54 423/6/1.
28 'Japanese citizens purchasing maps of New Guinea in Sydney', report, NAA: C443/P1, item J423.
29 Bullard, *Japanese Army Operations in the South Pacific Area*, p. 110.
30 Chinnery collection, map numbers 12, 16, 22, 24, 34 & 37, NLA map room.
31 CIB report, pt 3, NAA: A981/1, item Jap 101.
32 Cheesman, 'New Guinea'.
33 Cheesman, *Two Roads of Papua*, pp. 29 & 63.

34 Ibid., pp. 30, 55, 88 & 100.
35 Joseph Anton Hofstetter, naturalisation papers, NAA: AI 1921/21091.
36 Tom Lega and Carlo Cavalieri, telephone interviews, 22 August & 20 November 2006.
37 'Japanese activities in relation to the goldfields of New Guinea in conjunction with attempted occupation of Port Moresby', report, 26 March 1942, pp. 1–3, AWM54 13/5/5.
38 Gavin Long papers, AWM67 10/59; McCarthy, *South-West Pacific Area*, p. 63.
39 Report on the Japanese attack on Mubo, pp. 1–2, AWM54 587/7/20.
40 Folio of Hofstetter maps, pt 2, AWM54 423/4/106.
41 Ibid.
42 Analysis of the Hoffstetter maps, p. 3, AWM54 423/4/99.
43 Translated document, 30 April 1943, bulletin no 1137, p. 3, AWM55 1/22.
44 War Office, *The Complete Guide to Military Map Reading*, chs 3, 4 & 5.
45 Tsuji, *Singapore 1941–1942*, p. 33.
46 Coulthard-Clark, *Australia's Military Map-Makers*, pp. 88–90.
47 Ham, *Kokoda*, pp. 55 & 130.
48 Paull, *Retreat from Kokoda*, p. 23.
49 Harold Jesser, interview by son Peter Jesser, 1997, p. 5. Copy in author's collection.
50 21st Brigade war diary, 16 August 1942, AWM52 8/2/21.
51 21st Brigade report on operations, AWM52 8/2/21/17.
52 McAulay, *Blood and Iron*, p. 107.
53 2/27th Battalion war diary, appendix A, AWM52 8/3/27.
54 25th Brigade war diary, September–October 1942, map appendix, AWM52 8/2/25.
55 25th Brigade war diary, patrol report, 29 September 1942, AWM52 8/2/25.
56 Intelligence summary, 21 September 1942, general staff intelligence HQ NGF, September 1942, AWM52 9/2/4.
57 Yazawa Regiment, staff report, enemy publications no 28, 17/8/42, AWM55 5/3.
58 Folio of Hofstetter maps, pt 2, AWM54/423/4/106.
59 Kanamoto, *Nyuginia senki, Taiheiyô Senki* [Account of the New Guinea campaign, Pacific War], pp. 92–3.
60 IJN Flight Sergeant Nemoto Kumesaka, diary, p. 25, AWM54 253/4/11.
61 Koiwai, *Nyuginia Senki* [Battle history of New Guinea], p. 80.
62 Folio of Hofstetter maps, pt 2, map GX 1696, 14/7/42, AWM 54 423/4/106.

4 THE NANKAI SHITAI

1 Nankai Shitai intelligence report no 21, current translations no 42, p. 3, AWM55 3/4.
2 *Hohei Dai 144 Rentai Senki* [Battle records of 144th Infantry Regiment], NIDS 302.9.H, p. 44.

3 Daugherty, *Fighting Techniques of a Japanese Infantryman 1941–45*, pp. 44–5; Rottman, *The Japanese Army in World War II*, pp. 25–34.

4 *Hohei dai 41 Rentai Nyuginiasen senkyo hokoku* [Battle records of 41st Regiment in New Guinea], NIDS, 301.9.S, p. 12; 17th Army document captured at Guadalcanal, AWM54 423/4/67, item 24343; Franks, *Guadalcanal*, pp. 631–6.

5 War Department, *Handbook on Japanese Military Forces*, p. 18.

6 Captured documents, organisation and equipment, AWM54 722/4/11; report on operations, intelligence summary no 16, AWM54 123/270; United States War Department, *Order of Battle of the Japanese Army Dec 42*, end pocket chart.

7 *Hohei Dai 144 Rentai Senki* [Battle records of 144th Infantry Regiment], NIDS 302.9.H, p. 44; SWPA enemy publications, p. 22, AWM54 423/4/158.

8 IJN Flight Sergeant Nemoto Kumesaka, diary, p. 23, AWM54 253/4/11; ATIS current translations no 77, pp. 25–6, AWM55 3/7; Bullard, *Japanese Army Operations in the South Pacific Area*, pp. 33 & 47–8.

9 49th Battalion war diary, AWM52 8/3/88.

10 ATIS current translations no 42, p. 15, AWM55 3/4.

11 Second Lieutenant Noda Hidetaka, 3/144, diary, p. 1, AWM54 577/7/26 [hereafter Noda, diary]; company record of 5th Company, 2/144th, current translations no 15, p. 21, AWM55 3/1; captured documents, organisation and equipment of Japanese infantry in 1942, AWM54 722/4/11.

12 Noda, diary, AWM54 577/7/26, p. 2.

13 Review of the Papuan campaign, estimate of Japanese casualties, AWM123 609, pp. 31–3.

14 Bullard, *Japanese Army Operations in the South Pacific Area*, pp. 47–8.

15 Ibid., p. 7; Lieutenant-General Sir Sydney Rowell, report on operations, intelligence summary, no 16, AWM123 270.

16 ATIS bulletin no 75, p. 1, AWM55 1/1, ATIS enemy publications no 41, p. 1, & no 38, pp. 1–2, AWM55 5/3.

17 *Hohei Dai 144 Rentai dai 3 daitai Sento Sosho* [Detailed battle records of 3rd Battalion, 144th Regiment], NIDS, *Nanto zenpan* 174, p. 26; Review of Papuan campaign, AWM 123 270.

18 ATIS current translations no 42, p. 7, AWM55 3/4; ATIS bulletin no 9, p. 4, AWM 55/1/1; ATIS current translations no 4, p. 40, AWM55 3/1; ATIS current translations no 5, pp. 24–5, AWM55 3/1.

19 ATIS bulletin no 53, p 2, AWM55 1/1.

20 *Hohei dai 41 Rentai Nyuginiasen senkyo hokoku* [Battle records of 41st Regiment in New Guinea], NIDS, 301.9.S, p. 12.

21 Koiwai, *Nyuginia Senki* [Battle history of New Guinea], p. 63.

22 *Nankai Shitai Efogi minamigawa ni okeru sento* [Battles of the Nankai Shitai south of Efogi], NIDS, Nanto, Solomon Bisumarruku, 130 npn.

23 ATIS bulletin no 9, p. 4, AWM55/1/1.

24 ATIS current translations no 72, p. 23, AWM55 3/6.

25 Private Kato Kumio 15 IER, interrogation report no 87, p. 4, AWM 55 6/3.

26 Review of Papuan campaign, estimate of Japanese casualties, AWM 123 609.

27 *Hohei Dai 144 Rentai dai 3 daitai Sento Sosho* [Detailed battle records of 3rd Battalion, 144th Regiment], pp. 11–12, NIDS, *Nanto zenpan* 174; *Hiho to Tomoni-Sanpohei dai 55 Rentai senshi* [With fire: The war history of 55th Mountain Artillery Regiment], pp. 20–1, NIDS 302. 9.S; Bullard, *Japanese Army Operations in the South Pacific Area*, p. 244; ATIS current translations no 44, pp. 13–21, AWM55 3/4; Military Intelligence Service, *Order of Battle of the Japanese Army, December 1942*, p. 301; War Department, *Handbook on Japanese Military Forces*, p. 61.

28 ATIS current translations no 65, p. 39, AWM55 3/6.

29 ATIS current translations no 6, p. 17, AWM55 3/1.

30 5 Yokosuka SNLP diary, bulletin no 17, pp. 1–2, AWM55 1/1.

31 ATIS current translations no 62, AWM55 3/5; ATIS bulletin no 96 p. 1, AWM55 1/1.

32 Yamamoto Kiyoshi, medical officer 5 Yokosuka SNLP, diary, p. 3, AWM 3drl 8027.

33 ATIS bulletin no 17, pp. 1–2, AWM 55 1/1; ATIS bulletin no 40, p. 2, AWM55 1/1; Milner, *Victory in Papua*, p. 100.

34 ATIS bulletin no 20, p. 1, AWM55 1/3; ATIS bulletin no 25, p. 1, AWM55 1/1; ATIS bulletin no 9, p. 4, AWM55/1/1; ATIS current translations no 44, AWM55 3/4.

35 *Senshi gyousho, nanto houmen kaigun sakusen* [War history records, navy operations in south-eastern area], pp. 408–9, NIDS 392.18B. 9245; *Nanto homen chijo butai no heiryoku oyobi hensei ni kansuru shiryo* [Strength and composition of Japanese ground forces, south-eastern area, 1941–44], pp. 10–11, NIDS gohoku zenpan, 78; ATIS interrogation report no 152, p. 3, AWM55 6/4; ATIS spot report no 15, p. 1, AWM55 2/1; ATIS bulletin no 20, p. 1, AWM55 1/3; ATIS bulletin no 51, p. 4, and bulletin no 66, p. 1, AWM55 1/1.

36 *Senshi gyousho, nanto houmen kaigun sakusen* [War history records, navy operations in south-eastern area], pp. 408–9, NIDS 392. 18B 9245; Toyoda & Nelson, *The Pacific War in Papua New Guinea*, p. 218; ATIS bulletin no 11, p. 1, AWM55 1/1; ATIS bulletin no 51, p. 4, AWM55 1/1; ATIS bulletin no 51, p. 2, AWM55 1/1; translation of report of chief surgeon, 8th Fleet HQ, September 1942, AWM54 423/4/41.

37 ATIS spot report no 62, AWM55 2/1.

38 Paull, *Retreat from Kokoda*, p. 45.

39 Professor Hank Nelson, email to author, 3 October 2007.

40 Franks, *Guadalcanal*, pp. 631–6.

41 Ham, *Kokoda*, p. 205.

42 Franks, *Guadalcanal*, p. 634.

43 Records of 67 LOCH, enemy publications no 24, pp. 32 & 62, AWM55 5/2.

44 Tsunoda Kazuo, 32 Air Flotilla, documents in collection of and interview, 3 June 2004.

45 Military Intelligence Service, *Order of Battle of the Japanese Army, December 1942*, p. 348; ATIS bulletin no 47, p. 2, AWM55 1/1; Zeitz, 'No half-hearted soldiers', p. 187.

46 Ham, *Kokoda*, p. 146; Brune, *A Bastard of a Place*, p. 99; Keogh, *The South West Pacific 1941–45*, p. 280; McCarthy, *South-West Pacific Area*, p. 531.
47 Record of 67 LOCH, enemy publications no 24, pp. 1, 37, 46 & 87, AWM55 5/2.
48 Brune, *A Bastard of a Place*, p. 99; McCarthy, *South-West Pacific Area*, p. 146.
49 39th Battalion war diary, August–September 1942, captured documents appendix E, AWM52 8/3/78; review of the Papuan campaign, estimate of Japanese casualties, pp. 31–3, AWM 123 609.
50 War Department, *Handbook on Japanese Military Forces 1944*, p. 18.

5 FROM THE LANDING TO DENIKI

1 *Senshi Gyousho Nanto houmen Kaigun sakusen* [War History records, navy operations in south-eastern area], pp. 408–9, NIDS 392.18B, 9245; Yokoyama operational order no 1, 20 July 1942, sheet no 9, AWM55 3/4 449.
2 Yokoyama operational order no 2, 22 July 1942, spot report no 45, pp. 50–1, AWM55 3/4.
3 War history of 144th Regiment, p. 4, papers of Lieutenant Salmon, AWM PRO 0297.
4 File of Yazawa Butai orders, enemy publications no 28, p. 46, AWM55 5/3.
5 39th Battalion war diary, 1–7 August 1942, AWM52 8/3/78.
6 War History of 144th Regiment, p. 4, papers of Lieutenant Salmon, AWM PRO 0297.
7 Robinson, 'Villagers at war', pp. 201–3.
8 Austin, *To Kokoda and Beyond*, p. 87.
9 7th Division, messages dealing with Maroubra Force, p. 4, AWM54 577/6/4.
10 *Hohei Dai 144 Rentai Senki* [Battle records of 144 Infantry Regiment], attached list of 144th Regiment war dead, NIDS 302.9.H.
11 Brune, *Those Ragged Bloody Heroes*, p. 40.
12 39th Battalion war diary, 25 July 1942, AWM52 8/3/78.
13 PIB war diary, 21–30 July 1942, AWM52 8/4/4; 39th Battalion war diary, 26–30 July 1942, AWM52 8/3/78.
14 File of Yazawa Butai orders, p. 50, enemy publications no 28, AWM55 5/3.
15 Australian Imperial Force, Owen Stanleys Campaign, Battle Casualties, Kokoda to Imita, [hereafter Battle Casualties, Kokoda to Imita], pp. 1–2, AWM54 171/2/48; Australian Imperial Force, Owen Stanleys Campaign, Battle Casualties, Imita to Wairopi [hereafter Battle Casualties, Imita to Wairopi], pp. 1–2, AWM54 171/2/47.
16 ATIS current translations no 13, p. 25, AWM55 3/1; file of Yazawa Butai orders, enemy publications no 28, p. 50, AWM55 5/3.
17 Ham, *Kokoda*, pp. 49–53.
18 39th Battalion war diary, July–September, translated documents appendix F, pt 2, AWM52 8/3/78.
19 File of Yazawa Butai orders, enemy publications no 28, p. 46, AWM55 5/3.
20 War History of 144th Regiment, p. 5, papers of Lieutenant Salmon, AWM PRO 0297; ATIS current translations no 21, p. 17, AWM55 3/2.

21 Watanabe Toshio, 1st Company 1/144th, diary, current translations no 4, p. 5, AWM55 3/1. Watanabe misdates the entry by several days; *Hohei Dai 144 Rentai Dai 1 Chutai jinchu nisshi* [War diary for 144th Regiment 1st Company], NIDS, *Nanto higashi nyuginia* 282.

22 Sublet, *Kokoda to the Sea*, p. 25; Austin, *To Kokoda and Beyond*, p. 95.

23 39th Battalion war diary, 29 July – 2 August 1942, AWM52 8/3/78; Maroubra Force to NGF, signal, 2 August 1942, and B Company casualty returns, 24–29 July 1942, AWM54 171/2/20.

24 Gavin Long papers, relating to McCarthy, *South-West Pacific Area*, pp. 124 & 127, AWM67 2/17.

25 *Nankai Shitai shireibu Toyufuku shosa kowa* [Lecture of Major Toyufuku, headquarters, Nankai Shitai], p. 21, NIDS *nanto zenpan* 168.

26 Moreman, 'A triumph of improvisation', p. 133.

27 39th Battalion war diary, 6 August 1942, AWM52 8/3/78.

28 War History of 144th Regiment, p. 6, papers of Lieutenant Salmon, AWM PRO 0297.

29 Paull, *Retreat from Kokoda*, p. 71.

30 PIB war diary, 21–30 July 1942, AWM52 8/4/4.

31 Powell, *The Third Force*, pp. 47–9.

32 McCarthy, *South-West Pacific Area*, pp. 130–1; Austin, *To Kokoda and Beyond*, p. 109; Battle Casualties, Kokoda to Imita, AWM54 171/2/48.

33 WO J.O. Wilkinson, ANGAU, interview, October 1943, Gavin Long papers, AWM67 2/15.

34 Powell, *The Third Force*, pp. 47–9; McCarthy, *South-West Pacific Area*, p. 132.

35 PIB war diary, 8 August 1942, AWM52 8/4/4.

36 File of Yazawa Butai orders, enemy publications no 28, pp. 50–1, AWM55 5/3. This source gives the wrong date: 8 September 1942 instead of 8 August 1942.

37 Ibid.

38 ATIS current translations no 17, pp. 2–3, AWM55 3/2.

39 McCarthy, *South-West Pacific Area*, p. 137; WO J.O. Wilkinson, ANGAU, interview, October 1943, Gavin Long papers, AWM67 2/15.

40 Summary of operations, New Guinea, Kokoda–Ioribaiwa, 21 July – 3 October 1942, pp. 2–3, AWM54 577/7/29; 39th Battalion war diary 14 August 1942, AWM52 8/3/78.

41 Estimate based on 150 interviews by the author with Australian and Japanese New Guinea veterans.

42 14th Australian Field Ambulance in Papua, p. 1, AWM54 481/12/68.

43 ATIS current translations no 13, p. 25, AWM55 3/1; ATIS enemy publications no 28, p. 56, AWM55 5/3.

44 Battle Casualties, Kokoda to Imita, pp. 1–4, AWM54 171/2/48.

45 39th Battalion war diary, appendix E, AWM52 8/3/78; 39th Battalion report on operations in Kokoda area, July–August 1942, pt 19, pp. 3–4, AWM54 577/7/29.

46 39th Battalion report on operations Kokoda area, July–August, pt 19, pp. 3–4, AWM54 577/7/29.

47 Paull, *Retreat from Kokoda*, p. 75; 39th Battalion war diary, 8 August 1942, AWM52 8/3/78.
48 Johnston, *War Diary 1942*, pp. 134–5.

6 ISURAVA

1 Fitzsimons, *Kokoda*, p. 283; Honner, *Sydney Morning Herald*, 3 August 2002.
2 Brune, *A Bastard of a Place*, p. 135; Doornan, *The Silent Men*, p. 114; Ham, *Kokoda*, p. 163.
3 Edgar, *Warrior of Kokoda*, p. 145; Brune, *A Bastard of a Place*, p. 151.
4 7th Division messages dealing with Maroubra Force operations, npn, AWM54 577/6/4.
5 Report of ADMS visit to Maroubra Force, appendix A, AWM54 481/12/17.
6 Maroubra Force battle casualties, messages, npn, AWM54 171/2/20.
7 Koiwai, *Nyuginia Senki* [Battle history of New Guinea], p. 79.
8 Kawate Ryozo, interview, Hiroshima, 20 March 2005.
9 File of Nankai Shitai orders, enemy publications no 38, pp. 14–15, AWM55 5/3.
10 ATIS current translations no 15, pp. 15–21, AWM55 3/1.
11 ATIS current translations no 29, p. 52, AWM55 3/3; Noda, diary, pp. 2–3, AWM54 577/7/26; ATIS current translations no 51, pp. 12–18, AWM55 3/5.
12 Nishimura Kohkichi, NCO 2/144, interview, Tokyo, 6 March 2004.
13 21st Brigade war diary, 15–27 August 1942, AWM52 8/2/21; 55/53rd Battalion war diary, 7 August 1942, AWM52 8/3/91.
14 *Hohei Dai 144 Rentai dai 3 daitai Sento Shoho* [Detailed battle records of 3rd Battalion, 144th Regiment], p. 22, NIDS, *Nanto zenpan 174*.
15 Ibid., p. 23; ATIS current translations no 6, p. 17, AWM55 3/1.
16 Imanishi Sadaharu, company sergeant major, 1/144th, interview, Motoyama, Shikoku, 23 March 2004.
17 Major Horie Masao, interview, Tokyo, 8 March 2004.
18 *Hohei Dai 144 Rentai Senki* [Battle records of the 144th Infantry Regiment], NIDS 302.9.H.
19 Nankai Shitai intelligence summaries, no 15, AWM55 5/3.
20 Chester Wilmot report in Blamey, wallet no 29, p. 2, AWM 3DRL/6643; 21st Brigade report on operations, p. 3, AWM54 577/7/3.
21 39th Battalion war diary, 14 August 1942, AWM52 8/3/78.
22 30th Brigade war diary, 13 August 1942, AWM52 8/2/30.
23 21st Brigade report on operations, p. 3, AWM54 577/7/3; 7th Division, messages dealing with Maroubra Force, 29 August 1942, AWM54 577/6/4.
24 Nankai Shitai operational order A, no 102, current translations no 42, p. 17, AWM55 3/4.
25 'War History of 144 Regiment', p. 14, papers of Lieutenant Salmon, AWM PRO 0297.
26 Nankai Shitai operational order A, no 102, current translations no 42, p. 17, AWM55 3/4.

27 McCarthy, *South-West Pacific Area*, p. 206.
28 Quoted in Austin, *To Kokoda and Beyond*, p. 146.
29 21st Brigade report on operations, p. 29, AWM52 8/21/17.
30 MacDonald, *Chester Wilmot Reports*, p. 299.
31 Chester Wilmot report, Blamey, wallet no 29, p. 2, AWM 3DRL/6643; McCarthy, *South-West Pacific*, pp. 202 & 208.
32 Budden, *That Mob*.
33 'War History of 144 Regiment', p. 8, papers of Lieutenant Salmon, AWM PRO 0297.
34 Lieutenant Hirano, 1/144th, diary, current translations no 17, p. 4, AWM55 3/2; Japanese artillery plan, Isurava, current translations no 50, p. 32, AWM55 3/4.
35 *Hohei Dai 144 Rentai dai 3 daitai Sento Shoho* [Detailed battle records of 3rd Battalion, 144th Regiment], p. 23; NIDS, *Nanto zenpan* 174.
36 'War History of 144 Regiment', pp. 12–14, papers of Lieutenant Salmon, AWM PRO 0297; Hidetaka, diary, p. 1, AWM54 577/7/26.
37 Ham, *Kokoda*, p. 172.
38 *Hohei Dai 144 Rentai dai 3 daitai Sento Shoho* [Detailed battle records of 3rd Battalion, 144th Regiment], pp. 23–4; NIDS, *Nanto zenpan* 174: ATIS current translations no 50, p. 32, AWM55 3/4; Edgar, *Warrior of Kokoda*, pp. 143–5.
39 *Hohei Dai 144 Rentai dai 3 daitai Sento Shoho* [Detailed battle records of 3rd Battalion, 144th Regiment], pp. 23–4; NIDS, *Nanto zenpan* 174; ATIS current translations no 29, pp. 53–4, AWM55 3/3.
40 Lindsay Mason, interview, Plenty, Tasmania, 17 December 2005.
41 *Hohei Dai 144 Rentai dai 3 daitai Sento Shoho* [Detailed battle records of 3rd Battalion, 144th Regiment], p. 15. NIDS, *Nanto zenpan* 174.
42 Takamura Jiro, diary, current translations no 77, pp. 25–6, AWM55 3/7.
43 File of Nankai Shitai operational orders, enemy publications no 33, 30/8/42, AWM55 5/3.
44 Sitrep no 1, 30 August 1942, npn, AWM54 171/2/20.
45 ATIS 575, p. 33, AWM55 3/5.
46 Nankai Shitai intelligence summary no 15, AWM55 5/3; Horii operational order A, current translations no 42, pp. 13–14, AWM55 3/4.
47 *Hohei Dai 144 Rentai dai 3 daitai Sento Shoho* [Detailed battle records of 3rd Battalion, 144th Regiment], p. 23. NIDS, *Nanto zenpan* 174.
48 ATIS current translations no 29, p. 53, AWM55 3/3.
49 *Hohei Dai 144 Rentai dai 3 daitai Sento Shoho* [Detailed battle records of 3rd Battalion], pp. 17–18. NIDS, *Nanto zenpan* 174.
50 Lieutenant-Colonel Honner, interview, Melbourne, 27 September 1944, npn, Gavin Long papers, AWM67 2/50.
51 39th Battalion war diary, 30 August 1942, AWM52 8/3/78.
52 Sitrep, 7th Division messages dealing with Maroubra Force, npn, AWM54 577/6/4.
53 *Hohei Dai 144 Rentai dai 3 daitai Sento Shoho* [Detailed battle records of 3rd Battalion, 144th Regiment], p. 18. NIDS, *Nanto zenpan* 174.

54 ATIS interrogation report no 34, p. 94, AWM55 5/3.
55 *Rikugun tsushin no Gaikan* [Overview of army correspondence], npn, NIDS, Bunko Jiku, 469.
56 Dornan, *The Silent Men*, p. 139; Ham, *Kokoda*, p. 178.
57 Brune, *A Bastard of a Place*, p. 146
58 'War History of 144 Regiment', p. 9, papers of Lieutenant Salmon, AWM PRO 0297.
59 Private Watanabe Toshio, 1st Company 1/144th, diary, current translations no 4, p. 5, AWM55 3/1.
60 Takamura Jiro, diary, current translations no 77, p. 26, AWM55 3/7.
61 Noda, diary, p. 4, AWM54 577/7/26.
62 Lindsay Mason, interview, Plenty, Tasmania, 17 December 2005.
63 *Azuma Shigetoshio* [List of war dead of 144th Regiment], author's collection, p. 1; *Hohei Dai 144 Rentai dai 3 daitai Sento Shoho* [Detailed battle records of 3rd Battalion, 144th Regiment], p. 25, NIDS, *Nanto zenpan* 174; ATIS current translations no 15, p. 17, AWM55 3/1/193.
64 ATIS enemy publications no 24, p. 32, AWM55 5/2.
65 Imanishi Sadaharu, 1/144th, interview, Motoyama, Shikoku, 24 March 2004.
66 Nishimura Kohkichi, 2/144th, interview, Tokyo, 14 March 2004.
67 Koiwai, *Nyuginea Senki* [Battle history of New Guinea], p. 80.
68 Noda, diary, p. 17, AWM54 577/7/26.
69 'Notes on Operations, Isurava Area', p. 33, AWM54 577/7/5.
70 Koiwai, *Nyuginia Senki* [Battle history of New Guinea], p. 79.

7 GUADALCANAL AND MILNE BAY

1 Japanese monograph, no 98, p. 8, NLA mfm 1383.
2 Hyakutake to Horii, 28 September 1942, in Bullard, *Japanese Army Operations in the South Pacific Area*, pp. 156–7.
3 Translation of OKI group [17th Army] order, part 8, item 1167, 'A' no 10 of 18 June, AWM54 423/4/41.
4 Brune, *A Bastard of a Place*, p. 210; Collie & Marutani, *The Path of Infinite Sorrow*, p. 96.
5 Hyakutake to Horii, 28 September 1942, in Bullard, *Japanese Army Operations in the South Pacific Area*, pp. 156–7.
6 Bullard, *Japanese Army Operations in the South Pacific Area*, p. 131.
7 Sugiyama, Chief of Army General Staff, to Hyakutake, 29 September 1942, in Bullard, *Japanese Army Operations in the South Pacific Area*, p. 157.
8 Japanese monograph, no 98, p. 8, NLA, mfm 1383.
9 Milner, *Victory in Papua*, p. 69.
10 Brune, *A Bastard of a Place*, p. 199; Edgar, *Warrior of Kokoda*, pp. 301–2.
11 Stanley, *Invading Australia*.
12 Collie & Marutani, *The Path of Infinite Sorrow*, p. 59; Ham, *Kokoda*, p. 109.
13 Bullard, *Japanese Army Operations in the South Pacific Area*, p. 118.
14 Ibid., pp. 116–17.

15 McCarthy, *South-West Pacific Area*, p. 153.
16 Lieutenant-General Shuichi Miyazaki, interview, pt 15, pt 10, AWM54 423/4/41, p. 13.
17 Franks, *Guadalcanal*, pp. 142–3.
18 Lieutenant-General Kato, Chief of Staff, 8th Area Army, questionnaire, pp. 2–4, Gavin Long papers, AWM54, 423/6/8; Japanese officers, interview, p. 2, AWM67 11/29; Japanese monograph, no 37, p. 17, NLA, mfm 1383.
19 Franks, *Guadalcanal*, pp. 142–3.
20 Japanese monograph, no 98, p. 8, NLA mfm 1383.
21 Franks, *Guadalcanal*, p. 145.
22 Translation of OKI group [17th Army] order 'A', no 10 of 18 July, part 8, item 1167, AWM54 423/4/41.
23 Bullard, *Japanese Army Operations in the South Pacific Area*, p. 156.
24 Japanese monograph, no 98, p. 8, NLA, mfm 1383.
25 Bullard, *Japanese Army Operations in the South Pacific Area*, p. 177.
26 War Department, *Handbook on Japanese Military Forces*, p. 56.
27 SWPA captured documents no 43, item 2, AWM54 423/4/156.
28 Seventeenth Army HQ planning document captured on Guadalcanal, AWM54 423/4/130, item 2.
29 Japanese report on Kokoda airfield, ATIS enemy publications no 28, p. 48, AWM55 5/3.
30 Bullard, *Japanese Army Operations in the South Pacific Area*, p. 169.
31 Ibid., pp. 111–12.
32 General Adachi, Lieutenant-Colonel Tanaka, Lieutenant-Colonel Ota, Lieutenant-General Kato and Navy Captain Sanagi, interview, p. 2, Gavin Long papers, AWM67 11/29.

8 THE JAPANESE BUILD-UP

1 McAulay, *Blood and Iron*, p. 30; Ham, *Kokoda*, p. 109.
2 Sinclair, *Arteries of War*, p. 103.
3 Creveld, *Supplying War*, p. 152.
4 Sinclair, *Arteries of War*, p. 81.
5 Creveld, *Supplying War*, p. 212.
6 Lynn, *Feeding Mars*, p. 22.
7 The 215 men of 2/1st Australian Field ambulance weighed an average of 71 kilograms whereas the average weight of Japanese soldiers (graduates of the Ichigaya IJA Academy) was 58 kilograms. 2/1st Field Ambulance, war diary, 1942, AWM52 11/12/10; Dunnigan & Nofi, *Pacific War Encyclopedia*, p. 455.
8 Creveld, *Supplying War*, p. 34.
9 Sedgwick, *The Russo-Japanese War on Land*, p. 134.
10 Rowell, report on operations, AWM54 591/6/60, p. 13.
11 Military Analysis Division, 'The effect of air action on Japanese ground logistics', pp. 62 & 89; report on Japanese logistics, p. 11, AWM54 917/7/1. Sometimes *kaisenbun* referred only to ammunition, but just as often the term referred to all supply requirements of the force.

12 Great Army Instruction no 1153 in Bullard, *Japanese Army Operations in the South Pacific Area*, p. 96.
13 Military Analysis Division, 'The effect of air action on Japanese ground logistics', exhibit T, p. 89.
14 Ibid., pp. 6 & 18.
15 Zeitz, 'No half-hearted soldiers', pp. 41–2.
16 Hamley, *Operations of War*, p. 351; report on Japanese logistics, p. 6, AWM54 917/7/1.
17 Tsuji, *Singapore, 1941–1942*, p. 93.
18 Gross tonnages and cargo capacities calculated from Lloyd's *Register of Shipping*; Jordan, *The World's Merchant Fleets 1939*; documents captured on Guadalcanal, p. 2, AWM54 423/4/130, item.
19 Military Analysis Division, 'The effect of air action on Japanese ground logistics', p. 18.
20 *Nankai Shitai shireibu Toyufuku shosa kowa* [lecture of Major Toyufuku, headquarters, Nankai Shitai], NIDS *nanto zenpan* 168, p. 20; Military Analysis Division, 'The effect of air action on Japanese ground logistics', p. 18.
21 Military Analysis Division, 'The effect of air action on Japanese ground logistics', pp. 91 & 94, table 6.
22 Anchorage report, enemy publication no 28, p. 44, AWM55 5/3.
23 Sakigawa tai report, enemy publications no 1, pp. 11–14, AWM55 5/3; ATIS enemy publication no 33, p. 3, AWM55 5/3.
24 ATIS spot report no 62, p. 1, AWM55 2/1.
25 ATIS interrogation report no 30, p. 1, AWM55 6/1; Bullard, *Japanese Army Operations in the South Pacific Area*, p. 157.
26 Baker, *Transportation of Troops and Material*, pp. 135–6.
27 Kanemoto, *Taiheiyô Senki* [Account of the Pacific War], pp. 7–9.
28 Paulson, 'Light infantry', pp. 81–8.
29 Report on Japanese logistics, pt 3, npn, AWM54 917/7/6.
30 ATIS enemy publications no 39, pp. 1–2, AWM55 5/3.
31 Onda, *Tobu New Guinea Sen* [Advance in New Guinea], p. 179.
32 *Senshi gyousho, nanto houmen kaigun sakusen* [War history records, navy operations in south-eastern area], NIDS 392.18B. 9245, pp. 408–9; ATIS enemy publications no 39, p. 4, AWM55 5/3.
33 ATIS interrogation report no 9, AWM55 6/1; ATIS no 292, p. 13, AWM55 3/2.
34 ATIS no 110, p. 17, AWM55 3/1.
35 Bullard, *Japanese Army Operations in the South Pacific Area*, p. 114.
36 Boyd, *Supply Handbook for the Army Service Corps*, pp. 29, 79 & 94–7; Creveld, *Supplying War*, pp. 111–13.
37 ATIS enemy publications no 28, pp. 56–7, AWM55 5/3; Military Analysis Division, 'The effect of air action on Japanese ground logistics', p. 126.
38 Dr Michael Burke, interview, 8 August 2006; CSIRO report no 32, 'Land forms, types and vegetation of East Papua', series, no 10.
39 Lynn, *Feeding Mars*, p. 23.
40 Rottman, *The Japanese Army in WWII*, p. 35: ATIS current translations, no 5, p. 23, AWM55 3/1; Military Analysis Division, 'The effect of air action on Japanese ground logistics', p. 38, table 30.

41 Report on operations in New Guinea, supplies by air transport, appendix B, AWM54 917/3/11.

42 ATIS current translations, no 6, appendix, p. 2, AWM55 3/1.

43 Ibid.; ATIS enemy publications, no 28, pp. 56–7, AWM55 5/3; Bullard, *Japanese Army Operations in the South Pacific Area*, p. 158.

44 Bulletin nos 20 & 23, both AWM55 1/1, p. 2, and 'Problems of supply encountered by the Australian and Japanese forces on the Kokoda trail', p. 7, AWM MSS 701 item 1.

45 ATIS current translations no 24, pp. 12–14, AWM55 3/2.

46 Japanese monograph no 127, p. 26, NLA, mfm 1383.

47 Onda, *Tobu New Guinea Sen* [The advance to New Guinea], p. 139; ATIS current translations no 25, p. 12, AWM55 3/2; ATIS interrogation report no 37, AWM55 5/3; ATIS enemy publications no 33, pp. 21–2, AWM55 5/3; ATIS current translations no 62, AWM55 3/5; Japanese monograph no 121 pp. 24 & 45, NLA, mfm 1383; Japanese monograph no 122, document 60877, NLA, mfm 1383.

48 Creveld, *Supplying War*, p. 124.

49 Ham, *Kokoda*, p. 303.

50 ATIS current translations no 24, p. 12, AWM55 3/2.

51 Military Analysis Division, 'The effect of air action on Japanese ground logistics', p. 124; ATIS enemy publications no 28, p. 47, AWM55 5/3.

52 *Nankai Shitai shireibu Toyufuku shosa kowa* [lecture of Major Toyufuku, headquarters, Nankai Shitai], p. 19, NIDS *nanto zenpan* 168.

53 Dr Bryant Allen, interview, 8 August 2006; ATIS current translations no 54, p. 4, AWM55 3/5.

54 Professor Hank Nelson, interview, 1 August 2006.

55 Allen, 'Agricultural systems of Papua New Guinea', p. 30.

56 *Territory of Papua Report, 1937–38*, NAA: A518/1, FI 112/1, p. 45; Dr Michael Burke and Dr Bryant Allen, interview, 8 August 2006.

57 Allen, 'Agricultural systems of Papua New Guinea', table 1, npn; 'Papua New Guinea Census Preliminary Bulletin no 2', pp. 16 & 80.

58 Dr Michael Burke, interview with author, 8 August 2006.

59 Onda, *Tobu New Guinea Sen* [The advance to New Guinea], p. 142.

60 ATIS current translations no 24, map facing p. 26, AWM55 3/2; folio of maps, pt 2, AWM54 423/4/106.

9 FIRST EORA–TEMPLETON'S

1 Vernon, war diary, July–November 1942, pt 1, AWM54 253/5/8.

2 *Hohei dai 41 Rentai New Guinea senkyo hokoku* [War records of 41 Infantry Regiment], p. 12, NIDS, *Nanto higashi nyuginia* 255.

3 Yazawa Butai documents, current translations no 33, p. 20, AWM55 3/3. *Hohei dai 41 Rentai New Guinea senkyo hokoku* [War records of 41 Infantry Regiment], pp. 14–15, NIDS, *Nanto higashi nyuginia* 255.

4 ATIS bulletin no 24, p. 3, AWM55 1/1.

5 Sublet, *Kokoda to the Sea*, p. 58.

6 Summary of operations, p. 4, AWM54 577/7/29. Battle Casualties, Kokoda to Imita, pp. 1–3, AWM54 171/2/48.

7 Koiwai, *Nyuginia Senki* [Battle history of New Guinea], p. 81.

8 Major Okamoto Takahisa, 66th Infantry Regiment, interview with author, 20 March 2004.

9 Watanabe Kukuichi, 2/41st Regiment, notebook, current translations no 22, p. 11, AWM55 3/2.

10 Koiwai, *Nyuginia Senki* [Battle history of New Guinea], p. 83.

11 7th Company 2/41st Regiment, battle report, current translations no 25, p. 11, AWM55 3/2.

12 *Daiichi Nyuginiea sen rentai sento kodo gaiyo hohei dai 41 Rentai* [First New Guinea campaign, 41st Regiment], pp. 14–15, NIDS, Higashi Nyuguinea, 156.

13 Battle Casualties, Kokoda to Imita, pp. 1–3, AWM54 171/2/48.

14 Koiwai, *Nyuginia Senki* [Battle history of New Guinea], pp. 86–8.

15 Ibid., pp. 100–1.

16 Sublet, *Kokoda to the Sea*, pp. 63–4; Uren, *A Thousand Men at War*, pp. 136–43.

17 Koiwai, *Nyuginia Senki* [Battle history of New Guinea], pp. 91–2.

18 Ibid., p. 92.

19 Sublet, *Kokoda to the Sea*, p. 66.

20 21st Brigade war diary, AWM52 8/2/21.

21 Koiwai, *Nyuginia Senki* [Battle history of New Guinea], p. 93.

22 Lieutenant Morimoto Yoshiyuki, diary extracts, AWM55 3/165.

23 Koiwai, *Nyuginia Senki* [Battle history of New Guinea], p. 98.

24 *Daiichi Nyuginiea sen rentai sento kodo gaiyo hohei dai 41 Rentai* [First New Guinea campaign, 41st Regiment], pp. 14–15, NIDS, Higashi Nyuguinea, 156; Records of 67 LOCH, enemy publications no 24, p. 32, AWM55 5/2. The records of the Japanese 67th Line of Communication Hospital have been thought to be only partial accounts of Japanese wounded and sick treated at Giruwa, hence not useful in determining overall Japanese casualties. However, it is apparent from comparing the hospital records with other Japanese sources that they are fairly complete accounts, for the periods they cover, of battle casualties and the sick.

25 Battle Casualties, Kokoda to Imita, pp. 1–2, AWM54 171/2/48. The number given here excludes those who were casualties during this period, but not at this engagement, for Japanese patrols already searching the flanks occasionally clashed with Australian parties dispersed as a result of Isurava.

10 EFOGI

1 Rowell to LHQ, 8 September 1942, New Guinea Force messages and reports, AWM54, 577/6/3.

2 Drea, *MacArthur's Ultra*, ch. 2; report on New Guinea operations, p. 5, AWM123 270.

3 Milner, *Victory in Papua*, p. 51.
4 McAulay, *Blood and Iron*, pp. 83 & 113.
5 Department of External Affairs cablegram, 22 September 1942, AWM123 270.
6 21st Brigade report on operations, p. 12, AWM54, 577/7/3.
7 File of Nankai Shitai operational orders, enemy publication no 33, order, 4 September 1942, AWM55 5/3.
8 39th Battalion war diary, July–September 1942, appendix G, p. 4, AWM52 8/3/78. Lieutenant Onogawa of the 1/144th could be misread to say the battalion was present at Efogi, but he refers not to the battalion's own casualties but to the casualties the battalion was tasked to carry to the rear. Another Japanese document in the collection in appendix G has been mistranslated to imply that 5th Company, 41st Regiment fought at Efogi. In fact it refers to 5th Company, 144th Regiment, which was present.
9 Lieutenant Hirano, diary, current translations no 17, p. 5, AWM55 3/2.
10 Yazawa Butai documents, current translations no 33, p. 22, AWM55 3/3.
11 *Nankai Shitai Efuogi minamigawa ni okeru sento* [South Seas Force operations to the south of Efogi], p. 5, NIDS Nanto Soromon/Bismaruku, 130.
12 Commander, 5th Company, 2/144th, diary, current translations no 15, p. 17, AWM55 3/1.
13 21st Brigade war diary, 27 August 1942, AWM52 8/2/21; Burns, *The Brown and Blue Diamond at War*, pp. 112–13; McCarthy, *South-West Pacific Area*, p. 220.
14 Sublet, *Kokoda to the Sea*, p. 70.
15 7th Division messages dealing with Maroubra Force, AWM54 577/6/4.
16 Potts to Rowell and Rowell to LHQ, AWM54 577/6/3.
17 James, *Field Guide to the Kokoda Track*, p. 225; Edgar, *Warrior of Kokoda*, p. 164; Brune, *A Bastard of a Place*, p. 200.
18 *Hohei Dai 144 Rentai dai 3 daitai Sento Sosho* [Detailed battle records of 3rd Battalion, 144th Regiment], p. 33. NIDS, *Nanto zenpan* 174.
19 Ibid., p. 40.
20 Japanese army notes on infantry weapons of 1942, AWM54 320/3/19.
21 *Hohei Dai 144 Rentai Senki* [Battle records of 144th Infantry Regiment], appendix of regimental deaths, NIDS 302.9.H; unknown Japanese officer, diary, p. 6, AWM54 577/7/26.
22 *Hohei Dai 144 Rentai dai 3 daitai Sento Sosho* [Detailed battle records of 3rd Battalion, 144th Regiment], p. 3,. NIDS, *Nanto zenpan* 174.
23 Paull, *Retreat from Kokoda*, p. 192.
24 *Hohei Dai 144 Rentai dai 3 daitai Sento Sosho* [Detailed battle records of 3rd Battalion, 144th Regiment], p. 34, NIDS, *Nanto zenpan* 174.
25 Burns, *The Brown and Blue Diamond at War*, p. 117.
26 *Hohei Dai 144 Rentai dai 3 daitai Sento Sosho* [Detailed battle records of 3rd Battalion, 144th Regiment], p. 35, NIDS, *Nanto zenpan* 174.
27 James, *Field Guide to the Kokoda Track*, p. 247.
28 Nishimura Kohkichi, interview, Tokyo, 14 March 2004. Nishimura knew the area well having spent several weeks camped on Brigade Hill after the war recovering Japanese dead.

29 2/27th Battalion war diary, map appendix B, AWM52 8/3/27; ATIS current translations no 21, AWM55 3/2; ATIS current translations no 29, p. 56, AWM55 3/3.

30 MFHQ has been used as a covering term for Maroubra Force Headquarters combining 21st Brigade HQ and elements of 30th Brigade HQ.

31 NGF HQ sitrep, 7 August 1942, intelligence summary no 79, AWM52 9/2/4; Major G. Lyon, interview, 15 August 1944, p. 12, Gavin Long papers, AWM67 1/6.

32 Uren, *A Thousand Men at War*, p. 146.

33 *Hohei Dai 144 Rentai Senki* [Battle records of the 144th Infantry Regiment], list of war dead, pp. 625–726.

34 *Hohei Dai 144 Rentai dai 3 daitai Sento Sosho* [Detailed battle records of 3rd Battalion, 144th Regiment], p. 65, NIDS, *Nanto zenpan* 174.

35 *Hohei Dai 144 Rentai Senki* [Battle records of 144th Infantry Regiment], pp. 98–9, NIDS 302.9.H. *Hohei Dai 144 Rentai dai 3 daitai Sento Sosho* [Detailed battle records of 3rd Battalion, 144th Regiment], p. 41, NIDS, *Nanto zenpan* 174; *Nankai Shitai Efuogi minamigawa ni okeru sento* [South Seas Force operations to the south of Efogi], p. 5, NIDS Nanto Soromon/ Bismaruku 130.

36 Uren, *A Thousand Men at War*, p. 147; ATIS current translations no 15, p. 21, AWM55 3/1; *Hohei Dai 144 Rentai dai 3 daitai Sento Sosho* [Detailed battle records of 3rd Battalion, 144th Regiment], p. 41, NIDS *Nanto zenpan* 174; ATIS current translations no 51, p. 21, AWM55 3/5.

37 *Nankai Shitai Efuogi minamigawa ni okeru sento* [South Seas Force operations to the south of Efogi], p. 6, NIDS Nanto Soromon/Bismaruku 130.

38 ATIS current translations no 29, p. 56, AWM55 3/3.

39 James, *Field Guide to the Kokoda Track*, pp. 231 & 236.

40 *Azuma Shigetoshio* [List of war dead of 144th Regiment], author's collection, pp. 2–3.

41 Records of no 67 LOCH, enemy publications no 24, AWM55 5/2.

42 ATIS interrogation report no 34, p. 94, AWM55 5/3.

43 Rowell to Long, Gavin Long papers, AWM67 3/167.

44 Ibid.

45 39th Battalion war diary, 16 August 1942, AWM52 8/3/78.

46 McCarthy, *South-West Pacific Area*, p. 225.

47 Rowell to Long, Gavin Long papers, AWM67 3/167.

48 Edgar, *Warrior of Kokoda*, pp. 176 & 301.

1 1 IORIBAIWA

1 Notes on operations, AWM54 577/7/29, p. 2.

2 Crooks, *The Footsoldiers*, p. 157.

3 Laffin, *Forever Forward*, p. 90.

4 *Hohei Dai 144 Rentai dai 3 daitai Sento Sosho* [Detailed battle records of 3rd Battalion, 144th Regiment], p. 65, NIDS, *Nanto zenpan* 174.

5 ATIS current translations no 15, p. 21, AWM55 3/1.

6 Kusunose order of 16 September 1942, current translations no 42, pp. 25–7, AWM55 3/4; data on Japanese mountain artillery organisation, no 66, AWM54 423/4/28.

7 Records of 67 LOCH, enemy publications no 24, p. 32, AWM55 5/2.

8 *Hohei Dai 144 Rentai dai 3 daitai Sento Sosho* [Detailed battle records of 3rd Battalion, 144th Regiment], p. 48, NIDS, *Nanto zenpan* 174.

9 25th Brigade war diary, 12–17 September 1942, AWM52.

10 McCarthy, *South-West Pacific Area*, p. 228.

11 Current translations no 17, AWM55 3/2, and interrogation report no 23, Pte Chiya Haruyoshi, AWM55 6/1.

12 File of Nankai Shitai operational orders, enemy publications no 33, 16 August – 15 October, AWM55 5/3, p. 12, and Yazawa Butai documents, current translations, no 33, AWM55 3/3, pp. 23–4.

13 Dr Shindo Hiroyuki, military historian, NIDS, interview, 6 March 2005.

14 Japanese monograph no 37, p 18, NLA, mfm 1383.

15 ATIS interogation report no 157, AWM55 6/4.

16 Yazawa Butai documents, current translations, no 33, p. 26, AWM55 3/3.

17 See folio of maps, AWM54 423/4/106 pt 2, and AMF analysis of the Hoffstetter maps, p. 3, AWM54 423/4/99.

18 General staff intelligence, New Guinea Force, September 1942, situation report no 153, 14 September 1942, AWM52 9/2/4.

19 RAAF War History Section Combined Operations Centre situation report, interim report no 378, 2/1st Pioneer Battalion patrols, AWM66 10/1/5, p. 2.

20 2/1st Pioneer Battalion war diary, 10–20 September 1942, AWM55 8/6/1.

21 File of Nankai Shitai operational orders, enemy publications no 33, 16 August – 15 October 1942, order of 14 September 1942, p. 22, AWM55 5/3.

22 21st Brigade war diary, 18 September 1942, AWM52 8/2/21.

23 McCarthy, *South-West Pacific Area*, pp. 250–3.

24 Horii bulletin no 10, current translations no 42, p. 29, 21 September 1942, AWM55 3/4.

25 ATIS spot report no 3, p. 1, AWM55 2/1.

26 39th Battalion war diary, appendix G, p. 4, AWM52 8/3/78.

27 Translation of captured documents, no 92, AWM54 422/7/8.

28 Nankai Shitai order, current translations no 42, pp. 22 & 24, AWM55 3/4.

29 *Hohei Dai 144 Rentai dai 3 daitai Sento Sosho* [Detailed battle records of 3rd Battalion, 144th Regiment], pp. 45–8, NIDS, *Nanto zenpan* 174.

30 Nankai Shitai order, current translations no 42, 11 September 1942, pp. 22–5, AWM55 3/4; file of Nankai Shitai operational orders, enemy publications no 33, p. 22, 14 September 1942, AWM55 5/3.

31 *Hohei Dai 144 Rentai dai 3 daitai Sento Sosho* [Detailed battle records of 3rd Battalion, 144th Regiment], p. 48, NIDS, *Nanto zenpan* 174.

32 25th Brigade war diary, 17 September 1942, AWM52 8/2/25.

33 *Hohei Dai 144 Rentai dai 3 daitai Sento Sosho* [Detailed battle records of 3rd Battalion, 144th Regiment], p. 50, NIDS, *Nanto zenpan* 174.

34 ATIS current translations, p. 1, AWM55 3/1/193. There were two 3-inch mortars with 2/25th Battalion.

35 3rd Battalion war diary, 15 September 1942, situation report appendix B, AWM52 8/3/39.

36 2/33rd Battalion war diary, 15 September 1942, AWM52 8/3/33.

37 ATIS enemy publications, no 5, p. 59, AWM55 5/1.

38 *Hohei Dai 144 Rentai dai 3 daitai Sento Sosho* [Detailed battle records of 3rd Battalion, 144th Regiment], p. 54, NIDS, *Nanto zenpan* 174.

39 Battle Casualties, Kokoda to Imita, AWM54 171/2/48.

40 Records of 67 LOCH, enemy publications no 24, p. 32, AWM55 5/2.

41 *Hiho to Tomoni-Sanpohei dai 55 Rentai senshi* [With fire: The war history of 55th Mountain Artillery Regiment], p. 25, NIDS 302. 9.S; *Azuma Shigetoshio* [List of war dead of 144th Regiment], author's collection, p. 2; Bullard, *Japanese Army Operations in the South Pacific Area*, p. 166.

42 Records of 67 LOCH enemy publications no 24, September admissions chart, npn, AWM55 5/2.

43 *Hohei Dai 144 Rentai dai 3 daitai Sento Sosho* [Detailed battle records of 3rd Battalion, 144th Regiment], p. 65, NIDS, *Nanto zenpan* 174.

44 Ham, *Kokoda*, p. 255.

45 *Hiho to Tomoni-Sanpohei dai 55 Rentai senshi* [With fire: The war history of 55th Mountain Artillery Regiment], p. 25, NIDS 302. 9.S; Bullard, *Japanese Army Operations in the South Pacific Area*, p. 166.

46 *Daitoa senso minami taiheiyo homen ni okeru sento* [East Asia War, South Pacific Area], npn, NIDS, Nanto Zenpan.

47 ATIS current translations, no 29, p. 62, AWM55 3/3.

48 Records of 67 LOCH, enemy publications no 24, PCB figures for September 1942, AWM55 5/2.

49 Rowell, report and attached documents and intelligence summaries, War Cabinet minute p. 2, 6/10/42 AWM123 270; graph AMF and AIF battle casualties, New Guinea June 1942 – February 1943, AWM54 171/1/2.

50 Battle casualties, Kokoda to Imita, p. 7, AWM54, 171/2/48.

51 2/33rd Battalion war diary, 16 September 1942, AWM52 8/3/33.

52 25th Brigade war diary, 17 September 1942, AWM52 8/2/25.

53 Paull, *Retreat from Kokoda*, p. 230; Ham, *Kokoda*, p. 304.

54 *Hohei Dai 144 Rentai dai 3 daitai Sento Sosho* [Detailed battle records of 3rd Battalion, 144th Regiment], p. 56, NIDS, *Nanto zenpan* 174.

55 Ibid., pp. 46 & 61.

56 7th Division Report on Operations, 13 August to 2 December 1942, pp. 8–9, AWM54 577/7/34.

57 25th Brigade war diary, 16 September 1942, AWM52 8/2/25.

58 2/25th Battalion war diary, 16 September 1942, AWM52 8/3/25.

59 Horner, *General Vasey's War*, pp. 212–13.

60 Ham, *Kokoda*, p. 243.

61 Nankai Shitai operational orders, enemy publications, no 33, p. 15, AWM55 5/3.

62 Vernon, war diary, pt 1, p. 19, AWM54 253/5/8.

63 McCarthy, *South-West Pacific Area*, p. 232.
64 Ibid.
65 Howard, *The Franco-Prussian War*, p. 98.

12 JAPANESE ARTILLERY

1 Bullard, *Japanese Army Operations in the South Pacific Area*, p. 157.
2 James, *Field Guide to the Kokoda Track*, pp. 184–5.
3 McCarthy, *South-West Pacific Area*, pp. 203, 296–8, 318–25; Ham, *Kokoda*, p. 170.
4 File of documents dealing with captured enemy equipment, npn, AWM54 320/2/7.
5 Brune, *A Bastard of a Place*, p. 135.
6 For example see AWM54 320/2/1.
7 NGF General staff intelligence summary, intelligence summary no 79, 7 September 1942, AWM52 9/2/4; NGF General staff war diary, attached situation reports, AWM53 1/5/51.
8 File of Yazawa Butai intelligence records, enemy publications no 28, p. 82, AWM55 5/3.
9 ATIS current translations no 29, p. 65, AWM55 3/3.
10 NGF intelligence estimate, 1 November 1942, AWM54 581/7/21.
11 Japanese divisional orders of battle, AWM54 320/3/7.
12 ATIS interrogation report no 49, p. 1, AWM55 6/1.
13 Nakanishi, *Nihon no hohei kaki* [Japanese infantry weapons], pp. 52–9.
14 *Hohei dia 41 rentai New Guinea senkyo houkou* [Battle reports of 41st Infantry Regiment, New Guinea], p. 72, NIDS, *Nanto higashi Nyuginea*, 255.
15 ATIS current translations no 68, pp. 3–4, AWM55 3/6.
16 ATIS current translations no 58, p. 17, AWM55 3/5.
17 Private Chiya Haruyoshi, gun platoon 1/144, interrogation report no 23, p. 3, AWM55 6/1.
18 Report on type 92 gun, AWM54 320/4/27; Nakanishi, *Nihon no hohei kaki* [Japanese infantry weapons], p. 54.
19 Kawakubo Yasuichi, interrogation report no 49, p. 1, AWM55 6/1.
20 Nakanishi, *Nihon no hohei kaki* [Japanese infantry weapons], pp. 46–53.
21 Bullard, *Japanese Army Operations in the South Pacific Area*, p. 157.
22 Military Analysis Division, 'The effect of air action on Japanese ground logistics', chart, p. 89.
23 ATIS current translations no 74, p. 42, AWM55 3/7.
24 Nankai Shitai orders, enemy publication no 33, 16 August 1942 to 15 October 1942, order no 102 of 24 August 1942, p. 7 AWM55 5/3; ATIS enemy publications no 28, p. 48, AWM55 5/3.
25 *Nanto taiheiyo homen sakusen kiroku, Nankai Shitai no Sakusen* [Operations record in south-eastern Pacific area, operations of the Nankai Shitai], p. 47, NIDS, *Nanto zenpan* 297.

26 Lieutenant Naka Masao, interrogation report no 48, p. 2, AWM55 6/1; 2/16th Battalion war diary, August–October 1942, attached report, p. 4, AWM52 8/3/16.

27 Major-General Paul Cullen, interview, Marulan, NSW, 12 December 2004.

28 McCarthy, *South-West Pacific Area*, p. 289.

29 Ibid., p. 297.

30 2/4th Field Ambulance war diary, 20 October 1942, AWM52 11/12/13.

31 Major C. Sims, 2/27th Bn, interview, Gavin Long papers, p. 7, AWM67 2/97.

32 Private Tsuno Keishin, interrogation report no 20, pp. 2–4, AWM55 6/1.

33 'Combat principles of the infantry gun', current translations no 59, pp. 2–4, AWM55 3/5.

34 Cooper, *The Little Men*, p. 117; chart, artillery deployment, enemy publications no 5, p. 59, AWM55 5/1.

35 Shibata Shinichiro, interrogation report no 151, p. 7, AWM55 6/4; ATIS enemy publications no 26, p. 2, AWM55 5/2.

36 Assistant Chief of Air Staff, 'Air action in the Papuan campaign', appendix 6.

37 Report of Captain W. McLaren, p. 2, AWM54 481/2/48; Dunnigan & Nofi, *Pacific War Encyclopedia*, pp. 143–4.

38 Grogan, 'The operation of forward surgical teams in the Kokoda–Buna campaigns', pp. 68–73.

39 2/27th Battalion war diary, AWM52 8/3/27; Burns, *The Brown and Blue Diamond at War*, pp. 110–17; Sublet, *Kokoda to the Sea*, p. 72.

40 Burns, *The Brown and Blue Diamond at War*, pp. 115–17.

41 *Hohei Dai 144 Rentai dai 3 daitai Sento Sosho* [Detailed battle records of 3rd Battalion, 144th Regiment], p. 166, chart 2, NIDS, *Nanto zenpan 174*.

42 Ibid., p. 52. McCarthy, *South West Pacific Area – First Year*, p. 231. General staff intelligence report, New Guinea Force, situation report no 153, AWM52 9/2/4. 21st Brigade war diary, AWM52 8/2/21. Uren, *A Thousand Men at War*, p. 153.

43 Department of Veterans' Affairs, 'Kokoda Track: The Australian Veterans' Accounts', http://kokoda.commemoration.gov.au/australian-veterans-accounts/veterans-accounts.php.

44 Clausewitz, *On War*, book 5, pp. 285, 287 & 291.

13 MALARIA AND DYSENTERY

1 Zissner, *Rats, Lice and History*, p. 153.

2 Brune, *A Bastard of a Place*, p. 210.

3 NGFHQ intelligence summary no 86, 3–7/10/42, p. 1, AWM52 9/2/4.

4 Okada, *Lost Troops*, p. 24.

5 49th Battalion war diary, AWM52 8/3/88.

6 Notes on dysentery, malaria and casualties, 30/1/43, p. 3, AWM54 267/3/9.

7 Professor Frank Fenner, interview, 4 October 2006.

8 Professor Ian Clarke, interview, 4 April 2006.

9 Japanese monograph no 37, pp. 19–20, ANL mfm 1383.

10 Bullard, 'The great enemy of humanity', pp. 208–9.

11 'Papuan campaign: Malaria in the Japanese forces', report, pt 8, p. 2, AWM54 243/17/3.

12 Walker, *The Island Campaigns*, p. 280.

13 Noda, diary, p. 2, AWM54 577/7/26; ATIS bulletin no 36, p. 3, AWM55 1/1.

14 Items of medical interest compiled from captured Japanese documents, pp. 1–3, AWM54 423/4 88.

15 Reports dealing with medical organisation and medical problems, pp. 1–2, AWM54 481/2/48; New Guinea campaign, extracts from medical appreciations, pp. 1–4, AWM54 329/2/4.

16 Kingsley Norris, *No Memory for Pain*, pp. 146 & 150.

17 'Papuan campaign: Malaria in the Japanese forces', report, p. 1, AWM54 243/17/3, pt 8.

18 Professor Frank Fenner, interview, 4 October 2006.

19 ATIS current translations no 30, p. 3, AWM55 3/3.

20 Interrogation report no 19, AWM55 6/1.

21 'Papuan campaign: Malaria in the Japanese forces', report, p. 1, AWM54 243/17/3, pt 8.

22 ATIS current translations no 17, p. 3, AWM55 3/2.

23 *Hohei Dai 144 Rentai dai 3 daitai Sento Sosho* [Detailed battle records of 3rd Battalion, 144th Regiment], pp. 25, 41 & 64, NIDS, *Nanto zenpan* 174; ATIS current translations no 26, p. 6, AWM55 3/3.

24 Records of 67 LOCH, enemy publications no 24, pp. 1–7, AWM55 5/2.

25 Nankai operation order A no 133, current translations no 42, pp. 11 & 17, AWM55 3/4; Records of 67 LOCH, enemy publications no 24, pp. 1–2, AWM55 5/2; ATIS enemy publications no 38, pp. 14–15, AWM55 5/3.

26 Nankai Shitai operational orders, 10 October 1942, enemy publications no 33, AWM55 5/3.

27 Report of ADMS visit to Maroubra Force, appendix A, AWM54 481/12/17.

28 39th Battalion war diary, 26 August 1942, AWM52 8/3/78.

29 14th Australian Field Ambulance, Papua, report, pp. 128–9, AWM54 481/12/68; NGF medical notes, New Guinea campaign, p. 2, AWM54 481/12/48; Casualties evacuated from Maroubra Force, AWM54 577/7/13; 'Brief account of activities of 7th Australian Division', p. 2, AWM54 481/12/13.

30 Walker, *The Island Campaigns*, p. 36.

31 2/25th Battalion war diary, September–October, esp. 17 October 1942, AWM52 8/3/25/18; 21st Brigade report on operations, pt 5, p. 12, AWM54 577/7/3.

32 McCarthy, *South-West Pacific Area*, p. 276.

33 NGF, medical notes, New Guinea campaign, p. 2, AWM54 481/12/48.

34 Captain J.M. Oldham, 2/6th Field Ambulance, medical report, p. 3, AWM54 481/12/26.

35 Vernon, war diary, July–November 1942, pt 1, pp. 39 & 56, AWM54 253/5/8.

36 Australian 7th Division, messages dealing with Maroubra Force operations, 30 September 1942, AWM54 577/6/4.

37 Maroubra Force, analysis of admissions, AWM54 481/7/50; Australian
   7th Division, messages dealing with Maroubra Force operations, AWM54
   577/6/4; 'Brief account of activities of 7th Australian Division', p. 10,
   AWM54 481/12/13; Records of 67 LOCH, enemy publications no 24,
   pp. 30, 46 & 63, AWM55 5/2.
38 ATIS current translations no 30, p. 6, AWM55 3/3.
39 7th Division Adjutant and Quartermaster General Branch, war diary,
   March–December 1942, AWM52 1/5/15; Walker, *The Island Campaigns*,
   p. 98; *Nankai Shitai shireibu Toyufuku shosa kowa* [Lecture of Major
   Toyofuku, Headquarters, Nankai Shitai], p. 30, NIDS, *Nanto zenpan* 168.
40 Reports dealing with medical problems, Papuan campaign, p. 3, AWM54
   481/2/48.

14 THE JAPANESE SUPPLY CRISIS

1 Ham, *Kokoda*, p. 305.
2 Rainfall charts, Kokoda–Buna region 1906–73, Papua New Guinea
   Meteorological Service.
3 ATIS enemy publications no 11, p. 5, AWM55 5/14.
4 Kasis Inape, Papua New Guinea Meteorological Service, email.
5 Hawthorne, *The Kokoda Trail*, pp. 128 & 158.
6 Yazawa Butai intelligence records, record no 35, p. 95, AWM55 5/3.
7 ATIS enemy publication no 24, p. 43, AWM55 5/2; ATIS enemy publication
   no 28, pp. 8 & 71, AWM55 5/3.
8 Records of 67 LOCH, p. 1, enemy publication no 24, AWM55 5/2.
9 Yazawa Butai intelligence records, record no 28, p. 8, and record 31, p. 90,
   AWM55 5/3.
10 HQAAF SWP area intelligence summary no 27, p. 6, AWM66 2/5/1.
11 Yazawa Butai intelligence report, enemy publications no 28, pt 2, p. 68,
   AWM55 5/3.
12 Japanese monograph no 34, p. 108, NLA, mfm 1383; Japanese diary, p. 1,
   AWM55 3/7/841.
13 Nankai Shitai orders, enemy publications no 39, p. 21, AWM55 5/3.
14 IJA, 'Lessons from New Guinea operations July 42–April 43', pp. 3 &
   12–13, AWM54 423/4/156.
15 Furse, *Provisioning Armies in the Field*, pp. 265–7.
16 Koiwai, *Nyuginia Senki* [Battle history of New Guinea], p. 80; Bullard,
   Japanese Army Operations in the South Pacific Area, p. 163.
17 21st Brigade report on operations, p. 3, AWM54 577/7/3.
18 Ibid.
19 *Rikugun tsushin ni gaikan* [Overview of army correspondence] npn, NIDS,
   Bunko jiku, 469.
20 21st Brigade report on operations, p. 4, AWM54 577/7/3.
21 Report on Operations in New Guinea, supplies by air transport,
   subappendix 8, AWM54 917/3/11.
22 21st Brigade report on operations, p. 4, AWM54 577/7/3.

23 McCarthy, *South-West Pacific Area*, pp. 130–2, 140–1 & 197–8.
24 NGF HQ intelligence summary no 79, sitrep 8/10/42, AWM52 9/2/4.
25 'War History of 144 Regiment', p. 11, papers of Lieutenant Salmon, AWM PRO 0297.
26 21st Brigade report on operations, p. 21, AWM54 577/7/3.
27 Vernon, war diary, July–November 1942, pt 1, p. 17, AWM54 253/5/8.
28 ATIS enemy publications no 292, p. 53, AWM55 3/2.
29 Koiwai, *Nyuginia Senki* [Battle history of New Guinea], p. 52.
30 ATIS, enemy publications no 33, p. 9, AWM55 5/3.
31 ATIS, current translations no 13, AWM55 3/1; ATIS current translations no 39, p. 4, AWM55 5/3.
32 Ibid.
33 Report on Operations in New Guinea, supplies by air transport, AWM54 917/3/11.
34 Japanese monograph no 37 p. 17, ANL, mfm 1383.
35 *Boeicho boei senshishitsu, Senshi sosho, minami taiheiyo rikugun sakusen* [War history series, South Pacific Area army operations], vol. 1, p. 586.
36 ATIS enemy publications no 33, p. 16, AWM55 5/3; ATIS current translations no 42, p. 20, & no 141, pp. 3–4, AWM55 3/4.
37 2/25th Battalion war diary, 8 October 1942, AWM52 8/3/25/18.
38 ATIS enemy publication no 33, AWM55 5/3.
39 *Hohei Dai 144 Rentai dai 3 daitai Sento Sosho* [Detailed battle records of 3rd Battalion], p. 71, NIDS, *Nanto zenpan* 174; ATIS enemy publications no 39, p. 21, AWM55 5/3.
40 ATIS current translations no 25, AWM55 3/2.
41 ATIS current translations no 29, p. 21, AWM55 3/3.
42 ATIS current translations no 42, pp. 22 & 25, AWM55 3/4; ATIS current translations no 31, p. 1, AWM55 3/3.
43 ATIS current translations no 33, p. 26, AWM55 3/3.
44 ATIS current translations no 29, p. 62, AWM55 3/3.
45 ATIS current translations no 439, p. 22, AWM55 3/3.
46 *Argus*, Melbourne, 3 November 1942.
47 *West Australian*, Perth, 8 October 1942.
48 25th Brigade war diary, 13 October 1942, AWM52 8/2/25.
49 Notes from theatres of war, New Guinea, July 1942 – January 1943, p. 138, AWM54 519/6/51.
50 Koiwai, *Nyuginia Senki* [Battle history of New Guinea], p. 161.
51 Records of 67 LOCH, enemy publications no 24, p. 61, AWM55 5/2.
52 ATIS interrogation report no 86, p. 1, AWM55 6/3.
53 ATIS interrogation report no 25, p. 6, AWM55 6/1.
54 Papers of Lieutenant F. Winkel, p. 1, AWM PRO 3106; Vernon, war diary, July–November 1942, pt 1, p. 24. AWM54 253/5/8.
55 2/4th Field Ambulance war diary, October–December 1942, 3/11/1942, 8/11/1942, AWM52 11/12/13.
56 *Boeicho boei senshishitsu, Senshi sosho, minami taiheiyo rikugun sakusen* [War history series, South Pacific Area army operations], vol. 1, p. 339; ATIS current translations no 29, pp. 2–4, AWM 3/3.

57 *Nankai Shitai shireibu Toyufuku shosa kowa* [Lecture of Major Toyufuku, headquarters, Nankai Shitai], pp. 29–30, NIDS *nanto zenpan* 168.

58 Ibid., pp. 29–30.

59 Estimated from ATIS current translations no 49, p. 44, AWM55 3/4; ATIS bulletin no 78, p. 2, AWM55 1/1; ATIS enemy publications no 28, p. 66, AWM55 5/3; McAulay, *Blood and Iron*, p. 408.

60 Vernon, war diary, July–November 1942, pt 1, p. 24, AWM54 253/5/8.

61 2/25th Battalion war diary, 8 October 1942, 18 November 1942 and end of November report, AWM52 8/3/25/18.

62 General staff intelligence, NGF, HQHGF, sitrep no 275, 13/11/42, AWM52 9/2/4; NGF to land forces sitrep 14 November 1942, AWM 54 423/12/3; Wick, *Purple over Green*, p. 237.

63 Bourne, *Nutrition and the War*, p. 8.

64 Dr Christopher Forbes-Ewan, Defence Nutrition Research Unit, Scottsdale, Tasmania, interview and emails, October 2006.

65 Marriott, *Food Components to Enhance Performance*, p. 487.

66 Paton, *Army Rations*, p. 5.

67 Air Vice-Marshal Bostock to Major-General Kenney, letter, 30 August 1942, AWM54 964/4/2; Robertson, 'Problems of supply encountered by the Australian and Japanese forces on the Kokoda Trail, and the question of morale', p. 25.

68 Burns, *The Brown and Blue Diamond at War*, pp. 122–30 & 134.

69 '2/14th Battalion standard of fitness', report, 3 October 1942, p. 1, AWM54 481/2/25.

70 Masters, *The Road Past Mandalay*, p. 279.

71 Bullard, *Japanese Army Operations in the South Pacific Area*, p. 202.

72 Lieutenant Hayashi Yiroyuki, diary, current translations no 62, p. 1, AWM55 3/5.

15 Second Eora–Templeton's

1 ATIS enemy publications no 33, p. 22, AWM55 5/3.

2 Japanese monograph no 37, p. 19, NLA, mfm 1383.

3 Questions addressed to General Kengoro Tanaka, p. 5, AWM MSS 701, item 2.

4 Bullard, *Japanese Army Operations in the South Pacific Area*, pp. 206–8.

5 Ugaki, *Fading Victory*, p. 215; Japanese monograph no 37, pp. 18–19, NLA, mfm 1383.

6 File of Yazawa Butai intelligence records, enemy publications no 29, p. 88, AWM55 5/3; ATIS current translations no 14, p. 5, AWM55 3/1; ATIS current translations no 33, p. 29, & no 34, p. 32, AWM55 3/3.

7 Milner, *Victory in Papua*, p. 92; Gailey, *MacArthur Strikes Back*, pp. 110–12.

8 Newspaper article filed with report on operations by Lieutenant-General Sir Sydney Rowell, 24/9/42, AWM123 270.

9 Nankai Shitai Intelligence report no 21, current translations no 42, AWM55 3/4.

10 MacDonald, *Chester Wilmot Reports*, pp. 276–88 & 388; file of Yazawa Butai intelligence records, intelligence record no 28, pp. 84 & 87, AWM55 5/3; Nankai Shitai intelligence report no 21, 9 October 1942, p. 2, current translations no 42, AWM55 3/4.

11 File of Yazawa Butai intelligence records, intelligence record no 37, p. 97, AWM55 5/3; Matthews, *Shadows Dancing*, pp. 92 & 218–19.

12 ATIS enemy publications no 24, p. 75, AWM55 5/2; Japanese monograph no 37, p. 17, NLA mfm 1383.

13 Horii operational orders, order no 123, 1 October 1942, p. 32, current translations, no 34, AWM55 3/3; Nankai Shitai order, 4 October 1942, current translations no 42, p. 5, AWM55 3/4, ATIS current translations no 42, 3 October 1942, p. 4, AWM55 3/4.

14 Milner, *Victory in Papua*, p. 92.

15 7th Division Report on Operations, 13 August to 2 December 1942, p. 16, AWM54 577/7/34.

16 James, *Field Guide to the Kokoda Track*, p. 285; Sublet, *Kokoda to the Sea*, p. 96.

17 3rd Battalion war diary, 14 October 1942, AWM52, 8/3/39.

18 7th Division Report on Operations, 13 August to 2 December 1942, p. 16, AWM54 577/7/34.

19 Crooks, *The Footsoldiers*, pp. 211–13 & 215.

20 25th Brigade war diary, 11 October 1942, AWM52 8/2/25; 16th Brigade war diary, October sitreps and messages, 14 October 1942, AWM 52 8/2/16.

21 Nankai Shitai intelligence report, no 21, pp. 3–4, current translations no 42, AWM55 1/1; ATIS bulletin no 24, p. 7, AWM55 3/4.

22 ATIS current translations no 30, p. 6, AWM55 3/3.

23 *Hohei dai Rentai New Guinea Senkyo Houkou* [War reports of 41 Regiment in New Guinea], pp. 20–1, NIDS, Nanto higashi New Guinea, 255; ATIS current translations no 17, p. 63, AWM55 3/3.

24 ATIS current translations no 17, p. 7, AWM55 3/2.

25 Report, Blamey papers, series 2, wallet 47, p. 1, AWM 3 DRL/6643.

26 2/25th Battalion war diary, 13 October 1942, AWM52 8/3/25.

27 Sublet, *Kokoda to the Sea*, pp. 98–100.

28 *Hohei Dai 144th Rentai Senki* [War record of 144th Regiment], appended list of regimental war dead, NIDS 302.9.H; *Azuma Shigetoshio* [List of war dead of 144th Regiment], author's collection, p. 2; Battle casualties, Imita to Wairopi, pp. 1–6, AWM54 171/2/47.

29 Sublet, *Kokoda to the Sea*, p. 98.

30 Japanese order, messages, sitreps relating to the period 1 October – 10 November 1942, Owen Stanleys, AWM54 577/7/9.

31 Lieutenant Hirano diary, p. 8, current translations no 17, AWM55 3/2.

32 File of Nankai Shitai orders, 16 August – 15 October, order A, no 127, p. 24, enemy publications no 33, AWM55 5/3.

33 Japanese order, messages, sitreps relating to the period 1 October – 10 November 1942, Owen Stanleys, AWM54 577/7/9.

34 2/33rd Battalion war diary, 13 October 1942, AWM52 8/3/33.

35 Lieutenant Hirano diary, ibid.

36 ATIS bulletin no 24, p. 7, AWM55 1/1.
37 Japanese order, messages, sitreps relating to the period 1 October – 10 November 1942, Owen Stanleys, AWM54 577/7/9.
38 *Hohei Dai 144th Rentai Senki* [War record of 144 Regiment], appended list of regimental war dead, NIDS 302.9.H.
39 ATIS current translations no 29, p. 66, AWM55 3/3.
40 Ibid., p. 63.
41 *Hohei Dai 144th Rentai Senki* [War record of 144 Regiment], appended list of regimental war dead, NIDS 302.9.H, p. 17.
42 Headquarters New Guinea Force, G branch, war diary, 31 October 1942, AWM52 1/5/51; Marshall, *Nulli Secundus Log*, p. 218; McCarthy, *South-West Pacific Area*, pp. 276 & 300.
43 *Hohei Dai 144 Rentai dai 3 daitai Sento Shoho* [Detailed battle records of 3rd Battalion, 144th Regiment], p. 74. NIDS, *Nanto zenpan* 174; 'War History of 144 Regiment', p. 16, papers of Lieutenant Salmon, AWM PRO 0297; ATIS current translations no 52, p. 35. AWM55 3/5.
44 Koiwai, *Nyuginia Senki* [Battle history of New Guinea], p. 145.
45 Japanese order, messages, sitreps relating to the period 1 October – 10 November 1942, Owen Stanleys, AWM54 577/7/9.
46 Major-General Paul Cullen, battalion commander, 2/1st Battalion, interview, Marulan, NSW, 4 April 2003.
47 *Hohei Dai 144 Rentai dai 3 daitai Sento Shoho* [Detailed battle records of 3rd Battalion, 144th Regiment], p. 82, NIDS, *Nanto zenpan* 174, and McCarthy, *South-West Pacific Area*, p. 76.
48 Koiwai, *Nyuginia Senki* [Battle history of New Guinea], p. 146.
49 File of Nankai Shitai orders, enemy publications no 39, p. 6, AWM55 5/3.
50 ATIS current translations no 29, p. 68, AWM55 3/3.
51 *Hohei Dai 144 Rentai dai 3 daitai Sento Shoho* [Detailed battle records of 3rd Battalion, 144th Regiment], p. 78 NIDS, *Nanto zenpan* 174; McCarthy, *South-West Pacific Area*, p. 303; Koiwai, *Nyuginia Senki* [Battle history of New Guinea], pp. 148–9.
52 Japanese monograph no 37, pp. 19–20, NLA, mfm 1383.
53 *Hohei Dai 144 Rentai dai 3 daitai Sento Shoho* [Detailed battle records of 3rd Battalion, 144th Regiment], chart 1, p. 84, NIDS, *Nanto zenpan* 174.
54 Battle casualties, Imita to Wairopi, pp. 2–6, AWM54 171/2/47.
55 *Hohei dai 41 Rentai New Guinea Senkyo Houkou* [War reports of 41st Regiment in New Guinea], p. 25. NIDS Nanto higashi New Guinea, 225; *Hohei Dai 144 Rentai dai 3 daitai Sento Shoho* [Detailed battle records of 3rd Battalion, 144th Regiment], chart 1, p. 84, NIDS, *Nanto zenpan* 174; *Azuma Shigetoshio* [List of war dead of 144th Regiment], author's collection, pp. 2–3.
56 McCarthy, *South-West Pacific Area*, p. 290.
57 Major-General Paul Cullen, battalion commander, 2/1st Battalion, interview, Marulan, NSW, 4 April 2003.
58 ATIS enemy publications no 24, pp. 60 & 75, chart 9, AWM55 5/2; *Azuma Shigetoshio* [List of war dead of 144th Regiment], author's collection, pp. 2–3.

59 McCarthy, *South-West Pacific Area*, p. 299.
60 File of Nankai Shitai orders, enemy publication no 39, p. 7, AWM55 5/3.
61 Braga, *Kokoda Commander*, pp. 243–7; Ham, *Kokoda*, p. 367; Brune, *A Bastard of a Place*, p. 611.
62 Battle casualties, Imita to Wairopi, pp. 2–6, AWM54 171/2/47; Sublet, *Kokoda to the Sea*, pp. 99–100.
63 Braga, *Kokoda Commander*, p. 239.
64 McCarthy, *South-West Pacific Area*, p. 290.
65 Blamey to Allen, 26 October 1942, Blamey papers, series 2, wallet 47, AWM 3drl/6643.
66 Blamey to MacArthur, 5 October 1942, messages and reports, AWM54 577/6/3.
67 Ibid., 7 October 1942.
68 Rowell to Gavin Long, letter, 1957, pp. 10–13, AWM67 3/167.
69 Ibid.
70 Braga, *Kokoda Commander*, pp. 229 & 231.
71 Rowell to Gavin Long, letter, 1957, pp. 10–13, AWM67 3/167.
72 Braga, *Kokoda Commander*, p. xvi.
73 Koiwai, *Nyuginia Senki* [Battle history of New Guinea], p. 145.

16 OIVI–GORARI

1 Brune, *A Bastard of a Place*, p. 419.
2 Nankai Shitai orders, enemy publications no 39, p. 6, AWM55 5/3.
3 Bullard, *Japanese Army Operations in the South Pacific Area*, pp. 198–9.
4 Nankai Shitai orders, enemy publications no 39, p. 6, AWM55 5/3.
5 Koiwai, *Nyuginia Senki* [Battle history of New Guinea], pp. 159–62.
6 MacDonald, *Chester Wilmot Reports*, p. 279.
7 Bullard, *Japanese Army Operations in the South Pacific Area*, p. 203.
8 Map of Oivi, *Daitoa senso minami taiheiyo nomen ni okeru sento* [Battles in the South Pacific Area in the Greater East Asia War], npn, NIDS, Nanto Zenpan.
9 'War History of 144 Regiment', papers of Lieutenant Salmon, pp. 31–2, AWM PRO 0297.
10 Koiwai, *Nyuginia Senki* [Battle history of New Guinea], p. 163.
11 Colonel Yazawa to Lieutenant-Colonel Tomita, 21 October 1942, current translations no 30, p. 34, AWM55 3/3.
12 *Daiichiji Nyuginea sen rentai sento kodo gaiyo hohei dai 41 rentai* [Battles of the 41st Regiment in New Guinea], pp. 145–6, NIDS, higashi nyuginea 156.
13 Nankai Shitai orders, bulletin no 82, p. 2, AWM55 1/1.
14 39th Battalion war diary, August–September 1942, captured Japanese documents, appendix E, AWM52 8/3/78; Report on operations in New Guinea, AWM54 577/7/2; ATIS Current translations, no 29, p. 69, AWM55 3/3. ATIS current translations no 4, p. 40, AWM55 3/1.
15 Other detachments with 7th Division and not shown in table 16.1: 2/5th Field Company, 185 men; 12th Guard Platoon, 47; 2/4th Field Ambulance,

163; 2/44th Light Aid Detachment, 14; provost detachment, 16; 2/5th Army Service Corps, 352; postal detachment, 5.

16 Report on operations in New Guinea, serial 16, AWM54 577/7/29.

17 Crooks, *The Footsoldiers*, p. 221.

18 Koiwai, *Nyuginia Senki* [Battle history of New Guinea], pp. 160–3.

19 Private Tamura Hikoichi, interrogation report no 21, p. 1, AWM55 6/1.

20 7th Division Report on Operations, 13 August to 2 December 1942, p. 25, AWM54 577/7/34.

21 AAF operational survey no 1, part 3, p. 1, AWM66 2/3/1.

22 Nankai Shitai orders, enemy publications no 39, p. 17, AWM55 5/3; 'War History of 144 Regiment', p. 27, papers of Lieutenant Salmon, AWM PRO 0297.

23 McCarthy, *South-West Pacific Area*, p. 321.

24 *Hohei 144 Rentai dai 3 daitai sento shoho* [Detailed battle reports of 3rd Battalion, 144th Regiment], pp. 90–1, NIDS, *Nanto zenpan*, 174.

25 Koiwai, *Nyuginia Senki* [Battle history of New Guinea], p. 161.

26 Nankai Shitai orders, enemy publications, no 39, pp. 18–19, AWM55 5/3.

27 Koiwai, *Nyuginia Senki* [Battle history of New Guinea], p. 175; ATIS bulletin no 45, p. 2, AWM55 1/1; Records of 67 LOCH, enemy publications no 29, p. 10, AWM55 5/3.

28 'War History of 144 Regiment', pp. 27–31, papers of Lieutenant Salmon, AWM PRO 0297.

29 Brune, *A Bastard of a Place*, p. 419.

30 *Rikugun tsushin no Gaikan* [Overview of army correspondence], npn, NIDS, Bunko jiku 469.

31 Australian Imperial Force, Battle casualties, Owen Stanley Campaign, Imita to Wairopi, pp. 2–6, AWM 54 171/2/47.

32 Colonel Buttrose, interview, 28 March 1943, AWM54 577/7/32; 7th Division Report on Operations, 13 August to 2 December 1942, p. 26, AWM54 577/7/34; James, *Field Guide to the Kokoda Track*, p. 400.

33 *Hohei 144 Rentai dai 3 daitai sento shoho* [Detailed battle reports of 3rd Battalion, 144th Regiment], p. 106, NIDS, *Nanto zenpan* 174.

34 *Hohei Dai 144 Rentai Senki* [Battle records of 144th Infantry Regiment], appendix of regimental war dead, NIDS 302.9.H; *Azuma Shigetoshio* [List of war dead of 144th Regiment], author's collection, pp. 2–3.

35 New Guinea Force situation report, no 272, 12 November 1942, AWM52 9/2/4.

36 Tanaka, *Operations of the Imperial Japanese Armed Forces in Papua New Guinea during WWII*, pp. 139 & 142.

37 *Rikugun tsushin no Gaikan* [Overview of army correspondence], npn, NIDS Bunko jiku 469.

38 Milner, *Victory in Papua*, p. 120.

39 Precise figures for Japanese wounded are not always available so estimation is sometimes required. Japanese wounded to killed were one killed for one and three-quarters wounded during the Japanese advance, and one killed for one wounded in the retreat. Japanese casualty estimates, AWM54 12/4/1; 7th Division report on operations, appendix D, AWM54 519/6/58.

40 7th Division Report on Operations, 13 August to 2 December 1942, p. 26, AWM54 577/7/34.

41 Horner, *General Vasey's War*, p. 212.

42 Frank, *Guadalcanal*, p. 534.

43 Bullard, *Japanese Army Operations in the South Pacific Area*, p. 199.

44 Ibid.

17 THE WAR IN THE AIR

1 Historical study no 17, *Air Action in the Papuan Campaign 21 July to 23 January 1943*, p. 1.

2 Gillison, *Royal Australian Air Force 1939–1942*, pp. 473 & 478.

3 Munday, *USAAF Bomber Units, Pacific 1941–45*, p. 8.

4 AAF operational survey no 1, p. 1, AWM66 2/3/1; air operations, appendix 1, p. 1, AWM54 519/6/58.

5 AAF operational surveys 1–50, AWM66 2/3/1; HQ AAF SWP area intelligence summaries no 29–50, AWM66 2/3/1.

6 Mossman, *The Effect of Air Interdiction*, p. 1.

7 Craven, *The Army Air Forces in WWII: Guadalcanal to Saipan*, p. 24.

8 US Army Air Force, statistical digest, WWII, <www.usaaf.net/digest/t140>

9 Records of 67 LOCH, enemy publications no 24, p. 75, AWM55 5/2.

10 ATIS current translations no 25, pp. 3–6, AWM55 3/2.

11 Daily log of 2/47th FAAAB, current translations no 17, pp. 19–25, AWM55 3/2.

12 Daily log of 5 Yokosuka SNLP, current translations no 26, pp. 1–7, AWM55 3/3.

13 Hellion, *Strike from the Sky*, pp. 263–4.

14 Mossman, *The Effect of Air Interdiction*, p. 2.

15 Questions addressed to General Tanaka Kengoro, p. 6, item 2, AWM MSS 701.

16 Assistant Chief of Air Staff, 'Air action in the Papuan campaign', p. 42.

17 ATIS bulletin no 51, p. 3, AWM55 1/1.

18 Japanese order, messages, sitreps relating to the period 1 October – 10 November 1942, Owen Stanleys, AWM54 577/7/9.

19 HQAAF SWP area intelligence summary no 40, 6 October 1942, pp. 10–11, AWM 66 2/5/1.

20 HQAAF SWP area intelligence summary no 47, 30 October 1942, pp. 6 & 10, AWM66 2/5/1.

21 RAAF War History Section, Combined Operations Centre situation reports, nos 376 & 378, AWM66 10/1/5.

22 Questions addressed to General Tanaka Kengoro, p. 6, item 2, AWM MSS 701.

23 Hellion, *Strike from the Sky*, pp. 163–6.

24 IJA, 'Lessons from New Guinea operations July 42–April 43', p. 4, AWM54 423/4/156.

25 Dunnigan & Nofi, *Pacific War Encyclopedia*, p. 107.

26 Military Analysis Division, 'The effect of air action on Japanese ground army logistics', p. 42.

27 Dunnigan, *How to Make War*, p. 120.

28 Lieutenant Hayashi Hiroyuki, diary, current translations no 62, p. 1, AWM55 3/5/685.

29 Bullard, *Japanese Army Operations in the South Pacific Area*, p. 165.

30 *Hohei Dai 144 Rentai Senki* [Battle records of 144th Infantry Regiment], appendix of regimental deaths, NIDS 302.9.H; Noda, diary, p. 6, AWM54 577/7/26.

31 *Hohei Dai 144 Rentai dai 3 daitai Sento Sosho* [Detailed battle records of 3rd Battalion, 144th Regiment], p. 32. NIDS, *Nanto zenpan* 174; 'War History of 144 Regiment', p. 11, papers of Lieutenant Salmon, AWM PRO 0297.

32 Private, 144th Regiment, diary entry, p. 1, AWM55 3/4 461; ATIS current translations no 15, p. 19, AWM55 3/1; Noda, diary, p. 6, AWM54 577/7/26.

33 Keogh, *South West Pacific*, p. 210; McCarthy, *South West Pacific*, p. 221.

34 Paull, *Retreat from Kokoda*, p. 192.

35 James, *Field Guide to the Kokoda Track*, p. 224; Ham, *Kokoda*, p. 231.

36 Japanese officers General Adachi, Lieutenant-General Cato, Lieutenant-Colonel Tanaka, Lieutenant-Colonel Ota and naval Captain Sanagi, interviews, p. 5, Gavin Long papers, AWM67 11/29.

37 ATIS current translations no 22, p. 11, AWM55 1/2.

38 ATIS interrogation report no 249, p. 16, AWM55 12.

39 Assistant Chief of Air Staff, 'Air action in the Papuan campaign', p. 1.

40 Ibid., pp. 29 & 42.

41 Bullard, *Japanese Army Operations in the South Pacific Area*, p. 199; Japanese officers General Adachi, Lieutenant-General Cato, Lieutenant-Colonel Tanaka, Lieutenant-Colonel Ota and naval Captain Sanagi, interviews, p. 5, Gavin Long papers, AWM67 11/29; Military Analysis Division, 'The effect of air action on Japanese ground army logistics', p. 174.

18 CONCLUSION

1 McCarthy, *South-West Pacific Area*, p. 225.

2 Ham, *Kokoda*, p. 520.

3 Fitzsimons, *Kokoda*, p. 388.

4 Hamley, *Operations of War*, p. 411.

5 Report on operations, part 4, p. 25, AWM54 519/6/58.

NOTE ON SOURCES

1 *Hohei dai 41 Rentai Nyuginiasen Senkyo Hokoku* [Battle Records of 41 Regiment's Battles in New Guinea], NIDS, 301.9.S; *Hiho to Tomoni-Sanpohei dai 55 Rentai Senshi* [With fire: The war history of 55th Mountain

Artillery Regiment], NIDS 302.9.S; *Hohei Dai 144 Rentai Senki* [Battle records of 144th Infantry Regiment], NIDS 302.9.H.

2 For example, *Hohei Dai 144 Rentai Tsushin Chutai Shi Hensan Iinkai* [History of the 144 Regiment Signals Company], NIDS 302.9.I.

3 Accessibility to the ATIS collection has been considerably improved by the cataloging work of Lex MacAulay.

4 The Japanese monographs are at NLA, mfm 1383.

5 NLA, mfm 1383, nos 33 & 37.

6 Bullard, *Japanese Army Operations in the South Pacific Area*, p. 165.

7 Okada, *Lost Soldiers*, p. 14.

8 Ibid, pp. 15–18.

9 Military Analysis Division, 'The effect of air action on Japanese ground army logistics'.

10 Bergerud, *Touched with Fire*, and *Fire in the Sky*; Dunnigan & Nofi, *The Pacific War Encyclopedia*.

11 Clift, *War Dance*; Burns, *The Brown and Blue Diamond at War*; Laffin, *Forever Forward*; Crooks, *The Footsoldiers*.

12 Ross, *Armed and Ready*. See also Pratten, *Two Seconds*, and Moremon, 'Most deadly jungle fighters?'

13 Zeitz, 'No half-hearted soldiers'. See also Raudzens, 'Testing the airpower expectations of the Kokoda campaign'.

Bibliography

Interviews

Allen, Dr Bryant, ANU, 8 August 2006

Baker, Clive, Kokoda Track guide and author, October 2006

Bisset, Stanley, veteran, 2/14th Battalion, 23 June 2004

Burke, Dr Michael, ANU, 8 August 2006

Cavalieri, Carlo, veteran, NGVR and 2/5th Independent Company, 22 August 2006, 20 November 2006

Clarke, Professor Ian, ANU, 4 April 2006

Cullen, Major-General Paul, veteran and ex-battalion commander, 2/1st Battalion, 12 December 2004

Fenner, Professor Frank, ANU, 3–4 October 2006

Forbes-Ewan, Dr Christopher, Defence Nutrition Research Unit, October 2006

Forrester, Arnold, veteran, 39th Battalion, 3 February 2002

Hayashi, Major-General Yoshinaga, director of military history, NIDS, 7 March 2005

Horie, Major Masao, veteran, Eighteenth Army, and East New Guinea Comrades Association president, 8 March 2004

Imanishi, Sergeant Sadaharu, veteran, 1/144th Battalion, 23 March 2004

Inape, Kasis, meteorologist, PNG Bureau of Meteorology, 5–7 June 2007

Jesser, Peter, son of Captain Harold Jesser, 1st Papuan Infantry Battalion, 15 December 2004

Jones, Reginald, veteran, 2/25th Battalion, 12 December 2002

Kohkichi, Nishimura, veteran, 2/144th Battalion, 14 March 2004

Lega, Tom, veteran of NGVR, worked with Josef Hofstetter, 22 August 2006, 20 November 2006

Lock, Lester, prewar resident of Efogi, 9 November 2006

Mason, Lindsay, veteran, 2/14th Battalion, 17 December 2005

Moran, Desmond, veteran, 2/31th Battalion, 4 February 2002

Nakamura, Captain Kokichi, veteran, 66th Infantry Regiment, 14 March 2004

Nelson, Professor Hank, ANU, 1 August 2006, 3 October 2007

Okamoto, Major Takahisa, veteran, 66th Infantry Regiment, 20 March 2004

Raike, Lieutenant-Colonel John, 22nd Construction Regiment, 20 October 2007

Shevak, Major Michael, formerly Royal Australian Artillery, 1 February 2006

Shindo, Dr Hiroyuki, research office, NIDS, 6 March 2005

Shinoda, Lieutenant-Colonel Masuo, veteran, 66th Infantry Regiment, 23 March 2004

Shoji, Dr Junichiro, chief of research office, NIDS, 6 March 2005
Taylor, Frank, Kokoda Track guide, August 2005
Tsunoda, Lieutenant Kazuo, Tainan Air Group, Papua 1942, 3 June 2004

SOURCES IN JAPAN

National Institute for Defence Studies

NIDS gohoku zenpan 78, Nanto homen chijo butai no heiryoku oyobi hensai ni kansuru shiryo [Strength and composition of Japanese ground forces, south eastern area]

NIDS nanto zenpan 102, Daitoa senso minami taiheiyo homen ni okeru sento [East Asia war, south Pacific area]

NIDS nanto Soromon Bisumaruku 130, Nankai Shitai Efogi minamigawa ni okeru sento [Battles of the Nankai Shitai south of Efogi]

NIDS higashi Nyuginea 156, Daiichi Nyuginea sen renatai sento kodo gaiyo dai 41 Rentai [First New Guinea campaign, records of 41st Regiment]

NIDS nanto zenpan 168, Nankai Shitai shireibu Toyufuku shosa kowa [lecture of Major Toyufuku, of Nankai Shitai headquarters]

NIDS nanto zenpan 174, Hohei dai 144 Rentai dai 3 Daitai sento sosho [Detailed battle records of 3rd Battalion 144th Regiment]

NIDS nanto higashi Nyuginea 225, Hohei dai Rentai Nyuginea senkyo houkou [War reports of 41st Infantry Regiment]

NIDS nanto higashi Nyuginia 255, Hohei dai 41 Rentai Nyuginea senkyo hohoku [War records of 41st Infantry Regiment]

NIDS nanto higashi Nyuginea 282, Hohei dai 144 Rentai dai 1 Chutai jinchu nisshi [War diary of 1st Company, 144th Regiment]

NIDS, 301.9.S, Hohei dai 41 Rentai Nyuginiasen senkyo hokoku [War records of 41st Regiment's battles in New Guinea]

NIDS 302. 9.S, Hiho to Tomoni-Sanpohei dai 55 Rentai senshi [With fire: The war history of 55th Mountain Artillery Regiment]

NIDS 302.9.I, Hohei Dai 144 Rentai Tsushin Chutai Shi Hensan Iinkai [History of the 144th Regiment Signals Company]

NIDS 302.9.H, Hohei Dai 144 Rentai Senki [Battle records of 144th Infantry Regiment]

NIDS 392.18B.9245 Senshi gyousho, nanto houmen Kaigun sakusen [War history records, Navy operations in south eastern area]

NIDS bunko jiku 469, Rikugun tsushin no gaikan [Overview of army correspondence]

National Diet Library

Hohei Dai 144 Rentai Senki Henshu Iinkai [editorial committee of the 144th Infantry Regiment history], *Hoei Dai 144 Rentai Senki* [History of 144 Infantry Regiment], Kochi, 1974

Hohei Dai 144 Rentai Tsushin Chutai Shi Hensan Iinkai [Compilation Committee History of the Signals company of the 144th Infantry Regiment], *Hohei Dai Tsushi Chutai shi* [History of the 144th Regiment Signals Company]

Ide Masao, *Hohei Dai 41 Rentai Nyuginiasen senkyo hokoku* [Report of the 41st Regiment's battles in New Guinea], 1970

Nyuginia Hien Kai [New Guinea Hein Association], *Dai 14 Hikodan Butai Shi* [History of the 14th Air Unit], Kobe, 1977

Saihonei Kaigun Hodobu (ed.), *Minami taiheiyo kokusen* [Aerial Warfare in the South Pacific], Bungei Shunjusha, Tokyo, 1977

—— *Tsubaki Eiji Chosho nariyamazu Nankai Shitai no eiko to shuen* [The funeral stops ringing: The glory and demise of the South Seas Force], Showa, Tokyo, 1980

Yamamoto Katsue, *Sanpotai dekunobo monogatari:aru nomin heishi no taika* [Useless mountain artillery: A farmer soldier's experience], Senshi, Tokyo, 1985

Yamamoto Kiyoshi (ed.), *Yoko 5 Toku: Yasuda Butai Buna Gyokusai no Tenmatsu* [5th Special Landing Party: The Story of the Glorious Sacrifice of the Yasuda Naval Unit at Buna], Senshi Kankokai, Tokyo, 1985

Japanese articles

Hashimoto, H., 'Stanree sakusen' [Owen Stanley Operation] *Himeraretaru Senki* [Secret history of the Pacific War], Mainichi Shinbunsha, Osaka

Ishikawa, S., 'Rabauru zerosen kusenki' [Battle records of the Rabaul Zero Unit] *Tokushu Maru* [Maru special edition], vol. 2, no. 1, Ushio Shobo, Tokyo

—— 'Sutanree sanjo P40 tono gekito' [Fierce battle against P40s over the Owen Stanley Range], *Maru*, vol. 14, no. 2, Ushio Shobo, Tokyo

Koya, C., 'Hyoko 3000 metoru no Sutanre Sangaku sen: Poto Moresubi Nankai Shitai no gekiteki sento to saigo' [Campaign on the Owen Stanley Ranges over 3000 metres high: Dramatic battles and the end of the South Seas Force that close in on Port Moresby], *Maru*, vol. 13, no. 9, Tokyo, Ushio Shobo, 1960

Okada, S., 'Poto Moresubi sakusen no shinso' [The truth about the Port Moresby operation], *Maru*, vol. 10, no. 13, Ushio Shobo, Tokyo

Shikano, I., 'Gekito Moresubi kaido no hibike waga zero no zessho' [Fierce battle: The sound of Zeroes over the road to Port Moresby], *Maru*, vol. 31, no. 1, Ushio Shobo, Tokyo, 1978

Yanagiba, Y., 'Tosa Rentai Poto Moresubi koryakuki' [History of the Tosa Regiments offensive against Post Moresby], *Taiheiyo senso shogen shirizu*, *Maru Bessatsu* [Testaments of the Pacific War supplement], no. 2, Ushio Shobo, Tokyo, 1986

Sources in Australia

Australian War Memorial

AWM42 Records of the librarian to the official history research team

AWM49 Interwar army records

AWM52 Australian Military Forces, formation and units diaries, 1939–45

AWM54 Written records, 1939–45 war

AWM55 Allied translation and interpreter section

AWM64 RAAF formations and unit records

AWM66 RAAF miscellaneous records

AWM67 Official History, 1939–45 War: Records of Gavin Long
AWM82 Captured Japanese documents
AWM123 Special collection II, Defence Committee records
AWM124 Navy historical collection
AWM173 RAAF war history section documents
AWM188 Navy history section research files
3DRL 6643 Papers of Field Marshal Sir Thomas Blamey
DRL 6763 Papers of Lieutenant General Sir Sydney Rowell
MSS 0679 Kitamoto, M., *A Record of Marathon Adventures in the New Guinea War*.
MSS 701 Robinson, A., Problems of supply encountered by the Australian and Japanese forces on the Kokoda trail and the question of morale
MSS 0733 Okada, S., *Lost Soldiers*
MSS 0734 Yoshihara, K., *Southern Cross: An Account of the East New Guinea Campaign*
MSS 1089 Account of Lieutenant General Imamura Hitoshi
PR 84/370 Papers of Lieutenant General Sir E.H. Berryman
PRO 0297 Papers of Lieutenant Salmon
PRO 3106 Papers of Lieutenant F. Winkle
R 940 541 b3360 Official names of the battles actions and engagements fought by the land forces of the Commonwealth

National Archives of Australia

A518 Correspondence files
A816 Correspondence files
A981 Correspondence files
A5954 Shedden collection
A9186 RAAF unit history files
C443 Consular investigation files
CA18 Department of External Affairs, Central Office
CA19 Department of Defence, Central Administration
CA35 Department of the Air
CA46 Department of Defence
CA822 Territories Branch, Prime Minister's Department
CA904 Investigation Branch, New South Wales

National Library of Australia

Japanese monographs mfm 1383
Map room, Chinnery collection

BOOKS

Army, Department of the, *Service Ration Scales and Ration Packs*, Directorate of Supplies and Transport, Food Science Establishment, Melbourne, 1962
Austin, V., *To Kokoda and Beyond: The Story of the 39th Battalion 1941–43*, Melbourne University Press, Melbourne, 1988
Baker, Major C., *Transportation of Troops and Material*, Franklin Hudson Publishing, Kansas City, 1905

Bergerud, E., *Touched with Fire: The Land Warfare in the South Pacific*, Penguin, New York, 1996

—— *Fire in the Sky: The Air War in the South Pacific*, Westview Press, Boulder, CO, 2000

Bourcet, J., *Principles of Mountain Warfare*, publication details unknown, c. 1770

Bourne, G., *Nutrition and the War*, Cambridge University Press, Cambridge, 1940

Boyd, Lieutenant-Colonel J., *Supply Handbook for the Army Service Corps*, Royal United Service Institute, London, 1895

Braga, S., *Kokoda Commander: A Life of Major-General 'Tubby' Allen*, Oxford University Press, Melbourne, 2004

Brune, P., *A Bastard of a Place: The Australians in Papua*, Allen & Unwin, Sydney, 2003

—— *The Spell Broken: Exploding the Myth of Japanese Invincibility*, Allen & Unwin, Sydney, 1997

—— *Those Ragged Bloody Heroes: From the Kokoda Trail to Gona Beach 1942*, Allen & Unwin, Sydney, 1991

—— *We Band of Brothers: A Biography of Ralph Honner, Soldier and Statesman*, Allen & Unwin, Sydney, 2000

Budden, F., *That Mob: The Story of the 55/53rd Australian Infantry Battalion AIF*, self-published, Sydney, 1973

Bull, S., *WWII Jungle Warfare Tactics*, Osprey, Oxford, 2007

Bullard, S. (trans.), *Japanese Army Operations in the South Pacific Area: New Britain and Papua Campaigns 1942–43*, AWM, Canberra, 2007

Burns, J., *The Brown and Blue Diamond at War: The Story of the 2/27th Battalion AIF*, 2/27th Ex-Servicemen's Association, Adelaide, 1960

Byrnes, G., *Green Shadows: A War History of the Papuan Infantry Battalion*, private publication, 1989

Center of Military History, *The Papuan Campaign*, United States Army, Washington, DC, 1990

Chamberlain, H., *Japan over Asia*, Duckworth, London, 1938

Clark, S., *The Kokoda Track*, Kangaroo Press, Kenthurst, NSW, 1997

Clausewitz, C., *On War*, Princeton University Press, Princeton, NJ, 1976

Clift, K., *War Dance: The Story of the 2/3 Australian Infantry Battalion*, 2/3 Battalion Association, Kingsgrove, NSW, 1980

Coles, M. (ed.), *Military Logistics: A Primer on Operational, Strategic and Support Level Logistics*, Australian Defence Studies Centre, Canberra, 1996

Collie, C. & Marutani, H., *The Path of Infinite Sorrow: The Japanese on the Kokoda Track*, Allen & Unwin, Sydney, 2009

Coulthard-Clark, C.D., *Australia's Military Map-Makers: The Royal Australia Survey Corps 1915–96*, Oxford University Press, Melbourne, 2000

Creveld, M. van, *Supplying War: Logistics from Wallenstein to Patton*, Cambridge University Press, Cambridge, 1980

Crooks, W., *The Footsoldiers: The Story of the 2/33rd Infantry Battalion AIF in the War of 1939–45*, Printcraft, Sydney 1971

Cross, J., *Jungle Warfare*, Guild, London, 1989

Daugherty, L., *Fighting Techniques of a Japanese Infantryman 1941–45: Training, Techniques and Weapons*, Spellmount, Staplehurst, UK, 2002

Day, D., *Reluctant Nation: Australia and the Allied Defeat of Japan 1942–45*, Oxford University Press, Melbourne, 1992

Deane-Butcher, W., *Fighter Squadron Doctor: 75 Squadron RAAF New Guinea, 1942*, self-published, Sydney, 1989

Dornan, P., *The Silent Men: Syria to Kokoda and on to Gona*, Allen & Unwin, Sydney, 1999

Dunnigan, J., *How to Make War: A Comprehensive Guide to Modern Warfare in the Twenty-first Century*, Quill, New York, 2003

Dunnigan, J. & Nofi, A., *The Pacific War Encyclopedia*, Checkmark Books, New York, 1998

Du Picq, A., *Battle Studies: Ancient and Modern Battle*, Military Service Publishing Company, Harrisburg, PA, 1958

Dupuy, T., *Understanding War: History and Theory of Combat*, Nova, Falls Church, VA, 1987

Edgar, B., *Warrior of Kokoda: A Biography of Brigadier Arthur Potts*, Allen & Unwin, Sydney, 1999

English, J. & Gudmundsson, B., *On Infantry*, Praeger, London, 1994

Fairclough, H., *Equal to the Task: The History of the Royal Australian Army Service Corps*, F.W. Cheshire, Melbourne, 1962

Fitzsimons, P., *Kokoda*, Hodder, Sydney, 2004

Foch, F. Marshal, *The Principles of War*, Chapman & Hall, London, 1920

Forty, G., *Japanese Army Handbook 1939–45*, Sutton Publishing, Thrupp, UK, 1999

Franks, R., *Guadalcanal*, Penguin, New York, 1990

Fuller, Major General J.F.C., *Lectures on Field Service Regulations*, Sifton Praed, London, 1931

Furse, Colonel G., *Provisioning Armies in the Field*, William Clowes & Sons, London, 1899

Gailey, H., *MacArthur Strikes Back: Decision at Buna, New Guinea 1942–43*, Presidio Press, Novato, CA, 2000

Gill, G.H., *Royal Australian Navy, 1939–42*, Australian War Memorial, Canberra, 1958

Gillison, D., *Royal Australian Air Force, 1939–42*, Australian War Memorial, Canberra, 1962.

Giveney, E., *The First at War: The Story of the 2/1st Australian Infantry Battalion 1939–45*, Association of First Infantry Battalions, Earlwood, NSW, 1987

Gregory, B., *Mountain and Artic Warfare from Alexander to Afghanistan*, Patrick Stephen, Wellingborough, UK, 1989

Grogan, R., 'The operation of forward surgical teams in the Kokoda–Buna campaigns', *Australian and New Zealand Journal of Surgery*, vol. 68, issue 1, January 1998

Hall, T., *New Guinea 1942–44*, Methuen, Sydney, 1981

Hallion, R., *Strike from the Sky: The History of Battlefield Air Attack 1910–1945*, University of Alabama Press, Tuscaloosa, 2010

Ham, P., *Kokoda*, HarperCollins, Sydney, 2004

Hamley, General Sir E., *Operations of War*, Blackwood & Sons, Edinburgh, 1914

Harries, M. & S., *Soldiers of the Sun: The Rise and Fall of the Imperial Japanese Army*, Random House, New York, 1991

Hawthorne, S., *The Kokoda Trail: A History*, Central Queensland University Press, Rockhampton, 2003

Hayashi, S. Kogun, *The Japanese Army in the Pacific War*, Marine Corps Association, Quantico, VA, 1959

Hetherington, J., *Blamey: Controversial Soldier*, Australian War Memorial, Canberra, 1973

Hooker, R. (ed.), *An Anthology of Maneuver Warfare*, Presidio, Novato, CA, 1993

Horner, D., *Blamey, Commander in Chief*, Allen & Unwin, Sydney, 1998

—— *Crisis of Command: Australian Generalship and the Japanese Threat, 1941–43*, Australian War Memorial, Canberra, 1978

—— *General Vasey's War*, Melbourne University Press, Melbourne, 1992

—— *High Command, Australia and Allied Strategy 1939–1945*, Allen & Unwin, Sydney, 1982

Howard, Michael, *The Franco-Prussian War*, Methuen, London, 1985

Ienaga, S., *The Pacific War 1931–45: A Critical Perspective on Japan's Role in WWII*, Pantheon, New York, 1978

James, B., *Field Guide to the Kokoda Track*, Kokoda Press, Sydney, 2006

Johnston, G., *War Diary 1942*, Collins, Sydney, 1984

Jomini, A.H., *The Art of War*, Telegraph Press, Harrisburg, PA, 1958

Jordan, R., *The World's Merchant Fleets 1939: The Particulars and Wartime Fates of 6000 Ships*, Chatham Publishing, London, 1999

Kennedy, C., *Port Moresby to Gona Beach: 3rd Australian Infantry Battalion 1942*, Colin Kennedy, Canberra, 1992

Keogh, E.G., *The South West Pacific 1941–1945*, Grayflower, Melbourne, 1965

Kingsley Norris, F., *No Memory for Pain: An Autobiography*, Heinemann, Melbourne, 1970.

Koiwai, M., *Nyuginia Senki* (Battle History of New Guinea), Ushio Shobo, Tokyo, 1957

Kress, M., *Operational Logistics*, Kluwer Academic Publishers, Boston, 2002

Laffin, J., *Forever Forward: The Story of the 2/31st Infantry Battalion, 2nd AIF 1940–45*, 2/31st Australian Infantry Battalion Association, NSW Branch, 1994

Lindsay, P., *The Spirit of Kokoda: Then and Now*, Hardie Grant Books, Melbourne, 2002

Loroch, K., *Vessel Voyage Data Analysis: A Comparative Study*, Cornell Maritime Press, Cambridge, MD, 1966

Lundstrom, J.B., *The First South Pacific Campaign: Pacific Fleet Strategy, December 1941–June 1942*, Naval Institute Press, Anapolis, MD, 1976

Lynn, J. (ed.), *Feeding Mars: Logistics in Western Warfare from the Middle Ages to the Present*, Westview Press, Boulder, CO, 1993

McAllester, J., *Men of the 2/14th Battalion*, 2/14 Battalion Association, Melbourne, 1990

McAulay, L., *Blood and Iron*, Hutchinson, Melbourne, 1991

McCarthy, D., *South-West Pacific Area – First Year: Kokoda to Wau*, Australian War Memorial, Canberra, 1959

McDonald, N., *War Cameraman: The Story of Damien Parer*, Lothian, Melbourne, 1994

—— *Chester Wilmot Reports: Broadcasts that Shaped WWII*, ABC Books, Sydney, 2004

Marks, R., *Queensland Airfields World War Two: Fifty Years On*, R. & J. Marks, Brisbane, 1994

Marriott, B., *Food Components to Enhance Performance*, National Academies Press, Washington, DC, 1994

Marshall, J., *Nulli Secundus Log: 2/2nd Australian Infantry Battalion, AIF*, Sydney, 1946

Masters, J., *The Road Past Mandalay*, Cassell, London, 2002

Matthews, T., *Shadows Dancing: Japanese Espionage in the West, 1939–1945*, St Martin's Press, New York, 1994

Mellor, W.F. (ed.), *History of the Second World War: Casualties and Medical Statistics*, Her Majesty's Stationery Office, London, 1972

Milner, S., *Victory in Papua*, Office of the Chief of Military History, Department of the Army, Washington, DC, 1957

Mossman, B., *The Effectiveness of Air Interdiction during the Korean War*, Department of the Army, Washington, DC, 1966

Nakanishi, Ritta, *Nihon no Hohei Kaki* [Japanese Infantry Weapons], Dainippon Kaiga, Tokyo, 1998

Nelson, H., *Black, White and Gold: Goldmining in Papua New Guinea, 1878–1930*, Australian National University Press, Canberra, 1976

Onda, S., *Tobu New Guinea Sen* [The Advance in New Guinea], Kodansha Bunko, Tokyo, 1988

Paton, D.N., *Army Rations: Their Bearing on the Efficiency of the Soldier*, His Majesty's Stationery Office, London, 1920

Paull, R., *Retreat from Kokoda*, Heinemann, Melbourne, 1958

Powell, A., *The Third Force: ANGAU's New Guinea War, 1942–46*, Oxford, Melbourne, 2003

Pratten, G., *Two Seconds: The Australian Militia Experience 1941–1945*, AWM, Canberra, 1995

Richmond, K., *Japanese Forces in New Guinea During World War II: A Primer in Logistics*, privately printed, 2003

Robertson, J. & McCarthy, J., *Australian War Strategy, 1939–45: A Documentary History*, University of Queensland Press, St Lucia, 1985

Ross, A., *Armed and Ready: The Industrial Development and Defence of Australia 1900–1945*, Turton & Armstrong, Sydney, 1995

Rottman, G., *Japanese Army in World War II: Conquest of the Pacific 1941–42*, Osprey, Oxford, 2005

Rowell, S.F., *Full Circle*, Melbourne University Press, Melbourne, 1974

Russell, W.B., *The History of the Second Fourteenth Battalion*, Angus & Robertson, Sydney, 1957

Sakai, S., *Samurai*, Pocket Books, New York, 1996

Scott, G., *The Knights of Kokoda*, Horowitz, Sydney, 1963

Sinclair, J., *Arteries of War*, Airlife, London, 1992

Stanton-Hicks, Brigadier Sir E., *Who called the Cook a Bastard? A Personal Account of a One Man's Campaign to Improve the Feeding of the Soldier*, Keyline Publishing, Sydney, 1972

Steinberg, R., *Island Fighting*, Time Life, New York, 1978

Sublet, F., *Kokoda to the Sea: A History of the 1942 Campaign in Papua*, Slouch Hat Publications, McCrae, Vic, 2000

Sun Tzu, *The Art of War*, Wordsworth, UK, 1993

Sweeney, T., *Malaria Frontline: Australian Army Research during WWII*, Melbourne University Press, Melbourne, 2003

Tanaka, K., *Operations of the Imperial Japanese Armed Forces in Papua New Guinea During WWII*, Japan Papua New Guinea Goodwill Society, Tokyo, 1980

Thompson, J., *Lifeblood of War: Logistics in Armed Conflict*, Brasseys, London, 1998

Trigellis-Smith, S., Zampatti, S. & Parsons, M., *Shaping History: A Bibliography of Australian Unit Histories*, private publication, 1996

Tsuji, Masanobu, *Singapore 1941–1942: The Japanese Version of the Malayan Campaign of World War II*, OUP, Melbourne, 1988

Uren, M., *A Thousand Men at War: The Story of the 2/16th Battalion*, Heinemann, Melborune, 1959

Waiko, J., *A Short History of Papua New Guinea*, Oxford University Press, Melbourne, 1993

Walker, A.S., *Clinical Problems of War*, Australian War Memorial, Canberra, 1952

—— *The Island Campaigns*, Australian Army War Memorial, Canberra, 1957

War Department, *Field Service Regulations – Larger Units*, US Government Printing Office, Washington, DC, 1942

—— *Japanese Infantry Weapons*, Military Intelligence Division, Washington, DC, 1943

War Office, *Field Service Regulations, Operations – Higher Formations*, vol. 3, His Majesty's Stationery Office, London, 1935

White, O., *Green Armour*, Angus & Robertson, Sydney, 1945

Wick, S., *Purple over Green: The History of the 2/2nd Australian Infantry Battalion 1939–1945*, 2/2 Australian Infantry Battalion Association, Brookvale, NSW, 1977

Wigmore, L., *The Japanese Thrust*, Australian War Memorial, Canberra, 1957

Wilson, D., *Jackson's Few: 75 Squadron RAAF Port Moresby March to May 1942*, private publication, 1988

—— *The Decisive Force: 75 and 76 Squadrons at Port Moresby and Milne Bay 1942*, Banner, Melbourne, 1991

Zissner, H., *Rats, Lice and History*, Macmillan, London, 1985

Journal articles

Anonymous, 'They held the Japs on the Kokoda Track', *Mufti*, vol. 19, no. 4, 1979

Anonymous, '25th anniversary of New Guinea epic: The Kokoda Trail 1942', *Reveille*, vol. 40, no. 10, 1967

Author unknown, 'Mountain operations', *Military Review*, vol. 32, no. 6, June 1952

Bridge, P., 'Eora Creek', *First Post*, vol. 5, no. 2, 1967

Buckley, J., 'Australia's perilous year: January 1942 – January 1943', *Defence Force Journal*, no. 72, 1988

Bullard, S., 'The great enemy of humanity: Malaria and the Japanese medical corps in Papua 1942–43', *Journal of Pacific History*, vol. 39, no. 2, 2004

Cantor, S., 'Return to Kokoda', *Mufti*, vol. 6, no. 8, 1963

Cheesman, E., 'New Guinea', *Geographical Journal*, vol. CI, no 3, 1943.

Cranston, F., 'The Battle of the Beach Heads, November 1942 – January 1943', *Sabretache*, vol. 34, no. 2, 1993

Cullen, P., 'The Owen Stanley campaign', *First Post*, vol. 3, no. 2, 1966

Downey, M., 'The Kokoda Trail 1982', *Sabretache*, vol. 24, no. 2, 1983

Edmonds, A., 'First AIF looks at battlefields of Second AIF: Port Moresby and Kokoda', *Reveille*, vol. 32, no. 3, 1958

Halliday, D., 'The Jacka tradition: A history of the 2/14 Infantry Battalion', *Reveille*, vol. 35, no. 8, 2005

Higginbottom, R., 'The RAASC in New Guinea', *Royal Army Service Corps Review*, vol. 1, no. 5, 1952

Honner, R., 'The 39th at Isurava', *Australian Army Journal*, July 1967

Horner, D., 'Defending Australia in 1942', *War and Society*, vol. 11, no. 1, 1993

Hutton, G., 'Lessons of New Guinea', *Army Education Journal*, vol. 5, no. 5, 1942

Kinsley, N., 'The New Guinea campaign', *Stand To*, vol. 5, no. 3, 1955

McCarthy, D., 'Kokoda revisited', *Stand To*, vol. 4, no. 6, 1954

Millet, A., Murray, W. & Watman, K., 'The effectiveness of military organizations', *International Security*, vol. 11, no. 1, 1986

Moda, H., 'From the other side: Success then death on the Kokoda Track', *Australian Military History*, no. 3, 1994

NX 84902, 'Looking back 43 years', *Mufti*, vol. 24, no. 4, 1984

O'Conner, M., 'Kokoda: The lessons remain valid', *Australian Defence Force Journal*, no. 98, 1993

Paulson, O., 'Light infantry: A perspective on load carrying and the soldier past and present', *Australian Army Journal*, vol. 3, no. 2, 2006

Pearson, R., 'The 2/3rd Australian Infantry Battalion 16th Brigade, 6th Division, Australian Imperial Force', *Despatch*, vol. 33, no. 3, 1998

Pilger, A., 'Courage, endurance and initiative: Medical evacuation from the Kokoda Track, August–October 1942', *War and Society*, vol. 11, no. 1, 1993

Raudzens, G., 'Testing the air power expectations of the Kokoda campaign, July to September 1942', *Journal of the Australian War Memorial*, no. 21, 1992

Shindo, H., 'Japanese air operations over New Guinea during World War II', *Journal of the Australian War Memorial*, no. 34, 2001

Tanaka, H., 'Japanese naval operations against Australia', *Journal of the Australian War Memorial*, no. 30, 1997

Tracey, R., 'General Blamey and Australia's role in WWII', *RMC Historical Journal*, vol. 1, 1972

Wada, K., 'Into the jaws of death: Kokoda', *Review*, July 1972.

Theses, reports and papers

Allen, B., 'Agricultural systems of Papua New Guinea', working paper no. 16, Northern Province, Department of Human Geography, ANU, 2002.

Assistant Chief of Air Staff, 'Air action in the Papuan Campaign 21 July 1942 to 23 January 1943', Army Air Forces Historical Studies no. 17, Historical Division, Maxwell Air Force Base, Alabama, 1944

Bureau of Statistics, 'Papua New Guinea census, preliminary bulletin no. 2', Konedobu, 1966

CSIRO, 'Land forms, types and vegetation of east Papua and lands of the Buna and Kokoda area', report no. 32, no. 10, Land Research Series, 1964

Military Analysis Division, 'The effect of air action on Japanese ground logistics', United States Strategic Bombing Survey, War Department, Washington, DC, 1947

Moreman, J., 'A triumph of improvisation: Australian Army operational logistics and the campaign in Papua, July 1942 to January 1943', PhD thesis, University of New South Wales, Sydney, 2000

Moremon, J., 'Most deadly jungle fighters? Australian infantry in Malaya and Papua, 1941–43', BA (Hons), University of New England, Armidale, NSW, 1992

Ogino, T., 'The supply plan for Guadalcanal 1942', unpublished manuscript, author's collection

Purcell, W.R., 'The nature and extent of Japanese commercial and economic interests in Australia 1932–1941', PhD thesis, University of New South Wales, Sydney, 1980

Robertson, A., 'Problems of supply encountered by the Australian and Japanese forces on the Kokoda Trail, and the question of morale', BA (Hons) thesis, Department of History, University of Melbourne, 1973

Robinson, N., 'Villagers at war: Some Papua New Guinea experiences in WWII', Pacific Research Monograph no. 2, ANU, Canberra, 1979

Tonna, D., 'Wantok warriors: An analysis of the activities of the Pacific Island Regiment in Papua New Guinea during the Second World War', University of New South Wales, Sydney, 1993

Zeitz, L., 'No half-hearted soldiers: The Japanese army's experience in the south west Pacific', MA thesis, University of New South Wales, Sydney, 1992

Internet resources

AIF project, December 2010, <www.adfa.edu.au>

Australia Japan Research Project, June 2009 <http://ajrp.awm.gov.au/AJRP/AJRP2.nsf/Web-Pages>

Australian War Memorial, June 2009 <www.awm.gov.au>

Bayonet Strength, 'Battalion organization during the Second World War', March 2009, <www.bayonetstrength.150m.com>

Department of Veterans' Affairs, 'The Kokoda track: Exploring the site of the battle fought by Australians in World War II', April 2011, <http://kokoda.commemoration.gov.au/about-the-kokoda-track/index.php>

US Army Air Forces Statistical Digest, 'US Army Air Force in World War Two', January 2011, <www.usaaf.net/digest/index.htm>

INDEX

Printed by Printforce, United Kingdom